Making a Killing

*Chicana Matters Series*
*Deena J. González and Antonia Castañeda, editors*

*Chicana Matters Series focuses on one of the largest population groups in the
United States today, documenting the lives, values, philosophies, and artistry
of contemporary Chicanas. Books in this series may be richly diverse, reflecting
the experiences of Chicanas themselves, and incorporating a broad spectrum
of topics and fields of inquiry. Cumulatively, the books represent the leading
knowledge and scholarship in a significant and growing field of research and,
along with the literary works, art, and activism of Chicanas, underscore their
significance in the history and culture of the United States.*

# Making a Killing

Femicide, Free Trade, and *La Frontera*

EDITED BY ALICIA GASPAR DE ALBA
WITH GEORGINA GUZMÁN

University of Texas Press ◆ *Austin*

Requests for permission to reproduce material from this work should be sent to:
  Permissions
  University of Texas Press
  P.O. Box 7819
  Austin, TX 78713-7819
  www.utexas.edu/utpress/about/bpermission.html

♾ The paper used in this book meets the minimum requirements of ANSI/NISO
Z39.48-1992 (R1997) (Permanence of Paper).

**Library of Congress Cataloging-in-Publication Data**
Making a killing : femicide, free trade, and la frontera / edited by Alicia Gaspar de
Alba with Georgina Guzmán. — 1st ed.
    p.  cm. — (Chicana matters series)
  Includes bibliographical references and index.
  ISBN 978-0-292-72277-4 (alk. paper) — ISBN 978-0-292-72317-7 (pbk. : alk.
paper)
    1 Women—Crimes against—Mexico—Ciudad Juárez.  2 Homicide—Mexico—
Ciudad Juárez.  I Gaspar de Alba, Alicia, 1958–  II Guzmán, Georgina.
  HV6250.4.W65M3258  2010
  364.152′30082097216—dc22
                                                                2010018559

*For all the mothers who have suffered the loss of a child to violence*

*And in memory of Esther Chávez Cano (1933–2009)*

# Contents

# Alicia's Acknowledgments

I would like to express my gratitude to the University of California–Los Angeles Committee on Research and the Institute for American Cultures for several years of support for this project. Originally, this was going to be a compilation of the papers presented at the "Maquiladora Murders, Or, Who Is Killing the Women of Juárez?" Conference, which I organized in 2003 while serving as the associate director of the UCLA Chicano Studies Research Center. The more the crimes increased and the more scholars became interested in writing and teaching about them, the more apparent it became to me that the scope of the anthology needed to broaden to include the newer research being published in feminist and social justice journals along with the work of some of the presenters at the conference. I am indebted, still, to those three students who helped me organize the conference—Angélica Marín, Elena Aviles, Heather Masterton—without whom I certainly never would have been able to raise the $180,000 bottom-line cost of the conference, not to mention have kept my sanity.

Special thanks to all the contributors who promptly agreed to let me use their work in this collection and motivated me to continue advocating for the murdered women and girls of Ciudad Juárez.

Most of all, however, I want to bend at the knees and thank Georgina Guzmán for her four-year-long labor in helping me bring this book to light. She went far and above the normal work of any research assistant and became a translator, cowriter, and undercover agent. Thanks to Julián Cardona, J Guadalupe Pérez, and Rigo Maldonado for visually documenting the lives and deaths of exploited women on the border.

Special *gracias* to my wife, Alma López, for transforming the images to black and white and for her own amazing artwork.

I'd like to thank my assistant, Allison Wyper, and her dad, Tom Bryan, for all of their work in creating the timeline that appears in Appendix A to give us an idea about the binational and bilateral context in which the Juárez femicides have unraveled.

And finally, of course, my heartfelt gratitude and respect go to the mothers of the victims and to all of the grassroots organizations in Juárez, El Paso, Las Cruces, San Antonio, Los Angeles, and beyond that have struggled for so many years to bring an end to these gynocidal crimes.

# Georgina's Acknowledgments

I would like to thank Profe Alicia Gaspar de Alba and all the contributors for entrusting me with their very important work. My heart especially goes out to Eva Arce and Paula Flores, who are incredibly strong and courageous mothers; they are remarkable women with bold spirits. Gaspar—thank you for being an inspirational mentor, advisor, and friend. Thank you for trusting me with this project and bringing me aboard. It has been an unbelievable experience. *Gracias.* I'd also like to thank my husband, Raúl E. Moreno, my greatest partner in our pursuit of social justice.

# *Feminicidio:* The "Black Legend" of the Border

ALICIA GASPAR DE ALBA AND GEORGINA GUZMÁN

*Femicide is the killing of women qua women, often condoned by, if not sponsored, by the state and/or by religious institutions.*
—JILL RADFORD AND DIANA E. H. RUSSELL, EDS.,
FEMICIDE: THE POLITICS OF WOMAN KILLING

*The Black Legend (Spanish: La Leyenda Negra) is the depiction of Spain and Spaniards as bloodthirsty and cruel, intolerant, greedy, and fanatical.*
—WIKIPEDIA

I

Just because I published a novel called *Desert Blood: The Juárez Murders* (2005) does not mean the Juárez murders are fiction. Since May 1993, over five hundred women and girls have been found brutally murdered on the El Paso/Juárez border, and thousands more have been reported missing and remain unaccounted for, making this the longest epidemic of femicidal violence in modern history. The victims are known colloquially as "*las inditas del sur*," the little Indian girls from the south of Mexico—poor, dark-skinned, and indigenous-looking—who have arrived alone and disenfranchised in Ciudad Juárez to work at a twin-plant *maquiladora* and earn dollars to send back home. Not all of the victims are rural, not all of them are outsiders to the border metropolis, not all of them worked at a *maquiladora*, lived alone, or had indigenous features. But most of them are Mexican, impoverished, and young. And all of them are female, the victims of this particular crime wave.[1]

There was a time when no one knew about the Juárez femicides, as these

**Fig. i.1.** Jennifer Araújo © 2002, "Basura" (Trash). From "Las Hijas de Juárez" Exhibition, curated by Rigo Maldonado and Victoria Delgadillo. Social and Public Art Resource Center, Venice, Calif., 2003. Courtesy of Rigo Maldonado.

crimes have come to be called to signify the misogyny of the perpetrators. There was a time when little coverage could be found in newspapers or on television shows or on the Internet about what was happening in Juárez to poor, young, Mexican women. Nowadays, we know too much, and yet we continue to know nothing. In the process of learning; reading; researching; raising consciousness; signing petitions; writing stories, poetry, and music; making art; organizing conferences; and collecting anthologies, there are only two things that have changed. The number of victims continues to grow. And now the Juárez femicides have become a legend, the "black legend" of the border.

The Mexican government's new line, after years of inept investigations and covert maneuvers to derail progress on any of the cases, is that the femicides are nothing but an invention of some crazy feminists and the attention-grabbing mothers of a few dead prostitutes, a way of making Juárez look like a modern-day incarnation of the Spanish Inquisition out to hunt down, torture, and sacrifice young women, an image that city officials and merchants say is spoiling tourism to the city.[2]

Despite these negations of history, you have, by now, probably heard of the gendered death toll in Ciudad Juárez. You already know that between

1993 and 2008, more than five hundred poor Mexican women and girls, some as young as five, some in their sixties and seventies, were violently slain in Ciudad Juárez, across the border from El Paso, Texas. You know that their bodies were found strangled, mutilated, dismembered, raped, stabbed, torched, or so badly beaten, disfigured, or decomposed that the remains have never been identified. You know that many bore the signature of serial killers: the bodies half-clothed, hands tied behind their backs, evidence of rape, genital mutilation. You know that a majority of the victims shared the same physical profile: predominantly between the ages of twelve and twenty-three, young, slim, petite, dark-haired, and dark-skinned. You know that their brutalized bodies were dumped in deserted lots around Juárez as well as in landfills, motels, downtown plazas, and busy city intersections. You may even know that bodies were found inside trash dumpsters, brick ovens, vats of acid, and abandoned cars, as well as on train tracks, under beds in hotel rooms, and across the street from a police station or the headquarters of the Maquiladora Association. You know, perhaps, that the victims are also called "*maqui-locas*," assumed to be *maquiladora* workers living *la vida loca*, or *una vida doble*, of a border metropolis, coded language for prostitution.

In fact, you may know quite a bit about these dead women because, first of all, the bodies have been accruing since 1993, and, second, we now have a plethora of cultural products about the femicides. Since 1999, for example, a repertoire of songs has emerged from artists as diverse as Tori Amos, At the Drive-In, Lila Downs, Los Tigres del Norte, and Los Jaguares.[3] For online video fans, there are over twenty short films available on YouTube alone, including one by Amnesty International.[4]

Beyond the early documentaries, such as "Maquila: A Tale of Two Mexicos" (2000) and Lourdes Portillo's "Señorita Extraviada" (2001), which alone helped raise consciousness about the crimes all over the world, we now also have two Hollywood films,[5] one pulp Mexican film,[6] and at least three new documentaries.[7]

In print, other than my mystery novel and a collection of poetry about the murdered women of Juárez by Marjorie Agosín, we have a new fictionalized first-person account of life in the "capital city of murdered women,"[8] as well as two book-length journalistic accounts,[9] and a monograph.[10]

In the academic world, numerous panels have been presented at conferences such as the American Studies Association, the Modern Language Association, the National Association for Chicana and Chicano Studies, and MALCS (Mujeres Activas en Letras y Cambio Social). New Mexico State University, UCLA, Ohio State University, the University of Texas at

**Fig. i.2.** Rigo Maldonado © 2002, "Searching for Bodies in the Desert." Courtesy of Rigo Maldonado.

El Paso, the University of Nebraska, and Stanford University (to name a few) have all hosted conferences and symposia dedicated specifically to the Juárez femicides. And this is not to mention all of the writers, visual artists, and performance artists on both sides of the border who have lent their talents to a massive binational outrage over these crimes and the continued impunity granted the perpetrators.[11] Coupled with the investigative reports of major newspapers and television news shows across the country as well as across the world and the denunciations of organizations like Amnesty International, the Organization of American States, and the World Court, all of these cultural efforts have contributed to what you have learned about the femicides.

But there is another reason you know something about the dead daughters of Juárez. You know about them because they *are* dead, because they *are* part of this sensational, unresolved heinous crime wave that has taken the public by storm and has suddenly put this border on the radar of every human rights organization in the known universe. Ironically, the main signifier of their lives is a corpse half-buried in a sand dune. As Marjorie Agosín says in a poem from her collection about the murdered women of Juárez, *Secrets in the Sand*, "All we know about them / is their death" (25).

We did not know anything about these "*muchachas del sur*" (girls from the south) when they were alive, did not even realize they *were* alive or that they were living in such squalid and inhumane conditions just a stone's throw from El Paso, working at their mind-numbing, carpal tunnel–warping factory jobs, going to school some of them, struggling to support children or parents, to find a decent place to live in a squatter colony with no electricity, no running water, no sewage system, no paved streets, no city services whatsoever. Nothing about them was of any interest to us until they died, and even then, it took over three hundred bodies piling up over ten years and the noisy interventions of First World celebrities like Eve Ensler, Jane Fonda, Sally Field, and Christine Lahti (who in 2004 led us through the V-Day march in Juárez, which drew a crowd of thousands from both sides of the border) for us to really pay attention to the presence of these women in our midst. I myself—native of that very border, with family living on both sides of the Córdoba Bridge—did not find out about the crimes until 1998, five years after the bodies began piling up in the desert, when I read a story called "The Maquiladora Murders," by Sam Quiñones in the May/June issue of *Ms.* magazine.

Reading the story enraged me, not only because these crimes were happening right across the border from my hometown of El Paso and because very little about them had been reported in any major U.S. newspaper, or even the local papers of El Paso and Las Cruces, but also because, as a scholar of border studies and gender studies, as a native of that very place on the map in which the femicides were happening at a rate of two per month, I too had been caught in the web of silence that surrounds these crimes.

What was at the root of the silence? Surely such a crime spree would sell newspapers, if nothing else. In 1999, my search for media coverage on the femicides resulted in only a handful of stories. Other than the Sam Quiñones article in *Ms.,* I found an earlier piece by Debbie Nathan in *The Nation,* a piece in the *Los Angeles Times,* one in the *New York Times,* and a two-part, multiple-page-spread in the *Washington Post.* On television, only two news shows, *20/20* and *60 Minutes,* had broadcast exposés. After those eight bodies were discovered in a cotton field in November 2001, the U.S. media swarmed over the story, and suddenly we were reading about the Juárez femicides not only in the newspapers, but also in periodicals that ranged from left to right of the political scale: the *Utne Reader, Mother Jones, People,* and the *Texas Observer.* These were all signs of interest, finally, in a tragedy that has been accruing bones since 1993.

Nowadays, of course, the Internet and YouTube provide access to stories about the femicides worldwide, but when I first started my research after reading Quiñones's exposé, the Worldwide Web had precious little. I found a link to a story done by the BBC in London, another link to the Frontera NorteSur digest from Las Cruces, and, finally, a link to the now-defunct Sagrario Consortium (or Fundación Sagrario), named after one of the victims, Sagrario González Flores (daughter of Paula Flores, who has been very active in the mothers' struggle to end the femicides in Juárez and whose *testimonio* is included in this book). My research assistant in 1999 was informed by a reference librarian at the El Paso Public Library that the murders were "Juárez news, not El Paso news," and so the *El Paso Times* did not cover them. Media coverage in Mexican periodicals between 1993 and 1998, on the other hand, constituted a three-inch-thick archive of information.

Where were the academics, I wondered? Where were the Mexican, Chicana/o, and Latino/a academics, particularly those working on labor issues, immigration policy, the North American Free Trade Agreement (NAFTA), or the abuse and exploitation of women workers on the border? Why were they, especially my U.S. colleagues, not bringing their time, energy, and resources to this issue? Why was there so little scholarship on the crimes?[12] Was it fear or apathy that defined the silence?

In an effort to break that silence on the U.S. side of the border, I decided to write a mystery novel about the crimes—based on research and on what I knew from having grown up in that precise, paradoxical place on the map—to inform the broadest-possible English-speaking public about the femicides. When the novel was finished, I (with the help of a handful of students) organized an international conference called "The Maquiladora Murders, Or, Who Is Killing the Women of Juárez?" at UCLA in the fall of 2003, under the aegis of the Chicano Studies Research Center and cosponsored by Amnesty International. We brought together scholars, journalists, artists, activists, writers, forensic investigators, policy specialists, as well as mothers of the victims in a series of roundtable discussions and presentations. Cong. Hilda Solís, actor Eve Ensler, and then–University of California regent Dolores Huerta all gave keynote speeches. There were literary and dramatic presentations; a multimedia student exhibition of written, aural, and visual materials collected in a yearlong undergraduate research internship on the crimes; and a special altar of ceramic pieces by the San Antonio–based MujerArtes collective commemorating the lives and losses of the Juárez women. The pieces were sold at a silent auction, the full proceeds of which were donated to the nongovernmental organizations of the mothers who attended the conference.[13] The purpose of the conference was to facilitate more scholarly inquiry into the crimes and, in particular, to examine the social, political, economic, and cultural infrastructure in which the crimes were multiplying like another form of toxic waste on the border.

**Fig. i.3.** Rigo Maldonado © 2002, "Lo Que Quedó" (What Was Left). Courtesy of Rigo Maldonado.

The conference was held during the Mexican Days of the Dead, October 31–November 2, and more than fifteen hundred people from across Los Angeles, the United States, Mexico, and Europe attended. The conference generated twelve resolutions that echoed the demands of Mexican NGOs and policy makers in the United States for a binational task force that would help bring an end to the crimes and justice to the murdered women and their families. The resolutions became the "¡Ni Una Más!" petition, which called for an "End [to] Violence against Women and Children in Juárez and Chihuahua" and was addressed to both the U.S. and Mexican governments (it is still available online).[14]

Our conference logo, designed by Chicana digital artist Alma López,[15] was called *Coyolxauhqui's Tree of Life*, both to commemorate the primordial dismembered daughter of Aztec mythology, who was slashed to pieces by her brother, the War God, Huitzilopochtli, and to reconstitute her many pieces into a whole self.[16] My intention as the organizer of the conference was not only to raise consciousness about the crimes and provide a forum for discussing, analyzing, and taking action against the binational silence that had protected the perpetrators for so long, but also to re-member the sacrificed daughters of Juárez. I wanted to focus not so much on "who is killing them" as on, as Alma López's digital image suggests, how we could reassemble the pieces of the puzzle of their deaths to help us understand why they died and why they were killed with such viciousness directed at the brown female body. López's image suggests two other key questions: What war gods are being served by their deaths? and What "mother" or "father" are the killers—these modern-day Huitzilopochtlis who are wielding their own fiery serpents against their sisters—protecting?

There is so much we do not know. We do not know why there is a binational task force that includes immigration officers, Border Patrol agents, FBI agents, and police on both sides of the border—engaged in the collective task of trying to solve the pernicious problem of *car theft*—but not a similar binational effort to stop this epidemic of femicides. We do not know what role El Paso plays in either the investigation of the crimes or the protection of the perpetrators. We do not know how Mexico punishes sex crimes. We do not know, even, how many victims there actually are. Were there 254 murdered women in 2002, which is the statistic provided by the Juárez rape crisis shelter, Casa Amiga, or 320, which is the number reported by *El Paso Times* journalist Diana Washington Valdez, based on her own investigative research? Amnesty International's 2003 report on the Juárez murders, "Intolerable Killings: Ten Years of Abductions and Murders in Ciudad Juárez and Chihuahua,"[17] concludes that 370 young women

**Fig. i.4.** Alma López © 2003, *Coyolxauhqui's Tree of Life,* digital logo for "The Maquiladora Murders, Or, Who Is Killing the Women of Juárez" Conference. Courtesy of Alma López.

and girls had been killed on that border since 1993, "of which at least 137 were sexually assaulted prior to death." As reported in a Mexico City paper, the Chihuahua state government's response was that the Amnesty findings were "partial, slanted, distorted, and tendentious," and that the information presented in the report was both "inconsistent and decontextualized."[18]

Another thing we do not know: Can the DNA-testing techniques employed by the Chihuahua state authorities be trusted? In a shocking revelation by a group of Argentine anthropologists and forensics experts who came to Juárez in 2005 to lend their expertise to the DNA investigations—the same team "which gained fame by using advanced DNA-study techniques to identify people killed in Argentina's 'dirty war' of the 1970s"[19]—the mothers of two of those eight victims found in the cotton field in November 2001 learned that the remains they had been given were not those of their daughters.

Today, activists assert that the body count (that is to say, the found bodies, not the missing ones, which number in the thousands) has now exceeded five hundred. While attention has focused on the tangible murders, cases in which bodies have been discovered, the actual number of victims may be more than twice as high.[20]

Why have we not been made aware of their existence; why did they have to die for us to see them? Because they were women? Because they were poor, brown, young women? Because they were so low on the social totem pole that we all tacitly agreed the most polite thing we could do was to ignore them?

The essays and *testimonios* in *Making a Killing* make it difficult for us to continue to ignore the victims, or the murders, or the political, geographic, and economic context in which the crimes keep happening. Collectively, these essays are an intervention in the Freirian notion of *concientización*, offering as they do academic and personal reflection on a variety of factors that produce and sanction this gendered violence on an increasingly globalized U.S.-Mexico border, as well as analyses of actions being taken both to protest femicide and also to transform the social discourse that sees the victims as responsible for manufacturing their own deaths.

Readers will note that the numbers do not match in any of the essays in this book; the body count is always different. Indeed, that is one of the major issues with these crimes. There has been no systematic accounting of the victims or accountability by the authorities, which results in only more confusion, more impunity for the perpetrators, and less chance of resolution. Despite the discrepancy in the numbers, however, the contributors all agree with the activists and NGOs that have been working on these cases that the numbers given by "official" channels are much lower than the actual body count.

Who can hate these powerless women so much? What is it about them that they hate? What is so threatening about their presence on the border? What accounts for this level of misogyny? Is the poor brown female really an endangered species on the U.S.-Mexico border? What specific threats does she pose to the society, the economy, and the culture of the border? How can we explain the silence that continues to protect the perpetrators and haunt the mothers and families of the victims? What specific actions have been taken and must be taken to protest the impunity with which these crimes are committed, which is as much a signature of the criminals as of the authorities who refuse to bring justice to the daughters of Juárez? How do we put an end to the femicides?

## II

The essays in Part One, "Interventions," examine the murders in a socio-economic context, with a focus on evaluating NAFTA, border economic politics, and *maquiladora* working conditions and ethics. It is crucial to understand the "fatal indifference," as Elvia Arriola terms it, of corporations and governmental policies in regard to the border's vulnerable female workforce. In "Accountability for Murder in the *Maquiladoras*," Arriola examines NAFTA-related laws and the governmental policies that provide more rights for foreign investors than for the Mexican workers themselves. She argues that both the *maquiladoras* and the Mexican government are morally responsible for their workers' safety, but because they protect profit at any cost and privilege production before the laborer, the poor brown female *maquiladora* worker becomes "an insignificant cog in the wheel of production." Such analysis is bolstered by firsthand accounts from working women who describe the perilous conditions they face both on their way to work and at the *maquiladoras* themselves.

Subsequent essays trace the social ideologies that allow femicide to flourish with impunity. Rather than identifying individual culprits, the authors examine the traditional machismo and misogyny that pervade social attitudes toward the victims, who are represented as prostitutes responsible for provoking their own deaths. In this way, these articles collapse the simple binary of innocent and guilty by investigating the sociocultural devaluation of women rather than "whodunnit." Alicia Gaspar de Alba's "Poor Brown Female: The Miller's Compensation for 'Free Trade,'" for example, analyzes the complicitous roles of the media, the *maquiladora* industry, and the U.S. and Mexican governments in these murders. Gaspar de Alba shows how the *maquiladora* industry, from demeaning beauty pageants to monthly menstruation checks, dehumanizes its female labor force in the name of production efficiency; and yet, when these women go home, the corporations which make a killing in profits at their expense cannot provide proper lighting or background checks on the company shuttle drivers. "Safety," she argues, "is a commodity the workers cannot afford. Nor, it seems, can their employers, despite the huge profits they make on products assembled with cheap '*mano de obra*' (labor)." Moreover, "Poor Brown Female" examines topics that have not been studied in the literature of the femicides: the definitions and technicalities of rape and sex crimes found in Mexico's penal code, as well as the fact that, until 2002, El Paso was the largest dumping ground of registered sex offenders in the country, a possible lead in the investigations that neither government seems inclined to explore. In this way, Gaspar de Alba probes the misogynistic priorities and policies of two nations that can unite in an effort to find stolen cars but not missing women.

María Socorro Tabuenca Córdoba's "Ghost Dance in Ciudad Juárez at the End/Beginning of the Millennium" also probes the public discourse surrounding these murdered women and reveals how it serves to violate them both in life and after death. Tabuenca begins by examining the historical construction of Ciudad Juárez as a perverse border city—as the most "'unredeemable' of all the provinces"—and explores how such a stigma propagates and condones the image of the loose and discardable border woman. Analyzing public disdain for working women who "transgress" gendered public spaces, the 1995–1998 police department's so-called prevention campaigns, and the governors', district attorneys', and criminologists' statements about the victims (ranging from brutal indifference to downright condemnation), "Ghost Dance" seeks to contest the continual cultural disparagement of these women and shed light on the government's ludicrously ineffectual measures.

Continuing in Tabuenca's line of inquiry, Steven S. Volk and Marian E. Schlotterbeck's "Gender, Order, and Femicide: Reading the Popular Culture of Murder in Ciudad Juárez" provides one of the first comprehensive studies of the cultural production that has surfaced from the murders. Analyzing Alicia Gaspar de Alba's *Desert Blood: The Juárez Murders* and Tori Amos's songs on the women of Juárez as feminist counterpoints to the masculinist cultural texts by Julián Cardona, Carlos Fuentes, and Los Tigres del Norte, the authors argue that, while decrying and lamenting the deaths, these latter artists fix the cultural territory of the murders within a familiar set of patriarchal binaries: good girl/bad girl, virgin/whore. In this way, these masculinist cultural texts further perpetuate the notion that the murder of women will inevitably continue to happen until men's and women's proper roles and relations are reestablished, and thus they continue to propagate the hegemonic discourse of Juárez women as *maqui-locas* who were asking to get killed.

All of the pieces in Part Two, "¡Ni Una Más!" analyze the current ways in which femicide has been countered. They look at nongovernmental organizations and other grassroots forms of activism that have formed as a response to the crimes in Juárez and also call into question the motives of some of the activism. Kathleen Staudt and Irasema Coronado's "Binational Civic Action for Accountability" in particular examines how many NGOs, including El Paso's Coalition against Violence, have regarded the murders as a binational issue that requires binational task forces, given that the "border runs through the combined metropolitan area of Juárez/El Paso, complicating accountability relationships between people, victims and victims' families, and government." Their chapter discusses the multiple forms of activism on both sides of the border, such as V-Day marches, a myriad of independent films, the *Vagina Monologues'* fund-raising efforts, California representative Hilda Solís's Hispanic Caucus's trip to Juárez, and the Coalition against Violence's many rallies and meetings with officials in Ciudad Juárez. Examining the binational dimensions of these crimes, Staudt and Coronado argue, is to self-reflexively question how our own government and citizens might also be implicated in such atrocities.

Julia Monárrez-Fragoso's "The Suffering of the Other" complicates the current state of activism by exposing some unsettling obstacles in forging solidarity. She shows how the victims' families' suffering has become prized cultural capital for Juárez's powers-that-be, which have manipulated this legitimate pain as a means to divide the efforts of civil organizations. The result is that some mothers have demanded to separate the victims' families' organizations and the NGOs, wielding "their maternity as a symbol of power and accreditation." Far from being pessimistic, however, Monárrez-Fragoso raises our consciousness about the feigned empathy of the state and its malicious agendas of division and subjection. She also suggests strategies for more cognizant alliances between those who seek justice.

Clara E. Rojas's "The V-Day March in Mexico: Appropriation and Misuse of Local Women's Activism" perfectly complements Monárrez-Fragoso's chapter by showing how many celebrities, middle-class residents of Juárez (*juarenses*), and organizations have sought and gained recognition with their self-serving activism. Seeking to speak for others and to attain a charitable benefactor persona by way of these tragedies, these "agonistic" activists, as Rojas calls them, have made the victims into a modus vivendi for many self-interested people at the local, national, and international levels. Rojas poignantly explains the reasons why many local activists are now very cautious about what and whom they support publicly because of how their own efforts are appropriated, misused, and misrepresented.

Melissa W. Wright's "Femicide, Mother-Activism, and the Geography of Protest in Northern Mexico" continues this keen analysis of current activism by specifically focusing on mother-activist movements' current state in Ciudad Juárez and Chihuahua City. Wright explains that, although local activism seems to have faded in recent years, in part because of internal fissures, the northern Mexico antifemicide movement has broadened its efforts, joining forces with international and transnational movements (such as the Inter-American Commission on Human Rights and the Equipo Argentino de Antropología Forense (Argentine Forensic Anthropology Team). Regularly participating in academic, political, and human rights events around the world, Wright states that the movement's present strategy is to go "within and beyond Mexico to generate international political pressure on Mexican politicians in order to seek justice for the victims and their families and to prevent further crimes." Wright's point is that rather than regarding the decline of local activism as "failed movements," what is occurring is that the social movement is evolving out of previous forms as part of the ongoing materialization of social movements in Latin America. These international resistance strategies are corroborated by the mothers' actual experiences, which we read about in Part Three, "*Testimonios.*"

The first chapter in this part is Candice Skrapec's "The Morgue Was Really from the Dark Ages: Insights from a Forensic Psychologist." In remarks taped during an interview with filmmaker Lorena Méndez at the "Maquiladora Murders" conference at UCLA, Skrapec, who was invited in the early years of the crime wave to go to Ciudad Juárez to assist the state judicial police with the investigations, provides us with cultural, criminal, psychological, and forensic perspectives that enable us to obtain a more complete picture of why so many women have been murdered and why these crimes have gone unpunished. Skrapec describes the Mexican forensics and judicial systems' tremendous lack of resources and their consequent inability to identify, process, and store evidence and hence successfully prosecute cases with properly catalogued evidence. Moreover, through her interviews with perpetrators and her expertise as a criminologist, she explores the psychological makeup of the murderers and the anomaly of how "collective groups of men could come together for the purpose of killing repeatedly." For Skrapec, the social discourse of machismo is at the root of these crimes. She insists that, by not responding in any effective way, by not prosecuting cases and seeking justice, Juárez society essentially condones the femicides and enables *machista* and dysfunctional men to continue their misogynistic rape and murdering spree.

In the next two *testimonios,* two victims' mothers—Eva Arce and Paula Flores—discuss their early activism in local protest coalitions in Juárez as well as their current participation in the Inter-American Commission on

Human Rights and in their separate projects.[21] Paula and Eva also discuss the separation tactics that Monárrez-Fragoso addresses in her chapter and openly attest to the many ways in which the government has tried to silence and divide them with money, false promises, and, in Eva's case, indescribable violence. Eva has been offered money to keep quiet, but because she continues to investigate her daughter Silvia's disappearance, she has been followed, threatened, and beaten so badly she has ended up in the hospital. Paula discusses how the police have tried to make her sign forms affirming that she has received her daughter Sagrario's remains, but without DNA tests she cannot even be certain of whether it is indeed her daughter's body that she visits in that tomb. These harrowing testimonies allow us to see that the Juárez femicides are not fiction, statistics, or border folklore, but brutal tragedies that real people are suffering, and the mothers' stories allow us to hear the actual voices of that grief.

Moreover, these mothers' testimonies provide a glimpse of how, in Paula Flores's words, "the government has managed to keep [victims' families] confused and on the margins, so [they] won't be out protesting and seeking justice." Their experiences speak to many of the problems in grassroots organizing discussed in "¡Ni Una Más!" Paula and Eva describe how the authorities' hypocritical policy of "familial economic assistance" makes victims' families stop demanding answers from the government. This money, they say, is the greatest of insults, for the authorities are not only putting a price on their deceased daughters' lives, but they are also trying to substitute justice with money. Unfortunately, some impoverished families are forced to take the money out of necessity, and this undoubtedly creates tensions between victims' families. Paula recounts that, although these funds have enabled her and many other mothers to make a living by setting up a *tiendita* (little store), the result is that most mothers are now stuck in the store all day and are unable to go out and protest anymore. Eva refuses to accept any money, preferring to eke out a humble living on her own rather than accepting money from the authorities.

Reading these *testimonios*, it becomes clear that the authorities employ a three-pronged line of attack to try to fragment the mothers' protest movement: by buying their silence; by confining them to their private businesses; and by removing them from public arenas—not to mention by creating jealousies, rivalries, and resentments between the mothers who have received money and those who have not. But as Eva's and Paula's unified efforts to raise awareness prove, the authorities' vile tactics are not always successful in silencing or dividing these relentless crusaders for justice.

Paula Flores's and Eva Arce's lives have been shattered by violence, police indifference, and incompetence, but both have resiliently repieced those shards and sought justice as human rights and community activists. Paula was a part of Voces sin Eco (Voices without an Echo), the earliest of the antifemicide NGOs in Juárez, and now leads a community improvement organization named after her daughter, María Sagrario González Flores. Through her efforts with Fundación Sagrario, a preschool bearing her daughter's name was built in Lomas de Poleo, Juárez.[22]

Eva Arce works as a human rights activist and is a prolific poet. Her poetry, which has appeared in many journals, including *Chicana/Latina Studies: The Journal of Mujeres Activas en Letras y Cambio Social,* voices her outrage against the "high and mighty people who work in the government and think they can do anything."[23] Through their artistic and organizing efforts, Eva and Paula show that, rather than becoming inconsolable sufferers, it is crucial for mothers to become active social agents who combat the society that has increasingly come to normalize their daughters' brutal killings.

In the final *testimonio,* artist Rigo Maldonado continues to highlight the ways in which creative energies can and should be used to shed light on these tragedies and bring justice to the people of Ciudad Juárez. In describing his experiences as part of a group of Los Angelenos who traveled to Juárez in 1999 at a time when the femicides were still largely unknown to the American public, he poignantly relates how putting a face to what he thought was a mere urban legend had a tremendous impact on him. Consequently, he embarked on a mission to curate an exhibit that would expose the public north of the border to the femicides. As a Chicano artist, Maldonado shows us one of the many ways in which activists from both sides of the border are working in behalf of *las mujeres* of Juárez.

As one of the leading academic authorities on sex crimes and gender terrorism, Jane Caputi places the violence against Juárez women in a broader temporal and sociocultural scope. In her Afterword, "Goddess Murder and Gynocide in Ciudad Juárez," Caputi addresses the spiritual and ritualistic significance of the Juárez femicides. She posits that a possible reason for the impunity granted the perpetrators and the continuation of the crimes is the misogynistic teaching of ancient myths, which undergird the gendered beliefs and values of Mexican society. This is not to say that savagery runs in mestizo veins, but that we must assess the universal patriarchal tradition of destroying culturally powerful and socially defiant women (in Mexico, sixteenth-century Malinalli Tenepal and seventeenth-century Sor Juana Inés de la Cruz both come to mind).

Examining Aztec myths like that of Coyolxauhqui, the warrior Moon Goddess who was brutally dismembered by her brother Huitzilopochtli

**Fig. i.5.** Chisco © 2002, *Nacerán Flores* (Flowers Will Be Born), mixed media. From "Las Hijas de Juárez" Exhibition, curated by Rigo Maldonado and Victoria Delgadillo. Social and Public Art Resource Center, Venice, Calif., 2003. Courtesy of Rigo Maldonado.

(the Sun God) for rising up against the new world order that his birth represented for the Aztec nation, Caputi suggests that what is happening in Juárez today is a modern-day reenactment of ancient patriarchal rituals, whose cultural function is to perpetuate male supremacy. Facing economic displacement and its ensuing emasculation, or feeling the need to satisfy

**Fig. i.6.** Alma López © 2003, "La Llorona Desperately Seeking Coyolxauhqui," serigraph. Courtesy of Alma López. Special thanks to Coral López.

their grotesque misogynistic desires, or twisting the truth to blame the victims for their own deaths, the "high priests" of Juárez (the murderers themselves or the authorities invested in covering up their crimes) may be offering their blood sacrifices to what Mary Daly calls "the prevailing religion of the entire planet," that is, patriarchy. Caputi urges us to re-member the modern-day Coyolxauhquis in Juárez—as Alma López has done in her logo for the Maquiladora Murders conference—by reassembling her pieces on a tree of life, because the suffering of *las hijas* of Juárez translates into universal female suffering. Until we place these women in "their rightful symbolic place at the cosmic center," Caputi argues, we will continue to replicate patriarchal myths that punish women simply for being women.

It is of the essence that we re-member the dismembered Coyolxauhquis of Juárez, that we do something to stop the violence, to end the legal impunity, to help the victims, their families, and the hundreds of others who come to Juárez on a daily basis and continue to live in the blissful ignorance of hope and desire that we call the "American Dream." But we must also remember that they are more than victims. They were women and girls who lived and died among us. They had lives and names and histories, dreams and troubles of their own. They deserve our remembrance, our activism, our outrage, and our voices yelling out "¡Ni una más!" Not one more femicide on the U.S.-Mexico border, or anywhere else in the world!

## Notes

1. These crimes should not be confused with "narco-killings," which are crimes committed in the turf-and-power struggles of local drug cartels and which target mainly male victims.

2. North of the border, U.S. lawmakers' only response to this increased gender-targeted border violence has been to tighten homeland security measures. A resolution was introduced to the House of Representatives by Rep. Hilda Solís (D-CA) in 2003, and a similar one was introduced in the Senate by Sen. Jeff Bingaman (D-NM) in 2004 "to express sympathy for the families of the victims" and to get the U.S. government involved in a binational task force to address the crimes. The votes necessary for passage of the legislation were slow in coming, but in May 2006, Amnesty International reported that the joint resolution had at last been passed in the House. "Congress has now unanimously called on the secretary of state and the U.S. ambassador to Mexico to take specific steps to ensure that addressing these horrendous murders becomes a part of the U.S.-Mexico bilateral agenda." See http://www.amnestyusa.org/violence-against-women/page.do?id=1011012.

3. "Juárez," by Tori Amos on the album *To Venus and Back* (Atlantic, 1999); "Invalid Litter Department," CD single by At the Drive-In (EMI International, 2001); "La Niña de la Maquiladora," by Lila Downs on the album *The Border/La Línea* (Narada World, 2001); "Las Mujeres de Juárez," by Los Tigres del Norte on the album *Pacto de Sangre* (Fonovisa, 2004); "Madera," by Los Jaguares on the album *Crónicas de un Laberinto* (Sony International, 2005).

4. See www.youtube.com/watch?v=o5mlgmqy9oI&mode=related&search=.

5. HBO's *The Virgin of Juárez* (2006), directed by Kevin James Dobson and starring Minnie Driver; *Bordertown* (2007), directed by Gregory Nava and starring Jennifer López, Antonio Banderas, Martin Sheen, and Sonia Braga. In February 2009, Paramount released a Mexican production titled *Backyard/Traspatio*, written by Sabina Berman, directed by Carlos Carrera (*The Crime of Padre Amaro*), and star-

ring Jimmy Smits. For more details on the last, see http://news.newamericamedia
.org/news/view_article.html?article_id=910ba01693bec5c05fb4cd25a32d06fe.

6. *Las Muertas de Juárez*, directed by Enrique Murillo (Laguna Productions, 2002).

7. *Bajo Juárez: A City Devouring Its Girls*, directed by Alejandra Sánchez Orozco and José Antonio Cordero (Indymedia, 2006); *On the Edge: Femicide in Ciudad Juárez*, directed by Steve Hise (Illegal Art, 2006); and *Border Echoes*, directed by Lorena Méndez (Documentary Films, 2006).

8. See *Desert Blood: The Juárez Murders*, by Alicia Gaspar de Alba (Houston: Arte Público Press, 2005); *Secrets in the Sand: The Young Women of Ciudad Juárez*, by Marjorie Agosín, trans. Celeste Kostopulos-Cooperman (New York: White Pine Press, 2006); *If I Die in Juárez*, by Stella Pope Duarte (Tempe: University of Arizona Press, 2007).

9. See Diana Washington Valdez, *Cosecha de mujeres: Safari en el desierto mexicano* (Mexico City: Océano, 2005); and Theresa Rodríguez et al., *The Daughters of Juárez: A True Story of Serial Murder South of the Border* (New York: Atria Books, 2007).

10. See Melissa Wright, *Disposable Women and Other Myths of Global Capitalism* (New York: Routledge, 2006).

11. To name a few artists: Coco Fusco, Rubén Amavisca, Alma López, Laura Molina, Rigo Maldonado, Victoria Delgadillo, Daisy Tonantzin, Ester Hernández, Yreina Cervántez, Consuelo Flores, and Favianna Rodríguez.

12. For some of the earliest scholarship on the femicides, see Melissa Wright, "The Dialectics of Still Life: Murder, Women, and the Maquiladoras," *Public Culture* 11.3 (1999): 453–474; and "A Manifesto against Femicide," *Antipode* 33.3 (July 2001): 550–566; Rosa Linda Fregoso, "Voices without Echo: The Global Gendered Apartheid," *Emergences* 10.1 (May 2000): 137–155; Julia Monárrez-Fragoso, "La cultura del feminicidio en Juárez, 1993–1999," *Frontera Norte* 12.23 (January–June 2000): 87–118. For early pre-NAFTA scholarship on the *maquiladora* industry, see Norma Iglesias Prieto, *La flor más bella de la maquiladora* (Tijuana: Secretaría de Educación Pública, Centro de Estudios Fronterizos, El Colegio de la Frontera Norte, 1985). For early feminist scholarship on sex crimes, see Jane Caputi, "The Sexual Politics of Murder," *Gender and Society* 3.4 (December 1989): 437–456.

13. MujerArtes is a collective of elderly community ceramicists affiliated with the Esperanza Peace and Justice Center in San Antonio, Texas. Working under the direction of Verónica Castillo, MujerArtes created a community altar entitled *Lamento por las Mujeres de Juárez* (Elegy for the Women of Juárez), which included Verónica Castillo's *Maquilando Mujeres: Árbol de la Muerte* (Milling Women: Tree of Death) and twenty-six other pieces of ceramic art—plates, plaques, sculptures, and trees of life depicting scenes of violence, innocence, and mourning. *Lamento* opened as an exhibition at the Esperanza Center in July 2003 and was later transported to and installed at UCLA's Fowler Museum of Cultural History in the fall of 2003 as part of the museum's special exhibition on the Mexican cultural tradition of "trees of life," which featured the work of Verónica Castillo's family. The silent auction generated a $5,000 donation from MujerArtes to Amigos de las Mujeres de Juárez, which divided the funds among the victims' families that the group represents.

14. Access the petition at http://www.petitiononline.com/NiUnaMas/petition
.html. As of June 28, 2007, four and a half years after the petition went online, it

had garnered 10,700 votes from supporters from Europe, Latin America, and the United States.

15. See Jane Caputi's Afterword for a detailed deconstruction of the image.

16. The story of Coyolxauhqui, the Moon Goddess, links to the story of Coatlicue, her mother and the mother of all the gods, and is taken from the Florentine Codex. While Coatlicue was performing her ritual sweeping of a temple on the hill of Coatepec, she mystically became impregnated by a ball of falling feathers that she nestled to her breast. This pregnancy enraged Coyolxauhqui and her four hundred brothers and sisters—the stars—who made plans to attack and kill their mother on the hill of Coatepec. Coyolxauhqui, whose name means "the goddess of the bells on her cheeks," is the female warrior who led her siblings to their mother to mount the attack in response to feeling disgraced by their mother's unexplained pregnancy. Just as Coyolxauhqui and her siblings arrived, Coatlicue gave birth to the full-grown God of the Sun and God of War, Huitzilopochtli. Huitzilopochtli promised his mother that he would protect her from his sister's wrath. He armed himself with the Xiuhcoatl, the Fiery Serpent, and stopped his sister from killing their mother by decapitating Coyolxauhqui and hurling her body down the hill to smash into many pieces at the bottom. Huitzilopochtli then defeated the other siblings and claimed his title as the supreme ruler of the Aztecs, the God of War.

17. For an online summary of the report, see http://www.amnestyusa.org/document.php?id=3EC284DD25E3F2B080256D78005D4BB1. For an updated list of femicides in Juárez between 2004 and 2006, see the Web site of the Washington Office for Latin America (WOLA) at http://www.wola.org/index.php?option=com_content&task=viewp&id=474&Itemid=2.

18. See "Ciudad Juárez: Gobierno de Chihuahua desacreditó informe de AI," *Mujeres Hoy* (August 15, 2003), available online on the Nuestras Hijas de Regreso a Casa Web site, http://www.mujeresdejuarez.org.

19. Theresa Braine, "Argentine Experts Study Juárez Murder Remains," *Women's eNews* (April 16, 2006), http://www.womensenews.org/article.cfm/dyn/aid/2707/.

20. By 2003, copycat killings had started to crop up in other border cities such as Nogales, Matamoros, Mexicali, and Nuevo Laredo, and also in Chihuahua City, where over one hundred women and girls have been slain in the "Juárez style."

21. The mothers of Silvia Arce and Sagrario González, respectively. Both mothers shared a panel at the "Feminicide = Sanctioned Murder" Conference held at Stanford University on May 18, 2007.

22. Lomas de Poleo is one of the shantytowns where bodies of victims were found semiburied in trash. It lies just across the border and at the foot of the American Smelter and Refining Company (ASARCO) smelter smokestacks.

23. Eva Arce, "Calles," *Chicana/Latina Studies: The Journal of MALCS* 4.1 (Fall 2004): 112–113.

**PART ONE**

# INTERVENTIONS

# CHAPTER 1

# Accountability for Murder in the *Maquiladoras:* Linking Corporate Indifference to Gender Violence at the U.S.-Mexico Border

ELVIA R. ARRIOLA

*Claudia Ivette González might still be alive if her employers had not turned her away. The 20-year-old resident of Ciudad Juárez—the Mexican city abutting El Paso, Texas—arrived at her assembly plant job four minutes late one day in October 2001. After management refused to let her into the factory, she started home on foot. A month later, her corpse was discovered buried in a field near a busy Juárez intersection. Next to her lay the bodies of seven other young women.*
—DEBBIE NATHAN, *THE JUÁREZ MURDERS*

The *"maquiladora* murders" have become a popular subject for writing and activism by feminists, as well as the inspiration for numerous forms of art, literary fiction,[1] commentaries,[2] international conferences,[3] movies,[4] and marches[5] on both sides of the border. A 2003 conference held at the University of California–Los Angeles entitled "The Maquiladora Murders, Or, Who Is Killing the Women of Juárez?" drew worldwide attention to the cases of hundreds of young Mexican women who worked in *maquiladoras*—American-owned transnational factories—and met untimely, often brutal, deaths. Who killed them is still a mystery. What is not a mystery is that incidents of domestic violence and femicide in Ciudad Juárez have risen in the wake of heavy industrialization along the border;[6] that industrialization was a result of the signing of the 1993 North American Free Trade Agreement (NAFTA) between Mexico, the United States, and Canada.[7]

In less than a decade, a city that once had a very low homicide rate now reports that at least three hundred women and girls were killed in Ciudad Juárez between 1994 and 2000.[8] Some of the murders fall into a bizarre serial killer pattern.[9] Others are linked to illegal trafficking gangs.[10] Still others involve abductions of young female *maquiladora* workers who never made it to or from work and whose bodies were later found dumped in Lomas de Poleo, the desert that surrounds Ciudad Juárez.[11] They had been raped, beaten, or mutilated.

To be fair, the reference to *"maquiladora* murders" is a misnomer; not all victims have been workers for the vast number of American companies lining the two thousand–mile border that secures an interdependent economic bond between the United States and Mexico. However, while the exact number of victims is still unknown, of the estimated three hundred to four hundred unsolved murders, about one-third involve *maquiladora* workers.[12] Mexican government officials have not appreciated the negative press surrounding their largest export-processing zone and symbol of participation in the global economy.[13] And the public has not been happy, either, confused as it is by seemingly bungled and incompetent investigations. The lack of coordination among public authorities has only worsened the perception that the government is too corrupt, too indifferent, or too incompetent to address the problem of systematic violence against women.

In Mexico, the *maquiladora* worker is typically someone with little education or property and is often a migrant from even poorer regions of the country, which now hosts a conglomerate of factories owned by European, American, and Japanese multinational corporations. Thousands of workers in these factories eke out sad lives in shantytowns without water, electricity, or public lighting.[14] The most recent arrivals to the Mexican *frontera* find cities that are unable to meet their housing needs. Dozens of families may stake out plots of land near public utilities or industrial parks, where they pirate essential public services and live in shacks made of sticks, cardboard, rags, or discarded construction platforms. Some even make their homes next to trash dumps.

Public discourse on the Juárez murders intensified after the 2001 release of the documentary *Señorita Extraviada,* by former Juárez resident and filmmaker Lourdes Portillo. The documentary opens with various shots of factories bearing the names of familiar American companies that sell U.S. consumers everything from cell phones to televisions, stereo equipment, computers, electrical appliances, and toys. Juárez is portrayed as Mexico's symbol of the failed promises of free trade; in what activists refer to as the "race to the bottom" of the wage scale, investors compete globally and reap huge profits by creating new low-skilled and low-paying jobs for the working classes. Although a political and economic context is critical for grasping the breadth and depth of the gender violence that accompanies globalization, the film does not dwell on this context.[15]

Instead, *Señorita Extraviada* portrays Juárez as a city out of control, unable to respond to violence against poor working women. Highlighted are images of indigent, powerless, and grieving families confronting law enforcement and political systems that systematically fail them. The violence of poverty, graphically portrayed in *Señorita Extraviada,* generates rage and fury as the camera pans over crime scenes littered with the shoes, clothes, and jewelry of a girl's naked, bruised, or mutilated body discovered weeks after her disappearance. In another scene, a coroner confirms that one of the victims in a dual murder suffered massive cardiac arrest as a result of the terror she and the other young girl experienced in their final moments of life. Each story of grief produces waves of sorrow that spread over the families, the city, and the lost image of the characteristically family-oriented Mexican culture.

The bungled forensic efforts reinforce the violence against a young murder victim who left the house one day and never came home, leaving behind a family desperate for answers and comfort from their community leaders. The film highlights some of the outrageous official responses to the murders. For example, the governor of the State of Chihuahua is shown publicly criticizing the murder victims for the way they dressed or for frequenting nightclubs, thus blaming the victims for their fate and turning the demands for investigation into a mockery of justice. After public outcry, the state appointed a female special prosecutor. However, the state then failed to provide her with sufficient power or money to produce satisfactory leads.

While *Señorita Extraviada* portrays the problem as the systematic failure of law enforcement and the political system, Diana Washington Valdez, the reporter who has relentlessly tracked the murders since the early nineties, argues that true justice for the *maquiladora* murder victims may never come, because rampant corruption and secrecy surround efforts to track down the persons responsible for the most chilling serial- or ritualistic-type killings.

Yet, an important factor is constantly overlooked in the public discourse about the Juárez murders. Few seriously examine the relationship between systematic violence against women and the changes in the social environment of the city that have allowed such violence to occur. Along Mexico's border, and especially in Ciudad Juárez, many changes have resulted from the rapid industrialization produced by Mexico's intense participation in the global economy.[16] The unspoken element in the discourse is the multinational corporations' complicity with Mexican officials in disregarding the health, safety, and security needs of the Mexican women and girls who work in the *maquiladoras.* Multinational corporations come into Mexico, lease large plots of land, often run their factories twenty-four hours a day, pay no taxes, and do very little to ensure that the workers they employ will have a roof over their heads, beds to sleep in, and enough money to feed their families. Juárez, like many other border towns affected by NAFTA, may have factories and cheap jobs, but such employment has not enhanced peace and prosperity among the working class; instead, hostility against the poor working women—who form the majority of those employed by the *maquiladoras*—has intensified.

To the activists who advocate for justice in the *maquiladoras,* the undeveloped point that surrounds the phenomenon of the murders is the fact that the very girl whose body was found mutilated and dumped had worked hard, very hard, in one of those factories. She was trying to improve her lot in life, as well as that of her family, and no one, not even her own government, cares to take responsibility. What about the fact that the same attitude about the murders—"We are not responsible"—is also reflected in employment policies that encourage indifference to the workers' needs and human rights, whether in or out of the factories?

I argue that the Ciudad Juárez murders are an extreme manifestation of the systemic patterns of abuse, harassment, and violence against women who work in the *maquiladoras*—treatment that is an attributable by-product of the privileges and lack of regulation enjoyed by the investors who employ them under the North American Free Trade Agreement.[17] I begin by acknowledging the critical relationship between women, gender violence, and free trade that has been noted by some scholars. But I also seek to understand how the absence of regulations to benefit workers in standard free-trade law and policy perpetuates the degradation of *maquiladora* workers and creates environments hostile to workingwomen's lives, including discrimination, toxicity in the workplace, and threats of fatal assault. In "Missing the Story," noted feminist reporter Debbie Nathan rightly criticizes *Señorita Extraviada* for its failure to highlight the presence of the *maquiladora* industries and their power to set standards of worker treatment that encourage general hostility toward poor working women. The unquestioned right to exploit the mostly female working poor in Mexico, combined with the effects of rapid industrialization, incites increased gender violence while securing Mexico's significant role in the globalization of the economy at the U.S.-Mexico border.

In this chapter, I first present the argument, also made by activists at the border, that the Juárez murder phenomenon is a story about systematic abuse and violence against working-class employees; that abuse includes exposure to toxicity in the workplace, sexual harassment, and arbitrary disciplinary methods. This systematic abuse is the result of investor privileges guaranteed under NAFTA and repeated in the Central American Free Trade Agreement (CAFTA), which virtually immunize the transnational investor from accountability for harm to the worker, anticipated or not, when conducting business in Mexico.

Second, I illustrate the legal framework for addressing the questions of

**Fig. 1.1.** J Guadalupe Pérez © 2003, "Cruces en el Campo Algodonero, al Fondo el Edificio de la AMAC" (Crosses in the Cotton Field, with AMAC Building in the Background). Courtesy of J Guadalupe Pérez.

accountability that often arise when one is confronted with the realities of systematic violence against women in places like Ciudad Juárez and other locales that are newcomers to globalization.

Third, I return to the stories of workers at the border, with a focus on individual efforts by workers to bring about justice in the *maquiladoras*. Although it is important to improve economic globalization analysis with attention to women's experiences and struggles, it is also important to transcend the essentialist image of all poor working women as victims. Many workers in global factories do not passively sit by, accepting the attitudes of indifference crafted into free-trade law and policy and taken advantage of by some companies. There is much that is wrong with current free-trade policy and law that could be changed with amendments to NAFTA or CAFTA, or through litigation involving statutes targeting corporations as actors under the color of law. But even without those changes, some Mexican workers have found ways to empower themselves, like the legendary David against the giant Goliath corporation, by organizing and protesting against abusive employers to have their rights enforced.

Finally, I remind the reader that the phenomenon of the Juárez murders is inseparable today from the various forms of systematic abuse against mostly women workers who have populated the American factories since the pre-NAFTA days of industrialization at the Mexican border. Given the enduring fact that more women than men work in the factories, and the extreme example of abuse of women symbolized in the systematic killings of women and girls who are part of the city's poorest and most powerless, I make an appeal to the feminist activists who are busily creating awareness about the murders. I urge them to take more seriously the issue of the social and economic context of the Juárez murders so as to influence the shaping of improved public policies that can remedy the gross absence of regulation for corporate accountability and true protections of working women's rights under free-trade law.

### Gender and Globalization at the Mexican Border: Before and after NAFTA

Globalization has its fans and its critics. To some, like *New York Times* columnist Thomas Friedman, it is the way of the future, where people of different nations and cultures will interconnect easily through the Internet; markets and democracy will flourish; and all things stodgy, inefficient, and dictatorial will fade away.[18] Others are more cautious, calling for better regulatory oversight by the International Monetary Fund (IMF) and other financial players in the politics of free trade. Still others, like Amy Chua, see a deadly combination for nations whose transition to a market economy and democracy is too quick.[19] Most contemporary globalization talk, including that at the conference that produced this chapter,[20] focuses on the economic theories that either support or weaken the argument for it, such as free trade, capitalism, privatization, deregulation, and the relationship between market growth and social instability in new democracies.[21] Those who view gender and global trade as crucially related are still in the minority in academic discourse.

There is irony in knowing that females continue to dominate as ideal workers in export-processing zones while females are also the consumers most often targeted by ad campaigns to buy the goods coming from these exploitative zones. Carla Freeman argues that globalization discourse is "bereft" of gender analysis because it is hard to connect the "global" with women's stories and experiences or women-based movements for socio-economic change.[22] The problem may be that overall globalization politics appear loaded with masculine power and focus, and so the only way to see gender is to move away from the global to the local. There, in either production or consumption, one will see gender at work.

Women, especially poor women, continue to play a significant role in the work of global employment.[23] American companies have been relocating to Mexico since 1965,[24] and with the signing of NAFTA, cross-border trade has expanded, with new factories being built and jobs created. However, fewer rights for workers at the Mexican border have been guaranteed. As the workingwomen's group, Comité Fronterizo de Obreras (CFO, Committee of Workingwomen at the Border), wrote in its 1999 report, "Six Years under NAFTA," free trade had failed them. Under NAFTA, wages and working conditions for *maquiladora* workers had gone from bad to worse.[25]

One of the first systematic observations of the relationship between gender and the setup and operation of the *maquiladoras* at the Mexican border is a study, *La flor más bella de las maquiladoras,* by Norma Iglesias Prieto.[26] In her landmark study, Prieto sought to illustrate "a global phenomenon" encompassing both the *maquiladoras* and the life experiences of workers. She relied on the voices of experience from inside the factories in the pre-NAFTA period to illustrate how gender-based attitudes affected everything from recruitment and hiring (nearly 100 percent women) to the treatment of women in the workplace. When American electrical, television, and stereo component companies, such as General Electric and Panasonic, began relocating to Mexico,[27] women were blatantly preferred for the jobs. Why? According to Leslie Salzinger, women were seen as ideal workers because their smaller hands and fingers could better assemble the tiny parts of export goods such as light bulbs, cassette tapes, and recorders. The ideal *maquiladora* worker was thus a hybrid of stereotypes based on sex, race, and class—she was not only more docile and passive than Mexican men, but submissive, easily trainable, and unlikely to pose problems with union organizing.[28]

Not much has changed under NAFTA. Women have remained a higher percentage of the workforce; a younger woman in her teens is still preferred to an older, wiser, and more tired woman who is likely to question the bad pay and treatment or, even worse, try to organize workers. Prieto concluded that, in the pre-NAFTA period, it was clear that the main purpose for the poor treatment of the workers and low safety standards was to secure an easily discardable "reserve army of labor" rather than to offer career jobs or stable employment.[29]

Post-NAFTA, the workers confirmed the continuation of these policies; the CFO wrote that NAFTA had caused "a sharp drop in the standard of living; a marked intensification of the labor process through speed-ups and other tactics, and a sustained campaign to undermine unions, labor rights and social protections."[30]

The report also concluded that other long-standing problems identified with the *maquiladora* industries, such as the use of child labor and exposure of workers to toxic industrial waste, still plagued the border region. Other blatantly sexist practices, like forced pregnancy testing, only stopped after international exposure.

### Where the Violence Leading to Murder Begins: The Voices of Experience from Inside the *Maquiladoras*

In 2000, I visited the city of Piedras Negras, Coahuila, and met members of the Comité Fronterizo de Obreras and their coordinator, Julia Quiñónez Gonzales, a former *maquiladora* worker–turned–activist. I had just published "Voices from the Border," relying heavily on Iglesias-Prieto's work, and that of Devon Peña,[31] to capture the workers' voice of experience under NAFTA. I joined a delegation that was led by a new group calling itself Austin Tan Cerca de la Frontera (So Close to the Border), which formed after members heard the personal testimonies of several *maquiladora* workers who had come to share their experiences with local activist and faith-based community groups. Having just concluded my border study, it was a profound experience to see my research come to life and to meet someone whose testimony I had cited from an international women's rights conference. I was introduced to workers in their homes and listened to them describe bad pay, bodily injury caused by stress, long schedules, unsafe conditions, exposure to toxic chemicals, and feelings of betrayal by unions that took management's side.

Over the next few months, I visited several other cities where the CFO had volunteers and began to meet privately with primarily female workers

and to listen to them relate their experiences in the *maquiladoras*. I sometimes met workers in their homes, which were uniformly tiny and clean
but often without flooring, plumbing, or any electricity other than a single
light bulb.

"Fatal indifference" is the only way I can articulate the totality of the
patterns described by the workers—a systematic, structural disregard by
corporations and their agents for the humanity of the laborer. It is from
this perspective that I argue, along with the activists, that the phenomenon
of the Juárez murders begins with free-trade laws' licensing of a form of
corporate activity that exploits the physical and spiritual strength of a poor
country's people. However, the workers' stories also reveal an amazing courage and strength to survive abusive patterns of worker mistreatment and
discipline.

### The Unbearable Pace: "I Tolerated Them for a Total of Eight Years"

Amparo was thirty-eight years old and raising two teenaged boys when I
interviewed her in Piedras Negras. She was desperately trying to keep the
older boy in school so that he might avoid the destiny of the working poor—
beginning work in the factories at age fifteen and working ten-hour days,
on average, for little pay. Amparo had been fired for being outspoken about
the poor treatment of workers at Dimmit Industries, which is now defunct.
Amparo was hired at Dimmit to sew waistbands onto a minimum of twelve
hundred pairs of expensive dress slacks per day in order to receive the base
weekly wage of three hundred pesos and two hundred pesos in bonus (about
thirty-five dollars per week). To earn a salary on which she could live, she
pushed herself to produce 150 percent of the expected quota, or about eighteen hundred pairs of slacks per day, for approximately six years.

Amparo recalled that every day she walked out with a face blackened by
lint and dust due to the poor ventilation system in the plant. A common
complaint of the workers was the lack of adequate ventilation in the cheaply
built, windowless warehouses that were set up for factory operations. She
remembered the terrible cough she endured almost all of the time as a result
of the fibers, distinctly visible in the surrounding air, settling on her skin
and in her lungs. She also had to endure the exhaustion of the typical ten-
to-twelve-hour shift with only a half-hour break for lunch and a ten-minute
break in the morning. "I first thought, that's just the way working conditions are here at the border. In time I began to see injustices here." Amparo
was one of five workers who filed an unfair labor practice charge against

Dimmit after she was fired for complaining about the piecework policy that kept the wages so low.[32] Amparo knew she was in for a long haul by filing a claim, but she said it was worth it because "I've tolerated them for eight years."[33]

On that same trip, I met Juanita Torres, who had also been fired from Dimmit as a troublemaker and who was trying to organize new elections for a better shop steward—one who would not consistently side with management. Others I spoke with confirmed a pattern of abusive treatment. "Cuca" Torres, Juanita's sister, said, "They yell at us to hurry up," referring to the line supervisors. Cuca was working for Littelfuse Co., which employed mostly women to assemble thousands of light bulbs and fuses per day in the kind of factory Prieto describes in her study. Young Marina Briones, who was working for one of the many Aluminum Company of America (ALCOA) factories in Piedras Negras, said, "The typical workday [of ten-to-twelve hours] is so long that I come home too tired to do any housework or to talk to anyone."[34]

## Miserly Wages in Return for Exposure to Toxicity

Those who study, write, and think about globalization often understand at an abstract level that the pay is low, the working conditions are bad, and the workdays are long. But few ever confront and absorb in detail the depth and breadth of the physical, mental, and emotional pain the workers experience in the *maquiladoras* unless they can hear it from a worker. "I can never wear open shoes, and in hot weather I must have on cotton socks to prevent the humidity from encouraging the fungus to reappear," said María Elena García, a woman who, when I met her, had just begun to organize for the CFO in the city of Reynosa, Tamaulipas.

María Elena offered this story when I told her that I had come to learn more about the health effects of working in the *maquiladoras*. As we spoke, she pointed to dark scar tissue mostly on the top of her feet—old scratch marks and evidence of once-ruptured skin that she referred to as the symptoms of an unexplainable fungus. It was an infection that had broken out and rotted the skin so badly "that my own brothers and sisters would tell me to stay away from them because of the awful smell." The doctors concluded that the condition, which lasted for a year, was so bad that if she did not find a remedy and did not stop working in the environment that had obviously contributed to the infection, she would lose her feet to gangrene. Her mother told her, "Although I appreciate the help from your working, I don't want you to lose your feet." María Elena quit the job she had held for over two years—assembling one section of seat belts all day long—during which time she was exposed to fine chemical dust particles in the strap fabric. Those particles caused her serious foot condition, a condition for which there is no cure.[35]

María Elena's condition is only too common among workers. A variety of illnesses and conditions, including back problems, carpal tunnel syndrome, asthma, and disabling allergic reactions, typically accompany the privilege of working in a *maquiladora*. I recall the interview with Raquel Mendoza, who was fired along with her sister, Norma, from the Dimmit Factory in Piedras Negras. During the interview, Raquel remembered when she developed a severe bladder infection due to a lack of bathroom access—workers were fined or reprimanded for "abusing" the privilege of going to the bathroom during their time in the assembly line. "I had learned so well to ignore my need to go that now I could not go."[36]

Juanita Torres told how it was standard for employers to deny work-related injuries. It costs employers to have workers qualify for government disability programs, so the companies encourage them to use company doctors, whose tendency is to minimize any harm because of the potential liability employers face for occupational hazards under the Federal Labor Law.[37] On one occasion, an in-house medic denied that it was the chemicals in a particular pant fabric that had caused Juanita an upper body rash. On another occasion, she cut her finger on a machine, a frequent problem for workers because it was on "speed up"—a setting used by managers to increase a machine's output and to pressure workers to maintain a specific, hurried pace. That time it was a medic at the government clinic for workers, Seguro Social,[38] who botched the treatment and suggested the easy remedy of amputating her finger when she complained that the wound was not healing properly. Juanita said that she ran out crying, quit her job, and eventually healed her finger with home herbal remedies.

Some workers suffer injuries or spontaneous abortions in the workplace because occupational hazards, such as exposure to toxic chemicals or fumes, are given such low priority. On my visit to Ciudad Acuña, Pilar Marentes gave me a news article describing a recent chemical spill that had affected several women who were told to get back to work despite the fumes.[39] It was just like the story of Paty Leyva of Piedras Negras, who teared up when I began to ask questions about the health effects of *maquiladora* work. While talking about the stressful schedule, Paty remembered a miscarriage she attributed to the work pressures and constant exposure to toxic solvents at her job.[40]

## Low Priority on the *Maquiladora* Owner's Agenda: Basic Worker Safety

As previously noted, the percentage of female workers in *maquiladoras* is higher than that of males, but gender stereotyping accounts for a greater percentage of men in the automotive assembly factories. The same weekend I met Pilar Marentes, I met Nicolás. Nicolás built auto dashboards and, along with several dozen other workers, was trying to confront ALCOA management about a promise for medical care. This followed a report from the company during the 1990s that Nicolás and other workers had been exposed to a highly toxic chemical, referred to by the acronym MOCA.[41] Nicolás said that his great fear, as he showed me photos of his children, was that he and his wife had conceived the children during the period of exposure.

In October 2006, I led a delegation of law students interested in learning more about the effects of NAFTA from a human perspective. On this trip, we met workers in Reynosa, Tamaulipas (which borders McAllen, Texas), whose stories offered us insight into the systematic indifference to workers' humanity in the *maquiladoras*. Workers from the Emerson factory, which manufactures Maytag Co. washer and dryer motors and employs about eleven thousand workers, complained to the CFO about the total lack of safety precautions in the factory. Cuts and injuries on the job were frequent. A worker at this meeting who was on crutches explained that a safety latch on the assembly line loosened one of the motors, and it came crashing down on his leg. He did not receive proper medical care because the company diverted him to its doctor. The group described how another worker lost part of his finger because a safety latch broke and came down on his hand—the mechanic on duty was out, and it was over an hour before the injured worker's hand was dislodged. Doctors were unable to save part of the finger due to the delay in removing the hand from the heavy machine.

## NAFTA: Setting an Agenda for the Global Factories of the World

The *maquiladoras* thrive on the structure of a work week designed to produce the highest output. In the United States, the corporation that has factories at the border is likely to operate on the unchallenged standard of the forty-hour work week.[42] However, in the *maquiladoras*, the average is likely to be five to ten hours longer and not only avoids the schedule originally imposed by the Fair Labor Standards Act, but also creates a work culture that sees no problem with ten- and twelve-hour shifts, no overtime pay, and, in some factories, only one day off per week.[43]

In the delegation I led in October 2005 to Piedras Negras and Ciudad Acuña, we met and heard from Ángela, who had arrived from Veracruz seven years earlier. She earned 750 pesos (about $75.00) per week at the ALCOA factory and felt grateful not to have to work weekends. She said that her daughter was earning much more, about 950 pesos per week (about $95.00), but she had to work twelve-hour shifts, six days per week. With this kind of schedule, her daughter was forced to pay for child care and rely on Ángela's help on Saturdays. And supervisors made it clear that, with the exception of a half hour for lunch and two short breaks, all time in the shop was work time. One worker stated in an earlier published study: "It's really unreasonable because we work from 7 AM to 5:30 PM, Monday through Friday. To arrive on time, I have to get up at 5 AM, and at that hour you really don't feel like eating. At 9:30 they give us 10 minutes for breakfast, and half an hour for lunch at 1 PM."[44] The patterns of working conditions in the *maquiladoras* remain unchanged.

Global employment, whether in Mexico or elsewhere, falls into a familiar pattern—one in which the policies of worker treatment emphasize rapid production, not worker health and safety or improved living conditions.[45] As some critics note, the new wealth that comes with free trade often benefits a tiny privileged minority—not the general population of the poorer country.[46] The creation of another export-processing zone generates systems of employment and discipline designed to turn the "lazy," unskilled worker into an efficient production machine. Who the workers are, what they think, and how they feel about production methods, assembly, and export not only are irrelevant, but also can be a source of trouble.[47] Caring about people does not factor well into a business driven by commitment to the bottom line or a cost-benefit analysis.[48] If production is more important than people, then so is making sure that workers show up on time. When having workers show up on time is more important than their quality of life, then early work hours are the norm, as well as twenty-four-hour, seven-days-per-week operations.

Pilar Marentes and I talked about this as we discussed the issue of the Juárez murders in 2000. Pilar said that safety was always an issue for the poor, who had to rely on the bus to get to and from work. She further speculated that the Juárez killer was a bus driver for a factory. She said the bus drivers drove around at all hours and stuck to a certain route, so at "whatever block nearest to their home is where [the workers] get off. Sometimes it is three blocks . . . so for those three blocks, no one is protected because they are alone."[49]

On all of my trips since 2000, I have heard the same stories about the work schedules: ten-to-twelve-hour shifts, people getting off work at all hours of the morning and night, and women getting up in the dark of morning to get children ready for school and themselves for work, worried they might miss the company bus that delivers them to remote job sites. A common fear among workers is losing a day's pay if they come to work late, or being charged penalties on their paycheck for "abusing" the bathroom privilege during work hours.[50]

The stories told of a threadbare existence—people living in shacks, no running water, rough outhouses, dirt floors, and children exposed to all sorts of treacherous conditions because of unpaved roads and lack of street lighting. Children start working young because they begin to understand that their parents are working and that there is never enough. This means that children are leaving home at six and seven in the morning and walking either to or from work in the dark, or in dangerous conditions. For instance, two boys drowned after heavy rains and flooding in Ciudad Acuña because they walked home late at night after leaving the grocery store where they carried bags for mere tips.[51] Where poverty is the norm, so too is the violence of poverty.

The disciplinary methods, the production quotas that must be met at any cost, the speedups and injuries, the punishment for using the bathroom during work time, and the exposure to dangerous instruments or chemicals all flow directly from the signal by company owners and their agents to supervisors and managers that (1) workers' lives are less important than production schedules, and (2) the safety of workers is yet another cost that disturbs the projected return on investment.

Therefore, employee protections, such as adequate safety gear for employees who must work with toxic chemicals, lighting around the factory, and security for workers, are not as important as making sure workers do their tasks, supervisors meet the production schedule, and goods are exported and released into the stream of commerce, generating consumption and profits that will ultimately line the pockets of the owners and shareholders.[52]

These are the consequences of the privileges and rights enjoyed by employers under free-trade law and policy. It is a policy that does not care about workers, much less about a young woman like Claudia Ivette González, who was disciplined for being late to work by being told she must go home and would be docked a day's wage. In the world of corporate privilege, it does not matter that a young girl might be sent home in the dark, because discipline for the "lazy, irresponsible" worker is deemed more important than her life and physical safety. She is, after all, an insignificant cog in the wheel of production.

Even the corporations that own the *maquiladoras* see their employees as mere cogs. Therefore, when Lear Corporation representatives were asked by a reporter from *Salon* magazine about the lack of security for workers like Claudia (who was sent home and later found murdered), they responded, "The murder didn't happen on company property."[53] Technically, it had not, but a policy of fatal indifference to her safety and that of other similarly situated workers was already in place and enforced on the day of her disappearance. Legally, the company might not have been directly responsible for the abduction or murder, but morally?

In recent years, critical race-feminist scholars have argued that the discourse of human rights is missing a gender analysis.[54] Traditionalists view human rights as confined to matters like racial or ethnic persecution and torture. Arguments that sex discrimination and gender violence are also a human rights concern are viewed as suspect or as improper attempts to export cultural values.[55]

Yet, as Amnesty International reports have shown, the Juárez murders are being viewed internationally as a grave human rights problem for Mexico. In contrast, Mexican government officials, such as the governor of Chihuahua, resist these critiques with classic defensiveness—blaming the victims for their dress or referring to working girls who frequent bars and clubs as immoral.[56] They seem to think it is better to invoke sexism than to admit that the murders reveal a masculine attitude of power, subordination, and fatal indifference to the health and welfare of poor working women. When corporate rights are made superior to workers' rights, the activists for justice in the *maquiladoras* naturally see the Juárez murders as a mere continuation of how they are treated as employees.

## Corporate Activity at the Mexican Border and Questions of Accountability

Stories from workers in factories at the border disturb the abstract discourses on free trade and mutual economic benefits that supposedly flow from a free-trade agreement. The language in NAFTA reveals a skewed set of policies—more rights for the investor than for the worker or migrant laborer.[57] The imbalance explains why it is so difficult for corporations to be held accountable for their harmful activities in foreign countries.

In this section, I address the legal framework of corporate accountability by exploring the use of the law to improve workers' lives and, consequently, women's lives under free-trade law and policy. NAFTA, after all, was not easily passed. The North American Agreement on Labor Cooperation (NAALC) was a result of public pressure to do more for workers' rights. Though the enforcement mechanism can be frustrating and long, the NAALC may hold some promise as an organizing tool for the workers, if not a tool for awarding actual remedies (for wrongdoing). Public awareness that corporations abuse their position in other countries has generated considerable literature on the legal theories that might be used to make the corporate actor accountable under U.S. domestic law,[58] international law, or under the law of the host country. In this case, it would be Mexican tort law. The next section briefly explores these options.

## NAFTA'S Labor-side Agreement: The North American Agreement on Labor Cooperation

The NAFTA/NAALC complaint process is purely administrative. Still, workers might find it a powerful organizing tool, as it can be used to present evidence and personal testimony about the problems they face that are illegal under existing labor or health and safety laws. "NAFTA complaint" is actually a term of convenience that refers to invoking provisions under the NAFTA labor-side agreement, the NAALC, under which the parties to NAFTA (the United States, Canada, and Mexico) promise the improvement of "working conditions and living standards in each Party's territory."[59] The best way to understand a NAFTA complaint is to see it as a reminder to the party nations that they have promised to treat workers fairly in pursuit of free trade and open economic borders. Because it is about labor cooperation, the hearings that occur under the NAALC process are public and in theory open to the citizens of any country that has signed NAFTA. The following will provide only a bare sketch of the process. It is a process which is extremely technical, convoluted, and not designed to generate actual remedial measures to make injured workers whole.[60]

In theory, the matters that can be part of a complaint under NAALC include the following:

a. Freedom of association and protection of the right to organize
b. The right to bargain collectively
c. The right to strike
d. Prohibition of forced labor
e. Labor protections for children and young persons
f. Minimum employment standards, such as minimum wages and over-time pay, covering wage earners, including those not covered by collective agreements
g. Elimination of employment discrimination
h. Equal pay for men and women
i. Prevention of occupational injuries and illnesses
j. Compensation in cases of occupational injuries and illnesses and
k. Protection of migrant workers

Filing complaints under the NAALC is not like filing a lawsuit. While workers may be complaining about toxicity in the workplace, repetitive tasks that cause them severe disabling conditions, arbitrary production schedules, ridiculously low pay for incredibly long hours, or harsh (and high-risk) penalties for lateness, nothing about the NAALC complaint process really brings the corporation under scrutiny. Instead, if a *maquiladora* worker, or group of workers, is able to lodge a complaint, it is directed at Mexico. The complaint is filed with an agency known as the National Administrative Office (NAO) in Washington, DC. Hearings can be held anywhere outside of Washington. The NAO conducts its own investigation and then issues a report of findings on whether or not Mexico properly enforced its relevant labor, health, and safety standards.

The labor-side agreement has not been received well by labor activists.[61] It creates a labyrinth of procedure that sets no specific standard for enforcement, but instead merely asks the signed parties to enforce their own laws and tells interested parties to go to their appropriate local agencies for enforcement. Then, even if an NAO hearing produces a report that the host country violated NAFTA and the NAALC by not sufficiently enforcing the laws, the "remedy" is a fine that may not exceed .007 percent of the total trade in goods between the countries in the most recent year for which data is available. The fine is to be spent on enforcement of labor laws in the country against which the complaint was filed.

The Custom Trim/Auto Trim case is one of the few in-depth actions that progressed through all levels of the NAALC procedure and was filed pursuant to the NAFTA labor-side agreement on behalf of workers.[62] The case was brought on behalf of dozens of workers in auto parts assembly factories in the Matamoros, Mexico/Brownsville, Texas, region along the Texas/Mexico border. Monica Schurtman, a clinical-skills professor at the time with the Social Justice Center at Saint Mary's University School of Law in San Antonio, Texas, garnered the assistance of student attorneys and activists through the Coalition for Justice in the Maquiladoras to supervise the writing and filing of the more than one hundred–page complaint to the NAO.

The complaint invoked everything from relevant Mexican labor law to applicable international agreements and charged various Mexican labor-related agencies with failure to conduct legally mandated inspections relating to occupational health and safety; failure to enforce various laws regulating the use of chemicals, glues, and solvents that were the cause of specific worker injuries; and failure to inform and train workers about the health risks associated with exposure to various chemicals in use at the workplace. It also invoked the application of federal Mexican labor law and other Mexican health and safety statutes that apply to sanitation in the workplace, and it required diagnosis and treatment of work-related injuries. However, the complaint failed to force the Mexican government to impose sanctions on the employer—AutoTrim and CustomTrim/Breed Technologies Mexicana—which was operating in the Brownsville/Matamoros region.

Professor Schurtman has summarized the proceedings that followed filing the complaint, including a series of ministerial consultations and resolutions to create an intergovernmental working group to discuss the same deficiencies identified in the hearing, the NAO report, and the workers' complaint. She concludes that "the labor ministers of the NAFTA countries have failed to address workers' complaints directly, ignored worker recommendations to enhance enforcement of existing occupational health and safety laws, and neglected to take remedial measures. The labor ministers have also declined requests by workers and non-governmental organization's (NGO) petitioners to have a voice in the intergovernmental discussions prompted by [the complaint]."[63]

The NAFTA/NAALC/NAO procedure for workers presents a strong contrast with the rights and remedies for investors under NAFTA. NAFTA has never included workers' rights language; the NAALC simply tells the host government to enforce existing law. The infamous Chapter 11 of NAFTA, however, permits a corporation to sue for compensation when another government's regulatory conduct is deemed "tantamount to expropriation." Not only does this reflect an antiregulatory sentiment in NAFTA, it seemingly protects corporate activity and profit at any cost.

This is not to say investors should not have rights under free-trade agreements. But, currently, NAFTA and its successor version for Central American states, CAFTA, place investors' rights above workers' rights, health and welfare regulation, and consumer rights. A review of the NAALC process shows that investors are clearly favored over workplace policies meant to protect injured workers from the likelihood of bodily harm or even kidnapping and violent or fatal assaults near the workplace. Free-trade policy is about markets and profit, not about making corporations more socially responsible. Harmful consequences of corporate activity have become the price of doing business.

Today's global workers, whether in Mexico, Central America, India, or China, are doing work once performed by American workers.[64] It is a reversal of the emergence, in the nineteenth and twentieth centuries, of trade unions, collective-bargaining rights, minimum wage and maximum work laws, and protections from occupational hazards. Sadly, globalization and NAFTA or CAFTA mark either the end of an era of organized workers' strength in unions or a serious challenge to workers and activists to take back the right to work with human dignity.[65] As noted above, NAFTA's labor-side agreement, the NAALC, pays only lip service to workers' rights and creates no realistic remedies. It is as if all workers have been returned to the era of the at-will contract, when the employer could hire and fire for a good reason, or no reason at all.

There is something compelling about hearing the voices of experience describe the managerial styles, wages, and safety issues in the factories and then to recognize the product they make or the label of the employer in an advertisement directed at U.S. consumers. The difference between the cost of an item in the United States and the pennies earned by the workers conjures up the contracts theory of unjust enrichment. The workers say, "They use us, make money off of our hard labor, then they throw us away."[66] The major complaint of the CFO in "Six Years under NAFTA" is a lower quality of life because of the poor wages and the long hours; laborers were working harder for less money than ever before.

On a 2004 delegation to Nuevo Laredo, I remember hearing workers tell about the "discount coupon *maquiladoras*" that had come in for a brief time with an exploitive agenda. They hired very young workers for two months, made them work long hours, and then one night disappeared, leaving the workers, many of them as young as twelve and thirteen, unpaid. Since that visit, I have a hard time looking through the huge coupon inserts that come with my Sunday newspaper.

*Maquiladora* workers may need to think about suing their own government for its complicity in commercial activities that benefit privileged minorities while systematically harming the workers.[67] As a result of their experiences in Mexico, some workers are lured to cross the border to find something better than the pay and conditions in the U.S.-owned *maquiladoras*, only to then face terrorism by vigilantes and hostile American legislators, who view them as criminals for being desperate for work to meet their needs.[68]

Last, maybe the easiest path to accountability would involve putting NAFTA and the NAALC aside and simply suing the corporate employer—which negligently and recklessly sets in motion systematic policies and practices that deny workers their right to human dignity—in a Mexican court under Mexican law.

## Women's Bodies as Part of the Free-trade Deal?
## Women's Rights as Human Rights

It is against this backdrop of the institutional disregard for human rights that we should consider the fate of Claudia Ivette González. She could be sent home at any hour from the factory, despite the risk, in a city fraught with the systematic fatal assault of women, because her employer was not required to consider her safety under NAFTA. The policy of free trade is profit making, not the terms and conditions under which a poor woman is hired, worked, paid, or disciplined. Her body is essential for production. The investor is in her country to do business while paying lip service to the notion of improving social and economic conditions.[69] The license to cross borders for profit is set in motion by the Mexican business and political elite, who would rather cater to investors' interests than worry about citizens' health and welfare.

There was nothing unusual about Claudia's being handed the standard penalty for being a few minutes late—"Go home." To argue that this is simply an appropriate way to treat a chronically tardy worker would be to look at the tree, not the forest. The way in which Claudia was treated in October 2001 was no different from that of thousands of other global factory workers who work under a network of unreasonable standards for worker treatment at the hands of the global employer.

When I attended the UCLA "Maquiladora Murders" Conference, I was one of dozens of scholars and activists invited to explore the possibilities of empowering the grieving families with information, resources, and maybe even strategies for making the authorities accountable to them for what had happened to their daughters—some of whom had simply gone to work one day in an American factory and had never come home. I found myself thinking out loud about the possibilities of pointing the finger at a deep pocket—that of an employer—while I also acknowledged how extremely difficult it would be to blame the factories and their owners. If indifference toward Mexican workers means, statistically, indifference toward working women, then the problem lies not only in the probusiness political economy of the border, but also in the sexism of Mexico's free-trade players—both private and public. Until the lives of working women are deemed more important than, or at least as important as, participating in the global economy, little is likely to happen that effectively addresses their need for safety, not only inside the factories, but also in the communities that are dramatically affected by the presence of the factories.

And yet the difficulty of challenging a heavily male-dominated, probusiness, antiworker, sexist culture should not prevent us from asking, What if Claudia's family had decided that, in fact, her employer was partially responsible for putting her in the path of danger? What if they had wanted to contemplate the filing of a tort claim that might encourage the company to rethink the arbitrary use of a go-home policy on young female workers in a city plagued with gender violence and murder? Is this so unlikely a scenario for accountability?

When the investigations initially began, a theory was proposed that the chartered bus drivers who picked up and dropped off workers at the factories were responsible for the murders.[70] But that theory went nowhere. Undoubtedly, it is difficult to make the causal connection between the disciplinary measures for lateness at the Lear factory and Claudia's eventual abduction and killing. However, an employer who might be telling the world "We are socially responsible" might want to reconsider how an agent enforces a policy which, in theory, secures a reliable workforce but, in practice, endangers the safety and lives of working women and girls.

The spirit of social responsibility has generated a plethora of self-promoting campaigns by large corporations to claim a commitment to being socially responsible. Legislative activity directed at corporations that do business in other countries is virtually nonexistent.[71] Nor does the rhetoric of free trade ever seem to focus on the need to incorporate workers' rights into the trade agreements. One is more likely to encounter speculations for invoking the Alien Tort Statute (ATS),[72] which provides "original jurisdiction [to the federal courts] of any civil action by an alien for a tort only, committed in violation of the law of nations or a treaty of the U.S." This statute has generated a new body of law potentially applicable in the international labor context for suing multinational corporations that systematically treat workers in violation of the law of nations.[73]

In *Filartiga v. Peña-Irala,* a case which laid important groundwork for future ATS cases, the Second Circuit of the U.S. Court of Appeals emphasized how the international community had come to recognize the danger of ignoring "the flagrant disregard of basic human rights."[74] This decision, viewed by some scholars as the *Brown v. Board of Education* for the transnational public law litigant, provided a landmark ruling that approved of a unique type of lawsuit in American courts—one in which an alien citizen obtains jurisdiction in a U.S. federal court to seek damages for tortious conduct by another person in the noncitizen's own country. The court recognized such a claim when "deliberate torture perpetrated under color of official authority violates universally accepted norms of the international law of human rights, regardless of the nationality of the parties."[75]

Without replicating the well-developed body of literature on the potential use of the Alien Tort Statute, I can say that an alleged violation of the law of nations has to meet the *jus cogens* test—a peremptory norm that is accepted and recognized by all nations. These include genocide; slave trade; murder or causing the disappearance of individuals; torture or other cruel, inhumane, or degrading punishment; prolonged arbitrary detention; systematic racial discrimination; or a consistent pattern of gross violations of internationally recognized human rights.

Can the *maquiladora* worker qualify as a transnational public law litigant who can hold a multinational corporate employer liable for depriving workers of rights that fall under the category of the law of nations? I have argued that the murder of a worker on her way to or from work is an extreme manifestation of the corporate employer's attitude that the health, safety, and life of the worker is insignificant under the primary goals of NAFTA—the investor's right to profit without trade barriers. But whether the transnational employer's practices, like harsh disciplinary measures, rise to the level of violating the law of nations is a more difficult question. Under the ATS, it is necessary to provide evidence that the employer and the Mexican government are together cooperating to enforce employer policies and practices that are recognized as prohibited by all nations.[76]

The case law interpreting the law of nations has looked at more extreme examples of corporations cooperating with governments to produce inhumane conditions for workers, such as the forced slavery practices that were enforced by the Burmese government to aid the corporate activities of a global oil company. *Maquiladora* activists often decry the arbitrary imposition of extended work hours, on short notice and with the penalty of being fired if the worker refuses, just so a production schedule can be met. Such practices may be compared to the imposition of forced labor. Other systematic practices, such as the mandatory pregnancy testing that was eliminated only after international exposure followed investigation by a human rights group, could not have continued to occur for so long without the government's acquiescence.[77]

On the Reynosa delegation, we met a group of women who worked at the Delphi Electronics factory who were getting help from the CFO on a complaint involving the company's demand that they buy and wear special shoes. Over 230 workers had been suspended for wearing open-toed sandals, which they said were worn by most workers because they were all they could afford. They were frustrated that the company not only wanted them to wear safer shoes, but would not pay for them and threatened the workers with job loss if they did not stop wearing the sandals.[78] On that same delegation, a group of workers complained that safety was such a problem that injuries occurred regularly among the thousands of workers in the Emerson factory while the Mexican safety inspectors did and said nothing.

Should it be acceptable for a female worker to endure not just poor wages, but also systemic exposure to life endangerment while her own government looks the other way? Does the murder of a *maquiladora* worker, who would not have been put in the path of danger but for the policy in effect at her place of employment, qualify as "causing the disappearance of an individual" and therefore become a violation of the law of nations? When the host government does not question the use of policies that endanger the worker, is the employer now an actor under color of law? Is the multinational corporation which has a budget larger than that of several countries and whose presence causes massive social reorganization in social and public policy an actor under color of law, with or without the tacit approval of its practices by the host government?[79] These are questions I pose for the lawyer interested in creating new legal strategies on behalf of the *maquiladora* worker.

## From Passivity to Empowerment: Globalization and the Movement for Justice by Women Workers

> NAFTA was a swindle. It didn't keep its promise of more and better jobs, but rather the contrary. Now everything is more expensive: food, school supplies, transportation, everything.
> —TERESA HERNÁNDEZ, A WORKER IN MATAMOROS

In this section, I will highlight workers' efforts to bring about justice in the *maquiladoras*.[80] Although it is important to improve globalization analyses with attention to women's experiences and struggles, it is also important to transcend the essentialist image of all poor working women as victims. Many workers in global factories do not passively accept the attitudes of indifference that are crafted into free-trade law and policy and taken advantage of by some companies. In this section, I discuss the organizing philosophy and techniques of women workers, and I highlight individual stories of empowered workers.

Questions of legal accountability for the abuse of employees of multinational corporations, which benefit from free-trade agreements such as NAFTA,[81] are complex.[82] Since 1990, the world has been reorganized into borderless regions by a significant consensus—mostly among the financial leaders of the wealthiest nations—that freer trade among all nations in targeted regions will end poverty and promote democratic forms of government.[83] But for the workers, the promises of "*la globalización*" have been a lie. Instead, their experience includes increased stress and chronic illness associated with toxicity and demanding hours, an inability to make ends meet on pitiful wages, and the constant betrayal of government-backed unions siding with management.[84]

That said, the workers I have been privileged to meet do not easily give up the struggle for justice in the border industries. I am in awe of the organizing methods used by the CFO, which are premised on mutual respect, community, safety, and creating a sense of dignity in every worker no matter how old, young, or educated. Often, workers open up for the first time about their problems and concerns at a CFO meeting. It is not uncommon for a worker to meet another who also paid the price for standing up to an abusive supervisor. For example, the group from Dimmit that I met in 2000—Juanita, Raquel, Norma, Juan Pablo, and Amparo—did not know each other until they were all fired at the same time. Out of work, they received support from the CFO to organize and publicly protest their firing as other workers ended their shifts. At more meetings at the small CFO office, they learned about the basic elements of the CFO's strategies for social change within the *maquiladoras*.

The CFO organizes on simple principles. The first is to recognize the worth and dignity of every worker. Leaders arrive without a particular agenda, flyers, or advice to offer, instead listening to the workers, getting a sense of their needs, and only then beginning the process of introducing the workers to the idea that they have certain rights. These rights are printed in a copy of the compiled Mexican Federal Labor Law for the workers to review.[85] The first step in this educational process is powerful—it empowers the workers to connect the injustices they are enduring inside the factory to the existence of a rule of law that says this is illegal. Once that realization is reached, workers usually begin to talk even more, connect with each other, and understand the need for community, strategy, and patience.

In doing their work, CFO organizers may use techniques that include role-playing, humor, and encouraging workers to act out scenarios they can take back to the workplace. For U.S. allies, observing some of these educational exercises can be a sobering experience, especially those who see in the exercise known as "La Canasta Básica" (the basic market basket) how incredibly unjust the cost of living for a family is compared to the workers' take-home pay. In this exercise, there is a chart posted on a wall listing basic needs in terms of rent, utilities, food, clothing, and educational supplies for children. One chart itemizes essential expenses, while the other lists ideal expenses. The workers' wages barely meet the essential, while the ideal, including items like meat, cheese, poultry, and milk, fall into the "unaffordable" category.

The process of becoming aware, as well as the corresponding awakened sense of personal integrity, sparks transformational changes in some of the workers. "I used to be very timid like many of these workers we meet," said Juanita when I met her. "I would hold my head down and cry as the supervisors yelled at me." Juanita has become one of the best organizers in the CFO.[86] From such experiences, community is formed, trust is established, and large groups of workers, who once imagined they were the only ones suffering at the hands of an employer, are empowered.

The CFO volunteers constantly stress the importance of acting on the voice, cause, and interests of the workers. Nothing is done until many are committed. The CFO does not want to risk losing precious ground by having several key organizers fired from their jobs before a problem has been resolved. So they organize patiently, sometimes planning for several months before a critical mass is formed that can support a worker willing to stand up for justice.

Of course, there are challenges. María Elena García, the volunteer who began to work for the CFO in Reynosa and told me of her chronic foot rash, commented that organizing among largely poor and uneducated women is difficult and risky. She shared that supervisors say things like, "There you go again, you bunch of mediocre people . . . you go and you fight and you don't know what you're getting yourself into," in order to trigger the workers' fears and insecurities about being fired for protesting injustice. However, as the daughter of a woman who had fought for justice in the pre-NAFTA *maquiladoras*, María Elena was not about to give up fighting against labor injustice. She organized workers to challenge their employers' abusive practices. Reflecting on how hard it can be to organize workers fearful of losing their jobs, she said, "It is hard work, but . . . I also like it a lot."[87]

Workers empowered by the CFO have won victories. Some of the workers who have won labor board arbitrations have come out with generous lump-sum settlements that have allowed them to leave *maquiladora* work and open small businesses like beauty shops or food stands. A few years ago, several workers took a bold step and ventured into the world of fair trade.[88] With the help of the CFO and U.S. allies knowledgeable about business, they used their garment factory skills to create Fábrica Dignidad y Justicia, a fair-trade company run mostly by women who are working decent hours, earning a living wage, producing goods that people want (T-shirts and canvas bags), and engaging in labor they can love and be proud of every day.

### The Nemesis of Activist Workers: Hostile Governments and the Delusions of Global Democracy

I have noted that the phenomenon called "globalization" has both fans and critics, but that many people do not even question the idea of greater expansion of the global economy. It is simply assumed that when we expand the global interconnection with other countries, whether rich or poor, we are indeed expanding freedom throughout the world. Supporters are unlikely to take a closer look at the disparities that are present between trading partners based in wealthy First World countries and those in oftentimes extremely poor Third World countries. Former U.S. president George W. Bush made clear his support for more free-trade pacts and explicitly linked the expansion of markets for American entrepreneurs and farmers with greater freedom throughout the world.[89] He argued that increased free trade between countries, regardless of the size and wealth disparities between trading partners, would lead to the expansion of civil and political freedom. But, if there is in fact such a great benefit to be gained from globalization, and if the corporate investor is key to promoting globalization and global democracy, then I argue that it must meet the highest standards of conduct.[90]

Regardless of how and why free-trade pacts are promoted and set in place, it is mainly corporate CEOs and stockholders who reap the benefits of these treaties.[91] These pacts provide the legal framework that allows expansion of markets and reorganization of labor operations throughout the world. And as key actors in economic globalization, corporations stand symbolically in the place of governments that want freer trade, presumably to ensure the benefits promoted with open trading, such as international friendship and cooperation or new jobs and improved working conditions. The conspicuous presence of American enterprise (and military) in an expanding global economy should encourage Congress to enact measures that not only enhance free trade, but that also ensure a positive image of American global democracy by holding the American multinational employer to a higher standard of accountability than the weak standards currently found in documents like NAALC.

To date, the primary basis for holding MNCs accountable for violating international human rights law in a civil suit has been a finding that they acted in complicity with a government as "joint actors" guilty of raping, torturing, and otherwise abusing its own citizens. However, this basis requires evidence of aiding and abetting the government to violate the law of nations, or evidence that the MNC is deemed an actor under color of law, to be held separately liable under human rights norms as a state actor. These difficult questions have not been resolved and continue to be explored by courts and scholars.[92]

Scrutiny should be placed squarely on the multinational corporation, not on the complex relationship between the *maquiladora* worker and her government, or on other explanations for the gender violence (e.g., cultural patterns of sexism). Such focus is appropriate because

- many corporations are enormously wealthy and powerful enough to supplant governmental power and authority.
- these corporate leaders encourage their governments to pass laws that create a legal environment that promotes their objectives in the name of global democracy.
- in this capacity, these powerful and gigantic corporations might as well be quasi-governmental actors whose essence and function is to create the infrastructure and culture of new global democracies with their money, technology, construction, policing, and armies of independent contractors for multiple public services.[93]
- these corporate leaders stand to benefit from treaties that will allow them to venture forth in the name of global democracy and profit throughout the world via contracts with mostly Third World countries.

In the absence of an international governmental body truly respected by all nations and with the power to regulate and impose effective sanctions, the only hope is that a multinational corporate investor will choose to do the right thing and self-regulate instead of, for example, simply paying for expensive Web site pronouncements proclaiming that the company is socially responsible. Proglobalization advocates measure success only from the standpoint of markets. They do not address the questionable relationship between claims of benefits and increased costs for things that are priceless, such as a clean environment, secure families, and human life.[94]

Thus, when the policy for promoting globalization is structured to promote fatal indifference to the plight of global workers and left undisturbed and without effective amendments to future trade agreements, globalization of the economy will continue to guarantee less, rather than more, global freedom. Meanwhile, free trade, as opposed to fair trade, continues with more corporations and their highly paid directors raking in profits as they globe-trot in the corporate race to the bottom of the wage scale in Third World countries. And with increases in globalization, other developments that follow profits are likely to increase as well—developments such as the systematic abuse of workers and femicide in the *maquiladoras* of the world.

## Conclusion

I began this chapter by highlighting the intense feminist activism, primarily in the form of popular culture, that has surrounded the investigations of the Ciudad Juárez femicidal murders. I also postulated that the public discourse about systematic violence at the Mexican border says too little about the context within which the murders take place—the context being an extension of the gender abuses and violence that exist in some of the *maquiladora* factories. I realize that, for some, it is difficult to equate the abuses in the factories with violence. But I speak as one who has met workers and their families and witnessed courage and love amidst heartwrenching examples of despair, poverty, and illness wrought by the conditions of the workplace, which dramatically affect primarily working women at the border. Ciudad Juárez just happens to be one of the more extreme examples of an overwhelming level of powerlessness of the working poor that makes daughters, mothers, and sisters vulnerable to a violent environment, whether in the form of exploitative working conditions or in exposure to fatal assault on their way to and from work.

As a feminist living in the wealthiest country in the world—a country that is home to some of the largest multinational corporations and beneficiaries of globalization in the world—I encourage feminist activists to engage themselves more in the task of studying and changing the politics and policies of free trade. Along with an awareness of these murders, feminists need to be asking (1) why a working woman in a poor country should have to risk her life and health in order to make products that will ultimately be bought and consumed by more privileged women in a First World country; and (2) why there is so little regulation or accountability for the corporations that make and sell these products in the name of free trade and global democracy.

If the patterns of gender violence that accompany globalization are to be halted in other parts of the world, change needs to occur from a platform of global sisterhood, an idealistic concept that resonates with the feminism of the twentieth century, when women organized around the universality of unjust domestic and sexual violence in any part of the world where women and girls were subordinate to male supremacy. If feminists are going to take the time to produce literature, plays, movies, or other art forms that raise awareness of the *maquiladora* murders, they should also be studying ways to influence change in the politics and policies that promote free trade. As Amy Chua reminds us, that responsibility includes educating policy makers and electing legislators who will study the issue with nuances of the political economics of racism, classism, and sexism. Progressive globalization analysts, like the influential economist Joseph Stiglitz, also need to reexamine their critiques that focus only on economic disparities as a result of pushing more and more poor countries to participate in the global economy.

Feminists need to put the story of the Juárez murders in a context that appreciates the powerful attraction governments have to participation in the global economy. Meanwhile, critics of globalization need to consider the impact that globalization has on women's safety in the workplace and on their homes and communities,[95] and must question the integrity of the familiar argument that globalization benefits all. The fact that a Third World country is pressed by major economic institutions such as the World Trade Organization or the IMF or the World Bank to open its doors to foreign investors in exchange for new jobs and wealth, but also to abandon concern for basic human rights and safety for its citizens, is unconscionable. Yet it is a modern reality. Globalization of a poor nation's economy exacts a heavy price in guaranteeing the production and reproduction of gender-based violence and femicide.[96]

I have introduced some of the stories and testimony gathered on many visits to the border as an ally of women working in the *maquiladoras* and, more recently, as a committed educator trying to introduce students to the human face of free trade. What I have hoped to elucidate is how a combined host of variables, including typical corporate decisions about discipline for workers, as well as the clear bias that favors investors in free-trade

**Fig. 1.2.** J Guadalupe Pérez © 2003, "Pesquisa de María Teresa López, Centro Histórico de Juárez, al Fondo el Cinema Victoria" (Search for María Teresa López in the Historic Center of Juárez near the Victoria Cinema). Courtesy of J Guadalupe Pérez.

law and policy, produce a hostile work environment with a discriminatory effect on women and female children. What happened to Claudia Ivette González and other *maquiladora* workers is inseparable from the employers' indifference to the health and safety of working women inside the factories. If a company is not required to care about injuries and toxicity in the factory, why would it care about what might happen to a young woman who is sent out on foot in the early hours of the morning into unsafe areas of the city?

The role NAFTA has played in luring rural families north to the border towns and into the *maquiladoras* only to discover wages that are too low to support them, no place to make a home, and frightening social conditions that threaten their health and the safety of their families is widely ignored. Additionally, because of the historical presence of women in the *maquiladoras,* systemic and ignored patterns of gender discrimination well recognized throughout the industry (e.g., sexual harassment, mandatory pregnancy testing) have provided a foundation for the emergence of more violent forms of social chaos and gender violence to erupt in Juárez along with the city's development into a major export-processing zone.

Ciudad Juárez is still Mexico's shining star as an example of a successful export-processing zone. But it has also become a haven for violence against women in the form of systematic abuse inside the factories and in the production of subtle effects on the working and living environment for all women in the city. As the activists in the factories often note, the phenomenon of the murders is inseparable from the gross indifference to the health and safety of the workers employed by the large and powerful *maquiladoras*, whose activities are licensed by free-trade law and which are welcomed and unquestioned by the power elites of the host government. When gender abuse and violence, corporate power and indifference, and government acquiescence come together in the city of Juárez, they produce an environment hostile to women and hospitable to the rise of *maquiladora* murders.

Sadly, Claudia Ivette González became a martyr for justice in the *maquiladoras*, a place where workers have no expectation of safety in or out of the workplace and where supervisors can take action against workers that, collectively, becomes the structure of fatal indifference. Claudia's abduction, and that of so many of the victims of Juárez who were *maquiladora* workers, is the ultimate result of free trade and globalization. Her body may have been abducted and grossly violated by whoever found an easy target that morning, but the life preceding her brutal killing had already been defined as insignificant: a fleck in the fabric of global production.

## Notes

Author's note: I am grateful to the workers and volunteers of Comité Fronterizo de Obreras (www.cfomaquiladoras.org). Thank you also to many individuals who have helped with the production of this project: the members of the Board of Directors of Women on the Border; the members of Austin Tan Cerca de la Frontera; the various research assistants I have been privileged to work with on the topic of justice in the *maquiladoras*—Ed Campbell, J.D. (2003), Yvonne Lapp-Cryns, J.D. (2005), and Kelly Varsho, J.D. (2009)—and Cathy Chapaty for editorial assistance.

1. See, e.g., Alicia Gaspar de Alba, *Desert Blood: The Juárez Murders* (Houston: Arte Público Press, 2005).

2. See, e.g., Rosa Isela Pérez, "Ciudad Juárez: The Silence of Death," *Cuartoscuro* (February–March 2004), http://www.cuartoscuro.com/64/arteng1.html; Ed Vulliamy, "Murder in Mexico," *The Observer* (March 9, 2003); Laurence Pantin, "250 Murders Prompt Mexico Anti-Violence Campaign," *Women's E-News* (December 21, 2001); Evelyn Nieves, "To Work and Die in Juárez," *Mother Jones* (May–June 2002).

3. See, e.g., "Maquiladora Murders Conference," http://www.chavez.ucla.edu/maqui_murders/more.htm. In 2003, the UCLA Chicano Studies Research Center, in conjunction with Amnesty International, hosted a conference called "The Maquiladora Murders, Or, Who Is Killing the Women of Juárez?" [hereinafter Maquiladora Murders Conference].

4. See, e.g., *The Border* (Espinosa Productions, 2000); *Las Muertas de Juárez*

(Laguna Productions, 2002); *Maquila: A Tale of Two Mexicos* (Cinema Guild, 2000); *Performing the Border* (Women Make Movies, 1999); *Señorita Extraviada* (Xochitl Productions, 2001).

5. "Mexico Women March for Justice," *BBC News* (November 26, 2002); "Eve Ensler and Amnesty International March on Juárez to Stop the Murder of Young Women," *Village Voice* (February 17, 2004).

6. Julia Monárrez-Fragoso, "Feminicidio sexual serial en Ciudad Juárez: 1993–2001," *Debate Femenista* 13 (April 2002).

7. Inter-American Committee on Human Rights, "The Situation of the Rights of Women in Ciudad Juárez, Mexico: The Right to be Free from Violence and Discrimination" para. 42 (March 7, 2003) [hereinafter IACHR Report]. NAFTA was signed on January 1, 1994, by Pres. William J. Clinton (North American Free Trade Agreement, U.S.-Can.-Mex. [January 1, 1994], P.L. 103–182 or 107 Stat. 2057 [1993]).

8. IACHR Report, n7, p. 41. See also Monárrez-Fragoso, "Feminicidio sexual serial."

9. See Molly E. Moore, "Nightmare in a City of Dreams: Part I, Epidemic of Murder in a Free Trade Haven," *Washington Post,* special online feature, http://www.washingtonpost.com/wp-srv/photo/onassignment/juarez/.

10. See Diana Washington Valdez, *The Killing Fields: Harvest of Women* (Los Angeles: Peace at the Border, 2004).

11. Michael Newton, "Ciudad Juárez: The Serial Killer's Playground," Crime Library: http://www.crimelibrary.com/serial_killers/predators/ciudad_juarez/index.html.

12. A fairly detailed breakdown of the backgrounds and occupations of murder victims from 1993 through 2000 was produced by Julia Monárrez-Fragoso of the Colegio de la Frontera, a research institute located in Ciudad Juárez. See "Feminicidio sexual serial," 9–10 (tables 2 and 3).

13. The State of Chihuahua disavowed Amnesty International's report on the Juárez murders: "Ciudad Juárez: Gobierno de Chihuahua desacreditó informe de AI," *Mujeres Hoy,* http://www.mujereshoy.com/secciones/1123.shtml.

14. Elvia R. Arriola, "Looking Out from a Cardboard Box," *Frontera NorteSur* (December 2000–January 2001), http://www.nmsu.edu/~frontera.

15. Deborah M. Weissman, "The Political Economy of Violence: Toward an Understanding of the Gender-based Murders of Ciudad Juárez," *North Carolina Journal of International Law and Commercial Regulation* 30 (2005): 795.

16. Ibid., 823.

17. In the negotiations surrounding the North American Agreement on Labor Cooperation (aka NAFTA's labor-side agreement, or NAALC), however, the Clinton administration acceded to the demands of the Mexican authorities (and the multinational corporations) by deleting from the initial U.S. draft of the agreement the possibility of sanctions against a party that "persistently" failed to enforce its own laws and Constitution with respect to core worker rights of free association, collective bargaining, and the right to strike. The NAALC has, in contrast to the investment chapter of NAFTA, which invigorated investors' rights, been neutered.

18. Thomas L. Friedman, *The Lexus and the Olive Tree* (New York: Farrar, Straus, and Giroux, 2000).

19. For IMF analysis, see Joseph Stiglitz, *Globalization and Its Discontents* (New York: Norton, 2003). Also see Amy Chua, *World on Fire* (New York: Anchor Books, 2004).

20. The 2006 "South-North Exchange on Law, Theory and Culture" (SNX) convened in Bogotá, Colombia, May 18–20, 2006, to criticize the dogmas and consequences of "free-market fundamentalism." See generally http://www.law.du.edu/latcrit/portfolioofprojects/acadcom/southnorthexchange/snx2006colombia/snxcolombia(2006)(r1).pdf.

21. Hillary E. Maki, "Trade Protection vs. Trade Promotion: Are Free Trade Agreements Good for American Workers?" Notre Dame *Journal of Law, Ethics & Public Policy* 20 (2006): 883; Dianne Otto, "Challenging the 'New World Order': International Law, Global Democracy and the Possibilities for Women," *Journal of Transnational Law & Contemporary Problems* 3 (1993): 370–415.

22. Carla Freeman, "Is Local:Global as Feminine:Masculine? Rethinking the Gender of Globalization," *Signs* 26.4 (2001): 1007–1038.

23. See Miriam Ching Louise, *Sweatshop Warriors: Immigrant Women Workers Take on the Global Factory* (Cambridge, Mass.: South End Press, 2001).

24. The Border Industrialization Program (BIP), which followed the postwar Bracero Program, was designed to attract investors and to hire mostly migrant workers who had been coming into the United States as guest workers; see Pierrette Hondagneu-Sotelo, *Gendered Transitions: Mexican Experiences of Immigration* (Berkeley & Los Angeles: University of California Press, 1994), 30–31.

25. See Comité Fronterizo de Obreras, "Six Years under NAFTA: A View from Inside the Maquiladoras" (October 1999), http://www.cfomaquiladoras.org/seistlc.en.html.

26. Norma Iglesias Prieto, *Beautiful Flowers of the Maquiladora: Life Histories of Women Workers* (Austin: University of Texas Press, 1997).

27. See, e.g., John C. Stickler, "Mexico's 'Made to Order' Manufacturing Sites, Expansion Management," http://www.expansionmanagement.com/cmd/articledetail/articleid/14878/default/asp.

28. Leslie Salzinger, *Genders in Production: Making Workers in Mexico's Global Factories* (Berkeley & Los Angeles: University of California Press, 2003).

29. Prieto, *Beautiful Flowers.*

30. Comité Fronterizo de Obreras, "Six Years under NAFTA."

31. See Devon Peña, *The Terror of the Machine: Technology, Work, Gender and Ecology on the U.S.-Mexico Border* (Austin: Center for Mexican American Studies, University of Texas at Austin, 1997).

32. Amparo was part of a group of workers who filed a joint labor grievance in the summer of 2000 pursuant to rules and channels created to enforce the Federal Labor Law (Ley Federal del Trabajo).

33. Interview with Amparo Reyes, *maquiladora* worker in Piedras Negras, Coahuila, Mexico (September 10, 2000), http://www.womenontheborder.org/workers/amparo.htm.

34. Interview with Marina Briones, *maquiladora* worker in Ciudad Acuña, Coahuila, Mexico (September 2000), http://www.womenontheborder.org/articles_resources.htm.

35. Elvia R. Arriola, "Of Woman Born: Courage and Strength to Survive in the

Maquiladoras of Reynosa and Río Bravo, Tamaulipas," *Frontera Norte Sur* (April 2001), http://www.nmsu.edu/~frontera/apr01/feat2.html.

36. Interview with Raquel Mendoza, *maquiladora* worker in Piedras Negras, Coahuila, Mexico (September 2000), http://www.womenontheborder.org/articles _resources.htm.

37. The issue of employment-related hazards and potential liabilities is addressed in Title 9 of the Federal Labor Law. A version from the 1970 code is available at http://www.diputados.gob.mx/LeyesBiblio/pdf/125.pdf. See, generally, Francisco Breña Garduño, *Mexican Labor Law Summary*, 2d ed. (Mexico City: Breña y Asociados, 2006).

38. Seguro Social is short for the national health care program in Mexico known as Instituto Mexicano del Seguro Social (IMSS), which guarantees the right to good health, and medical assistance, inter alia.

39. Interview with Pilar Marentes, *maquiladora* worker in Ciudad Acuña, Coahuila, Mexico (October 2001), on file with Women on the Border, Inc., Austin, Texas.

40. Interview with Patricia Leyva Hernández, *maquiladora* worker in Piedras Negras, Coahuila, Mexico (September 2000), http://womenontheborder.org/ workers/paty_notes.htm.

41. Details of Nicolás's story and of his exposure to MOCA (a highly toxic component—4,4′-Methylene-bis[2-chloroaniline]—typically mixed with resins to make plastic molds that encase circuit wiring) were published previously: "Looking Out from a Cardboard Box: Workers, Their Families and the Maquiladora Industry in Ciudad Acuña, Coahuila," *Frontera Norte Sur,* http://www.nmsu.edu/~frontera/ dec00/feat4.html.

42. Scott D. Miller, "Work/Life Balance and the White-Collar Employee under the FLSA," *Employee Rights & Employment Policy Journal* 7.1 (2003): 5–35.

43. See Elvia R. Arriola, "Voices from the Barbed Wires of Despair, Women in the Maquiladoras, Latina Critical Legal Theory and Gender at the U.S.-Mexico Border," *DePaul Legal Review* 49 (2000) 729–816.

44. Ibid., 773.

45. NAFTA's preamble states that the agreement will "create new employment opportunities and improve working conditions and living standards in their respective territories." See North American Free Trade Agreement, http://www-tech.mit .edu/ Bulletins/Nafta/00.preamble.

46. Chua, *World on Fire*, 6.

47. See "Voices"; "Looking Out"; "Of Woman Born."

48. Lisa Heinzerling, *Priceless: On Knowing the Price of Everything and the Value of Nothing* (New York: New Press, 2005).

49. Interview with Pilar Marentes (October 2001), a *maquiladora* worker in Ciudad Acuña, a city known for its entrenched antiunion culture, where we discussed this issue extensively.

50. More than one interviewee talked about the problems that arose from trying to comply with the rigid shop floor attitudes that penalized workers for taking unscheduled bathroom breaks. One worker told me that before she understood how wrong it was to disregard her body's needs, she simply ignored the urge until she developed a toxic condition and bladder infection. Interview with Raquel Mendoza,

*maquiladora* worker in Piedras Negras, Coahuila, Mexico (September 2000) available at http://www.womenontheborder.org/articles_resources.htm.

51. See Arriola, "Looking Out."

52. Ibid.; and idem, "Of Woman Born."

53. See Debbie Nathan, "The Juárez Murders," *Amnesty International Magazine* (Spring 2003), http://www.amnestyusa.org/magazine/spring_2003/juarez/print .html.

54. Celina Romany and Katherine Culliton, "The UN Conference against Racism: A Race-Ethnic and Gender Perspective," *Human Rights Brief* 2.14 (2002); Leti Volpp, "Feminism versus Multiculturalism," *Columbia Law Review* 101.5 (June 2001) 1181–1218; Berta Esperanza Hernández-Truyol, "Sex, Culture, and Rights: A Reconceptualization of Violence for the Twenty-first Century," *Albany Law Review* 60 (1997): 607.

55. Celina Romany, ed., *Race, Ethnicity, Gender and Human Rights in the Americas: A New Paradigm for Activism* (Washington, DC: American University, 2001).

56. *Señorita Extraviada.*

57. The only reference to labor interests appears in the Preamble to NAFTA, in which the parties to the agreement (Canada, Mexico, and the United States) resolve to "protect, enhance, and enforce basic workers' rights." In contrast, the agreement, which covers in detail the rights and duties of the parties on matters of cross-border trade, treatment of investors, intellectual property rights, and other technical barriers to trade, has an entire part (Chap. 11) devoted to investors' rights. See North American Free Trade Agreement, U.S.-Can.-Mex. [January 1, 1994], Chap. 11, Arts. 1101–1139.

58. See, e.g., Maxi Lyons, "A Case Study in Multinational Corporate Accountability: Ecuador's Indigenous Peoples Struggle for Redress," *Denver Journal of International Law & Policy* 32 (2004): 701.

59. North American Free Trade Agreement, U.S.-Can.-Mex. [January 1, 1994], Chap. 11, Art. 16 (National Administrative Office Functions).

60. See Monica Schurtman, "*Los Jonkeados* and the NAALC," *Arizona Journal of International & Comparative Law* 22.2 (2005): 291–384.

61. See Commission for Labor Cooperation, NAALC—Review of the North American Agreement on Labor Cooperation, http://www.naalc.org/english/ publications/review_annex5_us.htm.

62. AutoTrim/Customtrim, U.S. NAO Public Submission 2000-01 (June 30, 2000), aka The Case of AutoTrim de México, S.A. de C.V., Matamoros, Tamaulipas, Mexico, and CustomTrim/Breed Mexicana, S.A. de C.V., Valle Hermoso, Tamaulipas, Mexico, in U.S. Department of Labor Reports, http://www.dol.gov/ ilab/media/reports/nao/submissions/ Sub2000-01pt1.htm [hereinafter AutoTrim Case].

63. Schurtman, "*Los Jonkeados*," 1.

64. Huck Gutman, "Outsourcing in the Developing and Developed," *The Statesman* (India) (March 26, 2004), http://www.countercurrents.org/glo-gutman 260304.htm.

65. See Andy Stern, *A Country That Works: Getting America Back on Track* (New York: Simon & Schuster, 2006).

66. Interview with Amparo Reyes (September 10, 2000).

67. See Chua, *World on Fire.*

68. A wave of anti-immigrant local ordinances has targeted immigrants by restricting their rights to housing and public benefits and by authorizing identity-verification mechanisms that violate civil rights. As of July 2007, over fifty cities and towns had enacted such hostile legislation. See Federation for American Immigration Reform (FAIR) at www. Fairus.org/site/PageNavigation/legislation/.

69. See *Maquila: A Tale of Two Mexicos* (Cinema Guild, 2000); *Maquilapolis: City of Factories* (Independent Television Service, 2006).

70. This is detailed in the film *Señorita Extraviada.* The chartered buses assure that workers who have no car or money for public transportation will show up for work.

71. Friends of the Earth International (FOEI) briefing, "Towards Binding Corporate Accountability," http://www.foei.org/publications/corporates/accountpr .html.

72. Claudia T. Salazar, "Applying International Human Rights Norms in the United States: Holding Multinational Corporations Accountable in the United States for International Human Rights Violations under the Alien Tort Claims Act," *St. John's Journal of Legal Comment* 19.1 (2004): 111–148.

73. Marisa Ann Pagnattaro, "Enforcing International Labor Standards: The Potential of the Alien Tort Claims Act," *Vanderbilt Journal of Transnational Law* 37 (2004): 203–263.

74. *Filartiga v. Peña-Irala,* 630 F. 2d 876, 890 (2d Cir. 1980).

75. Ibid., 890.

76. *Doe I v. Unocal Corp.,* 963. F. Supp. 880 (C.D.Cal.1997).

77. "Mexico: A Job or Your Rights, Continued Sex Discrimination in the Maquiladora Sector" (1998), Human Rights Watch, http://hrw.org/doc/ t=americas&c=mexico&document_limit=60,20.

78. "Project on the Study of Gender, Globalization, and Human Rights," http:// www.womenontheborder.org/niu_student_reflections.htm.

79. Rachel A. Conradt-Adams, "The International Expansion of Wal-Mart and Its Effects on Women to Signatory Nations to Free Trade Agreements" (December 26, 2006) (unpublished seminar to fulfill the NIU College of Law graduation writing requirement), http://www.womenontheborder.org/documents/. RachelPaperon WalmartandCAFTA.doc.

80. CFO, "Workers and Free Trade," http://www.cfomaquiladoras.org/english %20site/librecomercio_y_trabajador.en.html.

81. Adam Warden, "A Brief History of the Anti-Globalization Movement," *University of Miami International & Comparative Law Review* 12 (2004): 237–268.

82. See Sukanya Pillay, "And Justice for All? Globalization, Multinational Corporations, and the Need for Legally Enforceable Human Rights Protections," *University of Detroit Mercy Law Review* 81 (2004): 489–496.

83. Lori Wallach and Patrick Woodall, *Whose Trade Organization?: A Comprehensive Guide to the WTO,* 2nd ed. (New York: New Press, 2004).

84. Because of the history of poor representation by existing unions, the CFO is required to educate the workers about their rights under the labor law and constitution and to ask questions about the level of support from union representatives in the workplace. See CFO, "Temas del CFO" at http://www.cfomaquiladoras.org/ temas_cfo.es.html.

85. Ley Federal del Trabajo (April 1, 1970), http://www.diputados.gob.mx/LeyesBiblio/pdf/125.pdf.

86. In Elvia Arriola, "Becoming Leaders: The Women in the Maquiladoras of Piedras Negras, Coahuila," http:// www.nmsu.edu/~frontera/oct00/feat5.html.

87. Arriola, "Of Woman Born."

88. Ozay Mehmet et al., *Towards a Fair Global Labour Market: Avoiding the New Slave Trade* (London: Routledge, 1999).

89. Pres. George W. Bush, commencement address at the University of South Carolina (May 9, 2003), http://www.state.gov/p/nea/rls/rm/20497.htm.

90. See David D. Christensen, "Corporate Liability for Overseas Human Rights Abuses: The Alien Tort Claims Act," *Washington and Lee Law Review* 62 (2005): 1219–1270; Marc Rosen, "The Alien Tort Claims Act & the Foreign Sovereign Immunities Act: A Policy Solution," *Cardozo Journal of International & Comparative Law* 6 (1998): 461–483; idem, "The Alien Tort Statute: An Emerging Threat for National Security," *St. Thomas Law Review* 16 (2004): 627–668.

91. Nandini Gunewardena, "Reinscribing Subalternity: International Financial Institutions, Development, and Women's Marginality," *UCLA Journal of International & Foreign Affairs* 7 (2002): 201.

92. See, e.g., Anita Ramasastry, "Corporate Complicity: From Nuremberg to Rangoon, an Examination of Forced Labor Cases & Their Impact on the Liability of Multinational Corporations," *Berkeley Journal of International Law* 20 (2002): 91.

93. James Glanz, "The Struggle for Iraq: The Money; Auditors Find Widespread Waste and Unfinished Work in Iraqi Rebuilding Contracts," *New York Times* (January 31, 2007): A12.

94. Heinzerling, *Priceless.*

95. Regarding safety in the workplace, see "Voices"; Elvia Arriola, "Becoming Leaders: The Women in the Maquiladoras of Piedras Negras, Coahuila," *Frontera Norte-Sur* (October 2000), http://www.nmsu.edu/~frontera/oct00/feat5.html. Regarding safety in the home and community, see Allan Blackman, Michael Batz, and David Evans, "Maquiladoras, Air Pollution and Human Health in Ciudad Juárez and El Paso," *Research for the Future*, Discussion Paper no. 03-18, 2003, updated 2004 (on file with author).

96. See IACHR Report. See also Elvia R. Arriola, "Coffeehouse Musings on Post-Gutter Ironies: Promoting Diversity to Ensure Globalization," *St. Mary's University Scholar* 7 (2004): 3.

# CHAPTER 2

# Poor Brown Female: The Miller's Compensation for "Free" Trade

ALICIA GASPAR DE ALBA

*Pornographers, gang members, serial killers, corrupt policemen, foreign nationals with a taste for hurting women, immigration officers protecting the homeland— what did it matter who killed them? This wasn't a case of "whodunit," but rather of who was allowing these crimes to happen? Whose interests were being served? Who was covering it up? Who was profiting from the deaths of all these women?*

—ALICIA GASPAR DE ALBA, *DESERT BLOOD*

At the end of *Desert Blood,* my novel about the Juárez femicides, Ivon Villa, the protagonist and amateur sleuth, asks herself the foregoing questions, concluding that the real criminals are not just the perpetrators of the crimes, but the powers and interests that are being served by the brutal slayings of poor, brown females. What is clear in Ivon Villa's mind is that the femicides are not just a Mexican problem, they are a border problem, and they implicate the Border Patrol as much as the Juárez police, the *maquiladora* industry as much as the Texas Parole Board. Under the stony gaze of Mount Cristo Rey and the twin smokestacks of the American Smelter and Refining Company (ASARCO), both of which stand guard over the trickle of water that separates the First World from the Third, Ivon realizes that Mexican women workers have become as expendable as pennies in the hungry slot machine of transnational capitalism, and that the tragedy of the dead women's lives did not begin when their bones were dumped in the desert, but when they first set foot inside a *maquiladora*. As Melissa Wright notes, "their deaths are only symptoms of a wasting process that began before the violent snuffing-out of their lives."[1]

### "Maquilando Mujeres"

According to the 1990 Mexican census, 50 percent of the economically viable population was working at a *maquiladora,* and most of these workers were female. After the implementation of NAFTA in 1994, the number of female workers in the twin-plant industry increased dramatically. In 2006, in Juárez alone, approximately 330 *maquiladoras*—more than 75 percent owned by American corporations like Nike, Acer, RCA, Delphi, and General Motors—employ about 220,000 workers, of whom "approximately 60 percent are women."[2] Not all of them are sixteen, the legal working age; the only documents needed to apply for a factory job are a grade school diploma and a birth certificate—both of which can and are falsified by girls as young as twelve who are desperate for work. Indeed, hundreds of young women arrive daily from remote areas in Mexico and Central America, not prepared for the dangers of border life or the tragic exploitation that awaits them at work: slave wages; ten-to-twelve-hour shifts on their feet; working conditions that include dangerous levels of noise pollution, toxic fumes, and sexual harassment by management; manic production schedules and the constant threat of dismissal for not meeting quotas, for being late, for getting pregnant; demeaning beauty pageants disguised as work incentives and morale boosters; pregnancy testing at the time of hiring; enforced birth control through pill or injection or Norplant implants; and the strict monitoring of their reproductive cycles through monthly menstruation checks.

I wonder if it is general protocol for women factory workers in the United States to have to show bloody tampons or menstrual pads to the factory nurse each month to prove they are not pregnant or to submit to urine tests when they apply for a job.[3] Maybe it happens and is one of those untold stories of the manufacturing industry, but I do not think so. I doubt this kind of sexual surveillance is legal north of the border. In fact, in a January 13, 1998, article in the *New York Times,* Sam Dillon wrote that "the United States Labor Department reported today that thousands of border assembly plants administer medical tests to weed out pregnant applicants and harass pregnant workers to coerce their resignation."[4] The Labor Department's report was issued in response to a complaint from Human Rights Watch "that managers of Mexico's tax-free assembly plants, known as *maquiladoras,* routinely require female applicants to take urine tests and question them about their menstrual cycles and sexual activity to screen out pregnant women."[5] While the Labor Department stated that this was a form of sexual harassment and violated Mexican labor laws, the Mexican Labor Ministry argued that "administering pregnancy tests to job applicants was not illegal because

Mexico's labor laws protect workers only after they have been hired." This is the kind of doublespeak that NAFTA enables.

Of the victims whose occupation was known, Julia Monárrez-Fragoso tells us in "Serial Sexual Femicide in Ciudad Juárez, 1993–2001," nearly one in six were students, and at least a third were employed by or seeking employment from a *maquiladora*.[6]

And yet, the *maquiladoras* themselves, or, rather, the U.S. and other multinational corporations behind them, have seemed little interested in pursuing the investigation of these murders affecting the lives of their personnel, or in seeing justice prevail. To leave from or return to their *colonias*, the shantytowns where they live in cardboard and plywood shacks, the women employed at the *maquiladoras* must walk in the early morning or late night through the pitch-black desert to reach paved roads and city buses or personnel shuttles. More often than not, the drivers of these shuttles are not licensed bus drivers nor do the factories that employ them screen them for police records or evidence of drug addiction. Anything can and does happen in these *transportes de personal*, which carry the mostly female personnel back and forth between the industrial parks and the squatter colonies on the outskirts of town where the majority of the workers live. Safety is a commodity the workers cannot afford. Nor, it seems, can their employers, despite the huge profits they make on products assembled with cheap *mano de obra* (labor). They cannot afford to screen bus drivers to make sure they are not drug addicts or sex offenders or ex-convicts. They cannot provide money to the city to incorporate the *colonias* so workers can have the most basic of services, such as running water and electricity. Employers cannot even afford to provide some measure of economic assistance to the orphans of victims who were their employees.

In its 2003 report, "Intolerable Killings: Ten Years of Abductions and Murders in Ciudad Juárez and Chihuahua,"[7] Amnesty International denounced the disregard of the Mexican government, as well as the apathy of the transnational corporations that, thanks to NAFTA, have brought so many hundreds of young women from southern Mexico to look for the yellow-brick road of the American Border Dream: a job at a *maquiladora*, a paycheck, a shack of their own, money to send home. What hundreds of them have found, instead, is that Juárez is not the pass to the North or the ticket to a better life, but a ground zero of femicides where they and women who look like them find a gruesome and early death.

One little-known fact is that not all of the slain were Mexican citizens; at least six were U.S. citizens of Mexican descent from El Paso, Texas, and Las Cruces, New Mexico; one was from the Netherlands; and another from

Honduras. The Dutch woman was found under the bed in a seedy motel room on Juárez Avenue, raped, naked, and stabbed to death. Unlike the Mexican girls, Hester Van Neriop was easily identified. Her documents were left in the room, which had been rented to a man believed to be a U.S. citizen going by a Hispanic name and who was seen arriving at the hotel alone and on foot. No one knows how Hester got into the room. Of the *muchachas del sur,* or girls from the south, only their body parts or their clothing serve as identity markers: a severed foot inside a tennis shoe, a piece of a spinal column inside a Mervyn's shopping bag, a bloodstained bra or a factory smock with a name tag attached strewn in the mesquite.

To this day, despite the incarceration of several suspects in 1995, 1996, 1999, 2001, and 2004, the murders continue unabated, and hundreds more women wind up missing or turn up dead. Despite special task forces convened by Chihuahua's attorney general; interventions by Amnesty International, the United Nations, and the International Committee on Human Rights; candlelight vigils and protests by grassroots organizations; a worldwide online petition; massive demonstrations by Mujeres de Negro (Women in Black) in Mexico City and Washington, DC; and even a joint resolution of the U.S. House and Senate that was finally approved in May 2006, the crimes remain unsolved and unstoppable.

### Who Is Killing "*Las Hijas de Juárez*"?

Who is killing "las hijas de Juárez," to allude to the title of an exhibition at the Social and Public Art Resource Center (SPARC) in Venice, California, in 2003?[8] Theories range from an American serial killer crossing the border to commit his crimes, knowing that, even if he gets caught, there is no death penalty in Mexico; or perhaps it is a Satanic cult, because some of the bodies were found with ritual markings on the flesh; or maybe it is snuff films; or the underground market for human organs; or the corrupt police force in Juárez; or that Egyptian chemist who was arrested in October 1995 for assaulting a prostitute and who was later thought to be masterminding the crimes from his jail cell. Other theories accuse the detrimental effects of Americanization on Mexican family life, which causes the males to turn into good-for-nothing drunks and wife beaters or, worse, *cholos,*[9] and the females to leave their families and migrate north to work at the *maquiladoras.* Some accuse the factories themselves not only of luring or recruiting hundreds of workers to this dangerous border each day with the promise of a good job, but also of the measly $3.00 to $5.00 per day they pay, the unsafe working conditions, and their lack of protection.[10]

---

POPULAR THEORIES ABOUT WHO AND WHY

- Serial killers
- Satanic cults
- Snuff films
- Organ harvesting
- White slavery
- The Egyptian chemist "mastermind" (arrested in 1995)
- Los Rebeldes (local gang arrested in 1996)
- Los Choferes (band of bus drivers arrested in 1999)
- Corrupt Mexican police
- Well-protected sons of rich families
- Cartel killings
- The victims were leading double lives as prostitutes
- The victims dressed provocatively in short dresses and high heels
- Unemployed men are resentful of women getting jobs

---

To answer the question of "who is killing the daughters of Juárez?" both the authorities and the media employ the logic of blaming the victim. Accused of leading *una doble vida,* the double life of a good girl (student or employee) and a bad girl (sex worker) who goes out drinking and dancing after her shift at the *maquiladora,* the victims are seen as "asking for it," both because of the company they keep and the way they dress. Interestingly, not all of the murdered women were wearing short skirts, as has been the popular accusation. The book *El silencio que la voz de todas quiebra: Mujeres y víctimas de Cd. Juárez* was banned as a result of the public access the journalists who wrote it had to the police files of the first five years' of cases. The book divulges information that the authorities do not want made public, such as the fact that, although the victims were uniformly accused of dressing in provocative miniskirts, in actuality, 74 percent of the first 137 bodies that were found intact and still clothed were wearing long pants.[11]

When pressured to find a scapegoat to steer attention away from their incompetence and apathy, the police arrest likely suspects. The first to be arrested was Abdel Latif Sharif Sharif, a well-off Egyptian chemist who was responsible for a number of important patents for companies he had worked for in the United States, but who was employed at a *maquiladora* in Juárez. Sharif, tenacious journalists discovered, had a long record of sexual assaults in three U.S. states and had even served six years in a Florida prison for rape and battery. Because he had three strikes against him, he was to be deported back to his country, but at his deportation hearing in El Paso, his company's lawyers stepped in and got him removed to Mexico, instead, where he could help establish a twin plant for the company.

Sharif was Juárez's favorite scapegoat until David Meza, the cousin of one of the victims, Neyra Azucena Cervantes, stepped into the role in 2003.[12] From the time of his arrest until 1999, when Sharif was moved from El CeReSo, the Juárez social rehabilitation center, to the prison in Chihuahua City, the authorities attributed to the Egyptian a power of persuasion and mind control that makes Charles Manson seem like the little man behind the curtain in *The Wizard of Oz*. For example, in May 1996, six months after Sharif's detainment, a gang of teenaged drug runners and *cholos* named Los Rebeldes and led by a charismatic, fully tattooed fellow called El Diablo, were arrested in a sting operation in a downtown discotheque. According to briefings by the special prosecutor in charge of investigating the murders, a woman named Suly Ponce Prieto, Los Rebeldes had confessed that they were minions of the Egyptian, that Sharif was in fact paying them $1,200 per victim when they brought him the girls' underwear and a newspaper report as evidence of death. "This is a lot of money for a dead *indita*," a lot of people thought, especially when narco-related executions did not usually cost more than $500 a head.[13]

Sharif held press conferences from El CeReSo in which he denied any connection whatsoever with El Diablo and Los Rebeldes, although it was later discovered from a thorough perusal of the prison's visitors' log that one of the members of Los Rebeldes visited a cousin of his there quite regularly and would also meet with Sharif. No doubt, this is when the exchange happened: greenbacks for evidence of the killing. At least, that was the story.

When the press found out the teenagers were being beaten and threatened into "confessing," the government had to drop the charges, and all but El Diablo were released. El Diablo was the only one who was not a teenager, and besides, his dental impressions matched the teeth marks on the breast of one of the bodies. Nothing more has ever been said about him.[14]

Three years later, the story changed, and attention focused on a band of drug-addicted bus drivers called Los Choferes, who drove buses that transported the workers back and forth between their shantytowns and factories. Los Choferes got hauled in in 1999, when Nancy, a young woman they gang-raped, survived the attack and pressed charges. The supposed leader of Los Choferes was a violent alcoholic and crack addict who had two nicknames—El Tolteca and Dracula. He was not screened for drugs when he was hired. He left town after the attack on Nancy, but was so nervous about what he had done that he took it out on his pregnant wife and beat her to a pulp. The wife's mother pressed charges against him too, and the man with two nicknames was duly arrested, tried, and accused of all the murders that had taken place in Juárez except those that had already been pinned on the

Egyptian and Los Rebeldes. He named six or seven of his bus-driving buddies as accomplices, and all of them gave gruesome stories on the witness stand about how they would go out cruising for women to rape and kill after getting high.

But the conspiracy theories persisted. It was not that Los Choferes operated out of their own perverse power trips and misogyny, it was that they too, according to the special prosecutor, had been hired by the Egyptian to do his bidding. By then, however, the rate had gone down to $1,200 per pair of victims, or $600 a head.

Of course, neither the victims' families nor the general public, not to mention the local NGOs and women's groups, bought the conspiracy theories. And then photographs of the suspects came out in the Juárez newspapers, their bared stomachs showing signs of torture. Apparently, police were using everything from cigarette burns to electric prods to elicit the bus drivers' confessions. Only Dracula's charges held, because Nancy identified him in court as her rapist; the others were released and probably went back to driving personnel buses.

In 1999, the same year of the Choferes debacle, it was discovered that the Egyptian was living in luxury in the Juárez jail, his cell equipped with (among many other domestic conveniences) its own bathroom, a double bed, a small refrigerator, a microwave oven, a fax machine, and a cellular phone. A riot ensued in the jail when the Egyptian's privileges were made public. The warden resigned, a new warden stepped in, and order was restored, but the Egyptian was moved without explanation to the higher-security prison in Chihuahua. In 2000, charges were dropped against him on the basis of inconclusive evidence, which would have freed him from his thirty-year sentence. But just as suddenly, the charges were reinstated pending DNA analysis.

Sharif died in jail in 2006 of heart failure, we are told. His was the last in a series of mysterious deaths to plague the suspected perpetrators of the Juárez femicides. One of the two bus drivers who were arrested in 2001 for the murders of eight women whose bodies were discovered in a cotton field across from AMAC, the headquarters of the *maquiladora* association (and who were supposedly members of a convicted gang of rapists) died in jail in 2005. The official story was that he died of complications from a hernia operation, which his wife, in a video interview after his death, asserted he did not need. In 2002, his lawyer was shot down on a public street by police, who said they mistook him for a fugitive.

The organizations involved in protesting the police policy of scapegoating since the arrest of the Egyptian knew better, just as they knew that the bus drivers' confessions had been extracted under torture. The other bus driver had his charges dropped and was finally released after four years in jail, but only because the families of the victims and the families of the suspects had come together to decry the same injustice.

## The Numbers Game

There is much we do not know about the mechanics of femicide on the U.S.-Mexico border. For example, no one really knows the exact number of victims. Diana Washington Valdez in her 2002 *El Paso Times* exposé, "Death Stalks the Border" (nominated for a Pulitzer Prize), says her research shows 320 victims between 1993 and June of 2002; Casa Amiga shows 254 victims between 1993 and 2002; Mexico's attorney general's office (Procuraduría General de la República, PGR) calculates the number at 258 for the same time period. In a conference at New Mexico State University in November 2000, Suly Ponce Prieto, the special prosecutor in the cases of the murdered

**Table 2.1. Murders of Women in Ciudad Juárez, 1993–2002, Casa Amiga Estimates**

| Year | No. of Serial Murders of Women | No. of Other Murders of Women | Total No. of Murders |
|------|------|------|------|
| 1993 | 8 | 9 | 17 |
| 1994 | 7 | 11 | 18 |
| 1995 | 14 | 10 | 24 |
| 1996 | 9 | 19 | 28 |
| 1997 | 11 | 15 | 26 |
| 1998 | 12 | 18 | 30 |
| 1999 | 4 | 18 | 22 |
| 2000 | 7 | 22 | 29 |
| 2001 | 13 | 18 | 31 |
| 2002 | 1 | 28 | 29 |
| Total | 86 | 168 | 254 |

Source: Calculated from reports in *Diario de Juárez*, 1993–2002, by 8 de Marzo, translated by Maya Cone (Casa Amiga Web site: www.casa-amiga.org/Statistics.htm).
Note: For more information, including summaries in English of the newspaper's accounts of each murder, see www.casa-amiga.org/Statistics.htm.

Table 2.2. Murders of Women in Ciudad Juárez,
1993–2003, Chihuahua Attorney General Estimates

| Year | No. of Murders of Women |
|------|--------------------------|
| 1993 | 18 |
| 1994 | 19 |
| 1995 | 34 |
| 1996 | 32 |
| 1997 | 31 |
| 1998 | 29 |
| 1999 | 17 |
| 2000 | 31 |
| 2001 | 28 |
| 2002 | 13 |
| 2003 (January–March only) | 6 |
| Total | 258 |

Source: Chihuahua state attorney general's office.

Table 2.3. Murders of Women in Ciudad Juárez, 1993–June
2002, *El Paso Times* Estimates

| | |
|------|------|
| Total no. of murders of women | 320 |
| Sex-related serial murders of women | 90 |
| Number of convictions | 0 |

Source: *El Paso Times*, http://www.elpasotimes.com/borderdeath/page1-2.html.

women until 2001, reported 222 women killed between 1993 and 2000. Other reports by other official state entities cited 232 murders, later revised to 233, while media reports in 2000 cited 300 to 500 victims in the first ten years of the crime wave.

Finally, in August 2003, the Instituto Chihuahuense de la Mujer (Chihuahua Women's Institute), under the leadership of Victoria Caraveo, released a glossy and detailed report with four-color pie charts and statistical analyses of the bodies found and processed by the Homicide Unit of the State of Chihuahua. Entitled "Homicidios de mujeres: Auditoría periodística," the report is an audit of press coverage of the crimes from January 1993 to July 2003 and offers the "definitive" answer to the numbers game: 231 murders of women in ten years, of which 90 should be considered "sexual homicides" or, rather, homicides involving rape and other forms of sexual violation. Of these 90, according to the report, 43 percent (or 39 cases) were considered "resolved" while 56 percent (or 51 cases) were under investigation. Between 1995 and 1998, 12 to 15 women were sexually murdered per year; after 1999, the number dropped to 10 per year.

In a press release issued in September 2003, Amigos de las Mujeres de Juárez (Friends of the Women of Juárez, a Las Cruces, New Mexico–based NGO) countered the partial nature of the report and provided some important missing statistics:

> We have no desire to dispute the death of one more or one less woman, however, we would like to point out what is missing from the charts and statistics presented by the Chihuahuan Institute of Women. The homicide rate for women in Ciudad Juárez is at least 4 times that of any other border city. When one examines the rates by age, the difference is even more striking. For girls aged 5 to 14, Juárez has a murder rate 4 times that of El Paso and 20 times that of Tijuana. For women aged 15 to 24, Juárez has 11 times as many homicides as El Paso and 3.4 times as many as Tijuana.

The colorful charts and appendices of the "Auditoría periodística" report show statistics for a number of variables regarding the victims: how they died (28 percent, sexual homicides; 17 percent, crimes of passion; 14 percent, vengeance; and only 7 percent, narco-executions); how old they were (39 percent of the sexual homicides were between sixteen and twenty, while 20 percent were between eleven and fifteen, and 10 percent, between twenty-one and twenty-five); where they were from (of the total number of victims, 31 percent were from Ciudad Juárez, 13 percent from states outside Chihuahua, 41 percent, unknown); what their occupations were (36 percent of the total were employed, with their specific occupations listed in the appendices, the most common of which were dancer, factory operator, prostitute, and waitress; 20 percent were housewives; 9 percent were students); whether they were identified or not (86 percent identified, 13 percent not identified); and the number of cases investigated and resolved per year (102 resolved between 1993 and 1998, 103 resolved between 1998 and 2003). To this claim, Amigos de las Mujeres de Juárez responded in the same press release:

> Generally, homicide has the highest clearance rate of any crime. This clearance rate is the number of cases solved and brought to trial by police

forces. Generally, this rate is around 60 to 75 percent. While the Mexican government's study claims a similar rate, the conviction rate for the sexually motivated murders is only 0.05 percent. The claim that these cases have been solved is ludicrous in view of testimonies by those involved in the cases. One forensic expert resigned after being asked to manufacture evidence. There exists a recurring pattern of torture. The groups mentioned by the Chihuahuan Institute of Women as responsible for many of the crimes all allege they were forced to confess. There is credible evidence that this is the case. We, along with many of the family members and Mexican society as a whole, reject these people as the perpetrators of these crimes.

The "Auditoría periodística" report concludes that the actual number of sexual homicides is significantly lower than the numbers given in the local, national, and international media and that "la suerte de *leyenda negra* tejida en torno a Juárez en el sentido de que más de 300 mujeres fueron 'desaprecidas, violadas, y asesinadas' en el transcurso de los últimos 10 años, no encuentra sustento en la realidad."[15] The appendices, however, contradict the findings of the report, as the total number of victims listed by the Fiscalía Especial para la Investigación de Homicidios de Mujeres between 1993 and 2003 is 321.

What all the official channels seem to agree on is that ninety of the cases were sexual homicides. The methodology for determining whether the *"móvil,"* or motive, was sexual, vengeance, family violence, theft, a crime of passion, a fight, or narco-trafficking was attributed to criminological procedures and classifications utilized by the Violent Crimes Unit of the FBI.

The Juárez femicides entry in the Wikipedia online encyclopedia provides yet another set of numbers: until 2004, there were 295 cases of kidnapping and murder of women. Of these, 108 were already under investigation by previous task forces, 175 were in the justice system, and 12 had been remanded to the courts for crimes against minors. However, the entry also makes clear that there have actually been 332 victims of femicide in Juárez, of which 218 have supposedly been resolved: 104 by sentencing to prison, and 114 still being investigated. The Nuestras Hijas de Regreso a Casa (May Our Daughters Return Home) Web site lists the names of 286 victims plus 75 unidentified cadavers, for a total of 361 murdered women as of 2004.

None of these numbers include the hundreds of women and girls who have disappeared without a trace. According to a report presented by the National Commission on Human Rights in Mexico on November 25, 2003 (the International Day of No Violence against Women), two thousand women disappeared in Mexico between 1993 and 2003. Other sources say the number of disappeared women in Juárez alone is over four thousand.

In January 2006, the Mexican government issued its fourth report, or 400+-page "Informe,"[16] from the PGR. In this report the Fiscalía Especial para la Atención de Delitos Relacionados con los Homicidios de Mujeres en el Municipio de Juárez, Chihuahua (Special Prosecutor's Office for Attention to Crimes Related to Female Homicides in the Municipality of Juárez, Mexico) asserts that 63 percent of the 379 femicides committed between 1993 and 2005 have been resolved (for a total of 238 cleared cases) and that 177 perpetrators were arrested and sentenced in conjunction with these cases. Moreover, of the 379 murdered women, the report states that 345 have been identified and only 34 remain unidentified. The "Informe" also debunks the "myth" that over 4,000 women have been reported missing in Juárez, stating that only 47 missing women were actually reported between 1993 and 2005, of whom 11 were found, 2 were dead, and only 34 were still being sought.

Perhaps the most interesting of the charts presented in the "Informe" concerns the "*móviles*" for the murders. Of the 379 cases, 119 appear to have been murdered as a result of "social violence," including revenge, theft, and gang violence; 106 deaths were caused by domestic violence, including family violence and crimes of passion; 78 (or 21 percent) are listed as being the result of sexual violence; and 76 are listed as being of undetermined cause, which could include any or all of the previous motives. As Amnesty International notes in its February 2006 public statement in response to this fourth "Informe,"

> The PGR appears to have concluded that only those crimes involving sexual violence—approximately 20 percent of the 379 murders documented—amount to gender violence. Domestic violence appears not to be considered gender-based violence and also appears to be necessarily excluded from the category of sexual violence. Other murders are classified as resulting from *social violence*, a concept which appears to necessarily exclude, without explanation, the gender of the victim as a factor in the murder. Another element not given proper consideration is the role played by the climate of violence against women and impunity which may have facilitated the commission of crimes.[17]

Overall, the discrepancies in all of these statistics and reports adds to the general confusion that surrounds the crimes, that mystifies activists and authorities alike, increasing the sense that these cases are impossible to solve.

## The Sex Offender Capital of the United States

Other than multinational corporations and an exploited poor Mexican female workforce that is rapidly becoming, as Eve Ensler puts it in the *Vagina Monologues*, "an endangered species" in Mexico,[18] whom else has NAFTA brought to the border? According to a 1999 article in the *El Paso Times*, "since 1995, when sex-crime offenders were required by law to register with local law enforcement, more than 600 have registered in El Paso County."[19] A year later, police found a large number of the registered sex offenders in violation of the law. "El Paso police this week visited the residences of 620 registered sex offenders in El Paso County and found that 101 of them were not living where they had registered, as required by law."[20] If not living at their legal addresses, were all of these sexual predators running loose in El Paso or crossing over into what Simon Whitechapel in his troubling book about the femicides calls "the serial killer playground"?[21]

Indeed, while visiting the Piedras Street police station in El Paso, where I was interviewing Det. Andrea Baca as part of the research I was conducting for my novel on the Juárez femicides, I ran across a map of El Paso marking the supposed addresses of all the registered sex offenders and saw that many of them were clustered close to the downtown bridge that connects El Paso to Juárez: "The 500 block of West Missouri Street in Downtown El Paso is home to the largest concentration of registered sex offenders in the city. Out of 43 sex offenders registered in the 79901 zip code, 30 live in the 500 block of Missouri and nearby in the 300 block of Prospect."[22] Although sex offenders are not allowed to leave the state, much less the country, does this stop them from taking that five-minute walk over the Santa Fe Bridge and crossing into Mexico, especially when just across the border at any hour of the day or night they are sure to find at least one young woman walking alone in the desert? To what degree, I wonder, do U.S. immigration officials ignore or patently condone this illegal crossing of registered sex offenders, thus aiding and abetting their crimes?

By September 2000, the number of sex offenders living in El Paso had increased to 745, and the number jumped to 751 in the next year. In November 2001, Alexandra Flores was kidnapped from a Wal-Mart in the Lower Valley, and the perpetrator turned out to be a sex offender who had gone in to register at the Horizon City police station the day before he kidnapped, raped, and strangled the five-year-old girl. Diana Washington Valdez reported that "El Paso County Sheriff Leo Samaniego and other officials reeling from the Alexandra Flores case complain that El Paso has become a dumping ground for convicted sex offenders from other parts of the state."[23]

A January 2, 2002, letter to the editor of the *El Paso Times* decried the practice: "The number of convicted sex offenders paroled to El Paso County who are not from this community is a crisis. The system is failing us. Together, we must make some noise. I hope the outrage from El Paso County will be so loud that the echo of anger and disgust will reverberate from El Paso to Austin."

The wake-up call offered by the high-profile abduction and killing of Alexandra Flores motivated both community and state officials to oust sex offenders from El Paso back to their counties of origin. By February 2002, the number of sex offenders on parole in El Paso had dropped to 147, 112 of whom were not from El Paso.[24]

Is it a twist of fate that, until 2002, El Paso was the largest dumping ground for registered sex offenders in the country? Why were all of these sexual predators being sent to a place that was overpopulated with poor young women coming to work for the *maquiladora* industry and who lived in the most dangerous, desolate areas closest to the border, a place that, coincidentally, had been suffering the indignities of monstrous sex crimes against poor young women and girls since 1993? These are structural decisions made by the Texas Board of Pardons and Parole, not the personal choices of the perpetrators. I argue that the sex offenders too are part of the toxic fallout of the North American Free Trade Agreement, another type of vigilante army, like the Minutemen Project, working against the infiltration of the porous border by fertile brown female bodies.

## The Mexican Penal Code

How many of the victims were actually raped as well as slaughtered? Is it 137, as the Amnesty International report asserts, or 142, as Julia Monárrez-Fragoso claims,[25] or 90, which is the official number given by the State of Chihuahua? Could it be more than that, considering that the Mexican penal code defines rape as nonconsensual penile penetration?

We know there is no death penalty in Mexico, but what is the penalty for rape and other forms of gendered violence? The Mexican penal code makes a distinction between rape and sexual abuse. A sex crime is considered to be a "rape" if the "passive subject" is under fourteen or is a private citizen of sound mind or an infirm person forced into vaginal, anal, or oral copulation and is unable to resist the attack. Per the August 2001 reforms to the Mexican penal code, rape is punished with a prison sentence of three to twelve years and a fine of fifty to one hundred times the assailants' salaries. Cases in which a rape is perpetrated on a victim younger than fourteen or is carried out by two or more assailants are punished with a five- to fifteen-year prison sentence and a fine of eighty to two hundred times the assailant's salary. However, if the victim is at least twelve years old and is a "proven prostitute," no legal sanctions apply to the "active subject." A caveat was added in the August reforms to the penal code that diminishes the punishment for rape to one to six years in the case that the victim led the attacker on and then later refused to go through with the sex act.

Sexual abuse is defined as a sexual act other than copulation that takes place by force. The sentence for sexual abuse is six months to two years in jail and a fine of thirty to eighty times the assailant's salary. Sanctions increase to one to four years in prison and fifty to one hundred times the salary when the sexual abuse is perpetrated by two or more agents on nonprostitutes under fourteen years old or on persons of sound mind over age fourteen. Cases in which vaginal or anal penetration occurs with anything other than the penis, or *miembro viril,* are considered to be sexual abuse cases and are punished with a two- to six-year sentence, or a four- to twelve-year sentence if the crime is perpetrated against nonprostitutes under fourteen years old or on persons of sound mind over fourteen.

Under Mexican law, sexual abuse merits a lighter punishment than rape. Although in 2003 the Mexican legal system categorized only 98 of the then 320 violent murders of women and girls in Juárez as rape cases, many more of the bodies were found sexually violated in ways other than copulation. Victim number 16, for example, a fifty-year-old woman who was murdered in 1993 and found in her own home, had a deep wound in the skull and a piece of wood inserted in the vagina. The body of a much younger woman was found with a blanket inserted halfway into the anus. Neither of these cases would be considered rapes according to the Mexican penal code.[26]

## Divide and Conquer

To make the drama of the femicides just a little more compelling, a rift has developed among some of the NGOs in Juárez. Despite lack of equipment, lack of funding, the ongoing accumulation of bodies, and the daily struggle against apathy, legal impunity, and incompetence, these grassroots organizations have helped raise social consciousness about violence against women in Juárez and have decried the complicitous role played by the media, the *maquiladora* industry, and the Mexican government. In November 2001, when eight bodies were found in a cotton field in the southeastern sector of the city, the teacher of one of the victims organized a separate NGO, Nuestras Hijas de Regreso a Casa. This organization has a comprehensive multilingual Web site that features a significant (though selective) bibliography of articles, reports, books, films, images, songs, plays, poems, and blogs on and about the femicides. The Web site also includes an archive of everything published by the Mexican newspaper *La Jornada* post–November 2001, as well as the latest news, daily updates on what is and what is not happening in the investigations, and links to other Web sites and other actions being taken around the world in behalf of the women of Juárez.[27]

Unfortunately, problems, primarily based on social class, have arisen between Nuestras Hijas and some of the other mothers' collectives. Whereas the families of the victims are all poor or working class, the leaders of the early umbrella organizations—the ones that have raised funds and advocated for a number of the families, such as Victoria Caraveo's group, Mujeres por Juárez (Women for Juárez), established prior to her appointment as director of the Instituto Chihuahuense de la Mujer (Chihuahuan Women's Institute) or Esther Chávez Cano's 8 de Marzo (March 8) and Casa Amiga or the Las Cruces–based Amigos de las Mujeres de Juárez—are rich or middle-class women who are accused of using the femicides to draw public attention to their feminist causes and to make money for their organizations.

In an interview that I conducted with Victoria Caraveo in October 2002, she spoke about how the competition for resources had had a divisive effect on the groups. "We're in pieces," Caraveo asserted. When the state and federal governments started "compensating" families for the loss of their daughters, not as a way of taking responsibility for the crimes, but as a form of "humanitarian assistance" to the bereaved relatives, the mothers were also beholden to stop blaming the government for corruption or negligence in the matter of the investigations. Only those families that received no government funding, such as Nuestras Hijas and Amigos, have had the freedom to denounce their government the way Norma Andrade, Paula Flores, Eva Arce, and Ramona Morales have done.

### Activism or "Hacktivism"?

On her Web page, Coco Fusco says that the Internet is the most effective site for activist struggle and consciousness-raising in the case of the Juárez crimes. "The internet has generated a community of interest from different places in the world . . . and is being used by a grassroots organization in Mexico to circumvent repression and censorship by the Mexican government. An international virtual community thus becomes a political force field."[28] Thanks to the Internet, people the world over have found out about what is happening in Juárez. The Web techs who manage the Nuestras Hijas site wasted no time in tapping into that resource and eliciting that Net-based activist support.

For some of us, giving money to something is all we can think of doing, or all we have time to do. But what if that money which is supposed to be a way of strengthening a cause is either mismanaged or ends up splitting a community of activists that should all be working together to end violence and help provide a measure of support and solace? Is it just another example of divide and conquer?

Anything is possible in cyberspace. It serves the interests of victims and perpetrators alike. Notice what happens, for example, when you type the word "rape" into any search engine. Literally hundreds of sites come up with pages and pages of free pornography, many of them organized by ethnicity: Asian girls, Latin girls, Lolitas (girls under twelve years old). Available to anyone on the Worldwide Web, these sites offer multiple images of eroticized extreme violence against young women and girls of color: women being raped with guns to their heads, women being penetrated by steel pipes, women being gang-banged by men in uniform, girls engaged in bestiality. Some of the sites provide written commentary as well, sadistic, misogynistic language about controlling and overpowering the female body. Who says snuff has to come packaged in celluloid, especially when anyone with a Web cam and a computer can record a video and put it online?[29] So who profits from all of this "hacktivism," as Coco Fusco calls it? Is this yet another way of exploiting the poor brown female body?

When I was doing research for *Desert Blood* in 1999, I found a tourist Web site on Juárez called "Border Lines" (not to be confused with *border-lines,* an online publication of the International Relations Center's Americas Program).[30] There was a link on that page called "Those Sexy Latin Ladies," which took me to a listing of some well-known brothels in La Mariscal, as the red-light district is called, complete with pictures of dancers named Brenda and Becky and Eunice. There were two things about that page that particularly disturbed me: the flashing neon-yellow message, "Prostitution is legal here"; and the short descriptive paragraph of the kinds of "girls" likely to provide that service—"Every week hundreds of young Mexican girls arrive in Juárez from all over Mexico. Most of these young ladies are looking for work that will be a primary source of income for their families back home. While many will begin their careers in one of the various *Maquiladora* factories in the area, often they end up in the many bars and brothels."[31] There was even a map to the bars on Ugarte Street, with a downloadable coupon for a free drink at Club Panamá.

That stretch of Ugarte Street, I later discovered, was precisely the area where a number of victims had last been seen. They had been having a drink after work probably, or maybe moonlighting at one of those clubs to help supplement their substandard wages, and vanished into the night, to turn up days, weeks, months later with a neck broken, a right breast sliced off, a left nipple chewed off, a face beaten beyond recognition, legs spread-eagled, hands tied with cords or their own shoelaces.

Although it is possible that not every victim in the Juárez femicidal crime wave was raped, all of the victims—from the five-year-old who had her eyes removed to the seventy-year-old who died of twenty-three stab wounds—were brutalized, not "just" murdered. "In a significant number of cases, the brutality with which the assailants abduct and murder the women goes further than the act of killing and provides one of the most terrible examples of violence against women."[32]

Another example of how women's lives are devalued on that border: a ninety-one-year-old woman was found strangled in her home after being sexually assaulted on February 17, 2006. Her attacker confessed that he had intended just to rob her, but he decided it would behoove him to leave no witness, so he raped and killed her, as well. The judge in the case ordered his release a few weeks later.

## The Tres Marías Syndrome

The targets of the Juárez crimes are not *güeras del norte* (light-skinned girls from the north), but *muchachas del sur,* who in the patriarchal eyes of their society turn into *maqui-locas,* women who think they are independent because they work at a *maquila* when all they really are is so far from God, so close to the United States. Who are these *maqui-locas* in the eyes of the society that has been witnessing their brutal slaying since 1993, and in what context can we read that social discourse to understand how these vicious crimes operate as part of a technology of female annihilation in the patriarchal paradigm? According to the popular misconception, a *maqui-loca* is a *maquiladora* worker who, as a result of her close contact with the libertine ways of *el norte,*

- tries to behave like an American
- loses her good Mexican girl morality and, therefore, her value as a woman
- wears short skirts, high heels, and bright lipstick to attract or provoke men

- participates in beauty contests at her factory
- goes out with *cualquiera,* that is, any man who approaches her
- dances at nightclubs in the downtown bars and brothels of the city
- drinks alcohol and probably uses drugs
- allows herself to be fondled and photographed
- engages in unsafe premarital sex
- gets pregnant
- socializes with other *locas* like herself
- comes home in the early hours of the morning after staying out all night
- is asking for trouble and usually finds it

Read within the context of the Tres Marías Syndrome, the patriarchal social discourse of Chicano/Mexicano culture, which constructs women's gender and sexuality according to three biblical archetypes—virgins, mothers, and whores—the *maqui-locas* clearly fall into the third category. Linked to the three Marys who attended Jesus Christ at his crucifixion—his mother, the Virgin Mary, who despite her pregnancy remained a virgin because she was both immaculately conceived and impregnated; the "other" Mary, who is referred to simply as the mother of James and Joseph; and the reformed prostitute Mary Magdalene, from whom La Malinche, another illustrious foremother of Mexicano/Chicano culture (also known by the upper-crust Mexican intelligentsia as "la Chingada," or the fucked one) descended directly—the Tres Marías discourse outlines a code of ethics and behaviors that Mexican patriarchy prescribes for all of its women:

### MARÍA, LA MADRE
- La que vive por sus hijos y su familia/She who lives for her children and family
- La que siempre perdona/She who always forgives
- La que nutre, cuida y protege/She who nurtures, cares for, and protects
- La que hace todo/She who does it all
- La que da a luz al futuro/She who gives birth to the future
- La que participa en el sexo únicamente para procrear/She who has sex only to procreate
- La abnegada/She who is abject and abnegated

### MARÍA, LA VIRGEN
- La que obedece/She who is meek and obedient
- La que no se va con el novio/She who does not run off with her boyfriend

- La que se espera hasta que se casa para tener sexo/She who waits until her wedding night to have sex
- La que se viste y se porta decentemente/She who dresses and behaves decently
- La que vive con sus padres hasta que le piden la mano/She who lives with her parents until someone asks for her hand in marriage
- La que no conoce del sexo, ni consigo misma/She who has no knowledge of sex, not even with herself
- La que no llama la atención/She who doesn't call attention to herself
- La inocente/She who is innocent

### MARÍA, LA PROSTITUTA

- La que tiene sexo por placer/She who has sex for pleasure
- La que tiene sexo por oficio/She who sells sex
- La que toma anticonceptivos/She who takes birth control
- La que corrompe a los hombres/She who corrupts men
- La que avergüenza a su familia/She who shames her family
- La a que no le importa lo que dirán/She who does not care what people say
- La que se va con cualquiera/She who goes out with whomever
- La fácil/She who is loose and easy
- La que se merece lo que le dan/She who deserves what she gets

As archaic as it may seem, the Tres Marías Syndrome runs rampant in our twenty-first-century lives. My college-age female students at UCLA, for example, straight and lesbian alike, continue to be plagued by the fear of "lo que dirán," or, rather, being seen as whores, bad women, or bad daughters for enjoying sex with their boyfriends or, even worse, for desiring other women. They have internalized the message of the Tres Marías: there are only three ways to be a good Chicana or Mexican woman, and having sex for personal pleasure is not one of them: "In patriarchy, a woman's sex is the site of her deepest power (creation, which must be controlled and monitored at all times) and her deepest weakness (penetration, which must be punished). In between the mother and the whore that is La Malinche, there is the virginal condition, that ethereal state of womanhood, which can be owned, traded, and renamed."[33] A woman's function, in the revolution, the family, and the culture, is to procreate and produce sons for the Father, not to be an autonomous entity with an active sex drive. Sex empowers the body; sex is agency, the enactment of desire. In a patriarchy, the only ones permitted to enact their desires are men; women's sexuality has to be scrutinized, proscribed, protected, or punished at all times. As Jane Caputi explains in *The Age of Sex Crime*, the modern-day prostitute (or someone accused of being a prostitute), like the medieval witch, is the "archetypal projection of the patriarchal *bad* woman" who must be punished with torture, rape, and ritual destruction of the female body.[34]

Why are the Juárez women being killed *the way* they are being killed? This is an important point, *the way* they are being killed, because we have to understand that these crimes are more than murder; they are ritual acts of pure and unadulterated hatred and brutality toward the poor brown female body. In "Femicide: Sexist Terrorism against Women," Caputi and Diana E. H. Russell explain the many expressions of violent misogyny that can result in femicide:

> Femicide is on the extreme end of a continuum of antifemale terror that includes a wide variety of verbal and physical abuse, such as rape, torture, sexual slavery (particularly in prostitution), incestuous and extrafamilial child sexual abuse, physical and emotional battery, sexual harassment (on the phone, in the streets, at the office, and in the classroom), genital mutilation (clitoridectomies, excision, infibulations), unnecessary gynecological operations (gratuitous hysterectomies), forced heterosexuality, forced motherhood (by criminalizing contraception and abortion), psychosurgery, denial of food to women in some cultures, cosmetic surgery, and other mutilations in the name of beautifications. Whenever these forms of terrorism result in death, they become femicides.[35]

Caputi and Russell's rubric for understanding the wide parameters of what constitutes femicide in a patriarchal society helps underscore one fact: whether the victims in Juárez died at the hands of serial killers, sadistic policemen, or husbands and boyfriends—they are all victims of femicide. To argue that "only" ninety of the over five hundred murdered women in Juárez are victims of sexual violence, and that the majority of deaths are the result of domestic violence or social violence is to deny that all of these crimes are, as Caputi and Russell say, forms of sexual terrorism against women which resulted in their deaths. Hence, they are all femicides.

The Juárez femicides are no myth. That there are cruel, bloodthirsty, greedy, fanatical men killing young Mexican women and girls on the border for sport or profit is a historical truth. Collusion, conspiracies, trade agreements, drug trafficking, the human organ market, snuff films, serial killers, Satanists, a corrupt police force, the Partido de Acción Nacional (PAN, National Action Party) versus the Partido Revolucionario Institucional

(PRI, Institutional Revolutionary Party)—above all of this, two institutions remain free and clear of any blame, responsibility, or accountability: the *maquiladora* industry, and the Border Patrol. Therein, as Shakespeare would put it, lies the rub, and the rub, as Gloria Anzaldúa tells us, "*es una herida abierta* [is an open wound] where the Third World grates against the First, and bleeds."[36] Is it any wonder that *las hijas de Juárez* are mired in silence and a social apathy that has grown inured to the presence of slaughtered women on the border?

## The Miller's Compensation

In that complicity of silence in which all of us unwittingly partake, ignorance qualifies as innocence. As long as people do not realize or do not know what is going on in Juárez, it is not really happening, and nobody has to do anything about stopping the killers or figuring out what the real motives are for killing this very specific population of young women. When the news is too sensational to keep quiet—such as when a woman's dead and mutilated body is discovered wrapped in a blanket and dumped at the intersection of two major streets in Juárez—then it is time to blame the victim, because as the city council's and the police department's "prevention campaigns" imply,[37] "she asked for it," trashy, slutty, ignorant *indita* that the media and the social discourse make her out to be.

The transnational corporations that employ the victims as much as the government structures that are selling their souls to Uncle Sam's Faustian "free-trade" agreements and the border watchdogs positioned at twenty-yard intervals along the river with their infrared technology and their high-horsepower green trucks, are all pretending they have no responsibility for the crimes. Emma Pérez explains where this devil-may-care attitude originates on the U.S. side of the line:

> Many people have surmised that a particular clause in NAFTA precludes the Mexican government from holding the maquilas responsible in any way. The chapter 11 provision of the NAFTA agreement allows U.S. companies to sue the Mexican government for any monetary losses, which include both actual profits and *anticipated* profits, incurred on account of protective environmental laws, labor laws, or labor strikes. U.S. companies may pollute the environment in Mexico and treat workers as disdainfully as they please, without retribution from Mexico. In the meantime, we in the United States

can purchase inexpensive computers, cell phones, toys, and other products made in Mexico by women who have turned up dead.[38]

In "The Dead Women of Juárez," Sam Quiñones comments on the anonymity of the victims, which renders their murders unimportant and therefore not worth solving. "There is no resolution, no evil madman to pin it all on. The perfect murder is, it turns out, unusually easy to commit, especially when the victim is no one 'important,' an anonymous figure—and Juárez has enough of those."[39]

The following images are juxtapositions; they portray the contradictions that signify life on the U.S.-Mexico, post-NAFTA border. They exemplify the extremes between what is important and what is unimportant that all who cross and converge there must negotiate on a daily basis. Figure 2.1 juxtaposes one of the wealthy gated communities of the east side of Juárez with a shantytown dwelling in Puerto de Anapra on the west side. Figure 2.2 juxtaposes the (then) brand-new offices of the Juárez branch of the World Trade Center with a plywood shack from one of the *colonias* near the airport. Figure 2.3 contrasts the manicured lawns of the Delphi twin-plant factory in the Bermúdez Industrial Park with a billboard advocating for the municipal government to provide running water, the most basic of public services, in Puerto de Anapra. Figure 2.4 shows the barred grounds and glass walls of the IGMex *maquiladora* and the barred windows and homemade adobe bricks of another *colonia* dwelling. Finally, Figure 2.5 compares the French-accented Parque Eliseo (Elysian Fields) to the dirt road and trash-strewn sand dunes of Lomas de Poleo, where victims' bodies were dumped like so much garbage. What is especially ironic about the Parque Eliseo photo is that, although it looks like the kind of place to go for Sunday picnics or barbecues, there are skull-and-crossbones warning signs posted throughout that warn people not to light fires there as the park is constructed over the Chevron-Pemex petroleum pipeline.

Clearly, there is more wrong with the El Paso/Juárez border than the systematic destruction of poor brown women. For Ivon Villa at the end of *Desert Blood*, there are two self-evident truths: (1) that no matter who the actual killers are, multinational corporations through the *maquiladora* industry are making a killing from the globalization of poor brown female labor; and (2) that the North American Free Trade Agreement has created an epidemic of sexual terrorism and misogynist violence on the border.

I am reminded of the etymology of the word *"maquiladora,"* which I found on a Web site called "Maquila Portal": "'Maquiladora' or 'maquila'

**Fig. 2.1.** Alicia Gaspar de Alba © 2000, "No Trespassing!" Courtesy of Alicia Gaspar de Alba.

**Fig. 2.2.** Alicia Gaspar de Alba © 2000, "The Price of 'Free Trade'." Courtesy of Alicia Gaspar de Alba.

**Fig. 2.3.** Alicia Gaspar de Alba © 2000, "Let There Be Water." Courtesy of Alicia Gaspar de Alba.

**Fig. 2.4.** Alicia Gaspar de Alba © 2000, "A Piece of the Rock." Courtesy of Alicia Gaspar de Alba.

**Fig. 2.5.** Alicia Gaspar de Alba © 2000, "Elysian Fields." Courtesy of Alicia Gaspar de Alba.

is derived from the Spanish word 'maquilar' which historically referred to the milling of wheat into flour, for which the farmer would compensate the miller with a portion of the wheat, the miller's compensation being referred to as 'maquila.'" The modern meaning of the word evolved from its use to describe any partial activity in a manufacturing process, such as assembly or packaging carried out by someone other than the original manufacturer.[40]

If a *maquiladora* is the factory where the miller (the multinational corporations that own the twin-plant industry) grinds the wheat, and if the wheat represents the poor brown female labor force that is ground down, exploited, and discarded, are the murdered women and girls of Juárez the *maquila,* or miller's compensation—the extra ounce of revenue in a system that already profits in the billions? Or are they simply the price that Mexico (the farmer) is paying for the privilege of free trade?

## Notes

Author's Note: Portions of this chapter appeared previously in "The Maquiladora Murders: 1993–2003," *Aztlán: A Journal of Chicano Studies* 28.2 (Fall 2003): 1–17. Used by permission of the UCLA Chicano Studies Research Center.

1. Melissa W. Wright, "Dialectics of a Still Life: Murder, Women, and the Maquiladoras," *Public Culture* 11.3 (1999): 453–474, quotation on 459.
2. Ibid., 456. For latest statistics, see http://www.elpasoredco.org/juarez-maquilaemployment.aspx.
3. For more on this sexual surveillance, see ibid., 467. See also the Women on the Border Web site, http://www.womenontheborder.org/sexdiscrimination.htm. Indeed, this illegal practice is endemic to the *maquiladora* industry across the Americas, as we learn from the 2002 Human Rights Watch report, "From the Household to the Factory: Sex Discrimination in the Guatemalan Labor Force," http://hrw.org/reports/2002/guat/guat0102A.jude-03.htm#P646_139924: "Human Rights Watch found widespread sex discrimination in the maquila sector, in the form of questions or testing to determine reproductive status, post-hire penalization of pregnant workers, and failure to enforce maternity protections. . . . Although factories can be fined and even closed down for this blatantly illegal practice, ineffective monitoring by the social security system itself means that most factories never suffer any consequences. Even when they are affiliated with the system, many workers are unable to get permission from their employers to seek health care. This means that pregnant workers may not receive the prenatal care they need."
4. Sam Dillon, "Sex Bias Is Reported by U.S. at Border Plants in Mexico," *New York Times* (January 13, 1998): A8.
5. Ibid.
6. See Julia Monárrez-Fragoso, "Serial Sexual Femicide in Ciudad Juárez, 1993–2001," *Aztlán: A Journal of Chicano Studies* 28.2 (Fall 2003): 153–178.
7. The report can be accessed online at http://www.amnestyusa.org/document.php?id=3EC284DD25E3F2B080256D78005D4BB1.
8. For more information on the exhibition and reproductions of some of the artwork displayed in the show, see "Journey to the Land of the Dead: A Conversation with the Curators of the 'Hijas de Juárez' Exhibition," in the dossier section of *Aztlán: A Journal of Chicano Studies* 28.2 (Fall 2003): 179–202. See also the SPARC Web site archives at http://www.sparcmurals.org/.
9. Seen as criminals, gangbangers, drug addicts, and drug pushers, *cholos* embody and represent the Mexican imaginary of what happens to Mexicans under

the corrupting influence of the United States. *Cholismo,* or the practice of turning into *cholos,* is seen as a negative consequence of living too close to the border. The attitude is related to the long-standing Mexican animosity toward Chicanos and Chicanas, who, from the perspective of Mexican nationals, are said to have sold out their allegiance to Mexico and to pollute their native language and culture with Americanisms.

10. For a breakdown on salaries versus cost-of-living expenses for *maquiladora* workers, see the Women on the Border Web site, particularly Elvia Arriola's "Voices from the Barbed Wire of Despair: Women in the Maquiladoras, Latina Critical Legal Theory, and Gender at the U.S-Mexico Border," *DePaul Law Review* 729 (2000): 66. The full text of this article may be accessed online at the Women on the Border Web site at http://www.womenontheborder.org/Articles/ Voices%20From%20Barbed.pdf.

11. Rohry Benítez et al., *El silencio que la voz de todas quiebra: Mujeres y víctimas de Ciudad Juárez* (Chihuahua: Ediciones del Azar, 1999), 18. A chart in the book of the types of clothing worn by the victims shows that only 10 percent of them were wearing skirts or dresses, 16 percent, miniskirts.

12. David Meza was accused of killing his cousin, although he was in Chiapas at the time she was murdered. He spent close to three years in jail on false charges. To find out more about his story, see the documentary *Bajo Juárez: La ciudad devorando a sus hijas,* directed by Alejandra Sánchez Orozco and José Antonio Cordero (Indymedia, 2006). To read about Neyra Azucena Cervantes's abduction and the two families' joint struggle for justice, see "Feminicide and Torture in Ciudad Juárez and Chihuahua," available online at the *Witness* home page: http://www.witness .org/index.php?option=com_rightsalert&Itemid=178&task=story&alert_id=38.

13. See Gregorio Ortega, *Las muertas de Ciudad Juárez: El caso de Elizabeth Castro García y Abdel Latif Sharif Sharif* (Mexico City: Fontamara, 1999).

14. In *Bordertown* (2007), a Hollywood feature about the crimes, directed by Gregory Nava, the loose end of El Diablo is put to dramatic use by the local indigenous population of Juárez, who are depicted as naïve and superstitious in their belief that "the devil" is killing the women of Juárez.

15. "The fate of a black legend woven around Juárez in the sense that more than 300 women were 'kidnapped, raped, and murdered' over the last 10 years, has no basis in reality." See "Homicidios de mujeres: Auditoría periodística," 12.

16. For the full text of the "Informe," go to www.amigosdemujeres.org, click on "News," and scroll down to the Mexican government report.

17. For the full text of the statement, go to Amnesty International's Justice for the Women of Juárez and Chihuahua page: amnestyusa.org/document .php?id=engamr410122006.

18. Eve Ensler, *Vagina Monologues* (New York: Villard, 2000), 110.

19. Christina Ramírez, "Police Look to Track Sex Offenders," *El Paso Times* (May 9, 1999).

20. Laura Cruz, "101 on Sex Offender List Violated Rules, Police Say," *El Paso Times* (March 10, 2000).

21. Simon Whitechapel, *Crossing to Kill: The True Story of the Serial-Killer Playground,* 3rd ed. (London: Virgin Publishing, 2002). Although this is a problematic book on many counts, not the least of which is the author's last name, which alludes

to Jack the Ripper's Whitechapel murders, it was one of the first books published on the Juárez femicides and one of the first to pose the question of serial killers crossing into Juárez from El Paso.

22. Louie Gilot, "Some Neighbors Wary of Sex Offenders," *El Paso Times* (December 26, 2000).

23. Diana Washington Valdez, "Officials Say State Dumps Sex Offenders in El Paso," *El Paso Times* (December 8, 2001).

24. Louie Gilot, "Sex Offenders Trickle Out of El Paso," *El Paso Times* (June 19, 2002).

25. See Monárrez-Fragoso, "Serial Sexual Femicide," 169.

26. The sections on the discrepancy in numbers and on the Mexican penal code, as well as the chart on theories about who the perpetrators are, appeared originally in a policy brief I wrote entitled "The Maquiladora Murders, Or, Who Is Killing the Women of Juárez?" *Latino Policy & Issues Brief*, no. 7 (August 2003): 1–4, published by the UCLA Chicano Studies Research Center. Used by permission of the UCLA Chicano Studies Research Center.

27. See the Nuestras Hijas de Regreso a Casa Web site at http://www.mujeres dejuarez.org/.

28. See Coco Fusco's Virtual Laboratory, http://www.thing.net/~cocofusco/.

29. While writing this chapter and surfing the Nuestras Hijas Web site, an advertisement for Passion.com popped up on my screen showing pictures of half-naked "naughty" girls in southern California looking for sexy men.

30. See www.irc-online.org/americaspolicy/borderlines/index.html.

31. See the "Border Lines" Web site at http://www.blines.com/page1.html. Although the link to "Those Sexy Latin Ladies" was still available on the drop-down menu at the time of this writing, the URL to the link itself was no longer active.

32. See Amnesty International, "Intolerable Killings."

33. Alicia Gaspar de Alba, "Malinche's Revenge," in *Feminism, Nation and Myth: La Malinche*, ed. Rolando Romero and Amanda Nolacea Harris (Houston: Arte Público Press, 2005), 52.

34. Jane Caputi, *The Age of Sex Crime* (Bowling Green, Ky.: Bowling Green State University Popular Press, 1987), 95.

35. Jane Caputi and Diana E. H. Russell, "Femicide: Sexist Terrorism against Women," *Feminista!* 2.3/4; http://www.feminista.com/v2n3/Russell.html.

36. Gloria Anzaldúa, *Borderlands/La Frontera: The New Mestiza*, 2nd ed. (San Francisco: Aunt Lute Press, 1999), 25.

37. For more on the prevention campaigns, see Chap. 3 here.

38. Emma Pérez, "So Far from God, So Close to the United States: A Call for Action by U.S. Authorities," *Aztlán: A Journal of Chicano Studies* 28.2 (Fall 2003): 148.

39. Sam Quiñones, "The Dead Women of Juárez," in *True Tales from Another Mexico: The Lynch Mob, the Popsicle Kings, Chalino, and the Bronx* (Albuquerque: University of New Mexico Press, 2001), 152. Quiñones's chapter was originally published as "The Maquiladora Murders," *Ms.* (May/-June 1998): 11–16.

40. "Maquila Overview," http://www.maquilaportal.com/Visitors_Site.

# CHAPTER 3

# Ghost Dance in Ciudad Juárez at the End/Beginning of the Millennium

MARÍA SOCORRO TABUENCA CÓRDOBA
EDITED AND TRANSLATED BY GEORGINA GUZMÁN

*The border is both an international boundary and a discursive act. It is a barrier to be negotiated, exploited, and crossed, and a symbolic act to be contested.*
—VÍCTOR M. VALLE AND RODOLFO D. TORRES, *LATINO METROPOLIS: GLOBALIZATION AND COMMUNITY*

*The dead women of Ciudad Juárez are directly related to the state of sexism and the condition of women in Mexico.*
—CARLOS MONSIVÁIS, "LOS CRÍMENES CONTRA LA DEMOCRACIA"

## Charting the Border Space

Since 1993,[1] the crimes in Ciudad Juárez have made the city an obligatory news story in the world's top newspapers.[2] On the one hand, there are the serial murders of hundreds of young women together with a series of kidnappings, disappearances, rapes, and deaths of many more, who to date add up to more than four hundred.[3] On the other hand, many people have been killed by organized crime's endless vendettas; these victims' only offense was to be at the site of this violence, such as Gerónimo's Bar or Max Fim and King-Siu restaurants. Included within this news category are also the November 1999 reports on "narco-cemeteries," which disclosed that more than two hundred bodies were clandestinely buried.[4] From January 2008 to October 2009, another four thousand lives have been claimed by this continuing violence.

These events give way to numerous interpretations and points of view about how the border and its "black legend" have been constructed throughout time, via travel accounts, films, soap operas, journalism, and everyday discourse. Regarding this matter, Valle and Torres's epigraph could not be any more apt. Since the geopolitical demarcation between Mexico and the United States was instituted, it has been the subject of multiple interpretations with generally common concerns. Mexico's northern border has been regarded as a site of easy cultural penetration, through language, customs, or lifestyles produced by the close contact with the United States, and its inhabitants have been labeled, among other things, as sellouts, *pochos*, individualists, people without roots, or people who lack national identity. When the border's culture is imagined, it is conceived as "different from that which predominates in other regions,"[5] or it is deemed "inexplicable."[6] "From Mexico City's point of view, the northern border is imagined as perhaps the most 'unredeemable' of all the provinces' representations."[7]

In the United States, this image is hardly more positive, for, since the border's inception, the United States' expansionism has converted Mexicans—the ancient people of the region—into "the other."[8] Mexican otherness has been constructed as a cultural nemesis and has come to define everything non-Anglo-Saxon. Expansionist politics have displayed a zeal for civilizing lands distant from the center, for controlling everything that signifies barbarism: "sexuality, vice, nature, and people of color."[9] These first impressions, along with those of Mexican intellectuals, were perpetuated in texts, discourses, and public politics that were based on notions of difference and have since become lodged within both countries' nationalist social discourse.[10]

In this construction of "perverse cities" and Ciudad Juárez's stigmatization as a border town, one of the most pernicious stereotypes in our particular case has been that of women—and not just Mexican border women, but also Anglo women. The cinema of the 1940s propagated a generalized image of Anglo women as "libertines" that continues to this day, as we will see later.

Before the establishment of the *maquiladora* industry in Ciudad Juárez,[11] women were limited to the traditional role of mothering, and outside the home, they were employed by the service sector or were sex workers.[12] Before the Border Industrialization Program (BIP), women's employment possibilities were dictated by their relation to the city's economic life. These possibilities were well accepted by the city's residents. The city, in fact, had a clearly marked limited zone of tolerance where "decent people," especially the city's women, did not dare even to pass through.[13]

Nonetheless, after 1965, with the BIP now in full effect, the city started to become populated by other subjects: women who were incorporating themselves into the city and the country's productive life. Their arrival in masses produced a singular phenomenon in the people's discourse: the *ma-quila* was now regarded as a "savior" because it took the women out of the cabaret, but at the same time, there developed a stereotype of the *maquila* worker as a woman of dubious reputation, especially in the case of so-called single mothers.

With industrialization firmly planted in the city, this new social actor began to produce "contesting projects that [had] decolonization as their object—in the public, economic, and cultural sphere, and [had] survival strategies, such as informal economies, legal and illegal activities that elude[d] governmental regulation and control."[14] The *maquila* worker came to transgress different spaces in the city's (and the nation's) *usos y costumbres*, defying a social construction of gender. She shifted from being the daughter or the sister to being the household provider. It was she who went out from her city searching for sustenance, since it was she who had the possibility of finding a better-paying job than that which the men in her family could obtain. In the city, she adopted new ways of life and new, diverse spaces. With a certain economic autonomy, she had the possibility, with female co-workers, to purchase a car,[15] improve her formal education, and go out and have fun.[16]

These women workers' transgression of spaces and customs has been critical to the hegemonic discourse's evasion of responsibility before the inability to solve and stop the crimes against women in Ciudad Juárez. Likewise, that same discourse has created a certain stereotype that almost all of the murdered women were very young *maquiladora* workers, but "in this level of generalization, the different identities of all those women who didn't fit that description are lost. Moreover, using stereotypes makes society avoid regarding male violence against women with the seriousness and gravity that it requires."[17]

For the purposes of this chapter, it is important to revise those stereotypes, given the constant tension that exists between hegemonic discourse and the person who seeks to resist. It is impossible to speak of the murdered or of the vulnerable women in Ciudad Juárez and the atmosphere that surrounds them without speaking of class and gender prejudices; to be a woman (worker) in Juárez is to situate oneself in a "body and gender construction in a system of disadvantaged relations, in a city and a public space that renders women vulnerable, without growth politics and a system of power relations that confronts asymmetrical cultural forms."[18]

This chapter seeks to revise some of the images and discourses that have circulated about Ciudad Juárez and its women by examining how various governmental entities have responded to the crimes against women. To carry out this task, I will analyze the 1995–1998 Juárez City Council's and Police Department's advertisements and their so-called prevention campaigns. I will also examine the problematic statements made by Chihuahua governors, their respective attorneys-general, deputy attorneys, a Spanish criminologist who was hired to produce profiles of the murderer or murderers, and a former district attorney who specifically worked on the crimes against women in Ciudad Juárez. By critically assessing their statements, I seek to uncover in what way previous discourses construct images of possible victims, killers, and spaces in the city where murdered women's bodies have been found. I also seek to inquire how we should theorize about Ciudad Juárez, which has come to be known as a site of unspeakable violence.

One final aim of this chapter is to reconsider and attempt to contribute to the questions which Marc Zimmerman has raised in "Latin American Borders and Globalized Cities in the New World Disorder": "How can we conceptualize what is happening to us on a theoretical level and on an essential level, especially in a moment in which theorizations and even words we use to theorize have a tenuous relation to any 'reality'? . . . How have texts written about the city's repercussions been conceptualized, beyond classics such as Freud. . . . How have cities been conceptualized today and what relation does that conceptualization have with postmodernity and social movements of the future[?]"[19]

Within this dialogue, I would ask how we theorize about Ciudad Juárez if, since 1993, more than four hundred women have been murdered—some of them raped and mutilated after death. How do we theorize when there are more than five hundred missing men, abducted by or for their supposed connections to drug trafficking? How do I escape from those ghosts that dance through the streets that I pass through every day? How do we believe that this is—or is not—a vast "laboratory of postmodernity"?[20] How do I explain to others my ability to move about so calmly and fearlessly in these streets when "even the Devil is scared of living here"?[21] How are we to mesh theory with practice in this city of the dead and the living?

Before examining these discourses, it is important to note that this chapter's analysis takes into account the proposals set out by Norman Fairclough in *Language and Power*.[22] His project, part of what he calls the "critical study of language," allows us to observe the connections between language and the use of inequitable power relations. Fairclough's methodology encourages us to see language's significance in the production, maintenance, and change in power relations. One of his main concepts revolves around the idea that the use of power in our modern society is achieved through ideology and, in particular, through language's ideological work. That is why it is imperative to study the use of language as being part of the

**Fig. 3.1.** J Guadalupe Pérez © 2005, "Protesta de Mujeres en el Lote Algodonero de la AMAC" (Women's Protest in the Cotton Field by the AMAC). Courtesy of J Guadalupe Pérez.

production of our "realities." In Ciudad Juárez, there is a sexed and sexist discourse at work that employs metaphors about women in a discreet but crucial manner; it is this prevalent discourse and its underlying work and meaning, I argue, that we must further probe and examine. I should add that my work has a gender focus because "an inventory of the murdered women and girls in Ciudad Juárez that fails to take gender and political gender inequality into account would render what is occurring in this city unintelligible."[23]

## The Prevention Campaigns and the Partido Acción Nacional's Administration

The crimes against women in Ciudad Juárez began to be perpetrated in 1993, during the Partido Acción Nacional (PAN—National Action Party) administration's first term in office in the State of Chihuahua. The government and the media suggested that the murderer was someone hired by the Partido Revolucionario Institucional (PRI—Revolutionary Institutional Party) to tarnish Gov. Francisco Barrio Terrazas' administration (1992–1998) and Mayor Ramón Galindo's administration in Juárez (1995–1999) and to regain power in the 1998 state elections. Because the culprits were nowhere to be found and there were no leads by 1995, state authorities decided to act in two ways: they hired a Spanish criminologist and a former FBI agent who had experience in profiling both criminals and possible victims; and they set forth a prevention campaign to protect all women at risk.

The prevention campaign, like the federal and state authorities' statements, propagated the same historical discourse about women; both were very concerned with what was "moral and respectable" and with what had been rearticulated as "values" in the State of Chihuahua over the last few years.[24]

In other words, the investigations in Ciudad Juárez were already obstructed by two types of discourse that form part of Mexico's everyday life: that of women as inferior beings or objects; and that of values, as former assistant attorney general Jorge López Molinar affirmed in an interview with the newspaper El Nacional: "All the victims were mischief makers or even prostitutes." Such views were also expounded by former governor Francisco Barrio Terrazas.

How are we to expect an objective investigation if even the upholders of justice think that "she asked for it" or that "she deserved it"?

The prevention campaigns during Ramón Galindo's administration raise precisely the same questions. All in all, there were five prevention advertisements published in the two local newspapers—El Diario and Norte—during the first two weeks of January 1995. All five displayed different pictures, and three of them published the same discourse on prevention. These three differed only in the photograph and the caption they included. In one, there was an image of a "guardian angel" in the background, and the title asserted:

"He won't always be there to take care of you." In another, there appeared a photograph of a young man between twenty-five and thirty-five years of age who, despite having his eyes censored so as to render him anonymous, still resembled a soap opera hunk. The picture seemed to have been cut out of an American fashion magazine or hairstyle catalog. The main text read: "Single man looking for young woman, hard-working, who likes to go to parties on the weekend until dawn . . . INTERESTED WOMEN please approach any dark street or alley. Priority given to young women who arrive alone and make the least noise." The third ad had a picture of a body falling down a cliff or amidst clouds; it is hard to identify the background, but it is the body of a woman that is falling. The title, in capital letters, reads: "Be careful!" and the warnings were identical to the first and the second. All three ads share the same recommendations:

- Avoid dark or isolated streets
- Do not talk to strangers
- If you think someone is following you, turn around and look. If they are following you, scream, cross the street, and make your way to a police officer or a place where there are people
- Do not dress provocatively
- Carry a whistle
- When you leave home, let everyone know where you are going and when you will be returning
- Leave the lights on in your home
- Ask someone to wait for you at the bus stop or at your street corner
- Do not accept drinks from strangers
- If you are attacked, do not yell "Help." Instead, yell "Fire" so more people will pay attention to your cry
- Have the keys to your car or your home in your hand, for if you wait to look for your keys until you are at your destination, this will be a propitious time for an attack
- If someone in a car asks you a question, maintain a considerable distance so that they will not be able to pull you in
- Trust your instincts; if you believe that something is not right or you do not feel safe, leave the premises or ask for help
- Do not run the risk of becoming a statistic
- It is the Municipal Police's duty to prevent crime
- Help us by taking care of yourself

These ads convey the same image of the city that exists in movies such as *Aventurera* (1949) and *Espaldas Mojadas* (1953): a dark city whose life transpires at night—a site prone to crime and perdition. Its "decent" women maintain themselves in private spaces. But women who dare take to public spaces, which are reserved for men, and who like to go dancing "until dawn" put themselves at risk of becoming another statistic. The ads set forth the stereotype that the victims were young *maquiladora* workers and that the "single man" was seeking "hard-working" young women.[25]

One of the problems with this sign's representation of women is that it displays the image of the possible murderer as a privileged upper-class young man, and his victim is portrayed as a young, solitary, working-class woman who likes to go to nightclubs or bars until dawn, who is quiet, and who is willing to meet someone in a dark alley. Within this discourse there is a tension between gender and power relations. The discourse is reinforced by the virgin/whore binary, for, on the one hand, there is the young woman who is submissive and does not make noise, and on the other, there is the woman who likes to dance until way into the night, speaks to and accepts drinks from strangers, and walks alone through dark alleys.

The propaganda could have been effective in regard to class, but the rest of the text is handled disappointingly. Many of the victims belong to an impoverished lower class; according to Monárrez-Fragoso's statistics from 2002, from crimes designated only as sexual, there were fifteen *maquila* worker victims; nineteen sex worker victims, dancers, and bar employees; and twenty-six "unknowns."[26] However, the poster makes it seem that only working women who go to dance clubs and bars until dawn are victims. By failing to include other women, especially young women from the upper and middle classes, the ad implies that they go out accompanied and do not put themselves at risk by speaking to strangers and walking through dark alleys, for they, of course, travel in a vehicle. Consequently, poor/working women are portrayed as "loose."

The underlying discourse of this text is that *maquiladora* workers are not as "good" or "decent" as those women from the upper and middle class, and that is why they are killed. This discourse supports statements made by former governor Barrio Terrazas and former deputy state attorney general López Molinar. Therefore, it would be useful to stop and examine the relationship between public officials' words, their moralist attitudes, and the difference in social class that exists between them and the victims. The young women are doubly exploited: by an economic system's "social and political relations of power";[27] and by a social discourse that clings to a generalized image of them as "girls who go downtown to sell their bodies for money or food."[28]

Through the image of the guardian angel—an icon that is supposed to protect us and "never abandon us nor in the day or the night"—that par-

**Fig. 3.2.** J Guadalupe Pérez © 2003, "Performance del Colectivo Artístico Antígona en el Lote Bravo" (Antígona Artist Collective's Performance in Lote Bravo). Courtesy of J Guadalupe Pérez.

ticular notice utilizes the fear of God and implies that if a young woman does not strictly abide by all of the Municipal Police (Dirección General de Policía, DGP) warnings (the voice of authority), she will become a statistic. This notice, like the previous one, stems from the same presupposition: that these women climb into strangers' cars and walk through dark places, which can also be read as falling into temptation. This notice reinforces the hegemonic discourse of the God of the Old Testament: a God who punishes transgressors of the law by abandoning them. Just as Eve got what she deserved and was exiled from paradise for her disobedience, Juárez women who fail to obey the police warnings will be condemned to be kidnapped, raped, tortured, and murdered.

The third ad's main image and text differ from the one with the guardian angel, but it employs the same discourse. The falling body of a young woman and the text that cautions "Be Careful!" imply that if one does not follow the authorities' warnings, falling into a moral abyss, being expelled from paradise, and rape and death are assured.

The ad's final suggestion draws attention in this way: "If you are sexually attacked, induce vomiting. In this way, the aggressor will most likely be disgusted and flee." This last piece of advice goes beyond image and metaphor. On the one hand, it portrays a victim who, at the moment of sexual attack, will be able to marshal her thoughts enough to defend herself by inducing vomiting. On the other hand, it represents the aggressor as a fine and impeccable man who will flee on witnessing such a disgusting sight. This last suggestion seems ludicrous; it is almost as unbelievable and irresponsible as to denigrate the victims after their death.

The three ads I have examined seem to reinforce the cultural code that women are safer at home and that "strangers" are the only ones who can harm us. Yet in the case of Juárez femicides, by 1999, "thirty-four of the victims knew their murderer either because they were kin, friends, or neighbors; two were murdered by clients, and the rest's relation to the perpetrator remains unclear. In terms of those deemed serial murderers, there were two who each killed two women whom they knew."[29] Moreover, the portrayal of women who pass through dark alleys gives the impression that these women do so only for the purpose of engaging in some romantic affair or sexual act. This portrayal fails to specify that hundreds of working women—young and old—have to pass through dark alleys because they leave the factory late at night or have to start work at the break of dawn and must thus walk through the dark to get home or to reach public transportation.

In the fourth ad, a young boy states: "By this age, most boys have already learned how to tie their shoelaces, ride a bike, and mistreat women. Don't show examples of physical or emotional violence in your home. Don't set a bad example . . . for your children will most probably imitate it. Women have the right to say NO without any physical or emotional reprisals. If they suffer any type of violence, they have the right to report it and to be treated with respect and efficiency by the authorities." Everything about this ad draws attention: the photograph portrays a fair-skinned, straight-haired, well-nourished boy of about three or four. The ad's designer clearly has a set of prejudices that privilege a certain type of masculine beauty and social class. The designer seems unaware that these pictures conceive of the assailant with a certain image in mind. There is a tension between what is written and what is portrayed in the picture. If, on the one hand, the text implies that working women are loose women, on the other, it implies that handsome, well-dressed, blond or light brown–haired men are the potential murderers. One of the other implications of this ad is that bad conduct can be learned only in the home and that only boys who grow up in homes with domestic violence have the potential to become criminals.

All this contradicts the previous ads' message and perpetuates dominant cultural codes that women are safer within the home but boys are safer in the street, for if they stay at home they can be exposed to violence. These ads never examine the influence of the social environment, the neighborhood, the school, or the media.

The last two ads apparently seek to erase what was said in the previous ones which I have analyzed, for the earlier examples portray the image of the young working woman as a femme fatale, and these last examples give us the benefit of the doubt. In the earlier examples, women were warned not to dress in a provocative manner, not to walk alone through dark alleys, and not to dance on the weekends. In these last ads, women are given social and public permission to say no to any type of aggression, and they are granted the right to denounce any illicit act against them and to be efficiently served by the authorities—even if they are "loose women" or sex workers.

One has to ask, then, why the crimes against the women found in Lote Bravo, Lomas de Poleo, Campo Algodonero, Cerro del Cristo Negro, and other places in the city have yet to be solved—some of them after more than fifteen years. The answer must take into account the intimate ties between gender and class constructions, the politics of identity, and the intolerable negligence of the state.

The last ad depicts a very fit man and reads: "Very macho, very macho . . . One way of demonstrating our manhood is by taking care of our women. Let us avoid violence by taking care of our daughters, wives, and mothers." Then the Municipal Police's suggestions and warnings specifically address men: "Wait for your working or student women at the bus stop. They should always inform you where they will be and what time they will return home. Make sure you have emergency phone numbers handy. Make sure your home is well protected (well lit and with shut windows and gates). Change any loose or broken windows. Make sure to change locks that are in bad condition or are of poor quality."

The cultural construct that appears in the other ads is underscored here.

A woman is subject to a man's protection and is rendered practically useless on her own. These exhortations appeal to truly "very macho" men to protect, care for, accompany, and lock women in. This notice's discourse demonstrates that the city, within its social structure, continues to believe that "its" women must be kept in confinement, since the women who dared to go out at night to dance until dawn transgressed men's space and therefore died or deserved to die.

As we can see, the women whom the Municipal Police propaganda is addressing are those who have transgressed men's spaces and good social and moral values. They are working-class women who are violated both in their everyday life—facing exploitation in the factory and the home—and, symbolically, in these representations of them. Such images have been endorsed, as we have seen, by former governors, former attorneys general, and former district attorneys. José Antonio Parra Molina has reaffirmed these images in interviews in *Norte:* "On the border, women find themselves in a social environment where the feminine sex lives in a completely libertine state since it is but a few meters from the border with the United States, where women begin their sexual life at a much younger age, and they adopt this way of life, thus leading them to promiscuity."[30] Besides upholding the ideas set forth by the police ads, the criminologist's conclusions are based on a stereotyped view of the border—a vision that is partially grounded in the stereotype of the licentious Anglo American woman.

The border environment that Parra Molina imagines is that which Norma Iglesias examines in an analysis of Mexican films about the border. Using "Ciudad Juárez as a point of reference," she argues that these films depict "the border as a propitious place for organized crime and prostitution."[31] No one denies that there is prostitution and organized crime in Ciudad Juárez as well as in other border and nonborder cities, but our social reality is much more complex than Parra Molina's explanations, especially when he asserts that "the feminine sex lives in a completely libertine state since it is but a few meters from the United States border." His views are based on the construction of the other, and his assertions imply that all Mexican border women are "morally lost" because of U.S. women's bad influence.

These views are especially interesting, though, because Mexicans (both male and female) view Americans as the other. Rather than exploring lines of investigation with which to trap the criminals or sketching an objective and real(istic) profile of the victims or the women at risk, Parra Molina's narrative has only served to perpetuate centuries-old representations and images of women. Parra Molina etches the representation of possible victims, of *maquiladora* laborers: "I have personally witnessed what easy prey maquiladora working women are for murderers. When they get out of work, they stand outside the factory in large groups, and when they see someone with a nice car drive by they ask him for 'a ride.' They leave with whoever shows up at the premises without thinking about the consequences, and they often ask men to invite them for a 'little beer' and ask him out to dance."[32] The criminologist's narrative endorses the authorities' statements and prevention campaigns. In this representation, gender and class tensions continue to increase, for the murderer drives a "nice car" and treats women to beers and clubs. However, one wonders how Parra Molina corroborates what happens once the women are in the car. The criminologist never explains this.

Given the outpouring of criticism against the police's prevention campaigns, it seems the 1995–1998 City Council felt the need to hire an "authoritative voice" to defend them. As a result of my analysis, I believe that groups in power or groups with access to power are obviously manipulating the way in which working-class Juárez women (victims or potential victims) get represented: as fully responsible for the criminal acts unleashed on them.

The so-called prevention campaigns failed from the beginning. Rather than prevent anything, they only served to make the federal, state, and municipal authorities' misogynist and classist ideology all the more evident. This is precisely why they were removed from newspapers, for feminist groups, nongovernmental organizations, and academics immediately protested. In their defense, the authorities argued that "they had been designed by a woman" and that they had "generated them using FBI information." It is obvious that the woman who designed these ads was fully submerged in patriarchal ideology,[33] and that the images and metaphors that the Municipal Police and the FBI used to portray the city, the potential victims, and their possible murderers shared only a "tenuous relation with any 'reality' whatsoever."[34]

The narratives of the Municipal Police and the state attorney general have constructed an image of the victims and possible aggressors based on racial difference. Parra Molina fully employed notions of difference in regard to the murderers; knowing that this image would have a greater impact on Mexican society, the image he constructed was that of the foreigner, the "Oriental." In 1995, an Egyptian, Abdel Latif Sharif Sharif, was captured and charged with the serial killing of at least nine young women.[35] In 1996, members of Los Rebeldes, a gang,[36] were arrested and confessed to at least five of the crimes. Los Rebeldes also accused Abdel Sharif of being the mastermind behind many of the murders. In 1998, Parra Molina was hired to create profiles of the possible murderers; after simply reading Sharif's file, he endorsed the police narrative: "I believe serial killers exist in Juárez, beginning with Abdel Latif Sharif Sharif and the Los Rebeldes gang, but another serial killer coming from the United States, possibly from Texas, could have committed these acts since he would not risk committing these murders in Texas for fear of being detained and sentenced to death."[37]

Through this Spanish criminologist's discourse, it is interesting to see how identity politics are employed within the exercise of power and how vigorously they thrive in a society that does not consider itself racist. This drive to accuse the foreign other not only evidences exclusionist racial politics, but it validates the old stereotype of the border as a place where everything is permissible, as a stop on the way, or as a site of perdition. Moreover, it allows us to see that Parra Molina's notions of difference are clearly defined in respect to Americans, who in fact define his view of otherness. American men are the alleged murderers and American women are a "perverting" influence on young Mexican women. His words also convey that Mexico was perceived, not only by Sharif, but by the Spanish criminologist himself, as a place where such crimes could be committed with impunity.

## Ciudad Juárez, Its Murdered Women, and the Partido Revolucionario Institucional

Tensions between the center and the periphery in the State of Chihuahua have endured since the founding of Juárez and the naming of Chihuahua City as the state capital. Chihuahua City is constructed as the cradle of the old aristocracy, of ancestral families, of old money, and of good moral values. Juárez, by contrast, is the home "of all people,"[38] of dirty money, of bad girls, and of criminals. The state's identity politics have had repercussions on its public policy. During PRI governor Fernando Baeza's administration (1988–1992), the state restricted the business hours of local restaurants, nightclubs, bars, nightspots, and entertainment establishments and also restricted the hours that alcoholic beverages could be sold in supermarkets, convenience stores, and small local stores. These measures instituted by "Ferdinand the Catholic" (as he was called) were meant to reduce crime and, at the same time, improve the city's negative image.[39]

In 1998, Gov. Patricio Martínez García (1998–2004), also from the PRI, implemented the same measures, named the Zero Tolerance Program, at the outset of his term. In a statement to *El Diario* on November 18, 1998, he expressed the following: "I want Ciudad Juárez to go to sleep early; I want everyone to be home by 2:00 AM," as if "the nighttime were guilty of the violence and lack of safety; consequently all that is associated with night's negative image and its black legend is constructed as though it were natural."[40] As we can see, although political parties in Chihuahua may change, the image of the city and its women fails to alter substantially.

State and municipal government power struggles,[41] as well as disagreements over the various different police departments' roles, lead to every group blaming the other. On the one hand, Patricio Martínez's spokesperson, Jorge Sánchez Acosta, stated that "Francisco Barrio Terrazas's administration is responsible for the lack of investigations in the kidnapping and murder of women, [and] since October 4, when the new government was established in Chihuahua, there has been no more [legal] impunity."[42] Martínez's attorney general, Arturo González Rascón, declared that, during the previous administration, 83 of the 176 cases of murdered women were not solved and that of the 16 murders of women during Martínez's term, only 2 remained to be solved.[43]

On the other hand, at the Buried in the Border Conference at New Mexico State University in October of 1999, Javier Benavides, the former commissioner of the Municipal Police, claimed that "NGOs were magnifying the cases of murdered women and were neglecting incidences of murdered men, whose cases were also very lamentable."[44] Both parties' administrations have been criticized for their inefficiency and their failure to pursue investigations from a gender or class perspective. Javier Benavides diminishes the importance of the murdered women in Juárez as being simply a structural problem. As Carlos Monsiváis explains, "the great problem is that woman has always been victim . . . when one of them is kidnapped, raped, tortured, and murdered by a man, this no longer disturbs people or fills them with indignation because these aggressions have become customary." What is most lamentable about these events, Monsiváis argues, is the contrast: "we know of no woman who has equally hunted a man, raped him, killed him, and thrown him away."[45]

Reading Arturo González Rascón's statements, we find two types of discourse. In one he uses official language, and in the other he uses everyday language. When it comes time to discuss the murder of women, he has much more often employed the latter type of discourse. In an interview with Armando Rodríguez in which he was asked about the sex crimes in Ciudad Juárez, he reconstructed the city's black image, claiming that "it was more than a national problem—it was a cultural and situational problem."[46] González Rascón rearticulated the image of the border as the spiritual no-man's land that Vasconcelos branded, although the former tried to correct himself: "What happens is that right now we are all focused on Ciudad Juárez, and if one of these types of events happens in Chihuahua City, one does not notice . . . or in the State of Sinaloa, where, since January, ninety-six homicides have occurred, and it is not noticed."[47] This apparent revalorization of the city is reinforced by his words, for if one does not notice this happens in other places, it is because those places do not share the city of perdition's image. In this same interview, he returned to the discourse of power employed by Gov. Patricio Martínez: "I believe Ciudad Juárez and this border in particular have to rescue the image of security, a respectable place that all of Chihuahua's citizens have to give their city and that we are going to transform."[48]

True, most scholars and researchers are still unable to understand why these serial crimes are committed only in Ciudad Juárez. In the past, we considered it a phenomenon similar to drug trafficking and auto theft: the city simply lacked the proper infrastructure—in every sense—to keep up with its dynamic growth. For this reason, it was easy to go into hiding, become anonymous, change one's address, and even cross the border. Our main question then was: Why does this happen only in Ciudad Juárez and not in other border cities with the same dynamics, such as Tijuana? A possible answer had to do with the metropolitan zone and access to border crossing. In Tijuana, it is much slower and more complicated to walk or drive across the border. The sheer numbers of people crossing into El Paso are greater. Moreover, San Diego lies at least forty kilometers away. Ciudad Juárez and El Paso are situated in the same geographical space; they constitute a metropolitan zone of over 2.5 million people, and the longest distance between these two cities consists of the international bridges that connect them (approximately 200 meters). Either by foot or by car, crossing is much more accessible, and, it seems, there are much greater possibilities of losing oneself in anonymity once one crosses to the other side; this is especially the case since the income levels and standard of living of El Paso and Ciudad Juárez are more similar than those of San Diego and Tijuana, where $800,000 American homes contrast with poor *colonias* and make it virtually impossible for someone to blend in.[49]

Moreover, there is yet another answer that might be more accurate: there is a very powerful group behind the crimes, and there exists legal impunity in the city and the state, which has allowed such crimes to happen. Even though violence against women is not exclusive to Juárez,[50] the serial sex crimes here bring such violence to international attention because of the violence done to the victim's bodies, the legal impunity granted the criminal(s), and the silence and negligence of the state (be it municipal, state, or federal).

But in regard to the murderers, González Rascón's obsession with pinning them on the "other" hardly differs from Parra Molina's. In 1999, Jesús Manuel Guajardo, "El Tolteca," was apprehended after a rape survivor identified him as the aggressor. After his capture, the police arrested four presumed accomplices, known as "Los Choferes" or "Los Ruteros" (The Drivers, or the Route Drivers),"[51] and they were charged with the murders of twelve more women.

This case, as is the case of Sharif, is replete with cultural and political implications. Juárez society despises criminals, and even more so when they are from outside the city. Citizens of Juárez and Chihuahua City "proved" that "in Juárez we are not murderers,"[52] which supports the city's anti-immigrant prejudices. In El Tolteca's and Los Choferes' cases, the attorney general constructed a narrative similar to that used to prosecute Los Rebeldes: "After Sharif, 'Los Rebeldes' gang, hired by Sharif, committed many homicides. Then followed 'The Drivers,' led by Jesús Manuel Guajardo, aka 'El Tolteca,' who through Víctor Moreno, aka 'The Narco-trafficker,' received the payments he'd sent abroad, but the three cases were related."[53]

González Rascón generates his vision of the other by identifying the Egyptian Sharif as the leader of bands of rapists and murderers (Los Rebeldes, Los Choferes, and El Tolteca) and supports another anti-immigrant narrative in regard to El Tolteca, but he rejects the possibility that a Mexican national, Rafael Reséndez Ramírez, best known in the United States as "The Railroad Killer" or "The Railway Killer," might have murdered many women in Ciudad Juárez. This is a likely possibility, given that former FBI agent Robert Resler always maintained that Reséndez Ramírez was responsible for "at least six murders in Ciudad Juárez, if not a dozen."[54] Afterward, Resler stated that he did not understand why Mexican authorities had denied this. González Rascón alleged that they were not going to "elaborate on something for which they had no evidence."[55] Rather than following up on Resler's findings, it seems that González Rascón's greatest concern was to clean up the image of Mexicans abroad just as he was seeking to recover the image of Juárez for Chihuahua: "Although these multiple homicides are of Mexican origin, there is no reason to make generalizations about Mexican nationals going to the United States to commit crimes, or for there to emerge a negative image of the Mexicans who live abroad."[56]

González Rascón's narrative is comparable to José Parra Molina's every time he speaks of two assassins who were foreigners: an Arab and an American. We can observe a clear tension in their discourses of power and identity and within their process of authorization and nonauthorization. The Mexican attorney general, who employs notions of "I and us," and the Spanish criminologist's use of "I and the other" deauthorize the usual hegemonic discourse: the Anglo-Saxon one, the "other," which Resler embodies.

As a result of the NGOs' constant pressure, the Fiscalía Especial para la Investigación de Crímenes contra Mujeres (Special Prosecutor's Office for the Investigation of Crimes against Women) was founded in 1995 under Francisco Barrio Terrazas' administration. Since its beginning, "with five overburdened district attorneys and a shortage of staff and technical equipment, the office has faced great disapproval from the leading protest groups."[57] NGOs' protests have generally addressed the same issues: the authorities' ineptitude; the ever-so-slow investigations; the inefficiency; and, under Suly Ponce Prieto's administration (November 1998–August 2001), the arrogance toward and the disrespectful treatment of victims, their family members, and NGOs, reporters, criminologists, experts in victimology, scholars, and so on. Suly Ponce was in the eye of the storm and constantly engaged in a war of words with NGOs, especially with Voces sin Eco (Voices without an Echo), an organization made up of the family members of missing or murdered women.

I will examine but two events to make my case. The first example shows how Gov. Patricio Martínez and his attorney general, Arturo González Rascón, believed that the police investigations of the sex crimes in Juárez were conducted efficiently and with a focus on gender.[58] Suly Ponce noted that more than one hundred people were under investigation for crimes against women. This approach seemed "illogical" to the Instituto Chihuahuense de Criminología (Chihuahua Institute of Criminology) and to Esther Chávez Cano, director of the Casa Amiga crisis center. Chávez Cano considered this approach to be "a demonstration of inefficiency and a mockery of the people."[59] This statement stemmed from the last demonstration's events, when the people of Juárez sought to have Suly Ponce dismissed from office, but González Rascón argued that she was the best person for the job. As a result, protests led to rallies in front of the state attorney general's offices; people carried banners and posters that read, "If Suly is the best, then we Juárez citizens are truly unfortunate."

The second example best complements the discourses of power I have already discussed, as it is based on the district attorney's attitude and responses at the Primera Reunión Binacional "Crímenes contra Mujeres" (First Binational Crimes against Women Conference): "The district attorney [Suly Ponce] was upset because she felt attacked and besieged after a woman and her daughter confronted her for giving them scant attention when they went to her office to report a missing minor. Before the constant questioning, Suly Ponce scolded the little girl . . . and told her she had not given her any lines of investigation to follow,"[60] as if this was the family members' duty. After another question, Ponce said she would gladly give up her post, because "looking around for loose girls" took too much time away from her and her family.[61]

As we can see, this female special prosecutor's discourse hardly differs from that of the male authorities we have discussed, thus posing a larger problem for studies of gender and language. The fact that a woman is in charge of designing a campaign directed toward women, or that a woman is in charge of a special unit for the investigation of crimes against women, is not a guarantee that she will not be immersed in patriarchal discourse and ideology. Moreover, Suly Ponce's tirades reveal the incompatibility between her public and private spaces. For this special prosecutor, there was no site of negotiation between her "family obligations" and her obligation and commitment to the community.

## Final Reflections

From 1993 to the present, we have gained some spaces from which to seek justice for all these women. Whether it is functional or dysfunctional, at least we have a Fiscalía Especial para la Investigación de Crímenes contra Mujeres, as well as an Unidad Especializada de Delitos Sexuales (Specialized Unit for Sexual and Family Offenses), and an NGO crisis center. New forms of citizenship action have emerged. Alternative voices have dared to defy power, such as Voces sin Eco, Nuestras Hijas de Regreso a Casa (May Our Daughters Return Home), Mujeres de Negro (Women in Black), Justicia para Nuestras Hijas (Justice for Our Daughters), Madres en Busca de Justicia (Mothers in Search of Justice), Mujeres por Juárez (Women for Juárez), Fundación Sagrario, and the young woman at the binational conference who publicly called Suly Ponce a liar. There have been marches, demonstrations, vigils, and symposiums with the participation of NGOs, academic institutions, and social sectors. Many films and documentaries have been made. The tragic events have been on the front page of international newspapers, and the UN and Amnesty International have spearheaded two commissions. Endless telephone poles in the city have been painted pink and black as monuments to the victims. There are different monuments (pink crosses with the victims' names) in the places where bod-

**Fig. 3.3.** J Guadalupe Pérez © 2003, "Performance en Camión del Colectivo Artístico Antígona en el Lote Bravo" (Antigone Artist Collective's Performance on a Bus in Lote Bravo). Courtesy of J Guadalupe Pérez.

ies have been found. A federal special prosecutor and a special commissioner for violence against women in Juárez were appointed during Vicente Fox's administration.

Nonetheless, to this day, we do not know why such sex-related serial crimes have occurred for the most part in Ciudad Juárez or whether groups in Juárez are the only ones keeping a careful count of these kinds of hate crimes. We do not yet know whether it is because "the future arrived 30 years earlier in Ciudad Juárez,"[62] or whether, as Zimmerman explains, "the more cities become a part of global networks, the more their previous levels of organization are threatened, altered, or destroyed,"[63] or whether Juárez's citizens have not known how to completely negotiate spaces and/or identities. Or perhaps it is, because when we inscribe our geographies, we create artifacts that impose significance on the world.[64]

Ciudad Juárez, "another site of vice and perdition,"[65] has been unable to achieve the image of "Mexico's best border town," which Pres. Adolfo López Mateos propagated during the 1960s and which subsequent governments have proclaimed, especially in the 1980s, with the maquiladora boom. It might be that, because of Ciudad Juárez's border status, what "fuels the country's collective imaginary are images marked by the absence of the law,"[66] and we then decide to put this imaginary into practice. Perhaps we have not yet developed a full conscience in regard to how we use language, as Fairclough (1990) suggests, but when we acquire that conscience, it will help us in these processes of emancipation.

At this point, I do not know. As I regret and despise the state of legal impunity in which we live, and as I recall the words of Monsiváis—"no element is so decisive in its resonance or its lack of resonance as the historical appreciation of the value of unknown women's lives"[67]—I can only observe a ghost dance through the streets that I walk, calmly, solemnly, every day.[68]

## Notes

Author's note: The title of this chapter is borrowed from Jean Franco, "Ghost Dance in the Battlefields of the Cold War." The original version in Spanish was published as "Baile de fantasmas en Ciudad Juárez al final/principio del milenio," in *Más allá de la ciudad letrada: Crónicas y espacios urbanos*, ed. Boris Muñoz and Silvia Spitta (Pittsburgh, Pa.: Biblioteca de América, Instituto Internacional de Literatura Iberoamericana, 2003), 411–437. I have updated some data for this version.

1. Second epigraph from a talk presented at "1a Reunión Binacional: Crímenes contra Mujeres," organized by El Colegio de la Frontera Norte; the NGO Coordinator, New Mexico State University; and Semillas, November 3–4, 2000 (videotape).

2. Even though the crimes began to be recorded in 1993 and protests by local women's NGOs and scholars also began in this year, it was not until 1998 that these terrible events hit the international press.

3. Given that the statistics vary from one source to another, I am using the data from Julia Monárrez-Fragoso's PhD dissertation: "Feminicidio sexual sistémico, víctimas y familiares 1993–2005," Universidad Autónoma Metropolitana–Unidad Xochimilco. For updated statistics, see *Sistema socioeconómico y geo-referencial sobre la violencia de género en Ciudad Juárez: Análisis de la violencia de género en Ciudad Juárez, Chihuahua: Propuestas para su prevención* (El Colegio de la Frontera Norte [COLEF]/Comisión para Prevenir y Erradicar la Violencia contra las Mujeres en Ciudad Juárez [CPEVCMCJ], 2006), compact disc.

4. After investigating for more than two weeks, Mexico's Federal Office of the Attorney General and the U.S. Drug Enforcement Agency reported that "only nine bodies were found." The difference in "missing" and "found" numbers made Ciudad Juárez's municipal authorities and Chihuahua's state government begin a campaign for "the dignity of Juárez and its citizens." They asked the *Washington Post* to issue a public apology to Juárez's citizens for its yellow press. For more information, see *El Diario* and *El Norte* (Ciudad Juárez), November 29, 1999–January 30, 2000.

5. Alicia Castellanos Guerrero and Gilberto López Rivas, "La influencia norteamericana en la frontera norte de México," in *La frontera del norte: Integración y desarrollo*, ed. Roque González Salazar (Mexico City: El Colegio de Mexico, 1981), 68.

6. Carlos Monsiváis, "La cultura de la frontera," *Esquina Baja* 5.6 (May–August 1998): 43.

7. Debra Castillo, Gudelia Rangel Gómez, and Bonie Delgado, "Vidas fronterizas: Mujeres prostitutas en Tijuana," in *Nuevas perspectives desde/sobre América Latina: El desafío de los estudios culturales,* ed. Mabel Moraña (Pittsburgh: Instituto Internacional de Literatura Iberoamericana–Editorial Cuarto Propio, 2000), 245.

8. Norma Klahn, "Writing the Border: The Languages and Limits of Representation," *Travesía: The Border Issue Journal of Latin American Cultural Studies* 3.1–2 (1994): 29.

9. Ibid., 30.

10. Besides Norma Klahn, Gabriel Trujillo Muñoz, Víctor Zúñiga, Carlos Monsiváis, Jorge Bustamante, Guillermina Valdés-Villalva, José Manuel Valenzuela Arce, Claire Fox, and Tim Given, among others, have written on this subject.

11. The Maquiladora Program was fully established as the capstone of the Bracero Program, which was in place from 1942 to 1964. It was believed at the beginning of the 1960s that documented workers in the United States would return to Mexico in hordes and that, above all, border cities would be established. The Border Industrialization Program (BIP) did not induce workers to leave, as the majority of them stayed in the United States as undocumented workers. Nonetheless, what the BIP did do was attract specialized workers, especially women, from places south of the Mexican border states.

12. I define the service sector as employees working as secretaries, domestics, and restaurant workers.

13. Ricardo Aguilar and María Socorro Tabuenca Córdoba, "Lo que el viento a Juárez," *Testimonio de una ciudad que se obstina: Col. Papeles de Familia* (Torreón, Coah., Mex., and Las Cruces, N.M.: Universidad Iberoamericana–Laguna/Editorial Nimbus, 2000), 64.

14. George Yúdice, "Postmodernidad y capitalismo transnacional en América Latina," in *Cultura y postpolítica: El debate sobre la modernidad en América Latina,* ed. Néstor García Canclini (Mexico City: Consejo Nacional para la Cultura y las Artes, 1991), 64.

15. The population in Mexican border-belt cities can buy cars for better prices in the United States and then get special (border) license plates that are legal only thirty kilometers south of the border. Before the peso's devaluation in 1994, young working women would pool their money to buy a car so that they could go to work in the *maquiladoras* and then take turns driving it on the weekends.

16. Jorge Balderas Domínguez, "El estigma a la operadora de maquila: Salones de baile, antros y mujeres en la noche juarense," presentation at "1a Reunión Binacional: Crímenes contra mujeres," 5 (photocopy in author's possession).

17. Julia Monárrez-Fragoso, "La cultura del feminicidio en Ciudad Juárez, 1993–1999," *Frontera Norte* 12.23 (January–June 2000): 88–89.

18. Alfredo Limas, "Sexualidad, género, violencia y procuración de justicia," presentation at "1a Reunión Binacional: Crímenes contra Mujeres," 3 (photocopy in author's possession).

19. Marc Zimmerman, "Fronteras latinoamericanas y ciudades globalizadas en el nuevo desorden mundial," in *Nuevas perspectivas desde/sobre América Latina: El desafío de los estudios culturales,* ed. Mabel Moraña (Pittsburgh, Pa.: Instituto Internacional de Literatura Iberoamericana–Editorial Cuarto Propio, 2000), 294–295.

20. Néstor García Canclini, *Tijuana: La casa de toda la gente* (Mexico City: Instituto Nacional de Antropología e Historia–Escuela Nacional de Antropología e Historia/Programa Cultural de las Fronteras, 1989), 293.

21. Charles Bowden, "While You Were Sleeping: In Juarez, Mexico, Photographers Expose the Violent Realities of Free Trade," *Harper's Magazine* (December 1996): 44.

22. Norman Fairclough, *Language and Power* (London: Longman, 1990). Fairclough bases his methodology on Gramsci, Habermas, Bourdieu, Saussure, van Dijk, and Foucault, among others. In his methodology, Fairclough suggests observing sociolinguistic conventions, for they use language in its social context. In his proposal, he also includes the study of linguistics, pragmatism, cognitive psychology, conversations, and discourse.

23. Julia Monárrez-Fragoso, "La cultura del feminicidio," 89.

24. With the coming of the PAN to Chihuahua in 1993, Francisco Barrio Terrazas—head of Mexico's Comptroller's Office during the Fox administration—began a "recovering-values" campaign. This campaign has been highly criticized by progressive academics and people from the Left for its conservatism. This type of discourse continues to be used by the party. Let us not forget the controversy that took place when former labor secretary Carlos Abascal asked the principal of his daughter's high school to fire her literature teacher after she had recommended that the class read Carlos Fuentes's *Aura*.

25. The data shows that of the 162 murdered women, only 15 were *maquiladora* workers. See Monárrez-Fragoso, "La cultura del feminicidio," 110.

26. "Unknown" is Monárrez-Fragoso's designation. Not all of the women disappeared or were murdered as a result of sexual motives.

27. Valle and Torres, *Latino Metropolis*, Globalization and Community 7 (Minneapolis: University of Minnesota Press, 2000), 10.

28. Bowden, "While You Were Sleeping," 48.

29. Monárrez-Fragoso, "La cultura del feminicidio," 113.

30. Martín Orquiz, "Asesinatos de mujeres: La amenaza latente," *Norte* (August 1, 1998), 114.

31. Iglesias, *La flor más bella*, 29–31.

32. Orquiz, 114.

33. There is a notable difference between a woman and a woman who is aware of her gender. The awareness of gender construction leads women to deconstruct patriarchal ideologies.

34. Zimmerman, "Fronteras latinoamericanas," 294.

35. Sharif died in prison in June 2006. The authorities said he was the main suspect as the material and intellectual author of at least twenty-five crimes. However, he was charged only for one of the crimes, and that charge was based on circumstantial evidence. There were multiple inconsistencies in the investigation, which he pointed out. He always claimed he was innocent.

36. Los Rebeldes were accused of committing at least seventeen crimes. In 2005, they were formally sentenced: José Luis Rosales got twenty-four years for the rape and murder of Rosario García Leal; Sergio Armendáriz, Romel Ceniceros, Carlos Barrientos, Gerardo Fernández, and Jorge Contreras received forty years each for the rape and murder of Verónica Castro and two women identified as Lucy and

Tanya. As in Sharif's case, the convictions were based on circumstantial evidence. They later claimed that they had confessed because they were tortured.

37. Orquiz, "Asesinatos de mujeres," 114.

38. I borrow this phrase from García Canclini, *Tijuana: La casa de toda la gente.*

39. Never in Juárez's history was its image more "positive." The *maquiladora* boom of the 1980s created an atmosphere of confidence. Nightclubs in the city's downtown shared space with the middle- and working class, although there were nightclubs for each social class. The city's former vice-and-prostitution image was displaced by an economic bonanza, especially after 1985. See César Fuentes Flores, "Industrial Maquila Growth—Development Strategy? Maquiladora Workers and Nurseries: The Case of Colonia Toribio Ortega in Ciudad Juárez, Chihuahua" (photocopy in author's possession).

40. Balderas Domínguez, "El estigma," 15.

41. Although the PRI regained the governorship, the PAN continued to hold Juárez's city government until 2004, then the PRI again took over.

42. Alejandro Romero Ruiz, "Politizan casos de mujeres," *El Diario* (July 18, 1999).

43. Luis Rodríguez Vázquez, "Procurador de justicia: Desmienten a ONG's," *El Diario* (August 10, 1999).

44. Cristina Delgado, "Magnifican los crímenes contra mujeres," *Norte* (October 3, 1999).

45. In Raúl Flores Simental, "Suly Ponce: En vivo, sin máscara y por Internet" *Norte* (November 12, 2000).

46. Armando Rodríguez, "Son 'situacional' los crímenes, dice el procurador estatal," *El Diario* (February 24, 1999).

47. Ibid.

48. Ibid.

49. I thank the anonymous reader for this lucid observation.

50. See United Nations, "Integración de los derechos humanos de la mujer y la perspectiva de género: La violencia contra la mujer," in *Informe de la Relatora Especial contra la Mujer, Sus Causas y Consecuencias,* ed. Yarkin Ertürk (January 13, 2006).

51. El Tolteca and Los Choferes were captured in 1999, but it was not until 2005 that they were convicted and sentenced. Jesús Manuel Guajardo received a sentence of 113 years for the murder and rape of three women; José Gaspar Chávez, Víctor Moreno, and Agustín Castillo were sentenced to 40 years for the murder of four women; and Bernardo Hernández was found not guilty. During the process, El Tolteca declared to the press that he was tortured in order to make him implicate the other men as accomplices. Once again, there is no scientific proof that either El Tolteca or Los Choferes killed everyone they were accused of killing. El Tolteca did actually rape and attempt to murder the teenager who survived and accused him.

52. This was a slogan during the "Dignity for Juárez" march on December 18, 1999.

53. Rodríguez Vázquez, "Procurador de justicia."

54. We should recall that Reséndez lived in Ciudad Juárez, and in fact he was extradited from there after convincing family members to turn him in to U.S. authorities. Reséndez was convicted and executed by lethal injection in Huntsville, Texas, on June 27, 2006. See Alejandro Téllez, "También procurador desmiente a experto," *Norte* (July 15, 1999).

55. Ibid.

56. Ibid.

57. Luz del Carmen Sosa, "Fiscalía en entredicho," *El Diario* (March 4, 2001).

58. I am paraphrasing González Rascón during the announcement of the election of a new prosecutor, *El Diario* (November 7, 1998).

59. Tania Fernández and Roberto Ramos, "Cuestionan a Fiscal de Mujeres," *El Diario* (January 23, 2000).

60. Flores Simental, "Suly Ponce."

61. Ibid.

62. Bowden, "While You Were Sleeping," 48.

63. Zimmerman, "Fronteras latinoamericanas," 301.

64. Dennis Cosgrove and Mona Domosh, "Author and Authority: Writing the New Cultural Geography," in *Place/Culture Representation,* ed. James Duncan and David Ley (New York: Routledge, 1994), 37.

65. This phrase appears in the first scene to the 1953 film *Espaldas Mojadas.*

66. Carlos Monsiváis, quoted in Alejandro Quintero, "Urgen investigar a fondo crímenes contra mujeres," *El Diario* (November 5, 2000).

67. Ibid.

68. By November 2001, the date on which I finished editing this article for its original publication in Spanish, eight more bodies had been found in an abandoned lot called Campo Algodonero. For these crimes, Víctor Javier García Uribe, aka "El Cerillo," and Gustavo González Meza, "La Foca," were accused during Patricio Martínez's administration. González Meza died in prison under suspicious circumstances after a hernia operation, and García Uribe was freed in 2005. In 2004, four more bodies were found on the outskirts of Juárez in a place called Cerro del Cristo Negro.

CHAPTER 4

# Gender, Order, and Femicide: Reading the Popular Culture of Murder in Ciudad Juárez

STEVEN S. VOLK AND MARIAN E. SCHLOTTERBECK

*Ya se nos quitó lo macho o nos falta dignidad.*
—LOS TIGRES DEL NORTE, "LAS MUJERES DE JUÁREZ"

Lilia Alejandra García Andrade was last seen at 7:30 PM on February 14, 2001, by her coworkers as she walked toward an abandoned lot next to the *maquiladora* where she worked in Ciudad Juárez, Mexico. The seventeen-year-old mother of two crossed this same unlit, empty field every day to catch a bus home after work. That night she never arrived. Her mother reported her missing the next day. Her physically and sexually assaulted body was found in the lot one week later; she had been strangled to death. Those responsible for Lilia's death have not been arrested.[1]

The story of Lilia Alejandra is all too familiar in Juárez, Mexico's fourth-largest city, sprawled across the border from El Paso, Texas. Since 1993, more than six hundred young girls and women have been murdered in or near the city.[2] Some suspects have been arrested, including Abdel Latif Sharif Sharif ("The Egyptian"), members of Los Rebeldes gang, Édgar Álvarez Cruz, and a few bus drivers, but the bodies continue to appear in vacant lots throughout the city and on the town's outskirts, scattered like plastic bags blown by the desert wind. Juárez has become the city of femicide.

Diana Washington Valdez and other journalists have identified a number of likely suspects, but, she maintains, "not one of the true murderers [involved in] this long decade of serial sex crimes has been jailed."[3] As the murders continue unabated, not only have they generated a demand that the state act to end the killings,[4] but they have also triggered a dynamic cultural response. Videographers and filmmakers, novelists, poets, photojournalists, songwriters, and rock bands are but a few of the artists who have addressed the crisis facing Juárez's women.

The broadening significance of this cultural response is evident in two Hollywood films on the subject, *Bordertown* (2006, directed by Gregory Nava with Jennifer López as a journalist investigating the murders), and *The Virgin of Juárez* (2006, featuring Minnie Driver). Indeed, it is precisely because the state has failed so abjectly in stopping these murders that "fictional" narratives have become both the site where victims are mourned and the means by which justice can be restored. Cultural producers have filled the vacuum left by state officials who continue either to shun their responsibilities or to conceal the guilty.

This is not a novelty in historical terms. Unsolved murders, particularly on a large scale and targeting women, generate considerable social anxiety, which artists address—and sometimes exploit.[5] At the same time, these are works of the imagination, and even those authors most steeped in the forensic literature of the murders "solve" their cases only by leveraging what is known to arrive at well-informed speculations.[6] Significantly, we argue, what they disclose is often the very hypostasis of their social anxiety, and what is revealed is who, or what, at the most essential level, is responsible for a situation in which women continue to be killed with impunity.

Culture, Stuart Hall reminds us, is "concerned with the production and the exchange of meanings,"[7] and the meanings being produced about the murders are often about Juárez itself and thus fundamentally rooted in its location as both "border" and "borderland," as the frontier which unites and separates two nation-states, and as a contested zone in which identities, in this case, gender identities, are rearticulated. To read about the Juárez femicides therefore requires that we unpack the explicit geography of this particular "transitional" setting,[8] and that we specify the anxieties that women's location in that geography have created for the artists whose work we will examine here.

Our chapter examines three responses to Juárez and the murders—the photojournalism of Julián Cardona, a novel by Carlos Fuentes, and a song by Los Tigres del Norte—and concludes that even as these artists express a profound sympathy for the victims' plight, their representations, which are based on patriarchal binaries of male dominance and female submissiveness, often act to revictimize the women. We will suggest that, as many cultural producers locate women's active incorporation into the wage labor force as the engine which generated Juárez's "disorder," then "order" can be restored only when female passivity is reasserted. We also explore how the work of feminist critics, specifically Alicia Gaspar de Alba, challenges this approach by highlighting female/subaltern resistance and addressing the victims' basic rights while raising vital questions about gender identity on a highly militarized border.

## Borders, Borderlands, Juárez

Gloria Anzaldúa's foundational discussions introduced the border/borderlands as a doubled space, a physical zone where "two or more cultures edge each other," as well as a form of consciousness (*mestiza*) that promoted intimacy between cultures as it challenged the binary thinking central to western, masculinist thought.[9] Anzaldúa posits the border as a metaphorical construct of great potential, yet she never forgets that the "U.S.-Mexican border *es una herida abierta* where the Third World grates against the first and bleeds."[10]

While Anzaldúa had a profound impact on how later writers theorized the borderlands space,[11] many scholars have begun to deemphasize the physical reality of the border space, deterritorializing the border in favor of a reading which highlights its metaphorical possibilities as a nonspecific site of ethnic, racial, and gendered interactions.[12] Performance artist Guillermo Gómez-Peña, for example, maintains that geopolitical borders have "faded away," that Manhattan as well as Mexico City "look like downtown Tijuana on a Saturday night."[13]

We resist that perspective. If border theory has presumed to "erode the hegemony of the privileged center by denationalizing and deterritorializing the nation/state,"[14] the concrete reality of the U.S.-Mexico border reminds us of this move's limitations by providing a strikingly dramatic display of state power that reinforces territorial integrity and promotes nationalism. The U.S.-Mexico border is today one of the more militarized zones on earth, populated, on the U.S. side, by eleven thousand Border Patrol agents, on top of thousands of officials from Immigration and Customs Enforcement (ICE), the Drug Enforcement Agency (DEA), the Federal Bureau of Investigation (FBI), the U.S. military, state troopers, and local police, not to mention a growing population of civilian vigilantes (the "Minutemen" and others). On the Mexican side, the border teems with their counterparts, from federal soldiers and state judicial police (*judiciales*), all the way down to a virtual army of private security guards at local assembly plants.[15] The massive military presence on the border reflects a U.S. concern with immigration and drugs, but it is also directly linked to the integration of the U.S. and Mexican economies, particularly after the implementation of the North

American Free Trade Agreement (NAFTA) in 1994. This connection goes back even further in the case of Ciudad Juárez, which has operated as the primary center of export-based assembly plants (*maquiladoras* or *maquilas*) since 1965. It is this combination of state and private force alongside the machinery of late-capitalist, globalized production which suggests that the border on which the femicides are occurring exists both as a space where a new consciousness has generated challenges to traditional identities and a very real territory of power and violence.

In their insightful study, Debra Castillo and María Socorro Tabuenca Córdoba argue that the extent to which borderlands theorists emphasize the physicality of the border/borderlands space often tracks with the writers' own location. U.S. (Chicana/o) perspectives, they observe, often privilege the notion of the border as metaphor, thereby "eras[ing] geographical boundaries" between the United States and Mexico. Centrist Mexican perspectives, in contrast, will more often ignore theoretical issues (as well as women's literary production) while insisting on the importance of the geopolitical divide between the two countries. If these views circulate with greater (U.S. Chicana/o) or lesser (centrist Mexico) success, the authors continue, the views and voices of border writers themselves are rarely heard. Rosario Sanmiguel, Norma Cantú, Sheila Ortiz Taylor, and Rosinda Conde are little known by readers who may be quite conversant with the work of Carlos Monsiváis, Carlos Fuentes, Laura Esquivel, or Guillermo Gómez-Peña.[16] For Juárez/El Paso writer Rosario Sanmiguel, for example, personal and political borders shape her life and inflect her writing. The border "strikes at you from every angle," she observes. "The fact is that the United States is right next to us and the Migra is constantly watching. . . . The border is the way in which we dwell and walk through all its spaces."[17]

Our analysis takes from this perspective, insisting on both the physical and the theoretical aspects of the border/borderlands. To begin, we locate Ciudad Juárez, the scene of the murders, as a site-specific locale with an explicit history, political economy, and geography. At the same time, because our three primary examples of cultural responses to the femicides situate Juárez as a complex zone where gender roles and gender consciousness are formed and challenged, we also interrogate the city as a metaphorical space of identity transformation inherent in Anzaldúa's doubled notion of the borderlands. In this sense, as Alejandro Lugo has suggested, we cannot "separate 'border zones' as 'sites of creative cultural production' from 'border zones' as 'sites of lucrative manufacturing production' in the globalization of capital."[18]

To explore cultural responses to the Juárez crisis, we have chosen works that originate in each of Castillo and Tabuenca Córdoba's three sites of border literature. Los Tigres del Norte is a Chicano band from California; Carlos Fuentes, a novelist from central Mexico; and Julián Cardona, a photojournalist from the border town Ciudad Juárez. Of our examples, however, the work of the (centrist) Mexican writer, Fuentes, circulates immeasurably more widely than that of Los Tigres, which is, nevertheless, a highly popular band. Cardona's photographic work, characteristic of border producers, is the least well known of the three, mostly appearing in Juárez publications, although his photographs lately have gained visibility in wider artistic and political circuits. While the three cases have different access to public opinion, they do share important analytic roots, all developing their arguments about the Juárez murders from within the parameters of patriarchal discourse. Thus they are led to similar conclusions as to why the murders are happening and what needs to be done to restore "order" in the region.

Indeed, "order" and "disorder" occupy a critical terrain at the heart of the works of Los Tigres, Fuentes, and Cardona when they invoke the Juárez murders. Most bourgeois notions of order from Durkheim on have been constructed around a fear of "social disintegration" and "mob" rule. As Jane Flax has argued, "Western philosophers created an illusory appearance of unity and stability by reducing the flux and heterogeneity of the human and physical worlds into binary and supposedly natural oppositions. Order is imposed and maintained by displacing chaos into the lesser of each binary pair."[19] Explicitly or implicitly, these artists locate the root cause of Juárez's disorder (femicide) in a political economy that upended traditional order by placing women in men's roles as it generated the city's "subordinated modernity."[20] Even as they express a profound sympathy for the victims' plight, these cultural producers, to differing degrees, narratively revictimize Juárez's women by representing them within a framework of male dominance and female submissiveness, ultimately suggesting that it was women's substantial integration into the wage economy (and the changes this brought to the local sexual economy) that challenged Juárez's order and placed them in harm's way. If, for these cultural producers, female praxis generated disorder, then order will only be restored when female passivity is reasserted.

At the same time, not all the cultural responses to Juárez's femicides are organized within patriarchal binaries. A number of feminist writers, filmmakers, singers, and other artists have addressed the murders in important creative endeavors. The work of Lourdes Portillo, one of the earliest and most keenly sensitive feminist critics to interrogate the femicides, in her documentary, *Señorita Extraviada* (2001), has been widely reviewed.[21]

Here, as a counterpoise to the three primary examples, we discuss Alicia Gaspar de Alba's *Desert Blood* (2005), one example of an emerging literature which not only deplores the murders but highlights female/subaltern resistance, addresses the victims' basic rights, and raises vital questions about the responsibility of the state itself.

### Locating Juárez: Gender and Labor on the Global Assembly Line

Ciudad Juárez sits uncomfortably at the fractured intersection of late capitalism's globalized political economy and a sexual economy which remains stubbornly patriarchal. While historically the northern border was not of economic interest to the Mexican state, by the late 1950s, politicians in Mexico City were seeking to incorporate it more fully into the national economy through the Programa Nacional Fronterizo (PRONAF, National Border Program) and the Programa de Industrialización Fronteriza, or the Border Industrialization Program (BIP).[22] PRONAF (founded in 1961) was the state's response to stigmatized images of Mexican border towns as dens of vice servicing males from across the border,[23] but in 1965 it was overshadowed by the more explicitly development centered Border Industrialization Program, which ushered in the rapid growth of the *maquiladora* industry throughout the border region.[24] Implemented the year after the termination of the Bracero Program, the BIP was designed to resolve the problem of unemployment along the border as the United States tightened its immigration regulations. The problem was particularly acute in Juárez, where Mayor Félix Alfonso Lugo worried that the unemployed migrants who remained had "become a social and economic burden."[25]

Since 1965, when the first maquiladoras opened in Juárez, the quiet border town has seen its population explode as migrants from central and southern Mexico have flooded north in search of employment, pushing the city far out into the harsh Chihuahuan Desert. For the Mexican government, the *maquilas'* arrival was anticipated as the harbinger of a development plan that would spread capitalist modernization not just to the border, but to all of Mexico.[26] Value added by maquiladoras increased from one million pesos in 1974 to thirty-eight billion pesos in 2004. But instead of development, the maquiladoras generated what Luis H. Méndez terms "subordinated modernity" by vaulting over the historical project of industrialization in favor of late capitalism's model of globalized production.[27]

*Maquila* employment in Juárez rose from 3,135 in 1970 to 249,509 by 2000, but the population of the city itself increased nearly threefold, to

1.2 million.[28] Thus, while demand for wage labor grew dramatically, the BIP never significantly lowered Juárez's unemployment rates. Further, and contrary to assumed beliefs that returning migrant men would find work on the newly industrialized *frontera*, *maquiladora* managers turned to young Mexican women as their primary labor force. Indeed, *maquila*-based growth was predicated on a highly gendered economic formula that cast women both as producers charged with bringing modernity to Mexico through their labor on the global assembly line and as consumers in the modern markets that would (inevitably) accompany development. But the replacement of male with female workers challenged existing patriarchal structures and generated a deep well of male resentment and female vulnerability. In fact, *maquiladora* industrialization ultimately created a gendered and racialized political economy and shaped the city's geography in ways that facilitated, absorbed, and, perhaps, promoted femicide.

For employers, the ideal *maquila* worker was "docile, undemanding, nimble-fingered, nonunion and unmilitant."[29] These traits were seen as critical to maintaining a low-wage regime, the essential ingredient of the assembly plants' competitiveness in world markets, and they were read as "female" characteristics. Still, while women accounted for nearly 80 percent of Juárez's *maquiladora* workers through the early 1980s, by 2004 they were just over one-half of the workforce.[30] Scholars have suggested a number of reasons for this change, including industry restructuring and the fact that women in many plants began organizing to improve their working conditions and pay.[31] Tamar Diana Wilson argues that economic stringencies forced men to become the "docile, nimble-fingered" (i.e., "women") workers coveted by employers, and thus regendered, men began to be hired into jobs previously filled only by women.[32]

Wilson's argument is cogent, but it downplays the fact that women's labor and women's bodies are observed, managed, and threatened in ways that men's are not. Key here, of course, are issues of reproduction, manipulation of the sexualized body, and susceptibility to sexual attack. *Maquiladoras* are inordinately intrusive work sites for women, monitoring as they do female reproductive power from the moment of hiring (pregnant women are denied jobs) throughout their employment. In most plants, women must show supervisors their bloody tampons monthly to remain employed.[33]

At the same time that the plants continually monitor women's fertility, their sexualized bodies are literally paraded around in a steady cycle of employer-sponsored "beauty pageants."[34] Not surprisingly, male supervisors frequently demand sexual favors from female workers in return for (promises of) advancement, demands to which some women accede. As María Patricia Fernández-Kelly puts it, "women often find themselves in situations where they have to resort to their sexuality to gain a sense of precarious power in the labor market."[35] In the end, while the ratio of female to male *maquila* workers has tended toward parity, it is women who remain exceptionally vulnerable inside and outside the plants.

## The Geography of Danger

If Juárez's political and sexual economies meet within the *maquiladoras*, to what extent are the murders about the border assembly plants? Julia Monárrez-Fragoso of the Colegio de la Frontera in Tijuana, estimated that between 1993 and 2001 only 20 percent of the murdered women worked in the *maquilas*. In that sense, the exploitation of gendered bodies cannot adequately explain the murder of gendered bodies.[36] Nevertheless, the murders cannot be understood without recognizing the specific ways that *maquila* development has shaped both the political and the sexual economy of the border.[37] Gaspar de Alba makes the point exquisitely in "Kyrie Eleison for La Llorona," particularly in the startling enjambment between the third and fourth lines:

> You've gone the way of the alligators
> in San Jacinto Plaza.
>
> You've traded your midnight cry for the graveyard
> shift and a paycheck at the maquila.
>
> That mushroom cloud hovering
> over mount Cristo Rey
>
> is your shadow.[38]

The nature of *maquiladora* development increased the danger for *all* Juarense women whose subaltern status could not remove them from harm's way. This is evident in a number of examples. In the first place, high levels of female employment, by challenging pervasive notions of the male as primary wage earner, added to a reservoir of male resentment against all women. If, for women, entrance into the paid labor force often meant acquisition of greater independence, increased status within the family, and freedom to socialize outside the home,[39] it also underscored a process that required local and complex negotiations regarding how these changes would be understood and implemented. An early promotional tract boosting *maquiladora* industrialization spotlights the ways in which patriarchy would see the challenge of a female workforce: "Now, it is often the daughter, working in an industrial plant, who becomes the main source of family income. . . . When the father does work, it happens not infrequently that the daughter earns more. Certainly male egos, of fathers and would-be boyfriends, must suffer some deflation from this dramatic change in the economic influence of these young women."[40]

Hints of later tropes that would locate Juárez's social "problem" in its female workforce appeared as early as the 1970s, when *maquilas* were still expanding vigorously. Writing in the *New York Times* (February 22, 1979), John Crewdson detected a "dimming" of the *maquiladoras'* promise because "the plants employ few men . . . [F]or almost every woman who is lucky enough to find such jobs, there is a husband or a brother or a son who is likely to remain out of work." With women making up 80 percent of total assembly-line employment in 1982, Juárez, according to the president of the Asociación de Maquiladoras de Ciudad Juárez (Maquiladora Association), "had become a matriarchy,"[41] a characterization which stretches reality beyond recognition but offers a central image informing masculinist cultural production surrounding the Juárez murders. Thus, Juárez's mayor pointed to the "social disequilibrium" plaguing the city and embodied in men "who found themselves with nothing to do while their wives went to work." To the extent, then, that the failure of *maquiladora* development began to be written in terms of men's absence from the *maquilas,* women workers were cast as a problem rather than another exploited group within Mexico's struggling development plans, and all women became a target for male resentment.

Second, the rapid and speculative nature of *maquila* expansion created an urban geography which produced a form of marginality that ultimately affects all women who have no choice but to negotiate specific neighborhoods, a situation particularly acute for female *maquila* workers.[42] While Juárez's two main industrial parks are located south and east of the historical city center, most *maquila* workers live in *colonias,* poorly served shantytowns that sprang up in the desert and hills southwest of Juárez.[43] Many women begin or end their long commutes to the plants in darkness, walking through the poorly lit sprawl of the *colonias,* rendering them highly vulnerable to attack, then boarding a *maquila*-supplied or city bus, some of whose drivers have been implicated in sexual assaults.[44] At the same time, *maquila*-led development has generated a downtown geography which is dangerous to all women who cannot afford to cross it in a private vehicle.[45] The face of urban Juárez is pockmarked by empty lots (*lotes baldíos*) generated by the feverish land speculation that accompanied the first plants. Large parcels of urban space that never reached development stage were simply left vacant. In their movement through the city, poor women on foot traverse these *lotes baldíos*, spaces in which the bodies of murdered women are frequently found. As one journalist observed, "To walk through downtown Juárez is to know and deeply regret that you are a young woman."[46]

Third, *maquiladoras* are highly dependent on continual flows of migrant women from the center and south of Mexico. Migration north in search of (often illusive) assembly work severs the women's traditional communal ties and social networks; indeed, many of the murder victims are *anónimas*, recent arrivals who have no kin in the city. Esther Chávez Cano, director of Casa Amiga, the only women's shelter in Juárez, notes that women "have been taught to work. But they haven't been taught to live in a violent city with problems like this one. They come here very trusting, because in rural areas customs are much different."[47] Not only are women prey to the systematic misogyny of Juárez's patriarchal society, including the state, but their lack of kinship ties on the border means that their killers have little to fear from family retribution.

Finally, as a significant group of wage earners, women have become important consumers of urban entertainment (bars, discotheques, dance halls, restaurants, beer halls) and are no longer present solely as workers (prostitutes, waitresses) in that industry.[48]

The nightlife in the city's old downtown has reoriented from male-centered forms of entertainment to cabarets catering specifically to Juárez's new wage earners—young women with cash incomes. On weekends, women workers out for an evening of relaxation pack Juárez's clubs. Wondering how anyone who had spent a grueling forty-eight-hour week on a factory floor could look forward to a night of dancing, Fernández-Kelly was told by a *maquila* worker: "If you don't go out and have fun, you will come to the end of your days having done nothing but sleep, eat, and work."[49] And yet, as Kathleen Staudt has found, as women workers began to socialize outside the home and spend their own wages, they were quickly depicted by patriarchal society as "*maqui-locas*," sexually provocative and promiscuous women.[50]

While a number of ethnographers have pointed to the highly "precarious" path that women must walk when using sexuality as a means of advancement in the plants,[51] what is striking about the *maqui-loca* image is how *maquila* labor and sexuality are so often fused, ultimately making their way into explanations of the Juárez murders. When Debbie Nathan writes of "maquila sexuality [which] spills out of the plants during time off,"[52] and Charles Bowden connects the exploitable aspects of the female body by arguing that "the only cheap thing in Mexico is flesh, human bodies you can fornicate with or work to death,"[53] they come unwittingly close to reproducing the logic of Mexican officials who attempt to explain the disappearances of young women in Juárez. City officials have often asserted that the disappeared led *una doble vida,* a double life: "Many of the murdered women worked in factories during the week and as prostitutes during the weekend in order to make more money."[54] Portraying the victims as women who deceived their families by becoming prostitutes, Mexican authorities have both dismissed their deaths and made them responsible for their own murders.[55] In 1999, the Chihuahuan state attorney general darkly implied that "it is impossible not to get wet when you go outside in the rain; it is also impossible for a woman not to get killed when she goes out alone at night."[56]

If these factors alone were not enough to place Juárez's poor and working-class women in danger, the shift of *maquila* manufacturing to other low-wage producers, particularly China, has intensified the city's chaos. Between 2001 and 2004, prior to the economic crisis of 2008, over fifty thousand *maquila* workers lost their jobs in Juárez,[57] throwing the city's economy into a tailspin. Economically depressed and downwardly mobile cities are dangerous places for everyone, but in Juárez the generalized economic downturn has particularly increased women's vulnerability. To the extent that patriarchal society blamed women for occupying "male" positions in the wage economy, it also (ironically) looked to them as a fundamental part of Juárez's dream of modernization. When that project began to collapse in the face of Chinese competition, women became the scapegoats for its failure.

The Juárez femicides, then, represent a very specific disorder within a city already marked by a series of other convulsions. What is at stake when writers, photographers, singers, and other cultural producers take these murders on board, ultimately, is not just how they address the specifics of a gruesome history that stretches back more than a decade, but how (or if) they locate the murders within the broader set of circumstances that produced them. Their consideration of the Juárez murders reveals a diagnosis of the proper framework of order itself. In considering the work of Julián Cardona, Carlos Fuentes, and Los Tigres del Norte, we argue that, while decrying and lamenting the deaths, they fix the cultural territory of the murders within a familiar set of masculinist binaries. While the deployment of these binaries produces different results for each—orienting the photographic work of Cardona, dominating the novelistic work of Fuentes, and producing the female noncitizen in the musical work of Los Tigres—it indicates that, for an important set of cultural producers whose work circulates widely, order will return to Juárez only when the "proper" (i.e., patriarchal) relations between men and women are reestablished.

## Photographing the *Maquiladoras:* Julián Cardona's "Dying Slowly"

Julián Cardona, a writer and photographer based in Ciudad Juárez, is one of the city's keenest observers. His photography, which appears frequently in Juárez, has also been featured in influential articles about the femicides reaching audiences beyond the borderlands.[58] In his masterly photo essay "Morir despacio: Una mirada dentro de las plantas maquiladoras en la frontera Estados Unidos/México" (Dying slowly: A look inside the *maquiladoras* on the U.S.-Mexico Border),[59] Cardona pointedly juxtaposes scenes of well-ordered assembly plants with a text that foregrounds the structural violence of the *maquiladoras.* His images and text pose the argument that *maquila* women are "dying slowly" but just as steadily as the murder victims whose bodies appear in the desert. "On the assembly lines in Ciudad Juárez," Cardona writes, "one sees the faces of . . . 13- , 14-year-old girls who for five dollars a day give their lives to produce *world class product.*" Cardona not only satirically links assembly work and drug trafficking—the italicized words appear in English in the original—but he also discloses the allusive link between *maquilas* and murder: factory workers "give their lives" in the plant itself.

Cardona's photographs document the ways in which *maquila* industrialization shapes the lives of those on the assembly lines. His visual language is strongly informed by classical tropes that circulate widely in Hispanic Catholic society. The essay's opening image, "A Young Girl at Work," reveals a child-woman at her machine, her face and eyes lifted upward (see Fig. 4.1). Behind her, two male supervisors confer. If the viewer first reacts to her youth, it is the Christian imagery informing the photograph that will be most striking to a borderlands audience. Indeed, the young girl is a remarkable contemporary take on a compositional theme whose subject, the "Education of the Virgin," was popular among seventeenth-century Spanish painters. "Education," in this sense, implies upbringing, not formal instruction, and in Cardona's image, the two supervisors have taken over the young woman's tutelage from her mother. Significantly, images like this provide a central representation of Christian womanhood as one of chastity, submissiveness, and acquiescence to divine commandment.

Cardona returns to this theme at the series' close. In "A Young Girl and

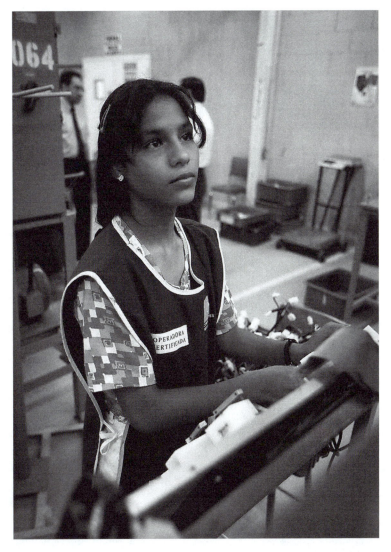

**Fig. 4.1.** Julián Cardona © 2000, "A Young Girl at Work, 1998." Reprinted by permission of Julián Cardona.

Her Future," we see an even younger girl in the *maquiladora* (see Fig. 4.2). The pigtailed *niña*, hands clasped tentatively behind her back, contemplates a satellite dish, likely assembled in the plant. An empty chair dominates the central space of the photograph. Cardona's intricate photograph captures both *the* future (instantaneous mass communications) and *her* future, perched on the no-longer-empty chair, tirelessly assembling products she

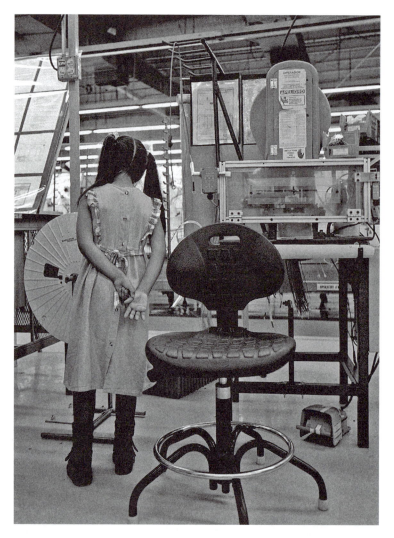

**Fig. 4.2.** Julián Cardona © 2000, "A Young Girl and Her Future, 1998." Reprinted by permission of Julián Cardona.

will never own. Unlike the first image in the series, in which the subject's personality is so richly displayed, the final image stuns us by its evacuation of the girl's identity; it is the only photograph in the series in which all we see of a worker is her back. Cardona's message is of an assembly process that drains the very life from its workers, again linking real deaths in the desert to the "slow deaths" of *maquila* workers.

Between the opening and closing photographs, of present and future workers, both suffused with visual markers of purity and innocence, Cardona elaborates *maquila* culture with a series of photographs featuring women and men at work as well as images suggesting the ways in which supervisors use the plants to showcase their female workers' sexuality. In one photograph, two women workers walk down a corridor lined with photographs of beauty pageant winners. They are followed and, by all appearances, watched by two managers. A second photograph is labeled in Spanish: "Trabajadoras se visten y maquillan para participar en el concurso de belleza Señorita RCA." The English translation, which is provided (Maquila Workers Getting Ready for Miss RCA Beauty Contest) misses one of Cardona's central ironies. In Spanish, "*maquillar*" is to put on makeup. Yet, to the extent that Cardona's essay is about the "*maquilas,*" it is hard to avoid his subtle argument that, while female workers are assembling "world class product," they are themselves being made up, reassembled (see Fig. 4.3).

Plant managers regularly hold beauty contests to reaffirm "traditional standards of feminine beauty and behavior" and to impress on women workers that the plants care about their "physical and emotional well-being."[60] Cardona's photograph displays a number of women preparing for the pageant. Most are dressed in formal gowns, while the worker in the foreground, who is being "assembled" (made up) by another worker, wears a traditional

**Fig. 4.3.** Julián Cardona © 2000, "Maquila Workers Getting Ready for Their Plant's Annual Miss RCA Contest, 1999." Reprinted by permission of Julián Cardona.

Mexican costume. Iglesias Prieto argues that the *maquilas'* promotion of beauty pageants is intended to "reaffirm women's subordination by promoting mildness, submission, and passivity."[61] But, as the dress indicates, they also work to instill a sense of tradition (nationalism) and unity, a sense that "we are all one big family," as a poster in one plant reminds its workers.[62]

How are we to read Cardona's essay? "Dying Slowly" begins and ends with images of virginal immaculacy, of innocent girls whose lives are draining away on the assembly line. The photographs in his essay remind us that sexuality is also assembled and displayed on the line. The iconography of sexuality in Latin America has long been dominated by a framework that centers on the binary of purity and carnality, the so-called virgin-whore continuum.[63] While the text of "Maquila Workers Getting Ready" suggests the ways in which *maquiladoras* continuously manage their female workers' bodies, it also reiterates this traditional cultural framework for representing women and sexuality. Cardona's essay avoids the innuendo generated by authorities who link female sexuality to rape and murder. But in his mapping of the ontogeny of the female *maquila* worker, Cardona portrays purity in binary opposition to sexuality. He handles his subjects with dignity—indeed, he elevates one to the level of the mother of God—but his photographs are grounded in the iconography of female passivity that, ironically, recapitulates the female "docility" which was at the heart of the *maquiladora* project.

In this way, Cardona's photographs, which provide a valuable look behind the closed doors of *maquiladoras,* continue to work not just within the Christian imaginary, but within a specific Mexican-Catholic binary elaborated by Octavio Paz and others. By dividing Mexican womanhood between the Virgen de Guadalupe and La Chingada (the "violated mother" or the "fucked one"), Paz not only plotted the virgin-whore binary, but also marked *both* sides by their submissiveness. "Guadalupe is pure receptivity," Paz writes, "the *Chingada* is even more passive."[64] Paz's approach informs Cardona's work, which, in its portrayal of Juarez's crisis, trades on the patriarchal binary. But it is Carlos Fuentes who drives this reading toward its ultimate conclusions.

### The Center Reassembles the Border:
### Carlos Fuentes's *The Crystal Frontier*

If Cardona's representation of Juárez speaks to the persistence of masculinist binaries among cultural producers closest to it (and most sympathetic to the plight of the city's women), these traditional binaries can even more stridently define the work of writers who do not know the city as well, who have never (unlike Cardona) walked on a *rastreo* (the search for bodies which private organizations conduct in the city's surrounding lands). When Carlos Fuentes addresses the border, not only does he deploy Paz's traditional binaries, but his distance from the subject and Paz's more resolutely patriarchal stance help shape a work that ultimately locates the roots of the femicides in an economic project which replaced men with women, and locals with southern migrants.

Fuentes's work circulates considerably more widely than Cardona's; indeed, Fuentes is typically seen as Mexico's preeminent writer, a status even more exaggerated outside Mexico, where he serves as "translator" of (central) Mexico's culture and history to English-speaking, U.S. audiences. And it is the difficult relationship between Mexico and the United States which is on display in *The Crystal Frontier: A Novel in Nine Stories* (1995), particularly as it highlights the reflective, distortive border that joins and separates the two countries.

Leonardo Barroso, the wealthy, business-savvy Mexican protagonist of the novel, much like Artemio Cruz before him, personifies the vast corruptions of contemporary capitalism in Mexico as generated by a mix of U.S. imperialism and homegrown greed. A *maquila* owner himself, Barroso cynically describes *maquilas* as the solution to Mexico's quest for modernity: "The progress of the nation can be measured by the progress of the maquiladoras," Barroso proclaims grandly to his U.S. backers.[65] Through Barroso, Fuentes showcases *maquiladoras* as symbolic of the ills of Mexican society, a theme that he explores in "Malintzin of the Maquilas," one of the nine stories, which narrates the lives of women *maquiladora* workers in Juárez. These women's histories are familiar. They have migrated from central and southern Mexico to Juárez to take up tedious assembly jobs, thereby becoming their families' primary breadwinners. They suffer the sexual harassment of male supervisors, who continually observe them from panoptic vantage points. And they are sustained by female camaraderie, which sweeps them outside the shop floor and into Juárez's vibrant cabarets and bars.

While Barroso is much more interested in accumulating wealth than in Mexico's overall economic development, he is quite happy to advertise the *maquiladoras* not just as way stations on the economic road forward, but as dedicated highways of progress for Mexican women. The *maquiladoras* "liberated women from farming, prostitution, even from machismo itself . . . because working women soon became the breadwinners of the family, and the female head of the family gained a dignity and a strength that set her free, made her independent, made her a modern woman. And that, too, was democracy—didn't his partners from Texas agree?"[66]

Barroso's argument foregrounds a metonymy which has been a familiar trope of *maquila* boosters and which is as old as the Mills' (father and son) work on India: "civilization" ultimately rests on the liberation of women from the oppression of "traditional" society. Even as Mexican capitalists and U.S. managers understand the quotidian reality of Juárez's female workers—the U.S. partner at one point skeptically wonders "how many times [Barroso has] staged" his "little act"[67]—they seek refuge in a narrative in which *maquila* industrialization stands as a signifier of progress for women and democracy for the nation.

Fuentes has been a vocal critic of NAFTA and Mexico's historical acquiescence to the interests of U.S. capital. Even the one-dimensional Barroso accepts that Mexico has been pulverized by globalization: "we dreamed we were in the first world and woke to find ourselves back in the third."[68]

Yet despite Fuentes's critical reading of globalization's impact on Mexico, his presentation of its repercussions on the female work force is freighted with traditional conceptions of a "proper" gendered order. The elemental social politics at play in "Malintzin of the Maquilas" is revealed one night when four *maquila* women head to the Malibú, their habitual rendezvous. The club is packed with working women absorbing the rock-and-roll dancing, ceremonies in which naked, dark-skinned Mexican women are "married" to gringos and Chippendale men in bow ties, boots, and jock straps. As Fuentes enters the Malibú, he engages the imagery of the *maqui-loca*, the "hypersexual" *maquila* worker targeted by authorities as the "real" cause of Juárez's problems. On this night, as one hunk dances toward the group of *maquila* friends, "the girls elbow one another. In my bed, just imagine. In yours. If only he'd take me, I'm ready. If he'd only kidnap me, I'm kidnappable."[69]

Perhaps one can overlook Fuentes's transposition of kidnapping fantasies from male murderers to female clubbers, for his novel was published just as the Juárez femicides emerged. But the tragedy he fashions in his story suggests that death is the legitimate price paid by women who threaten patriarchal society. While the *maquila* friends are enjoying themselves, Dinorah, a single mother, receives word that her young son, whom she left tied to a table in her shack, has strangled himself on the cord. In the scene of grief that follows in the *colonia*, an older male neighbor wonders, his voice heavy with nostalgia, "if they were right in coming to work in Juárez, where a woman had to leave a child alone, tied like an animal to a table leg. The poor innocent kid, how could he not hurt himself? The old people pointed out that such a thing wouldn't happen in the country—families there always had someone to look after the kids, you didn't have to tie them up, ropes were for dogs and hogs."[70]

For Fuentes, while *maquilas* are the visible sign of Mexico's dual failure to confront U.S. corporate interests and design an economy capable of sustaining its population, the tragedy of the *maquiladora* project, symbolized here by the death of a male child, is rooted in women's economic and sexual displacement of men. Both the new political economy (where women have become heads of households) and the new sexual economy (where *they* now stuff money into the *men's* g-strings) remove women from the home and challenge nostalgic visions of the extended and imagined (Mexican) community. As Dinorah's friends wrestle with how to console her, a gray-bearded voice of tradition observes, "My father used to tell me . . . that we should stay peacefully in our homes, in one place. He would stand just the way I am now, half in and half out, and say, 'Outside this door, the world ends.'"[71] Fuentes fails to recognize that, with the man standing in the doorway, it is the woman who remains trapped inside, the woman for whom the world begins outside the door.

Fuentes's portrayal of the Malibú reproduces the club as a familiar exotic location quite common in colonializing discourses.[72] Even though he populates it with working Mexican women and barely dressed men, Fuentes only reverses, without unpacking, the traditional trope of the border as a magnet for U.S. men searching out scantily clad Mexican women. In the hands of writers more familiar with Juárez and less beholden to male fantasy, the club scene on the border is more fully realized. This is clear in both ethnographic and literary accounts.[73]

When Rosario Sanmiguel takes her male protagonist into the Mona Lisa in the title story of *Callejón Sucre y otros relatos,* we enter a location that reflects the long history of Juárez and allows for introspection, revelation, and reality, not just the parading of fantasized stereotypes.[74] Similarly, when Alicia Gaspar de Alba's protagonist, Ivon, enters the bars on La Mariscal or Calle Ugarte in *Desert Blood,* she desensationalizes them by locating them within their own specific histories (Mariscal's name arising not from that of a famous general, but from the smell of seafood [*mariscos*] which wafted out of the brothels), and establishing them as sites where women act as more than sexual commodities. Leaving the Red Canary, Ivon, searching for her kidnapped sister, slaps the American boy demanding the attention of the "*puta*" tending bar.[75]

Fuentes's deployment of *maqui-loca* imagery inside the Malibú ("hair flying, breasts bouncing, asses shaking freely"), particularly when coupled with the innocent's death which occurs while all this shaking is going on, reveals his narrative as occupying the traditional masculinist iconography of a Mexico populated by saints and sluts.[76] Fuentes discloses his organizing binary in the chapter's seemingly curious title, "Malintzin of the Maquilas."

Marina is one of the four women who go clubbing and work together assembling television sets. Her parents named her after "their desire to see the ocean [*mar*],"[77] yet Fuentes relocates her historically and ideologically. Marina was the Spanish Christian name Cortés bestowed on his indigenous translator-mistress. The Aztecs called her Malinche, but her original name was Malintzin.

Fuentes has covered this territory previously, most suggestively in *Todos los gatos son pardos* (1977), where multiple naming evokes fractured identities: "Three were your names, woman . . . Malintzin, your parents said: witch, goddess of bad luck and of the blood feud . . . Marina, your man said, remembering the ocean by which he came to these lands . . . Malinche, your people said: traitor, mouthpiece and guide for the white man."[78]

If Malinche in *Todos los gatos* is a clever strategist who turns against Moctezuma's tyranny only to discover that both he and Cortés were "simple trinkets of two empires,"[79] and Marina is located in the promise of movement which the sea provides, of all the nominative possibilities, Malintzin is the most troubling. A "Goddess [*Diosa*], Malintzin," yes, but a dark one.[80] Many of the witchlike characters who populate Fuentes's novels are often drawn from his interpretation of the Aztec goddess Coatlicue, who possesses both life-giving and life-taking characteristics,[81] as evidenced by Teódula Moctezuma in *Where the Air Is Clean*.[82] In *Todos los gatos*, however, Malintzin is one-dimensional, an offshoot of Paz's Chingada, whose "taint is [seen to be] constitutional and resides in her sex."[83]

Of course, the representation of Coatlicue is deeply contested and occupies a certain foundational space within both Chicana/o and borderland studies.[84] Coatlicue, "Serpent Skirt," was a creator goddess in pre-Columbian Mesoamerica. Anzaldúa and others have argued that, as male-dominated forces came to control Azteca-Mexica culture, they ruptured the dualistic Coatlicue.[85] One aspect of Coatlicue hived away was Tonantsi, who became the "good mother" and, after the conquest, was absorbed into the Guadalupe/Coatlapopeuh identity, where she was desexualized, ultimately giving rise to the virgin-whore dichotomy. For Anzaldúa, Coatlicue "represents duality in life, a synthesis of duality, and a third perspective," and her call for the creation of a new *mestiza* consciousness rests on "unlearning" the *puta/virgen* dichotomy.[86] Fuentes, of course, insists on this binary in "Malintzin of the Maquilas," narrating the provocative/destructive Dinorah against a naïve/trusting Marina.

It is certain, as Lanin Gyurko has pointed out, that Fuentes sees the Malinche figure as the consciousness of the Mexican nation, not as a traitor[87] (in contrast to Paz, who insists that "the Mexican people have not forgiven [her] for her betrayal").[88]

It is highly significant, then, that in *The Crystal Frontier*, Fuentes has chosen to title his tale of *maquila* women "Malintzin of the Maquilas," for Malintzin is the witch, bringer of bad luck, sower of chaos. For Fuentes, *maquila* women are not traitors (as Nathan has suggested),[89] for they are incapable of Malinche's dramatic action. They are "Malintzins," signifiers of disorder. The tragedies that they bear witness to are calamities that they have brought on themselves. Goddesses of the blood feud, they have trespassed the boundaries of tradition and therefore share responsibility for the disaster that has befallen them, Juárez, and Mexico.

## A View from the North: Los Tigres del Norte and "Las Mujeres de Juárez"

Murders and *maquilas* have been recurrent themes in *corridos* and *norteño* music since the late 1990s, as well as becoming a part of U.S. and Latino/a folk and Mexican *rockera* music.[90] The cultural valence of this message is important not just because the singers draw large audiences, but because these songs are composed by critics of the *maquiladoras'* globalization project and staunch defenders of the rights of women and workers. The work of the popular *conjunto* band Los Tigres del Norte is characteristic of this, as it narrates explicit themes of resistance and reordering in its response to the femicides.

Los Tigres del Norte formed in the late 1960s around Jorge Hernández, the accordionist and main singer; his brothers; and their cousin Óscar Lara. Originally from Sinaloa, Mexico, they crossed into California as undocumented workers in 1968 and settled in San Jose. Fama Records offered them their first contract in the early 1970s, and, having contemporized their sound by adding electric instrumentation, Los Tigres soon achieved crossover success. Their identification as a progressive border band was solidified with the release of "Contrabando y Traición" (Contraband and Betrayal) in the mid-1970s, a hugely popular song which created the subgenre of the *narco-corrido*. In 1987, Los Tigres won a GRAMMY for "Gracias, América Sin Fronteras."

The band has attained significant critical standing within Chicano/a culture. Anzaldúa begins her paradigm-setting work, *Borderlands/La Frontera*, with an epigraph drawn from Los Tigres; José David Saldívar defines them as "mass cultural intellectuals" whose work deserves serious theoretical evaluation.[91]

In 2004, when the images of Juárez that circulated most widely were of young women's brutalized bodies, Los Tigres del Norte released "Las Mujeres de Juárez" (The Women of Juárez) on their *Pacto de Sangre* album.[92] The song, written by Paulino Vargas, sparked controversy when it was banned from radio play in Juárez because, local officials argued, it damaged the city's reputation. Band member Luis Hernández maintains that Los Tigres "always wanted to sing about this problem. But we didn't want to get too political. We wanted to . . . tell the [Mexican] government to do something, that we want a solution."[93] Jorge Hernández sings "Las Mujeres de Juárez" in classic *conjunto* style, marked by a strong polka backbeat played on the accordion. But the driving, upbeat tempo takes nothing away from the gravity of the theme. "The subject is serious," Luis insists, "so we tried to make that point by the way [Jorge] sings the song."

The song opens by arguing that the state's inability to solve the murders of Juárez's women is both suspicious—the lyrics speak of the state's "untouchable impunity"—and humiliating. As with much other cultural work on Juárez, it links the murders to the city's *maquiladoras,* describing the victims as

> Mujeres trabajadoras basto de maquiladoras
> cumplidoras y eficientes, mano de obra sin igual
>
> Homespun women *maquila* workers
> reliable and efficient, hired hands without equal.

While satirizing the corporate voice, the verse carries a second meaning: the victims are humble working women, not *maqui-locas.* The song delivers its principal message in the third stanza by revealing the "shame" and "humiliation" which "we" have come to feel in Mexico: "Ya se nos quitó lo macho o nos falta dignidad" (Either we have already lost our manhood or we lack dignity). It is hard to read the imagined "we" and "our" as other than male referents, given the prominence of *lo macho* in the text, and this is critical to the band's interpretation. The murder of Juárez's women is to be read as a sign of Mexico's squandered masculinity.

The precise nature of this attack on *lo macho* is elaborated in subsequent verses, which, spoken rather than sung, are delivered with two different inflections. The first part of the verse, pronounced in a direct reportorial voice, stages the murder victims within the iconic space of motherhood:

> Woman is a blessing and a miracle of faith, the fountain of creation
> She gave birth to the czar and she gave birth to the king and even
> Jesus Christ Himself was born of a woman.

By this move, Los Tigres removes the women of Juárez from their critical position within the city's political economy and relocates them as reproducers, their sole import within a sexual economy. María Herrera-Sobek has characterized the *corrido* as a "male-dominated genre" featuring male authors, "masculine-oriented themes," and a "strongly patriarchal ideology."[94] And Ramón Saldívar argues that one of the reasons for the decline of the *corrido* "as a viable resistance form" in the 1930s was its inability to break from Mexican patriarchal discourse.[95]

In that sense, "Las Mujeres de Juárez" remains firmly within traditional patterns of *corrido* representation, where women most often (but not always) appear as archetypal mother figures. What is notable in this song, however, is that the representation of women as mothers stands in unresolved tension with the view of the victims as "homespun *maquila* workers." If Cardona and Fuentes work within the *puta/virgen* binary, Los Tigres offers a contrast between reproduction and production.

The speaker's tone becomes more urgent and challenging as the song continues, rallying his listeners to action. As the state itself is implicated in the murders,

> It is the moment, citizens, to live up to our responsibility
> If the law does not resolve this, we must
> Punishing the cowards who abuse women.

It is possible that by calling on the "citizens" to take the law into their own hands, Los Tigres are exhorting both men and women to act. Yet, in the light of the band's representation of women primarily as mothers and victims, it seems hard to avoid the conclusion that both "citizens" and "we" refer only to the men of Juárez.

Chandra Mohanty's question, raised in a different context, is equally valid here: "Who are the insiders and outsiders in this community? What notions of legitimacy and gendered and racialized citizenship are being actively constructed within this community?"[96]

As the *corrido* resumes its *conjunto*-polka rhythm, the responsibility of *lo macho* is juxtaposed to, indeed, generated by the

> tears, laments, and prayers . . .
> of the agonized mothers . . .
> [who] cry on heaven to have pity
> that the bodies be given to them so that they can be buried properly.

Many of the victims' bodies have never been found, and thus these women enter into the painful narratives of the disappeared. The psychological burdens of mourning for a disappeared loved one have been well documented in the literature of the "dirty wars" of South and Central America.[97] While the lack of bodies and formal accountability have presented women's organizations in Argentina and elsewhere with an excruciating set of choices regarding the demands they bring to the state,[98] Los Tigres have removed the women and their organizations from these decisions. Only the men ("citizens") make the demands, appealing to the state to heed the tears of grieving mothers by producing the victims' bodies. The victims and their mothers are conflated, equally incapable of action.

The approach of Los Tigres found an unusual echo in the *rockera* band El TRI, which recorded a song of the same title, "Las Mujeres de Juárez," in 2004. The rock band, one of Mexico's most popular, emphasizes not only female passivity, but a traditional call for justice to be meted out in the next world: "biblical justice," the song argues, will punish the killers even if the police will not.

By setting the responsible male in apposition to the sorrowful female, Los Tigres redress the crime of femicide with an appeal to traditional gender roles. The force of the *corrido* comes from its demand that men take matters into their own hands and "punish the cowards who abuse [our] women." As such, the band would resolve these crimes by reasserting female passivity (as victims, sufferers) and male vigilantism. After all, it is better to be *chingones* than *chingadas*.

## Unlearning Dichotomy, Foregrounding Resistance: Alicia Gaspar de Alba's *Desert Blood*

Representations which present Juárez as a "matriarchy," the femicides as punishment for challenging patriarchy, and the solution to the crisis as the reassertion of male vigilantism and female submissiveness have attracted sizable audiences, but they are not the only cultural responses to the murders. Among the many artists who have disputed masculinist readings of the Juárez femicides are novelists (Gaspar de Alba), documentary filmmakers (Portillo, Ursula Biemann, Alejandra Sánchez Orozco), songwriters and singers (Lila Downs, Tori Amos, Los Jaguares), visual artists (Tania Acosta Ayala, Claudia Bernal), and poets (Juan Ríos Cantú, Emma Rueda). While space does not allow for a full examination of these resistant and contestatory narratives, one example can provide a sense of their challenge to patriarchal readings of the crisis.

Alicia Gaspar de Alba, who grew up on the El Paso/Juárez border, is a professor of Chicana/o studies and English at UCLA, where, in 2003, she organized a major international conference on the Juárez femicides. Her work includes poetry, historical novels, art criticism, short stories, and essays. Her first work of detective fiction, *Desert Blood: The Juárez Murders* (2005), employs traditional (if noirish) strategies of the genre to address the murders.

Gaspar de Alba's semiautobiographical main character, Ivon Villa, adumbrates Anzaldúa's *mestiza* consciousness; she is a citizen of a borderlands nation. The progeny of strong, stubborn women, perhaps even the great-great-granddaughter of Pancho Villa (adding to the sense that a new imagined community is being narrated), Ivon—who changed her name from Yvonne after she came out—left her El Paso/Juárez home to pursue her studies. She ends up in Los Angeles, finishing her dissertation and teaching women's studies. Returning to El Paso in order to adopt a baby from Juárez, Ivon finds herself drawn personally into the city's maelstrom when the still-pregnant mother of her soon-to-be-adopted child is kidnapped and brutally murdered, an act quickly followed by the kidnapping of Ivon's sixteen-year-old sister.

*Desert Blood* follows the standard lines of contemporary noir detective fiction: the state apparatuses charged with solving crimes are themselves actively complicit in them. In the face of this, Ivon becomes the detective, and her (fictional) investigations reproduce elements of actual inquiries carried out by journalists and local organizations as she draws the readers' attention to narco-traffickers, the local power elite (the "Juniors"), snuff-movie producers, and *maquila* owners.

*Desert Blood* parts company with the other narratives we have examined in a number of ways, not the least of which is its authorship by a lesbian feminist. While consistent with the demands of detective fiction to produce a culprit—Ivon ultimately discloses a vast web of depraved private and state agents—the novel ultimately concludes: "What did it matter *who* killed them? This wasn't a case of 'whodunit,' but rather who was allowing these crimes to happen?"[99]

This question orients her approach as she probes the relationship between sex and profit. *Desert Blood* reminds us that "not all the girls who have died were maquiladora workers,"[100] yet the social and economic realities created by the assembly plants provide the underlying dialectic for the murders. As

Father Francis, a sympathetic Catholic priest who works on the border, observes, "The women are being sacrificed to redeem the men for their inability to provide for their families, their social emasculation, if you will, at the hands of the American corporations."[101] Ivon's judgment when she comes upon a mutilated body in the desert is even more bitter: "The irony of it: an assembly worker disassembled in the desert."[102]

Thus, Gaspar de Alba's critique of the Juárez murders is much more systemic than that of Patrick Bard, another novelist who has engaged the Juárez murders via detective fiction (*La frontera*, 2004). Bard's journalist-detective uncovers a vast conspiracy at work without elucidating the basic economic and social forces that provide the oxygen for this murderous conflagration. It is Gaspar de Alba's Ivon who becomes a detective in the original sense of the word, not only discovering what has been "artfully concealed," but exposing it to the light of day.

Perhaps the most important manner in which *Desert Blood* departs from other texts we have examined is that, in narrating a history of women who are victims, the author populates her novel with strong and resistant women. Juárez may be far from a matriarchy, but in *Desert Blood* Gaspar de Alba has created her own gynocentric community inhabited by borderlands women who have "unlearn[ed] the *puta/virgen* dichotomy."[103] As with many noir tropes, the novel's "heroes" (including Ivon and her sister) are capable of acts that are exasperating, foolish, and dangerous to themselves and others, but they call on their internal strength and intelligence to survive. Unlike in traditional detective fiction, however, Gaspar de Alba's characters survive only because they are supported by a (largely but not exclusively) female community built around extended family, friends, and lovers. Significantly, this community stretches beyond fictional characters to include a very real cultural and political community. Tori Amos's song "Black Dove" provides Irene, Ivon's kidnapped sister, with a bridge to sanity and strength during her ordeal.[104] Amos writes that the nightmarish images of the song arose from her own sexual abuse as a child,[105] and her own gloss on the murders appeared the following year in "Juárez,"[106] a song written in the voice of the desert itself, which is about survival and truth even though "no angel came" to save the murdered women.

## Conclusion: Citizens and Rights

At its most basic level, as Mohanty suggests, what is at stake in the Juárez femicides is nothing less than the gendered and racialized boundaries of citizenship.[107] The masculinist virgin/whore binary which underlies the photographic work of Cardona and dominates the novelistic work of Fuentes ultimately produces the female noncitizen in the musical work of Los Tigres del Norte. That Los Tigres argues forcefully for redressing the murders of *las mujeres de Juárez* does not change the fact that their protection is a beneficence, not a right, and therefore depends on the generosity of (male) citizens.

Gaspar de Alba, Portillo, and others whose cultural treatment of the Juárez femicides is grounded in feminism ultimately root their critiques of this approach not just in the metaphorical territory of identity, but in the modernist concept of rights—the rights of women, of the living and the dead; the right to live peacefully and to be treated with dignity in death. Toward the end of Ursula Biemann's video *Performing the Border,* journalist Isabel Velásquez poignantly remarks, "It's not very difficult if you're watching the evening news to see the corpse of a girl right there. Even if she's dead, she has rights. Her image is her right, even if she's not here." In the same way, Chicana singer Lila Downs's beautifully rendered "La Niña" (The Girl) compels the listener to pay attention to the forces which have shattered the rights of her *niña,* Rosa María, a sad-faced *maquila* worker whose job is "finishing her off" and whose patron saint "is on vacation every day."[108]

In the end, we understand, rights are only won and held by action; "to be silent is to acquiesce."[109] By rejecting the deployment of patriarchy as a solution to the Juárez femicides, these resistant works push their audiences to think more deeply about both metaphorical borders and the forces that have produced the very real border which has become a nightmare for poor and working-class women. By doing so, the ultimate effect of these counternarratives is to return dignity and agency to the women of Juárez, both living and dead.

## Notes

Authors' note: The authors gratefully acknowledge the help and advice of Anuradha Needham and Pablo Mitchell of Oberlin College and, in particular, the insightful critiques and suggestions of the three anonymous readers. The final product and its conclusions remain, of course, the sole responsibility of the authors.

1. Diana Washington Valdez, *Cosecha de mujeres: Safari en el desierto mexicano* (Mexico City: Océano, 2005), 200–204; Irene Kahn, "Muertes intolerables: Diez años de desapariciones y asesinatos de mujeres en Ciudad Juárez y Chihuahua," *Resumen y casos de llamamiento del informe de Amnistía Internacional* (August 11, 2003). Amnesty International Mexico, Mexico City, AMR 41/027/2003, http://www.amnesty.org/es/library/info/AMR41/026/2003.

2. Ascertaining the exact number of femicides in Juárez has proven to be so

difficult that, in mid-2009, a Chihuahua state legislator proposed a resolution to the state legislature requiring it. The Procuraduría General de Justicia del Estado (PGJE, Chihuahua state attorney general's office) contends that there were 447 women murdered between 1993 and the end of 2008, but the media regularly references more than 600 deaths. The PGJE claims that it has prosecuted more than 60 percent of the cases, although in a suit heard in April 2009 by the Inter-American Court of Human Rights in Santiago, Chile, mothers of three victims charged that the Mexican government has consistently thwarted any attempt to resolve the femicides. The state's main suspect, Edgar Álvarez Cruz, was convicted of a single murder and is serving a twenty-six-year sentence. His family strongly denies the charges, challenging the state's reliance on the testimony of the accuser. See, among others, Frontera NorteSur, "Historic Femicide Trial Gets Underway," *http://www.newspapertree.com/news/3766-historic-femicide-trial-gets-underway;* and Diana Washington Valdez, "Decapitated Body among 100 Girls, Women Killed in Juárez in '09," *Elpasotimes.com,* October 14, 2009, http://www.elpasotimes.com/ci_13555924?IADID=Search-www.elpasotimes.com.elpsaotimes.com.

    3. Washington Valdez, *Cosecha de mujeres,* 237.

    4. See Patricia Ravelo Blancas, "Entre las protestas callejeras y las acciones internacionales: Diez años de activismo por la justicia social en Ciudad Juárez," *El Cotidiano* 125 (May–June 2004): 21–32.

    5. See Jane Caputi, *The Age of Sex Crime* (Bowling Green, Ky.: Bowling Green State University Popular Press, 1987).

    6. See Alicia Gaspar de Alba, *Desert Blood: The Juárez Murders* (Houston: Arte Público Press, 2005); Patrick Bard, *La frontera: Una novela de denuncia sobre las muertas de Juárez* (Mexico City: Grijalbo Intriga, 2004); and Enrique Murillo, *Las muertas de Juárez* (Granada Hills, Calif.: Condor Pictures, 2002).

    7. Stuart Hall, *Representation: Cultural Representations and Signifying Practices* (Thousand Oaks, Calif.: Sage Publications, 1997), 2.

    8. Renato Rosaldo, *Culture and Truth: The Remaking of Social Analysis* (Boston: Beacon Press, 1993), 207–208.

    9. Gloria Anzaldúa, *Borderlands/La Frontera: The New Mestiza* (San Francisco: Spinsters/Aunt Lute, 1987), pref., n.p., 79–80.

    10. Ibid., 3.

    11. Gloria Anzaldúa, ed., *Making Face, Making Soul: Haciendo Caras: Creative and Critical Perspectives by Feminists of Color* (San Francisco: Aunt Lute Books, 1990); Héctor Calderón and José David Saldívar, eds., *Criticism in the Borderlands: Studies in Chicano Literature, Culture, and Ideology* (Durham, N.C.: Duke University Press, 1991); José David Saldívar, *Border Matters: Remapping American Cultural Studies* (Berkeley and Los Angeles: University of California Press, 1997); Claire F. Fox, *The Fence and the River: Culture and Politics at the U.S.-Mexico Border* (Minneapolis: University of Minnesota Press, 1999); Scott Michaelsen and David E. Johnson, eds., *Border Theory: The Limits of Cultural Politics* (Minneapolis: University of Minnesota Press, 1997); Walter D. Mignolo, *Local Histories/Global Designs: Coloniality, Subaltern Knowledges, and Border Thinking* (Princeton: Princeton University Press, 2000); Debra Castillo and Maria Socorro Tabuenca Córdoba, *Border Women: Writing from La Frontera* (Minneapolis: University of Minnesota Press, 2002).

    12. Emily D. Hicks, *Border Writing: The Multidimensional Text* (Minneapolis: University of Minnesota Press, 1991), xxiii–xxxi.

13. Guillermo Gómez-Peña, "The New World (B)order," *High Performance* 15.58–59 (Summer/-Fall 1992): 58–65, quotation on 60.

14. Alejandro Lugo, "Fragmented Lives, Assembled Goods: A Study in Maquilas, Culture and History at the Mexican Borderlands," PhD dissertation, Stanford University, 1995, 45.

15. Timothy Dunn, *The Militarization of the U.S.-Mexico Border, 1978–1992: Low-intensity Conflict Doctrine Comes Home* (Austin: University of Texas Press, 1996); Peter Andreas and Thomas J. Biersteker, eds., *The Rebordering of North America: Integration and Exclusion in a New Security Context* (New York: Routledge, 2003); Peter Andreas, *Border Games: Policing the U.S.-Mexico Divide* (Ithaca, N.Y.: Cornell University Press, 2000).

16. Castillo and Tabuenca Córdoba, *Border Women*, 5–7.

17. Cited in ibid., 8.

18. Alejandro Lugo, "Reflections on Border Theory, Culture, and the Nation," in *Border Theory: The Limits of Cultural Politics*, ed. Scott Michaelsen and David E. Johnson (Minneapolis: University of Minnesota Press, 1997), 43–67, quotation on 57.

19. Cited in Mónica Torres, "'Doing Mestizaje': When Epistemology Becomes Ethics," in *Chicana Feminisms: A Critical Reader*, ed. Gabriela F. Arredondo, Aída Hurtado, Norma Klahn, Olga Nájera-Ramírez, and Patricia Azvalla (Durham, N.C.: Duke University Press, 2003), 195–203, quotation on 197.

20. Luis H. Méndez B., "Violencia simbólica en el territorio maquiladora fronterizo," *El Cotidiano* 125 (May–June 2004): 7–20, quotation on 8.

21. See, e.g., Rita González, "The Said and the Unsaid: Lourdes Portillo Tracks Down Ghosts in *Señorita Extraviada*," *Aztlán: A Journal of Chicano Studies* 28.2 (Fall 2003): 235–240; Lourdes Portillo, "Filming *Señorita Extraviada:* The New Killing Fields," *Aztlán: A Journal of Chicano Studies* 28. 2 (Fall 2003): 228–234; Alejandro Enríquez, "Lourdes Portillo's *Señorita Extraviada:* The Poetics and Politics of Femicide," *Studies in Latin American Popular Culture* 23 (2004): 123–136.

22. Oscar J. Martínez, *Border Boom Town: Ciudad Juárez since 1848* (Austin: University of Texas Press, 1978), 115–116, 152.

23. Leslie Sklair, *Assembling for Development: The Maquila Industry in Mexico and the United States* (San Diego: Center for U.S.-Mexican Studies, University of California, San Diego, 1993), 30.

24. Martínez, *Border Boom Town*.

25. Ibid., 198n52.

26. Sklair, *Assembling for Development;* Donald W. Baerresen, *The Border Industrialization Program of Mexico* (Lexington, Mass.: Lexington Books, 1971); María Patricia Fernández-Kelly, *For We Are Sold, I and My People: Women and Industry in Mexico's Frontier* (Albany: State University of New York Press, 1983); Devon G. Peña, *The Terror of the Machine: Technology, Work, Gender, and Ecology on the U.S.-Mexico Border* (Austin: Center for Mexican American Studies, University of Texas at Austin, 1997); Norma Iglesias Prieto, *Beautiful Flowers of the Maquiladora: Life Histories of Women Workers in Tijuana,* trans. Michael Stone with Gabrielle Winkler (Austin: University of Texas Press, Institute of Latin American Studies, 1997).

27. Méndez B., "Violencia simbólica," 8; Néstor García Canclini, *Consumers and Citizens: Globalization and Multicultural Conflicts,* trans. George Yúdice (Minneapolis: University of Minnesota Press, 2001), 49–65.

28. Sklair, *Assembling for Development*, 35, 99; Instituto Nacional de Estadística Geográfica e Informática (INEGI), *Industria maquiladora de exportación* (Mexico City, 2005), http://www.inegi.gob.mx.

29. Sklair, *Assembling for Development*, 172.

30. INEGI, *Estadística de la industria maquiladora de exportación, 1974–1982* (Mexico City, 1991), 6; idem, *Industria maquiladora de exportación*, 2005.

31. María Patricia Fernández-Kelly, *For We Are Sold, I and My People: Women and Industry in Mexico's Frontier* (Albany: State University of New York Press, 1983), 144–150; David Bacon, "Stories from the Borderlands," *NACLA Report on the Americas* 39:1 (July–August 2005): 25–30; Iglesias Prieto, *Beautiful Flowers*, 81–97.

32. Tamar Diana Wilson, "The Masculinization of the Mexican Maquiladoras," *Review of Radical Political Economics* 34.1 (Winter 2002): 3–17; Sklair, *Assembling for Development*, 173; Leslie Salzinger, *Genders in Production: Making Workers in Mexico's Global Factories* (Berkeley and Los Angeles: University of California Press, 2004), 54–55.

33. María Patricia Fernández-Kelly, "Maquiladoras: The View from the Inside," in *Gender in Cross-cultural Perspective*, ed. Caroline B. Brettell and Carolyn F. Sargent (Upper Saddle River, N.J.: Prentice Hall, 1997), 525–537; Elvia R. Arriola, "Voices from the Barbed Wires of Despair: Women in the Maquiladoras, Latina Critical Legal Theory, and Gender at the U.S.-Mexico Border," *DePaul Law Review* 49 (2000): 729–815; Iglesias Prieto, *Beautiful Flowers;* Rosario Sanmiguel, *Callejón Sucre y otros relatos* (Chihuahua: Ediciones del Azar, 1994).

34. Iglesias Prieto, *Beautiful Flowers*, 75.

35. Fernández-Kelly, *For We Are Sold*, 141.

36. Washington Valdez, *Cosecha de mujeres*, 57; Rosa Linda Fregoso, *MeXicana Encounters: The Making of Social Identities on the Borderlands* (Berkeley & Los Angeles: University of California Press, 2003), 7; Julia Monárrez-Fragoso, "La cultura del feminicidio en Ciudad Juárez, 1993–1999," *Frontera Norte* 12.23 (January–June 2000): 87–117.

37. Lugo, "Fragmented Lives."

38. Alicia Gaspar de Alba, *La Llorona on the Longfellow Bridge: Poetry y Otras Movidas* (Houston: Arte Público Press, 2003), poem on 106–108, quotation on 108; Suzanne Chávez-Silverman, "Gendered Bodies and Borders in Contemporary Chican@ Performance and Literature," in *Velvet Barrios: Popular Culture & Chicana/o Sexualities*, ed. Alicia Gaspar de Alba (New York: Palgrave Macmillan, 2003), 215–227, quotation on 225.

39. Kathryn Kopinak, "Gender as a Vehicle for the Subordination of Women Maquiladora Workers in Mexico," *Latin American Perspectives* 21.1 (Winter 1995): 30–48, esp. 31.

40. Baerresen, *The Border Industrialization Program*, 34.

41. *New York Times* (March 19, 1984).

42. Kathleen A. Staudt, "Economic Change and Ideological Lag in Households of Maquila Workers in Ciudad Juárez," in *Social Ecology and Economic Development of Ciudad Juárez*, ed. Gay Young (Boulder, Colo.: Westview Press, 1986), 97–120, esp. 115; Sergio Peña, "Recent Development in Urban Marginality along Mexico's Northern Border," *Habitat International* 29.2 (June 2005): 285–301; Méndez B., "Violencia simbólica."

43. William J. Lloyd, "Land Use Structure and the Availability of Services in Ciudad Juárez," in *Social Ecology and Economic Development of Ciudad Juárez*, ed. Gay Young (Boulder, Colo.: Westview Press, 1986), 47–64, esp. 48.

44. Washington Valdez, *Cosecha de mujeres*, 154–158.

45. Theresa Braine, "Murder in the Desert," *Business Mexico*, special issue (January 2004): 32.

46. Cecilia Balli, "Ciudad de la Muerte," *Texas Monthly* (June 2003): 108–117, quotation on 112.

47. Quoted in Sam Quiñones, *True Tales from Another Mexico: The Lynch Mob, the Popsicle Kings, Chalino, and the Bronx* (Albuquerque: University of New Mexico Press, 2001), 146.

48. Fernández-Kelly, *For We Are Sold*, 133–144; Tryon P. Woods, "Globalizing Social Violence: Race, Gender and the Spatial Politics of Crisis," *American Studies* 43.1 (Spring 2002): 127–153; Soledad González Montes, Olivia Ruiz, Laura Velasco, and Ofelia Woo, eds., *Mujeres, migración y maquila en la frontera norte* (Mexico City: El Colegio de México, 1995).

49. Fernandez-Kelly, "Maquiladoras," 535.

50. Staudt, "Economic Change," 116.

51. Fernández-Kelly, *For We Are Sold*, 133–144; idem, "Maquiladoras"; Iglesias Prieto, *Beautiful Flowers*, 74–80; Salzinger, *Genders in Production*.

52. Debbie Nathan, "Work, Sex and Danger in Ciudad Juárez," *NACLA Report on the Americas* 33.3 (November–December 1999): 24–30.

53. Charles Bowden, "While You Were Sleeping: In Juárez, Mexico, Photographers Expose the Violent Realities of Free Trade," *Harper's Magazine* (December 1996): 44-52, quotation on 48.

54. Cited in Rosa Linda Fregoso, "Voices without Echo: The Global Gendered Apartheid," *Emergences: Journal for the Study of Media & Composite Cultures* 10.1 (May 2000): 137–155, quotation on 138.

55. Ibid.

56. Cited in Woods, "Globalizing Social Violence," quotation on 143.

57. INEGI, *Industria maquiladora de exportación*, 2005.

58. Bowden, "While You Were Sleeping"; idem, *Juárez: The Laboratory of Our Future* (New York: Aperture, 1998); idem, "Camera of Dirt: Juárez Photographer Takes Forbidden Images in Foreign-owned Factories," *Aperture* 159 (Spring 2000): 27–33.

59. Http://www.almargen.com.mx/#.

60. Iglesias Prieto, *Beautiful Flowers*, 75.

61. Ibid.

62. Ibid., 80.

63. Norma Alarcón, "Traddutora, Traditora: A Paradigmatic Figure of Chicana Feminism," *Cultural Critique* 13 (1989): 57–97; Maylei Blackwell, "Contested Histories: *Las Hijas de Cuauhtémoc*, Chicana Feminisms, and Print Culture in the Chicano Movement, 1968–1973," in *Chicana Feminisms: A Critical Reader*, ed. Gabriela F. Arredondo, Aída Hurtado, Norma Klahn, Olga Nájera-Ramírez, and Patricia Zavella (Durham, N.C.: Duke University Press, 2003), 59–89.

64. Octavio Paz, *The Labyrinth of Solitude*, trans. Lysander Kemp (New York: Grove Press, 1947; reprint 1985), 85.

65. Carlos Fuentes, *The Crystal Frontier: A Novel in Nine Stories,* trans. Alfred MacAdam (New York: Farrar, Straus, and Giroux, 1995), 127.

66. Ibid.

67. Ibid., 134.

68. Ibid., 174.

69. Ibid., 136.

70. Ibid., 140.

71. Ibid., 140–141.

72. Castillo and Tabuenca Córdoba, *Border Women,* 68.

73. Fernández-Kelly, *For We Are Sold;* idem, "Maquiladoras."

74. Sanmiguel, *Callejón Sucre;* Castillo and Tabuenca Córdoba, *Border Women,* 59–68.

75. Gaspar de Alba, *Desert Blood,* 185, 199–206.

76. Fuentes, *The Crystal Frontier,* 135.

77. Ibid., 114.

78. Carlos Fuentes, *Todos los gatos son pardos,* 7th ed. (Mexico City: Siglo Veintiuno, 1977), 13–14.

79. Fuentes, *The Crystal Frontier,* 168.

80. Ibid., *Todos los gatos son pardos,* 14.

81. Ana María Carbonell, "From Llorona to Gritona: Coatlicue in Feminist Tales by Viramontes and Cisneros," *MELUS* 24.2 (Summer 1999): 53–74.

82. Gloria B. Durán, *The Archetypes of Carlos Fuentes: From Witch to Androgyne* (Hamden, Conn.: Archon Books, 1980).

83. Paz, *The Labyrinth of Solitude,* 85–86.

84. Anzaldúa, *Borderlands/La Frontera;* Adelaida R. del Castillo, "Malintzin Tenepal: A Preliminary Look into a New Perspective," *Encuentro Femenil* 1.2 (1974): 58–78; Blackwell, "Contested Histories."

85. Anzaldúa, *Borderlands/La Frontera,* 27ff.

86. Ibid., 46, 84.

87. Lanin Gyurko, "The Vindication of La Malinche in Fuentes' 'Todos los gatos son pardos,'" *Ibero-Amerikanisches Archiv,* n.s., 3.3 (1977): 233–266, quotation on 257; Sandra Messenger Cypess, *La Malinche in Mexican Literature: From History to Myth* (Austin: University of Texas Press, 1991), 121.

88. Paz, *The Labyrinth of Solitude,* 86.

89. Nathan, "Work, Sex and Danger," 28.

90. Musicians include Tori Amos, "Juárez"; Lila Downs, "La Niña"; El TRI, "Las Mujeres de Juárez"; Mujeres en Fuga, "El Boulevard de los Sueños Destrozados"; Ana Gabriel, "Tiempo de Actuar"; Mónica Vidal, "Ni Una Más, Sin Su Mirar"; and Alejandro Lerner, "De Mariposa a Cruz."

91. José David Saldívar, *Border Matters,* 1–4.

92. *Pacto de Sangre,* Fonovisa FDCD-51245.

93. *Chicago Sun Times* (April 4, 2004).

94. María Herrera-Sobek, *The Mexican Corrido: A Feminist Analysis* (Bloomington: Indiana University Press, 1990), xviii.

95. Ramón Saldívar, *The Borderlands of Culture: Américo Paredes and the Transnational Imaginary* (Durham, N.C.: Duke University Press, 2006), 177.

96. Chandra Talpade Mohanty, *Feminism without Borders: Decolonizing Theory, Practicing Solidarity* (Durham, N.C.: Duke University Press, 2003), 188–189.

97. Nancy Caro Hollander, *Love in a Time of Hate: Liberation Psychology in Latin America* (New Brunswick, N.J.: Rutgers University Press, 1997), 117.

98. Marguerite Guzmán Bouvard, *Revolutionizing Motherhood: The Mothers of the Plaza de Mayo* (Wilmington, Del.: Scholarly Resources, 1994).

99. Gaspar de Alba, *Desert Blood*, 333.

100. Ibid., 251.

101. Ibid., 252.

102. Ibid., 255.

103. Anzaldúa, *Borderlands/La Frontera*, 84.

104. Tori Amos, "Black Dove," *From the Choirgirl Hotel*, Atlantic/Wea, 1998.

105. *Die Zeit* (November 11, 1999).

106. Tori Amos, "Juárez," *To Venus and Back*, Atlantic/Wea, 1999.

107. Mohanty, *Feminism*, 188–189.

108. Lila Downs, "La Niña," *Border/La Línea*, Narada World, 2001.

109. Lourdes Portillo, *Señorita Extraviada*, San Francisco: Xochitl Films, 2001.

**PART TWO**

# ¡NI UNA MÁS!

# CHAPTER 5

# Binational Civic Action for Accountability: Antiviolence Organizing in Ciudad Juárez/El Paso

KATHLEEN STAUDT AND IRASEMA CORONADO

Since the early 1990s, civic activists in Ciudad Juárez, Chihuahua, and El Paso, Texas, have been gaining ground in raising awareness of and bringing attention to the femicides—the hundreds of unsolved murders of girls and young women in the region. In the context of Mexico's transition to democracy, activists have struggled to obtain political accountability, professional responses from the criminal justice system, or even respectful acknowledgment of public problems, particularly those affecting women and families from poverty. In fact, some activists have faced threats, harassment, and intimidation for their efforts to make problems visible and criticize governmental nonresponsiveness.

This chapter focuses on antiviolence organizing in the Ciudad Juárez/ El Paso population of two million people. The border is a violent place for men and women, but this chapter's focus is on the organizing efforts around the murders of girls and women in the 1990s (now numbering over four hundred deaths, a third of which involve rape and mutilation),[1] and on the events taking place in 2008 in Ciudad Juárez. Drug dealers are engaged in a turf war that has turned Ciudad Juárez into a militarized city, has rendered local government useless and ineffective. This wave of violence resulted in over five hundred deaths from January through June 2008 alone, of mostly police officers, federal government officials, and random other people.

Where are the activists now? What has happened to the antiviolence organizing in the region? Women's bodies are still found in Ciudad Juárez, mutilated, raped, and gunned down. Where was the outrage of feminist and antiviolence organizations when a high-ranking police officer who happened to be a female was gunned down in her home in front of her children or when a pregnant twenty-four-year-old died after witnessing the violent deaths of three men who were sitting outside her home?

We argue that the antiviolence movement has waned for a variety of reasons: (1) fear of reprisal from the state; (2) fear of being a target of drug traffickers for defending their perceived enemy or enemies; (3) U.S. citizens' concerns about being arrested in Mexico for violating Article 33 of the Mexican Constitution; and (4) hard-to-sustain, dramatic organizational performances that peaked in 2004 and became, in organizing terms, a hard act to follow.

Violence against men and women is reprehensible; however, activists have been silenced because the victims are seen as less worthy or as "bad people" who are involved in high-stakes activities that may result in loss of life. It is important to mention that this drug war is in part fueled by the consumption of illegal drugs in the United States and that over 90 percent of all arms being used to wage this war originate in the United States and are transported into Mexico.

We focus on the civic actions of nongovernmental organizations (NGOs), which press governments for accountability. The first section will briefly outline the facts and chronology of the Juárez murders and official responses. The second section examines the challenges of accountability in borderlands, which complicate public action. In the third section, cross-border civic action is analyzed. The fourth part of the chapter deals with civil society's response to the new wave of violence that has rampaged through Ciudad Juárez and the reactions to the "warfare." This section is followed by considerations of strategies for successful action.

The chapter draws on multiple sources: interviews, observations, and participant observation of antiviolence organizations, including the cross-border Coalition against Violence toward Women and Families involving activists and organizations from both Ciudad Juárez and El Paso. We also use local radio and television news programs and content analysis of blogs and newspapers in the region. Our underlying argument calls for "institutional shrouds" to provide leverage and resources for successful, systemic action, such as a human rights treaty, coupled with oversight by civil society. While Mexico and the United States have signed numerous agreements on topics that range from free trade and the environment to air traffic control and plant viruses, no human rights agreement exists to address public safety, sex-related serial killers, and the overall lawless climate in cities like Ciudad Juárez.

## The Juárez Murders and the Official Response

Borderlands are often characterized as wild frontiers. Ciudad Juárez, Mexico's fifth-largest city, is no exception. Juárez has long been considered a boom town.[2] The Border Industrial Program (BIP) of the 1960s and the growth of assembly-line production in the *maquiladora* industry served as a magnet to attract migrants from the interior and led to dramatic population increases.

Moreover, illegal drug trafficking is perhaps the city's major business, for it is home base to the Carrillo-Fuentes cartel. The Sinaloa cartel has gained ground in the city, fueling a turf war that led to the huge murder rate in 2008 and 2009. Once the U.S. War on Drugs made trafficking from Colombia through Florida more difficult, El Paso/Juárez became a major trafficking corridor.[3] However "wild and lawless" the characterization, borders coexist with heavy law enforcement and what has been called the "militarization of the border."[4] Law enforcement aims to regulate and control immigration, commerce and trade, firearms (the special concern of Mexico), and drug trafficking (the special concern of the United States). At the federal level, the U.S. Federal Bureau of Investigation (FBI) and the Drug Enforcement Agency (DEA), among others, all work in Mexico.[5]

Pres. Felipe Calderón sent the Mexican military to Ciudad Juárez in the spring of 2008. Juarenses are divided on this issue. Some are concerned that the presence of the military will lead to authoritarianism; others feel that they are giving up civil liberties for public order; and still others see the military as a saving presence that has come to clean up the city. The office of Mexico's attorney general, the Procuraduría General de la República (PGR), has offices in the United States. Binational cooperation in law enforcement exists at the higher echelons of government, setting precedents for such cooperation at all levels of government.

With this plethora of institutions working together, why is drug trafficking so prevalent, acts of violence so common, and lawlessness rampant? Some argue that corruption runs unchecked among law enforcement agencies on both sides of the border.

In the early to mid-1990s, Juarenses began to notice patterns in media reports about female homicide. The bodies of women (the majority of them teenagers), raped and mutilated before death, were found either in the desert or in fields inside the city. They fit a certain profile: slender, poor, young, with dark hair. Public officials, when questioned, discounted the value of the victims and appeared to blame them for "leading a double life" or "dressing provocatively" and "being out at night." Of course, victims dressed in a variety of ways and were killed day and night.

Partial information can be found in police files, all too many of them shoddy and incomplete:[6] most victims are women (the majority) and are young (eleven–twenty-one); they have died after being subjected to particular practices prior to death, such as being set on fire or having their breasts cut off.

The first to be charged was a foreigner, Abdel Latif Sharif Sharif, and the sentiment in the city was that "Mexicans don't do these things."[7] When the killings continued, the authorities charged members of the Rebeldes gang, claiming they took direction from Sharif. After that, bus drivers contracted to second- and third-shift *maquiladoras* were charged.

Mexico has a long tradition of forcing confessions,[8] and many suspects were mistreated; several have died in prison, one of an infection after knee surgery, and Sharif, of a heart attack. Some were released because of a lack of real evidence. Yet the killings continued, leading people to wonder whether multiple serial killers were responsible.

This early history is covered well in Lourdes Portillo's film, *Señorita Extraviada* (2001). Portillo focuses on the victims' families, the indifference of police and judicial authorities, and those who also denounced the police as active participants in the rape and torture killings.

Consciousness began to be raised through newspaper articles, and people painted pink crucifix-style crosses on black backgrounds in public spaces. A large wooden crucifix with nails representing the victims sits just in front of the downtown international crossing bridge. From the 1990s to 2005, media coverage on both sides of the border was extensive each time new bodies were found. In 2008–2009, coverage of drug-related violence and murder was also high. During the entire decade of the 1990s, the number of victims was in dispute, even by the Partido Revolucionario Institucional (PRI) and the Partido de Acción Nacional (PAN). By the year 2002, the figures from various entities included 254 (86 of them serial killings) claimed by Casa Amiga, the antiviolence counseling center in Juárez; 258 claimed by the Chihuahua state attorney general's office; and 320 (90 of them sex-related serial killings) claimed by the *El Paso Times*.[9] By this time, media coverage extended beyond the border, from Mexico City to U.S. dailies like the *New York Times*, the *Washington Post*, the *Los Angeles Times*, and the largest U.S. Spanish-language newspaper, the Los Angeles–based *La Opinión*. International coverage was extensive as well, with European newspapers and magazines sending journalists and photographers to the border.

At the state level, victims' families have been treated with disdain and disrespect.[10] Most families earn poverty-level wages (the minimum wage amounts to about US$5.00 per day). As of 2009, the official minimum wage was 53 pesos a day. The value compared to the U.S. dollar has fallen since the fall 2008 economic downturn and peso devaluation (in 2009, P13 = $1.00; in summer 2008, P10 = $1.00). The police have been careless about retaining the victims' clothing and remains. Participants from two cross-border coalitions assisted in desert searches to locate evidence, and they found underwear and other objects that the police had left behind.

Activists levy many charges against the police besides indifferences and intimidation: fabricated evidence; incomplete and lost investigation files; bone misidentification, causing victims' families to relive the murders over and over. Police do not provide straight or consistent stories to victims' families, undermining any trust that an already skeptical population might have in its law enforcement. A threatening message was left on the phone of a victim's family about dropping the issue: the caller identification showed that the state judicial police number was the source.[11]

During our research, family members have reported that, in some instances, they do not know even where to start to report their missing daughters. Poor and disenfranchised people have limited knowledge of and experience with governmental institutions, and, coupled with anguish over their missing daughters, they report high levels of frustration with law enforcement agencies at all levels. One mother indicated to us that she went to

one office, where we told them that our daughter had not come home. They made us wait, then sent us to an office where a man asked us all kinds of questions: name, age, address, where we worked, on and on. Then we finally got to our daughter, her name, how old, what she was wearing, etc. The man stated that we should not worry because many young women, like our daughter, usually go and spend the night in a hotel with their boyfriend and oversleep, and they usually return the next day. [I felt shocked, like a] pail of cold water was thrown at me.[12]

The official went on to tell her that, if their daughter did not return later in the day, to go to another office whose address he provided. "This is not where we deal with missing people," he told them.

Family members have also reported that public officials mistreated them. They also indicate that they have to take whole days off from work to go to the police when they want to follow up on their cases. Families that do not have telephones have a hard time getting through to the person who is in charge of their case, so they just present themselves in person with the hope that they will get information.

Despite the public attention to the cases, things have not changed much over the years, and corruption is routine. As one mother reported, "We were told by one police officer that they would look into my daughter's case a little more closely if we could provide him an incentive. Our family and friends gathered all the money that we could and gave it to him, hoping that they would be able to tell us where our daughter was. At the time, one is in so much pain and anguish that one is not thinking clearly, and I felt that it was the right thing to do because I really wanted them to find my daughter."[13]

Public officials received visits from victims' families, with pleas to "do something," following the supplication style of patron-client politics, to little avail. By the late 1990s, NGOs were formed by victims' families and women's and human rights activists acting in solidarity with the families. One of the first (later disbanded) was Voces sin Eco (Voices without an Echo), a group of family members. The first cross-border binational group to emerge was Amigos de las Mujeres de Ciudad Juárez (Friends of the Women of Ciudad Juárez), based in Las Cruces, New Mexico. Feminist groups, such as 8 de Marzo (March 8), articulated concerns. Other NGOs organized, such as Mujeres por Juárez (Women for Juárez), Nuestras Hijas de Regreso a Casa (May Our Daughters Return Home), and Mujeres de Negro (Women in Black), the last of which dresses in mourning at large public events. Mujeres de Negro solidarity actions have occurred in different U.S. cities and all over the world, often at Mexican consulates and embassy offices. The binational Coalition against Violence, discussed below, was born at a labor-solidarity event in Juárez in November 2001. Finally, in 2003, Amnesty International released a lengthy report on the murders, claiming a total of 370, 137 of them "sexual homicides"; Mexican feminists refer to these misogynistic crimes as *feminicidio*.[14]

By the turn of the twenty-first century, government officials were no longer blaming the victims, at least in public. Similar serial killings spread to other border locations and to the state capital in Chihuahua City.[15] But the municipal and state police acted with indifference, incompetence, or, to express the vox populi, in complicity with the killers, theorized as being the "juniors," sons of rich families, including from the cartels, who have money and influence to buy protection. Near Day of the Dead commemorations in 2003, *La Jornada* published a lengthy front-page article that named prominent Juárez families implicated by investigations.[16]

In Mexico, residents distrust the police and experience or expect corruption, and these concerns are worse in Juárez and the State of Chihuahua generally—one of several states in Mexico with high crime rates and rampant organized crime (including drug trafficking), according to the federal attorney general's office.[17] In the multination World Values Survey, approximately three out of ten Mexicans trust the police, and five out of ten trust the army.[18] Although dated, a Universidad Nacional Autónoma de México (UNAM; National Autonomous University of Mexico) study calculates that "cocaine traffickers spent as much as $460 million on bribery in

1993—far more than the annual budget of the Mexican Attorney General's Office in 1993."[19] After more than a decade since that report, the amounts have likely skyrocketed. Transparency International, an international NGO that reports an annual Corruption Perception Index for most countries, scores Mexico between 3 and 4 (higher than the lowest rated, from 1 to 2), but far from the top (between 9 and 10).[20] Mexican police at the municipal, state, and federal levels are regularly fired or suspended for corruption and drug charges.[21]

Threats, intimidation, and death have been the risks associated with criticism of government-granted impunity. In February 2002, state police officers shot attorney Mario Escobedo Anaya to death in Ciudad Juárez. Escobedo Anaya was defending one of two bus drivers accused of raping and murdering eight women found in an empty lot in November 2001. The young attorney and his father, Sergio Dante Almaraz (who was defending the other accused bus driver), had been interviewed along with the wives of the bus drivers by *20/20*, an ABC news show. Before the interview, both father and son had received death threats. As local police chased Escobedo Anaya through the streets of Ciudad Juárez, he managed to call his father on his cell phone. Conflicting details emerged regarding what happened that night: the attorney crashed and died; the police shot at him in self-defense; or, after the car wreck, police walked over and shot him. When his father arrived at the scene of the accident, state police were everywhere, and the young attorney was dead.[22]

Mexico's move to a multiparty system, pioneered on the northern frontier, undermined cooperation between the levels of the federal system. When PAN president Vicente Fox won the elections in 2000, PRI governor Patricio Martínez controlled the State of Chihuahua, and PANista Jesús Delgado controlled the municipal presidency in Juárez.

President Fox responded to the national and international pressure to act on the murders and official impunity granted accused perpetrators. In the summer of 2003, he authorized the stationing of hundreds of federal preventive police in Juárez, and in 2004, he appointed a special commission, with Guadalupe Morfín as its head and María López Urbina, a special prosecutor, as investigator.

## Border Accountability

The problem of violence against women is ancient and deep-seated, tolerated as a private matter for many centuries.[23] But since the 1970s in both Mexico and the United States (and globally), activists from the grassroots to the national and international levels have called attention to violence against women involving domestic assault and abuse, rape, and murder as a public problem.[24]

At borders, problem solving is compounded by national sovereignty, although many precedents have been set for cross-border, binational cooperation by official organizations like the International Boundary and Water Commission (IBWC)/Comisión Internacional de Límites y Aguas (CILA) and NGOs, whether registered tax-exempt nonprofit organizations or informal networks and coalitions.[25] Despite national sovereignty, both governments have cooperated over water, toxic waste, air quality, trade, and commerce.

The border runs through the combined metropolitan area of Juárez/El Paso, complicating accountability relationships between people, victims and victims' families, and government. The border regional context involves two sets of political institutions that, on the surface, appear similar (presidential forms of government with separate executive, legislative, and judicial branches, i.e., federalism), but operate quite differently. Periodically, binational cooperation transcends borders. Binational cooperation occurred in the late 1990s, with inconclusive reports after data was run through the FBI database at Quantico, Virginia.

Article 33 of the 1917 Mexican Constitution states that foreigners should in no way get involved in the political affairs of the country: "Los extranjeros no podrán de ninguna manera inmiscuirse en los asuntos políticos del país."[26] This produces a level of fear for activists: declaration as persona non grata; jail, with the risk of torture. During the V-Day activities that took place on February 14, 2004 (discussed below), with Jane Fonda, Christine Lahti, and Sally Field in attendance, a flyer circulated in the community reminding people of consequences that foreigners could face for their political activism in Ciudad Juárez. At the largest-ever cross-border solidarity march in the region that day, massive crowds, along with suit-wearing officials snapping photos, awaited the five thousand to eight thousand crossers.

Why is the killing a *binational* issue? Cross-border activists point to several factors. First, at least four of the victims are from the United States (specifically, El Paso) and others are from the Netherlands, Honduras, and Guatemala.[27] Furthermore, there are many more *desaparecidos,* disappeared people, than murder victims from *both* sides of the border as well as a cross-border organization called the Asociación de Familiares y Amigos de Personas "Desaparecidas" (Association of Family and Friends of Disappeared People).[28] It is impossible to know how many of these people have been murdered, their bodies yet to be found in the vast stretches of the Chihuahuan Desert surrounding Ciudad Juárez. The mother of a *desaparecida* from El Paso testified before members of a U.S. congressional delegation in October 2003 (discussed later).[29]

Second, the serial killers may be border crossers and their nationality uncertain, for the borderlands are porous. As the murders spread to Chihuahua City, the authorities forced a confession from a U.S. woman married to a Mexican.[30]

Third, the economies are linked, especially in the mostly U.S.-owned *maquiladoras,* where some of the victims worked, earning little more than the Mexican minimum wage of under US$5.00 daily. Some border scholars theorize that the notion of a cheap, "disposable" labor force contributes to the lawless climate in the city.[31] Ciudad Juárez has become a magnet for migrants since the inception of *maquiladoras* in 1965, and the *maquiladora* workforce grew to its high point in 2000: 250,000 workers (down to approximately 200,000 in 2003).

Chihuahua's legislature has passed a variety of laws addressing domestic assault, rape, and murder. The language is often vague, and the (under-reported) crime statistics are not disaggregated by gender (unlike in other states with seemingly better crime data record-keeping, such as Sonora). The lack of disaggregated data allowed then-governor Martínez to say casually that the murder rate in Juárez was not so bad compared to that of other big cities like New York. The rate of homicides of females per 100,000 population was glaringly high during Martínez's government, however, compared to that of other big cities in Mexico and elsewhere.[32] Thirty deputies serve in the state legislature, and in 2001, activists fought an effort to reduce the penalty for rape to a penalty that was less than that for hurting a cow (as headlines testified).[33] Committees do not appear to exercise significant oversight over particular bureaucratic agencies, such as judicial investigation agencies. In 2005, three women sat in a Congress of thirty, each from one of the three major parties. Despite partisan differences, they prioritize solutions for violence against women. Of course, public safety is not simply a "women's issue," and 10 percent never constituted a majority.

At the national level, Mexico created the Comisión Nacional de los Derechos Humanos (National Human Rights Commission) in the 1990s. Numerous reports about the violence against women have been made to the commission, but it lacks enforcement powers.

In 1994, Mexico reformed the Supreme Court to increase its autonomy from the executive branch (and political domination). But national reforms have not spilled over into the state level. According to UNAM professor José Luis Soberanes, the "delivery of justice in Mexico depends on a

**Fig. 5.1.** J Guadalupe Pérez © 2004, "Contingente de la Comunidad Chicana, Pasan de los EU a México durante el V Day, 2004" (Protestors from the Chicano Community, Crossing from the U.S. to Mexico during V-Day, 2004). Courtesy of J Guadalupe Pérez.

structure that is complicated, slippery, and often corrupt."[34] In a damning indictment, judicial experts have concluded that Mexico does not extend rights and protections based on "rule of law."[35]

How can accountability be increased? The next section analyzes cross-border civic actions and the gains they have brought. Although public awareness of the crimes has increased, the responses have thus far been meager and modest. The Coalition against Violence brings together disparate groups that share the common goal of ending the violence and locating the killers. However, other organized interests, such as the chambers of commerce, the downtown merchants, and the *maquila* industries, have only feebly pressed the government, because the image of Juárez could deter investments in the region. Instead, business voices, articulated in the media, say that the protestors make Juárez look bad.

## Cross-border Civic Actions

This section focuses on the cross-border Coalition against Violence toward Women and Families at the U.S.-Mexico border. It is a loose, binational alliance of organizations and individuals representing human and women's rights; labor; health, counseling and shelter organizations; and students. The chronological analysis below outlines its movement from regional, cross-border networking among activists with strong personal ties at its birth to a movement that gained leverage with what Granovetter calls "the strength of weak ties,"[36] that is, impersonal ties to other networks at the national and international levels in 2004. However, the personal and impersonal ties lack the "institutional shroud" of human rights laws, policies, and resources that include violence against women as a public safety issue worthy of rights protection.

## Cross-border Organizational Birth and Growth

Amigos de las Mujeres de Juárez was the pioneering cross-border network to emerge in 2001. Activists worked with victims' families, raising funds for them and other NGOs in Juárez. Amigos is a tax-exempt U.S. organization based in Las Cruces, New Mexico.[37] The Coalition against Violence emerged to mobilize visibility for the murders and to connect that visibility to systemic and policy change, particularly at the binational level.

At its birth, the Coalition against Violence emerged in solidarity with independent unions in Mexico. Many of these unions take a critical stance toward globalization, the North American Free Trade Agreement (NAFTA), and neoliberalism generally, yet activists work "within" capitalist economies and pursue reformist strategies. The coalition organized events associated with International Women's Day, connecting with organizations as far south as Chihuahua City. In 2002, hundreds of people on each side of the international border rallied and then met at the border. Some protesters dressed in dramatic and symbolic colors (mostly black, following the Mujeres de Negro), and the quasi-religious symbolic signs of death—black crosses on a pink background—were found everywhere.

The antiviolence coalition of cross-border activists built visibility for and momentum around binational cooperation among local police authorities and an international tip line with assistance from the FBI. Their challenge, repeated over and over to public decision-makers was this: "You cooperate over auto theft; why not over the murders of girls and women?"[38]

The Coalition against Violence called for a binational task force to foster cooperation in investigating the crimes, including greater FBI involvement. Besides local police cooperation in investigating auto theft, rampant at borders, both governments cooperate in a variety of other issues, from water

**Fig. 5.2.** J Guadalupe Pérez © 2006, "Cruces por Todos los Caminos de Juárez Recuerdan a los Transeúntes los Asesinatos, al Fondo el Puente Internacional Lerdo-Stanton" (Crosses on Juárez Roads and Highways Remind Passersby of the Murders, International Bridge between Lerdo and Stanton). Courtesy of J Guadalupe Pérez.

and air quality to business and commerce. For "radicals" in the coalition, however, it was unusual, even uncomfortable, to look to police or investigative agencies for solutions to problems. The coalition also approached Crime Stoppers—a nonprofit organization that receives and pays for tips that lead to solving crimes—to no avail. The coalition's board of directors expressed hesitation about actions that would imply criticism of law enforcement in Mexico.

There were also efforts to revise a document that frames and legitimizes health interventions through 2010. The official U.S.-Mexico Border Health Commission, comprising mostly MD political appointees from both countries, issued a report, *Healthy Borders 2010*, which contains no language about violence against women as a health issue or about other issues of concern to females, such as voluntary motherhood or gender-disaggregated data. Members of the Transborder Consortium on Gender and Health at the U.S.-Mexico Border supplied expertise and utilized contacts to draft a gentle critique that proposed new language and got it on the commission agenda, a feat in bureaucratic organizations. This is working its way through commission agenda setting and consideration (and is still unresolved at this writing).

The Coalition against Violence met with Texas state senator Eliot Shapleigh, key supporter of antiviolence actions, who has been willing to use his name and letterhead to push for binational cooperation. He is one of the few politicians who are proactive on this issue and willing to work for social justice.

Coalition archives contain numerous copies of letters Shapleigh sent to U.S. officials, from President Bush to the Departments of Justice and State and the FBI. Months passed before he received responses, and most of those defined the issue as a narrow judicial matter that Mexico must resolve on its own unless it asked for U.S. assistance. Through the good graces of the senator's office, coalition members met with FBI officials (and the FBI, in turn, gathered intelligence on activists' perceptions). The FBI expressed its willingness to cooperate again in 2002 (the first time was in 1998), but later relegated that cooperation to training rather than investigation.

Coalition against Violence members dressed in mourning at luncheons hosted by the Twin Plant Wives Association and the Republican Women's Club. Twin-plant wives, who reside in El Paso, are married to the managers and corporate executives of the largely U.S.-owned assembly plants in Ciudad Juárez. The murders were discussed and the wage inequalities critiqued. The keynote speaker, First Lady of Texas Anita Perry, was willing to be "pinned" with the symbolic black cross on pink, share names of staff, and brainstorm strategies, once even asking for a meeting (during her husband's reelection campaign in 2002) with coalition members on a trip to El Paso complete with body guards. In results or problem-solving terms, little came of these activities.

Only when coalition members staged dramatic public events, with full media coverage, did regional, national, and international networks mobilize to induce responsiveness from wider segments of the public. Media coverage in Mexico tended to be greater than in El Paso and the United States generally, especially from newspapers with more critical stances toward the government and the dominant political party (the PRI), the one that controlled state government in Chihuahua. Former governor Martínez appointed longtime activist Vicky Caraveo to head the Instituto Chihuahuense de la Mujer (Chihuahua Women's Institute), with a sizable budget. Little is known about budgetary priorities and spending, save the payment of stipends to some of the victims' mothers. Mexico's traditional "divide and rule" strategies and misinformation campaigns, in the context of nontransparency in government, had the effect of polarizing human rights groups. "Who profits from our pain?" was the question that some mothers asked.[39] For students of Mexican politics, manipulative co-optation has long been understood as a response to challenges from civil society.

Public educational events in which the Coalition against Violence participated were striking and dramatic, filled with symbols, colors, and icons. In April 2002, students in the Feminist Majority Leadership Alliance of the University of Texas at El Paso (UTEP) sponsored a silent mourning, holding large black-cross-on-pink placards in a well-traversed part of campus. Many newspapers snapped photos of the 150 mourners, including one dressed in full costume as the Grim Reaper.

In Ciudad Juárez, short, shocking guerrilla theater performances sparked awareness on the streets, solidarity at the international bridge and in cross-border actions. In early November, Day of the Dead commemorations have been held in both Ciudad Juárez and El Paso, displaying altars with candles, artifacts, and memorials to the deceased. At universities on both sides of the border, students have prepared elaborate altars to the murdered girls and women. However, when students graduate, leadership vacuums exist unless new leaders are mentored and their participation sustained.

Political films and theater performances offered extended public education opportunities with memorable visuals.[40] The award-winning *Señorita Extraviada* has been enormously important for expanding the visibility of the murders and police indifference. Fund-raising complemented some of these activities. Eve Ensler's play, the *Vagina Monologues,* has been performed several times in El Paso and Las Cruces. V-Day, organizing against violence, has offered a national and international link between the border region and the world. In 2003, Esther Chávez Cano, an antiviolence activist who runs Casa Amiga for violence victims in Ciudad Juárez, was named as one of "21 Leaders for the 21st Century—2003" in V-Day preparations. Eve Ensler visited Ciudad Juárez for a full day of cultural events, including guerrilla theater and marches, but also for meetings with state judicial officials. At the final event of the day, in front of the attorney general's office for the State of Chihuahua, Ensler spoke in English and her words were then translated.

Lourdes Portillo's film, *Señorita Extraviada,* focuses on the murders and especially the victims' families. The film is grim but respectful of the victims. Portillo is from Ciudad Juárez; she is not just a video/photographer/journalist/academic tourist. The film has been shown many times in the region, both for public education and for fund-raising for antiviolence services. The English version was shown on Public Television in the United States. Portillo was recognized in Mexico City with Academy Award–like honors in 2003. In interviews with coalition members, El Paso's city council members cite specific horrific details from the film, empathizing and worrying about sisters, mothers, and daughters.[41]

At the November 22, 2002, labor and antiviolence conference in Ciudad Juárez, a sequel to the meeting that birthed the coalition, much time and energy was invested in inviting speakers and building audiences. The mayor of El Paso was invited but neither attended nor sent a representative.[42] The municipal president of Ciudad Juárez was invited and came, but he left immediately after his short speech and did not leave staff behind to hear and learn about other ideas and strategies that could have been useful for follow-up. But solidarity was reinforced, with union leaders such as the *telefonistas* (telephone workers) offering to support antiviolence actions with strikes.

## From Local Regional Networks to Transnational and Global Networks

In February 2003, multiple victims were found in a single week, including several teenaged girls and a six-year-old child, all raped and mutilated before death. The death tally kept rising. Disagreements about numbers muddled the issue, as did blanket statements about *maquiladora* victims or whether all or some victims were mutilated before being killed.

Coalition against Violence members reacted to the girls' deaths with a press conference to which Mexican and U.S. media were invited. Coverage was widespread in the border region and the hemisphere (through Spanish-language coverage in the Americas by Univisión). In early 2003, the coalition spoke with city and county political representatives in order to get both a resolution passed concerning the violence and a proclamation for International Women's Day. The resolution had a narrow focus, calling for a binational task force, cross-border police resources and information, and other specifics. The proclamation was broad and general, but offered the ever-present opportunity to "educate" still-widening ripples of people, with official documentation and media coverage, about systemic gender inequalities and everyday life. Both the City Council and the County Commissioners Court in El Paso passed the resolution and proclamation, and media coverage was extensive. Political representatives were concerned about both human rights and the bad image of the border, which could deter investments.

Similar strategies were not available to NGOs focused completely on the Juárez side of the border, for the *cabildo* (municipal council) controls its agenda carefully, and its meetings are not open for public comment. Accountability tools and institutions vary in a binational setting.

At a press conference in March 2003, former mayor Caballero of El Paso announced, with the police chief, that joint cooperation would take place between judicial authorities on both sides of the border. Mexican officials were present as well, somewhat discomfited by a press conference format wherein journalists and NGOs asked challenging questions.

Once again in 2003, rallies and marches were held on International Women's Day. In the United States, rallies require considerable time investment for securing permits, paying fees, and seeking to waive other fees that would cost hundreds of dollars for El Paso police "protection" in case marchers disrupt traffic. In El Paso, at least one month of lead time was necessary for bureaucratic and council approval (in contrast to the opportunity for more spontaneous rallies in Ciudad Juárez, in a country wherein street protest is tolerated and expected). Again, hundreds turned out on both sides of the border, with many reporters and television crews. An AP wire reporter and photographer were also present, with outlets picking up the story across the United States.

Senator Shapleigh and Representative Norma Chávez introduced a joint resolution to the Texas Legislature on binational cooperation in investigations. In early April, both the House and Senate committees held hearings, audiotaped and videotaped and available online. The Coalition against Violence was invited to testify, and written remarks were prepared for the public record.[43] Austin-based activists, wearing coalition-supplied blackcrossed pink pins, testified as well. Representatives and senators listened to and read testimony. HCR 59 was passed during the Seventy-eighth Legislative Session.

Meanwhile, protests were organized at Mexican consulates around the world and in the region. Extensive cyberactivism created a flurry of e-mails and pictures documenting solidarity in Tokyo, Belgrade, Madrid, and many other places.

In March, the forty-seventh U.N. Commission on the Status of Women invited coalition participants to New York City. One university professor and one student participated.[44] This provided another event to put pressure on Mexican authorities and develop weak but committed network ties in distant locales.

However, human rights commissions generally report abuses rather than exercise authority to enforce solutions. NGOs in Ciudad Juárez have worked extensively to communicate with international NGOs like Amnesty International and with international organizations like the Organization of American States and its Inter-American Commission on Human Rights to get the Juárez murders on agendas.[45] The global Amnesty International finally joined the bandwagon of organizations focused on this issue. In the summer of 2003, it released a monograph on the history of the murders, the Mexican criminal justice system, and the government's failure to respond.[46]

The coalition was networked with not only international and inter-American connections, as noted above, but also with the Mexico Solidarity Network and antiviolence coalitions in other cities in both the United States and Mexico. U.S. representative Hilda Solís, responding to the many Juarenses in her Los Angeles constituency, took the lead in organizing the Hispanic Caucus to communicate with President Fox to push for federal involvement in the murders, with legal tools and precedents noted in her letter: Mexico's 1996 Federal Law against Organized Crime provides authority to transfer jurisdiction from the state of Chihuahua to the federal attorney general's office.[47] The El Paso–based coalition met with Cong. Silvestre Reyes's staff to encourage his signature on this letter and his support for hearings at the border. The Washington Office on Latin America helped organize the visit and later follow-up.

In October 2003, Solís led a delegation to the border, visiting victims' families, NGO activists, public officials, and gruesome sites where bodies were found. That visit spurred a great deal of print and television coverage. She introduced House Resolution 466, a bipartisan resolution that encouraged U.S. involvement in binational solutions, with three Republican and five Democratic cosponsors.[48]

Other universities also organized events that made the murders visible and extended the pressure on governments to act. In April 2003, Arizona State University–West sponsored the "Gender, Justice, and the Border" Conference. Students and faculty members decorated 320 dresses, one for each victim, and hung them on 320 crosses, three feet tall, in the central campus courtyard.[49] From October 31 through November 2, the University of California at Los Angeles hosted a conference, "The Maquiladora Murders: Or, Who Is Killing the Women of Juárez?" that drew over a thousand participants, with a range of speakers from experts to victims' family members and activists from both sides of the border.[50] Under the banner of Operación Digna (named after Digna Ochoa, the assassinated human rights lawyer), cyberactivists, particularly Coco Fusco at Columbia University, organized a "floodnet" to stream the conference and worldwide audience responses into the servers of Mexican government agencies. Before the conference, a lengthy fax outlining promises for new coordinating bodies was sent to conference organizers and summarized at the event.[51]

In Mexico, President Fox spoke out against the murders, appointed new federal officials, and coordinated intergovernmental investigations. New attention focused on Juárez in early 2004, when buried bodies were found in Juárez backyards, prompting the removal of complicit state police and binational attention (including Texas governor Perry's order to make the canine patrol, heretofore unavailable, available for investigation of the murders of girls and women). Investigative reports in the *Dallas Morning News* publicized victims "abducted, raped, and killed to 'celebrate' successful drug runs" and once again implicated the police.[52]

But the most visible attention to the murders of girls and women came during V-Week and especially V-Day, February 14, 2004. Students at the University of Texas at El Paso organized a daylong conference, men's workshops, art exhibits, and film series during the week prior to V-Day. On V-Day itself, an estimated five thousand to eight thousand marchers crossed the border from El Paso to Juárez in solidarity with victims of violence. This was *the* largest march across the border in the region's history. Many people came from outside the border region, as did reporters from as far away as Europe. Celebrities from both Mexico and the United States performed excerpts from the *Vagina Monologues*. Eve Ensler wrote an additional monologue about the murders in Juárez, and it has been performed at the border and in over one thousand cities around the world. This monologue will be a permanent feature in future productions of the *Vagina Monologues*.[53]

This chronological analysis from the birth of cross-border organizing and its maturation over time outlines how cross-border activists have helped move local, regional border organizing into national and international organizing around the murders of girls and women in Ciudad Juárez. By 2003, the cross-border groups still operated, but national and international networks overwhelmed those efforts and strengthened the process of making the murders visible and pressing governments for binational solutions.

But for all moves forward, there was backlash, and resistance continued. The business community has yet to respond visibly, save to blame organizers for fewer tourists in downtown Juárez and for the move of *maquiladora* jobs to China (a move caused by many factors, the most prominent being lower labor costs in China). Mainstream academic literature has been slim, save a sentence in Bailey and Chabat.[54] And the murders continue. And the violence continues.

### New Waves of Violence: Drug Wars and the Military

In the spring of 2008, a marked increase in the number of violent deaths was noted by the local press, activists, and the Mexican government. Pres. Felipe Calderón responded by sending in the military to establish order in the city. According to a Mexican government official, this was part of a broader strategy that the government was employing in order to stop drug traffickers.

The arrival of troops led to increased tensions between different local, state, and federal law enforcement agencies. It became obvious that the military had the upper hand, and it immediately started to "clean house" at the local police department. Police officers were arrested and killed;[55] they resigned en masse amid rumors that they were providing protection to the drug dealers.

Civil society responded in a variety of ways to the military presence in the community. Some people welcomed the soldiers, others were concerned about the loss of civil liberties. A march was organized on March 24 in order to raise awareness and to promote nonviolence. Participants dressed in white, and over 300,000 attended this event. Bumper stickers thanking the military for its presence and work were distributed, and the business community started to scramble so that investors would not be dissuaded from investing in Ciudad Juárez.

Certain sectors of civil society were mum, afraid of reprisals. The military set up an 800 number people could call to denounce any perceived illegal activity. This led to searches of homes and businesses based only on anonymous phone calls to this 800 number. The military justified its actions because judges were granting them search warrants that allowed soldiers to invade people's property.

Residents of El Paso reported that they were afraid to go to Ciudad Juárez, especially after an anonymous e-mail circulated in the community that on the last weekend in May 2008 "violence" would plague the city. This e-mail was probably a hoax or a warning by the drug traffickers to minimize civilian casualties. Yet innocent people were being caught in the cross fire more and more. Later e-mail messages would warn people to stay away from certain nightclubs and to avoid public places like Cielo Vista Mall in El Paso, a large shopping center frequented by residents of both cities and the region.

Three victims of the violence in Mexico ended up in El Paso County's Thomason Hospital. This led to the lockdown of the facility. Law enforcement officials expressed concern that the violence would spill over into El Paso and that the perpetrators of these crimes would cross into El Paso and finish the job at the hospital. Law enforcement officers monitored the entrance to the hospital, and patients and visitors had to go through metal detectors. County officials decried the cost of this extra security and demanded that the federal government foot the bill, all of which was covered widely in the local press.

Notably absent in all of this was the outcry of antiviolence organizations, possibly because they were afraid to publicly denounce the violence lest they become victims too.

## Conclusions and Strategies for Change

Cross-border organizing is an expression of civil society organizing and struggling to deepen democracy in problematic spaces such as the U.S.-Mexico border, where accountability relationships are rendered complex with the existence of national sovereignties and multiple institutions. Additional complications include threats to and intimidation of activists, lack of police professionalism, and low priority given to the problems that women and poor people face. Although NAFTA and numerous bilateral agreements form institutional shrouds that provide policy leverage and resources or subsidies that activists and officials may use to address common North American problems at borders, such shrouds do not exist for human rights and public safety. Binational cooperation has begun with several tentative steps, but much remains to be done if rule of law is to prevail and all people are to secure access to justice in the region.

Several categories of regional, national, and international strategies for change are recommended below. They include short- and long-term actions for Mexico, the United States, and the North American region generally.

In Mexico, activists should demand federal involvement in the more-than-decade-old unsolved murders of girls and women. Activists should also press for the use of federal revenue-sharing incentives to encourage reform at state and local levels (a long-standing tradition in Mexico).[56] These reforms include the freedom of information laws of 2003, now operating solely at the federal level; professionalism in state and local police operations; domestic-violence training for police; and gender-disaggregated data on all sexual assaults and domestic violence for better reporting and oversight capabilities.

In Ciudad Juárez and Chihuahua, the government should fund battered women's shelters. Until 2004, none existed in Ciudad Juárez. Oversight over and accountability by state agencies should emanate from state legislators, as well as from civil society. NGOs should have a voice not only in selecting the director of the Instituto de la Mujer but also in deciding the institute's priorities and spending priorities.

Rule of law does not exist in Mexico. To extend legal accountability, legal reformers should extend the ability of the *amparo* (protection) to provide collective justice in a class-action format that requires systemic policy and institutional change in cases of serious intransigence, such as hundreds of poorly investigated deaths.

Citizens should be able to file civil lawsuits against intransigent police departments for monetary damages or reparations, and damages should be provided to all victims' families, not just those the government curries favor with in the form of the long-standing "stipends" in Mexico's co-optation-based system.

Sporadic anticorruption measures need strengthening by the creation of independent agencies with enforcement powers. Torture and forced confessions should stop. Legal-literacy campaigns should clearly lay out the legal terrain of reports, complaints, charges, investigations, and court procedures so that all citizens can understand and access the system. Beyond that, streamlined legal steps may be in order, just as they have emerged for businesses seeking "one-stop shopping" for licenses and regulations.

Binational strategies are also important mechanisms for accountability. Activists, through high-visibility events, media attention, and symbols, should maintain pressure in both Mexico and the United States on their justice systems and their seriously flawed lack of professionalism with regard to the murders of girls and women in Ciudad Juárez. Both activists and policy makers should connect violence against women with public safety and public health policy actions and academic research. Civic coalitions should expand to include not only human rights activists, but also those interested in economic development, for the chaos and violence of the border region could deter stable investment.

Binational solutions should be funded with adequate resources to pursue several strategies. Resources for training, laboratory and DNA testing, and tip lines should be available to police departments and federal investigation agencies. *Maquiladora* managers should analyze workplace safety to include surrounding areas, security guards, and drivers, including those subcontracted. This would involve background checks and routine drug tests for drivers of company buses on which female victims ride. Managers should examine rigid schedules that have sent young workers to their deaths (as in the Lear Company case), as employees are forced to leave the factory if they arrive late rather than face paycheck deductions. *Maquiladora* managers could also fund workshops and self-defense classes for employees.

Public school curricula should integrate anti–domestic violence and anti–sexual violence themes for male and female students. Criminal hypermasculinity should be publicly criticized and no longer tolerated or celebrated as culturally acceptable. Institutional shrouds, with resources and enforcement capabilities, are essential for public security at borders. A strong human rights treaty for the North American region is essential.

Radical solutions include the legalization of drugs in both the United States and Mexico, funding for substance-abuse treatment facilities and education, and enforcement of money-laundering laws. The present policy benefits government employees who are employed under the guise of the U.S. War on Drugs. Substance-abuse facilities are limited and costly, especially in the border region. The availability of guns in the United States that find their way into Mexico needs to be curtailed by U.S. officials. The War on Drugs as it stands today benefits the drug dealers. Legalization would definitely put them out of business and minimize the violence.

## Notes

Authors' note: This chapter is an updated and revised version of "Binational Civic Action for Accountability: Anti-violence Organizing in Cd. Juárez–El Paso," in *Reforming the Administration of Justice in Mexico,* ed. Wayne A. Cornelius and David A. Shirk (South Bend, Ind.: University of Notre Dame Press, 2007), 349–368.

1. Diana Washington Valdez, "Death Stalks the Border," special insert, *El Paso Times* (2002), www.elpasotimes.com/borderdeath; Sergio González, *Huesos en el desierto* (Barcelona: Anagrama, 2002); Rohry Benítez et al., *El silencio que la voz de todas quiebra: Mujeres y víctimas de Ciudad Juárez* (Chihuahua: Ediciones del Azar, 1999); Kathleen Staudt and Irasema Coronado, *Fronteras No Más: Toward Social Justice at the U.S.-Mexico Border* (New York: Palgrave Macmillan, 2002), chap. 6; Marisela Ortiz, "Crímenes contra mujeres: Un desesperado grito de auxilio," *Chamizal* 2.1 (July–December 2002): 23–30. For full analysis that includes field research on domestic violence, see Kathleen Staudt, *Violence and Activism at the Border: Gender, Fear, and Everyday Life in Ciudad Juárez* (Austin: University of Texas Press, 2008).

2. Oscar J. Martínez, *Border Boom Town: Ciudad Juárez since 1848* (Austin: University of Texas Press, 1978).

3. Charles Bowden, *Down by the River: Drugs, Money, Murder and Family* (New York: Simon & Schuster, 2002). U.S. Department of Justice (USDOJ), 2004, congressional testimony, by Sandalio González, DEA special agent in charge, April 15, 2003. (Many similar articles are copied from annual reports and testimony and are found on www.usdoj.gov/dea).

4. Timothy Dunn, *The Militarization of the U.S.-Mexico Border, 1978–1992: Low-intensity Conflict Doctrine Comes Home* (Austin: University of Texas Press, 1996); selections in David Spener and Kathleen Staudt, eds., *The U.S.-Mexico Border: Transcending Divisions, Contesting Identities* (Boulder, Colo.: L. Rienner, 1998); Edward Williams and Irasema Coronado, "The Hardening of the United States–Mexico Borderlands: Causes and Consequences," *Boundary and Security Bulletin* 1.4 (1994).

5. Kent Paterson, "Deepening U.S.-Mexico Security Cooperation: As NAFTA's Anti-Narcotics Apparatus Focuses on Public Security, Human Rights Activists Grow Worried," *Borderlines* 9.11 (December 2001); http://americas.irc -online.org/borderlines/2001/bl84/index.html.

6. Cheryl Howard and Zulma Méndez, "Violence, Women and Work," Workshop EII, "Families and Their Insertion into Labor Markets," University of Texas–

Brownsville/Desarrollo Integral de la Familia, Matamoros, March 5–6, 1999, 48–51.

7. On serial killing in early-twentieth-century Mexico City, however, documenting homegrown varieties, see Pablo Piccato, "'El Chalequero' or the Mexican Jack the Ripper: The Meanings of Sexual Violence in Turn-of-the-century Mexico City," *Hispanic American Historical Review* 82 (2001): 623–651.

8. Human Rights Watch, *Systemic Injustice: Torture, "Disappearance," and Extrajudicial Execution in Mexico* (New York, 1999).

9. Alicia Gaspar de Alba, "The Maquiladora Murders 1993–2003," *Aztlán: A Journal of Chicano Studies* 28 (Fall): 1–17. See also www.casa-amiga.org/Statistics .htm; www.elpasotimes.com/borderdeath.

10. Staudt and Coronado, *Fronteras No Más*, chap. 6.

11. Field notes (FN) 2002–2004, Amigos de las Mujeres de Ciudad Juárez meeting with New Mexico legislators, U.S. consul, and Coalition against Violence, New Mexico State University, Las Cruces, 2003.

12. Ibid., FN 2002.

13. Ibid., FN 2004, Washington Office on Latin America (WOLA), www.wola .org February 25, 2004.

14. Amnesty International, "Intolerable Killings: Ten Years of Abductions and Murders of Women in Ciudad Juárez, Chihuahua" (2003), www.amnesty.org.

15. Alma Guillermoprieto, "Letter from Mexico: A Hundred Women: Why Has a Decade-long String of Murders Gone Unsolved?" *The New Yorker* (September 29, 2003): 82–93.

16. Diana Washington Valdez, "Ciudad Juárez: Así empezó todo," *La Jornada* (October 31, 2003); John Burnett, "On the Job: Chasing the Ghouls: The Juárez Serial Murders, and a Reporter Who Won't Let Go," *Columbia Journalism Review* 2 (March–April 2004), http://www.cjr.org/issues/2004/2/burnett-mexico.asp.

17. Summarized in Marcos Pablo Moloeznik, "The Challenges to Mexico in Times of Political Change," *Crime, Law & Social Change* 40 (2003): 7–20.

18. For reviews of other research in Mexico, see Marcos Pablo Moloeznik, "The Challenges to Mexico in Times of Political Change," *Crime, Law & Social Change* 40 (2003): 7–20; Marcelo Ciugale et al., *Mexico: A Comprehensive Agenda for the New Era* (Washington, DC: World Bank, 2001).

19. Peter Andreas, *Border Games: Policing the U.S.-Mexico Divide* (Ithaca, N.Y.: Cornell University Press, 2000), 62.

20. Transparency International, Corruption Perception Index, www.trans parency.org.

21. Andreas reports that 10 percent of the Federal Judicial Police were fired from 1992 to 1995; see *Border Games*, 64.

22. Http://www.nodo50.org/pchiapas/documentos/juarez2.html.

23. Laurel S. Weldon, *Protest, Policy and the Problem of Violence against Women* (Pittsburgh: University of Pittsburgh Press, 2002).

24. On national-level activism and response in Mexico, see Victoria Rodríguez, *Women in Contemporary Mexican Politics* (Austin: University of Texas Press, 2003), 170.

25. Staudt and Coronado, *Fronteras No Más*.

26. Http://www.georgetown.edu/odba/Constitutions/Mexico/mexico1917.html.

27. Washington Valdez, "Death Stalks the Border."

28. Staudt and Coronado, *Fronteras No Más*, 150–151.

29. FN 2003.

30. Guillermoprieto, "Letter from Mexico."

31. Ursula Biemann, "Performing the Border: On Gender, Transnational Bodies, and Technology," in *Globalization on the Line: Culture, Capital, and Citizenship at U.S. Borders*, ed. Claudia Sadowski-Smith (New York: Palgrave, 2002), 99–118. (Biemann also produced a film with the same title.)

32. However, between 2008 and 2009, under a different governor elected in 2006, and with the drug war, many more women were killed, but not with the "sexualized" profile. See Julia Monárrez-Fragoso, "Feminicidio sexual serial en Ciudad Juárez: 1993–2001," *Debate Feminista* 13 (April 2002). Monárrez-Fragoso also gave two lectures, at the El Paso Community Foundation in January 2002, and at the University of Texas at El Paso in April 2002, in which she showed charts of the homicide rate for females.

33. Alejandra Martínez-Márquez, "A Feminist Response to Changes in the Sexual Violence Law in the State of Chihuahua," unpublished.

34. Human Rights Watch, *Systemic Injustice: Torture, "Disappearance," and Extrajudicial Execution in Mexico* (New York: HRW, 1999): 46.

35. Pilar Domingo, "Rule of Law, Citizenship and Access to Justice in Mexico," *Mexican Studies/Estudios Mexicanos* 15.1 (1999): 151–191.

36. Mark Granovetter, "The Strength of Weak Ties," *American Journal of Sociology* 78.6 (1974): 1360–1380.

37. Amigos de las Mujeres de Juárez, 2004, www.amigosdemujeres.org.

38. FN 2002, 2003.

39. Ibid.

40. This section analyzes the chronology of growth of antifemicide movement organizing, which peaked in 2003–2004. *Vagina Monologues* is still performed annually but no longer focuses on femicide.

41. FN 2003.

42. Ongoing negotiations about other matters deterred his interest in the potentially awkward and embarrassing violence issue.

43. Kathleen Staudt, testimony before the Texas Legislature Border Committee, Austin, April 9, 2003.

44. Irasema Coronado was cochair of the coalition.

45. Marisela Ortiz, "Crímenes contra mujeres: Un desesperado grito de auxilio," *Chamizal* 2.1 (July–December 2002): 23–30.

46. Amnesty International, "Intolerable Killings."

47. Coalition against Violence toward Women and Families at the U.S.-Mexico Border, University of Texas at El Paso/Department of Political Science/Staudt and Coronado, 2003, field notes, Kathleen Staudt, UTEP.

48. Hilda Solís, "In Search of Justice," University of California at Berkeley *Center for Latin American Studies Newsletter* (Winter 2004): 3, 18–20.

49. Several dresses moved to the monthlong exhibit in the UTEP library commemorating Day of the Dead, October 2003.

50. "The Maquiladora Murders, Or, Who Is Killing the Women of Juárez?" Conference, University of California, Los Angeles, October 31–November 2, 2003, http://chavez.ucla.edu/maqui_murders.

51. FN 2003.

52. Alfredo Corchado and Ricardo Sandoval, "Juárez Slayings: Inquiry Indicates Police, Drug Ties. Disturbing Reports Say Women Were Tortured and Slain as Celebration," *Dallas Morning News,* reprinted in *STARS Voice* 2.1 (March 2004): 2–3.

53. Www.vday.org.

54. John Bailey and Jorge Chabat, eds., *Transnational Crime and Public Security: Challenges to Mexico and the United States.* (La Jolla: University of California at San Diego, Center for U.S.-Mexican Studies, 2002).

55. There is little investigation and prosecution in Mexico. Police are killed by cartel members and criminals, but sometimes they are employed by cartels.

56. Victoria Rodríguez, *Decentralization in Mexico: From Reforma Municipal to Solidaridad to Nuevo Federalismo* (Boulder, Colo.: Westview, 1997).

# CHAPTER 6

# The Suffering of the Other

JULIA E. MONÁRREZ-FRAGOSO
TRANSLATED BY GEORGINA GUZMÁN

*My subject: the discovery that self makes of the other.*
—TZVETAN TODOROV

The pervasiveness of femicide in Ciudad Juárez is a complex problem, and many groups of perpetrators are involved. As such, there are many manifestations of injustice to analyze. In this chapter, I want to examine the injustice through another, distinct, angle. I have chosen to reflect on how the *I* that does not suffer behaves before the *other* that suffers. The time frame I am analyzing includes the months of January, March, April, and July of 2004. The event is the recovery of fragments of historical memory from news reports regarding the victims' families' struggle for justice and how their demands were met with reprimands by the groups in power. The question I am posing is this: How does the hegemonic group of Juárez regard itself in the face of the victims' families' pain?

I recognize the particular influence that Tzvetan Todorov's *Abuses of Memory* and *Conquest of America: The Question of the Other* have had on my analysis; his story serves as a model for my own. My objective in this recovery of memory is not to lose the moral sense of the supposed acts of solidarity or of the pleas for justice which groups in power have made on behalf of victims' families.[1] Rather, I argue that we must be mindful that these groups are composed of men and women who occupy positions of privilege due to their gender and class status. To not recover this memory is to set aside critical and reflective consciousness—this applies to both those related to the victims and those who are not.

Devoid of this recovery, Ivone Gebara states, we avoid understanding the events' disillusionments, self-deceptions, betrayals, and ambiguities, and we are hindered from clear-headedly maturing into new forms of action from an ethical and feminist antiviolence politics. We must become aware of the errors, ailments, mistakes, complicities, and concrete violent acts which tangible men and women have performed in this violent state of affairs.[2] Only in this way "can we overcome the simplistic and dualistic standpoints that separate the guilty from the innocent."[3] Accordingly, each person will be able to assume the responsibility that corresponds to her or him.

From our feminist stance, we women need to be aware of all the agreements and understandings that exist between the perpetrating parties. Above all, we need to be aware of how political groups and groups in power have appropriated these events and how the interests for which we have struggled have been substituted or reversed in favor of others' interests or against our own. That is why I seek to assess the manner in which people in power evaluate subordinate groups and portray them through their particular class perspective, especially when these subordinate groups are afflicted with pain and injustice.

I believe that those who have felt excruciating pain in the flesh are the relatives of the women who have been murdered. Furthermore, components of the structure of violence combine within them: the voices that are not heard; the lack of money; the lack of power, which excludes them. In this sense, practices are adjusted and selected depending on the person's social position, and this gives her or him a certain social orientation or sense of place from which to articulate experience and produce classifiable acts, which are also acts of classification and which are themselves classified.[4]

I situate my analysis from this position and vis-à-vis the paradigms of patriarchal and capitalist hegemony, utilizing the Gramscian concepts of coercion and consensus. This perspective will shed light on the groups in power that approach the pain of the victims' families. The Gramscian concept of hegemony describes a double process wherein one social group's supremacy is obtained not only by physical force—what he calls domination and control—but also by the dominated people's consensual submission by way of the leadership or direction of people apparently unlinked to the state.[5]

Pierre Bourdieu argues that, even when domination is founded on the crudest of force, it always possesses a symbolic component. In symbolic violence, the acts of submission and obedience are present, and they are exerted by the support that the dominated cannot cease to grant to the dominant and the domination in general. The dominated does this because, when interacting with the dominator, she or he has no other way to do this but in the way that such interaction has been structured: this structure of power relations becomes an instrument for advancing hegemonic schemes that come to seem natural, such as the divisions between light skinned/dark skinned, rich/poor, knowledgeable/ignorant, male/female, victim/savior, good/bad, authentic/false, original/copy, orthodox/heretic, and so on. Such categorizations order and maintain social structures and perceptions, and they ultimately come to be defined by structures of inequitable capital.[6] Both groups perceive themselves within such categories: family members see themselves as the *excluded* group, as the *other;* hegemonic groups view themselves as the *distinguished* (the eminent), as the *I.* Both groups are divided into these social classes.

The comments made by privileged groups in 2004 richly display the social production around the murders and reveal the marked difference between distinct social classes. From these two indicators, I have been able to confirm how symbolic power constructs reality and how it establishes a set of beliefs that become legitimate knowledge. In the news stories that I analyze, we can discern three Marxist symbolic functions: (a) the dominant class group that affirms communication between its members and distinguishes them from other social classes; (b) the dominant class's feigned and conventional interpretation of the whole society; and (c) the legitimization of order established through hierarchies and distinctions and the endorsement of these distinctions through "titles of nobility" given to those who declare their worry, empathy, and feigned sorrow.[7]

This poses consequences for the attainment of justice, for socially dominant bodies stubbornly produce generalized value judgments. At the same time, dominant culture serves to establish subtle differences in the perception of otherness and confers on social agents a certainty in the "we," which serves as a lens through which to interpret reality and impede the victims' and their families' access to justice.[8]

## The Other

The relatives of the victims of femicide in Ciudad Juárez have not remained silent, forgone movement organizing, or remained devoid of justice-seeking action.[9] But the final solution to the extermination of the female gender and identity is finding an explanation for the irrational violence of those who committed these acts.[10] Such a process forces these family members to risk seeking justice equality in a country where justice is a pipe dream for the majority of subaltern citizens. They lack the economic means and the understanding of social staging—that is, how social agents mobilize to "support" their calls for justice and how they incorporate themselves into the field of violence due to their greater experience with the public sphere.[11] Nevertheless, both groups' actions are products of human relations based on a class-based, gender-discriminating society.

Victims' families entered the public sphere and boldly called for justice for their daughters, sisters, and wives. Their words, which are "an attempt to restore justice in a societal structure of violence,"[12] frequently become contaminated or lost within the ideology of symbolic violence that their representatives, or "guardians of the law," generate. This is due to the fact that there is a fragmentation among the groups,[13] and without a unanimous or homogeneous response on behalf of family members and the different groups that have formed, relatives' differing expressions have been documented and presented as "the voice of the victims' family members" and nothing but. There is no single voice—there are multiple voices, which, when they are heard as such, make evident to those who hear them, that, if "practice and commitment are not well-founded, they risk being completely unintelligible and spurned,"[14] whether or not the listeners are in favor of their pleas for justice, human rights, and respect for life.

### Pain and Grief

The suffering of the victims' families, or the pain of the *other*, is transformed into grief by the distinguished, by the *I*. Borrowing from Ivone Gebara, I define this *painfulness* as the use and abuse of the family members' accumulated sorrow, anguish, suffering, and grief. Different *I*'s use these wrongs and injuries in a dramatized and collective manner with the objective of generating pity for, and ruining the reputations of, those found in the sphere of violence. This process, without remedying or vindicating their experience as victims, represents the victims as distorted figures, twisted and lacking logical reasoning beyond that of seeking to create a collective nuisance. As Gebara indicates, this process "maintains consciences in ignorance, dominated by the impossibility of changing such oppressive and unjust conditions."[15]

But this somber form of denunciation arises from a privilege that remains hidden and unnoticed, and which in itself constitutes an abuse of power exercised in the sphere of social institutions. Pain (suffered by the victims' families) functions as cultural capital for the institution. This pain obtains value as symbolic capital because the social and economic conditions that have produced it remain unexamined. This pain becomes a "source of material and symbolic benefits and instruments of domination and legitimization"

**Fig. 6.1.** Rigo Maldonado © 2002, "Crucifix of Nails, Downtown Bridge, Juárez." Courtesy of Rigo Maldonado.

that can be wielded in the interests of power by hegemonic entities against justice-seeking groups.[16]

## The I

The *I* that sees the suffering of the *other* (*la otra*) and consciously or unconsciously makes use of this suffering burst onto the scene in January 2004 in the offices of the Instituto Chihuahuense de la Mujer (Chihuahua Women's Institute), in a symposium organized by then-director Victoria Caraveo Vallina. Also in attendance were the state's attorney general, José Jesús Solís Silva (2001–2004); the governor's representative, Patricio Martínez; Álvaro Navarro Gárate; and thirty-two of the victims' mothers.[17] The mothers' petitions focused on "asking judicial representatives to force nongovernmental organizations (NGOs) to stop profiting from their daughters' deaths."[18] Rosario Montañés, a victim's mother, demanded, "I want this woman, Esther Chávez Cano, to listen to me. I ask her, are you a mother? How many children do you have? What do you know of the pain of losing a child? Because I do feel pain for my daughter." She also denounced a group of Chihuahua activists—Las Mujeres de Negro (Women in Black)—whom she asked, "With what morality do you go to the streets protesting the homicides when you have not been able to understand the pain that mothers feel at these losses?"[19] The course of action was clear: to categorically exclude and invalidate the voices of those women organizers and protesters who took their grievances before an international forum. In this discourse, the mothers wielded their maternity as a symbol of power and accreditation: if one is not a mother, one cannot feel how a mother feels.

Melissa W. Wright comments that Las Mujeres de Negro from Chihuahua City are nationally and internationally known for wearing large black cloaks and pink hats. They take to the streets to question the government about the impunity granted perpetrators of violence against women in Ciudad Juárez and Chihuahua City. This particular group has been the object of attacks by the government, which blames them for, among other things, Chihuahua's social decay and hence the violence against women. What is paradoxical is that Las Mujeres de Negro have responded to these indictments by emphasizing and justifying their status as family women who go out in search of social justice for victims whose status is that of "daughters."[20] Therefore, both groups, in the role of mothers or daughters, seek justice for the victims.

In the symposium with Attorney General Solís Silva, another mother,

Santos Macías García, said, "They hit her where it hurt the most when they killed her eldest daughter, and that is why she didn't hesitate to reveal her hatred, not only against those who gave her death, but also against those who try to take advantage of it."[21] These mothers' hostile conduct and spiteful denunciations arise from the privilege that remains hidden, ignored, and that in of itself contains an abuse of power produced in the institutional sphere. Others' pain and grief has functioned as cultural capital that has been manipulated by those who need to provide justice and by those who represent the politics of human rights for Chihuahua's women. In this way, legitimate pain has been transformed into the *painfulness* experienced by victims' families, and it has acquired a symbolic capital value that has come to be used by hegemonic groups against civil organizations that have protested against violence. But it also has grave implications for the mothers' struggle for truth and justice, since, as is the case for the mothers in Argentina, they "seem unable to recognize that they themselves have established a repressive system with their discourse in which virtually all other parties, except for the Mothers, are dismissed because of their inattention to or inaction in terms of the disappeared. The Mothers' discourse in essence denies the other, much as Argentina has denied the existence of the disappeared."[22] In refusing to acknowledge the activism of the women of these nongovernmental gender violence–fighting organizations, the mothers of Juárez's femicide victims resemble the Chihuahuan government, which denies the murder of their loved ones and their pursuit for justice.

And these disjointed family members' voices meet divergent voices that do not share their beliefs or desires; they do, however, converge with the voices of those who claim to represent them: those who are obligated to provide them access to justice. In this way, the family members' pain serves as an indispensable element that is (un)consciously used to reinforce the power of those who already possess it—the power to manipulate the family members' lives for the benefit of a minority that certainly has very concrete class interests: maintaining the image of a border city that sustains itself through economic progress. For these authorities, the mention of femicide is uninvited, for to mention it is also to shed light on the impoverished conditions in which the majority of these women lived and the impunity granted those involved in gender-based violence.

The family members' discourses on pain also served as the basis for Astrid González, from "Juárez contra el crimen," to insist and declare to the press that there was a need to separate the victims' family members and civic organizations (such as NGOs). González reprimanded some NGOs for "the great burden they carry: the shadowy and unclear way in which they run their organizations."[23] At the same time, she cited the example of Casa Amiga and argued that "their representatives must be aware that they and other associations must collaborate in regard to their resource management and the comings and goings of their groups and their treasurers."[24]

In her declarations, González stressed that the crimes against women had become a business and that it was "perverse that some should profit from the permanent pain of mothers who hope for justice, some of whom have been waiting for it eleven years, but it hasn't arrived."[25] And to underscore her arguments, she commented that she had witnessed the situation up close, citing firsthand testimonials from mothers who were upset at the exploitation of their daughters' names. She read a letter that Irma García, the mother of victim Elizabeth Castro, had sent her. A fragment of the letter, which addresses the organizations, states the following: "To the rest of the groups that are profiting from the death of our daughters, I would like to ask for a bit of respect for them. To take pieces of human flesh out onto the street seems to me like utter disrespect. What they have done with all this is a big political revelry and from which they have benefited from our pain. To whomever this letter reaches, please help us truly defend our daughters."[26]

Neither Astrid nor the newspaper mentioned the date on which this letter was received. This lack of information worked wonders for the purpose of breaking up NGOs and revalidating the mothers' and the legitimate representative's grief (*dolorismo*), and she articulated her "genuine demands for justice" alongside the hegemonic groups' demands for (in)justice.

These hegemonic groups' voices surfaced in the same newspaper story.[27] They alleged that the increased magnification of the crimes stigmatized the city and therefore caused its population social and economic damage. Ricardo Soto Carrillo, president of the Ciudad Juárez Asociación de Hoteles y Moteles (Association of Hotels and Motels), affirmed: "In 1997, there was a 75 percent room occupancy rate. Now, it is 50 percent because of the city's deteriorated image and the lack of will to resolve the problem."[28] The reality was, Servando Pineda argued, that in 2003 and 2004, three new hotels were constructed by major hotel chains in the city.[29] Héctor Lozoya, vice president of the National Chamber of Commerce's specialized sections, declared that "one cannot but sense that there is a problem, yet it is one of bad taste, and too much profit has been derived from the pain that we all feel."[30] What Héctor Lozoya really revealed was that the *others* exhibited bad taste, above all, in the threat that they posed to his good taste, which emerged from a distant social space that was secure in its particular sphere—good taste that was associated with a particular class and that ensured him the continuity of his individual and economic existence.

For these reasons, when some people justify themselves, they do it "in an entirely negative manner, by means of the rejection of other tastes."[31] I quote Astrid González once more: "The greatest impact has been the economic one, and unfortunately, the incomes most affected have been those of the working class and the neediest of people."[32] It is worth recalling that a great majority of the women murdered were poor working women.

But hegemonic groups can rest easy knowing the following: Ciudad Juárez attracted 53.9 percent of Mexico's national and foreign investment in 2004, and Applebee's restaurant chain and Cementos Azteca announced total investments of two million dollars in the region.[33] Investments come and go in a world of unequal economic development. What is certain is that they will always come as long as salaries do not buck the 1990–2004 trend—during these fourteen years, salaries rose from $11.90 to $45.24 Mexican pesos for a day's work.[34]

Óscar Legorreta Ito, then-president of the Cámara Nacional de la Industria de la Transformación (National Chamber of Transformational Industry)'s Ciudad Juárez delegation, demonstrated his voluntary complicity in his own words: "Some associations have exaggerated the problem to such a degree that they have greatly hurt the same community."[35] What we can gather from Mr. Legorreta's statements is that the number of women murdered is not important since they were not part of the community; therefore, the community should not pay heed to the suffering of the victims' families or the NGOs' calls for justice.

Salvador Urbina Quiroz, vice president of the Barra y Colegio de Abogados (State Bar and Law School), underscored his concern that, even though the femicides had been the lucrative subjects of documentaries and had been covered by large international communications companies, the victims' families had not received any of that money. In his view, "with the massive sums of money and volunteer time that has been donated, the victims' families should have had at least 100 houses constructed and their children should have college trust funds in the bank."[36]

Nonetheless, there are always discrepancies, and notwithstanding the withholding of justice, there remain worrisome omissions which must be explored. The local Partido Acción Nacional (National Action Party, PAN) representative, Pedro Martínez Cháirez, stated, "Yes, some NGOs have greatly hurt Juárez, but I believe that the victims' families have the right to denounce the impunity [granted the alleged perpetrators] and denounce how they have not been rightfully assisted." He then reminded the people that the Comisión de Diputados Locales para el Seguimiento de los Homicidios de Mujeres (Commission of Local Representatives for the Investigation of Homicide of Women), which he had been part of, "*has been a failure,*

*since more than a year after its formation, we have neither met with the victims'*
*family members nor met with the state's attorney to pursue any investigations"*
(emphasis mine).[37] First, his words present the image of a Ciudad Juárez
ravaged by perverse NGOs. Second, they exhibit the commission's failure
to treat the victims' family members properly, according to the established
rules that national and international human rights groups had given the
Mexican government and, especially, the government of Chihuahua.[38] In
this way, the federal and the state governments' granting of impunity was
ultimately thrust into the spotlight, and these hegemonic groups displayed
a marked fissure.

However, in April 2004, the song "Las Mujeres de Juárez," by Los Tigres
del Norte, debuted before the metaphoric stage of grief sanctioned by both
hegemonic groups and victims' family members.[39] This watershed event
opened a renewed public discussion concerning the city's image and the anguish of the victims' mothers. State representative and president of the state
Legislature, Víctor Valencia de los Santos, stated that "the Legislature will
present an energetic protest before these corresponding instances because
not only are they once again attempting to mar Ciudad Juárez's image, but
they are shamelessly profiting from this to the detriment of the victims'
families."[40] The representative's statement reveals the belief that the city's
image was of utmost importance whereas victims' families were secondary.
By bringing up the city's image first, public officers lost all sense of compassion, solidarity, and justice for the suffering other. Above all, Valencia's
statement demonstrates the legislative powers' feigned pain.

Thus, we can see that these networks of social and economic relations
occur in the face of global capital–related concerns and that these unions do
not require that reciprocity, equality, or a sense of community exist among
those who have less capital.[41] Above all, these social relations must be recognized in the different, disparately powerful hegemonic groups that join
in this crusade against violence—they may appear to support the victims'
families, but they do not, for what they defend are their political and economic interests.

When the national television network TV Azteca aired a series that
made the murder of Juárez women into a two-week drama titled *Tan In-*
*finito Como el Desierto* (As Infinite as the Desert),[42] the victims' families'
pain was once again at the forefront of new (un)concerned efforts by Salvador Nassri Chávez, president of the Ciudad Juárez Barra y Colegio de
Abogados. Nassri said that his association "could provide free legal advice
to victims' mothers through the social services program if they solicit it
from them [and that] both the city and the state government must support

these women in their legal battle against TV Azteca's transmission of the *telenovela Tan Infinito Como el Desierto*—a *telenovela* that uses the names of people and companies to harm their daughters' memory."[43]

What would be interesting to know is why this same association did not offer family members free services in their demand for justice and explanations for the murders of their daughters, mothers, wives, and sisters, or why the association did not demand the city and state government's support to offer free legal services. According to these hegemonic groups, the violence and suffering that the families experienced justified and perpetuated their suffering; it was the media that made them suffer rather than a lack of political will and an outdated justice system that was failing to provide justice for those who demanded it.

Victoria Caraveo expounded that the aforementioned television series represented a "serious problem, since much of the populace that watches it believes that it is a documentary that deals with the real problems of Ciudad Juárez, and that is not the case." Furthermore, she argued, "with this treatment of the information, some of the authorities' investigational lines might be cut off."[44] With this declaration, the director of the Instituto Chihuahuense de la Mujer echoed and endorsed the authorities' decade-long excuse: that they could not provide information or solve the cases of murdered women because lines of investigation could be lost or contaminated. At the same time, she also crushed any image of the city as opposing the eradication of violence against Juárez's women.

The discourses that hegemonic groups put forward in the field of violence served to oppress the victims' families, although within this field there was relative autonomy for the *other*. Norma Andrade, of Nuestras Hijas de Regreso a Casa, stated that her organization had to analyze what should be done in regard to the television series. Paula Flores, of Fundación Sagrario, spoke out against the corporate sectors' requests to take *Tan Infinito Como el Desierto* off the air. And regarding Los Tigres del Norte's song, Ramona Morales, mother of a victim, expressed this: "No one looked for my daughter, and what was worse is that they said she had been murdered because she was a prostitute. I will never be able to forget that. All of my family recognizes that this song must be advertised and made known."[45]

The declarations of these victims' relatives' are the genealogy that enables the articulation of the experience and knowledge of suffering and the disillusionment caused by the rampant impunity granted the alleged perpetrators. In this case, it is *erudite* knowledge that sanctioned the legitimacy of a *historical* knowledge of their struggles and their demands so that they would not be utilized and manipulated by hegemonic groups' tactics.[46] These

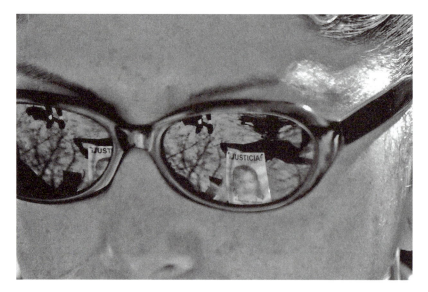

**Fig. 6.2.** J Guadalupe Pérez © 2007, "Mujer durante una Protesta en las Instalaciones de la Subprocuraduría de Justicia del Estado, 2007" (Woman during a Protest at the Headquarters of the Assistant District Attorney). Courtesy of J Guadalupe Pérez.

groups pretended to employ these tactics in the name of their supposed concern for justice, yet their true concern was misaligning the others' demands. At the same time, the symbolic violence that was committed against the victims' family members sought to discredit the victims and render them invisible. Also, according to Juan Carlos Segura, "it seeks to construct silent, subordinate identities [and it] establishes the victims' defenselessness. We are not witnessing a battle between two equal groups where the combat results in the massacre of the losing contender. The losing party is completely stripped of any characterization of collective identity; their identity has been 'erased.' The winning party remembers its victory and the grotesque image of its enemy's decomposition, which is the image of its strength. From one side, identity emerges reinforced. From the other, identity simply does not emerge."[47]

Nevertheless, we must always remember the suffering that, because of victims' families' alliances with groups that do not agree with them, becomes part of the bodies and minds of the victims' families and that becomes an ideology of subjection rather than one of liberation or relief. With victims' family members having entered such direct or indirect alliances with hegemonic groups and their representatives that pretend to represent their interests, I believe that a docile group, a disciplined group of victims' family members can be formed.

Under these circumstances, I argue that "the subaltern does not need a defender or a representative to speak for her and does not need special regulations to protect her."[48] She only needs for the justice system to fulfill its responsibilities and for her demands for justice or her (re)cognition of illegalities in respect to her daughter or sister not to be enshrouded in an obscure film of *submitted* knowledges, or to be classified by the authorities and other hegemonic groups as reckless, hierarchically inferior, and lacking "scientific knowledge."[49] These family members' experiences have been transformed into an immoral, degenerate, guilty, and corrupt knowledge—the knowledge of the worthless *other*—because it is the knowledge of the excluded women, of the *other*. But this knowledge is the knowledge of the people, which is, above all, a *particular* knowledge. It is a knowledge which remains and "owes its strength to the dividing line that opposes all those who surround it"[50] on this prolonged and indeterminate path that the people have advanced by seeking justice, honor, dignity, and a sense of life for those who are no longer with them and for themselves.

## Final Reflections

Activism, political consciousness, and the enjoyment of justice have to do with money, health, education, and privileged social relations; all these components form part of the symbolic capital which victims' families lack. Nevertheless, in entering this 'theater of grief,' these citizens run the risk of having their demands for social justice submerged beneath the demand for maintaining the city's pristine image. The city's hidden objective can serve to distance these families from the women's organizations that have battled against femicide—organizations that have sought to place more responsibility on society for the murder of women and that have contested the way that these women have been portrayed as immigrants with dubious backgrounds and as workers who bring the process of industrialization to a halt. Claiming that the murdered women tarnish the border environment also seeks to divert attention from the suffering that the structure of violence inflicts on its citizenry. Therefore, those who oppose the attainment of truth and of justice react to the perceived disgrace of their border city, whose pride has been hurt.

Because their existence disparages and discredits the city's culture of work, these murdered women and their families are presented by hegemonic groups as the city's prime enemies. It is the murdered women's and girls' fault that the poor are becoming poorer, because the former are the cause of decreased investments in their city.

This perception explains the violence that the dominant class has sponsored and financed. The state and other hegemonic groups have utilized all the power that they have at their disposal to coerce family members with the objective of making them accept the "access to (in)justice" that they themselves have afforded them. These groups have tried to mine the families' resistance and at the same time obstruct their claims to justice through socially organized groups with all the weight of domination that they have had.

Jointly, they have also utilized consensus. This phase in the same hegemonic process is more dangerous and difficult to attain; it presupposes the dissident group's subjugation through the subtle dissemination of the interests of the groups in power. This consensus emerges through family members or through the women themselves, through the mediation of the groups in power via their "moral and intellectual leadership." The latter exhibit so much concern for the families' physical, mental, and moral health and the economic pressures on them that the families' demands for justice appear to be lost or are lost. Consequently, their interests are alienated and their demands are presented in a seemingly narrow-minded, or obtuse manner. But their demands are organized and included in the dominant groups' demands, interests, and influences, and they become the same demand: the memory of the lie—the immoral closeness with which the I approaches the other's suffering.

## Notes

Author's note: I would like to thank María Socorro Tabuenca Córdoba and two anonymous readers for their comments regarding this chapter. This chapter was previously published in Spanish in Julia E. Monárrez-Fragoso and María Socorro Tabuenca Córdoba, eds., *Bordeando la violencia contra las mujeres en la frontera norte de México* (Mexico City: El Colegio de la Frontera Norte and Miguel Ángel Porrúa Editores, 2007), 115–137. It was translated from the Spanish and edited by Georgina Guzmán.

1. By recovery of memory, I am referring to the knowledge of the events and the causes that lead us to the truth and ethics of justice instead of to the use and abuse of the memory scars of those who suffer. See Tzvetan Todorov, *Los abusos de la memoria* (Barcelona: Paidós, 2000). Moral sense has to do with the actions that open fissures among a responsible citizenry: not doing for strangers what one would

do for oneself or those closest to one; liberating oneself from implied risks when one is involved in the search for truth and justice; not recognizing others' affliction after they have suffered an atrocity; closing one's eyes to sexual discrimination and the state's political terrorism against women; see Tzvetan Todorov, *Frente al límite,* trans. Federico Álvarez (Mexico City: Siglo XXI, 1993), 311; and idem, *La conquista de América: El problema del otro* (Mexico City: Siglo XXI, 2005).

2. Ivone Gebara, *El rostro oculto del mal: Una teología desde la experiencia de las mujeres* (Madrid: Editorial Trotta, 2002), 33–35.

3. Ibid., 36

4. Pierre Bourdieu, *La distinción,* trans. María del Carmen Ruiz de Elvira (Mexico City: Taurus, 2002), 477–478.

5. Douglas Litowitz, "Gramsci, Hegemony, and the Law," *Brigham Young University Law Review* 2(2000): 515–551.

6. Pierre Bourdieu, *Meditaciones pascalianas,* trans. Thomas Kauf (Barcelona: Anagrama/Colección Argumentos, 1999), 224, 227, 287.

7. Néstor García Canclini, "Introducción," in *Sociología y cultura,* by Pierre Bourdieu, trans. Martha Pou (Mexico City: Editorial Grijalbo, 1990), 38–39.

8. Rossana Reguillo, "The Social Construction of Fear: Urban Narratives and Practices," in *Citizens of Fear: Urban Violence in Latin America,* ed. Susana Rotker (New Brunswick, N.J.: Rutgers University Press, 2002), 187–206.

9. I use "el otro/la otra" without making a gender differentiation, since the victims' families are mostly women.

10. Elena Azaola, "La sinrazón de la violencia: Homenaje a las mujeres muertas en Ciudad Juárez," in *Violencia contra las mujeres en México,* ed. Marta Torres Falcón (Mexico City: El Colegio de México, 2004), 71–82.

11. The field of violence is a concept developed by Pierre Bourdieu. The concept mediates the comparison between structure and superstructure, between the individual and the social. The field of violence as social organizer takes into account class structures, class struggle for the appropriation of a common capital (whether it be experiences, sets of knowledge, beliefs, interests, or ideals about something, be it artistic, scientific, or religious, among other things). In this specific case, the suffering of victims' families is a common capital in the field of violence. The field is constituted by two elements: the existence of a common capital; and the struggle for its appropriation. In this sense, two positions are formed: those who have the capital, and those who aspire to possess it. Those who form part of the field of violence manage interests, language, and common causes in that struggle, within which are found positions that establish power or authority in the field of violence on behalf of the different groups that are part of the dispute (García Canclini, "Introducción," 17–19). These groups are also defined by their exclusion or distinction in the field's structure, depending on the distribution of their social positions (Bourdieu, *Meditaciones pascalianas,* 178). The field exists insomuch as it is not able to comprehend the capital or what is banned in the production of that same capital. But it can become an apparatus in the sense that the dominants annul the dominated's resistance (García Canclini, "Introducción," 45).

12. Gebara, *El rostro oculto,* 25.

13. The many different family member groups that have formed throughout the more than ten years of extermination of vulnerable women are Voces sin Eco (Voices

without an Echo), Nuestras Hijas de Regreso a Casa (May Our Daughters Return Home), Integración de Madres por Juárez (Mothers United for Juárez), Madres en Busca de Justicia (Mothers in Search of Justice), and Fundación Sagrario.

14. Gebara, *El rostro oculto*, 10.

15. Ibid., 156. I have defined the groups in power's form of presenting the victims as "the stage of the lacrimal tear."

16. Ibid., 106.

17. Ramón Chaparro, "Se reunen autoridades con madres de víctimas," *El Diario*, Ciudad Juárez, January 22, 2004.

18. Ibid.

19. Ibid.

20. Melissa W. Wright, "El lucro, la democracia, y la mujer pública: Estableciendo las conexiones," in *Bordeando la violencia contra las mujeres en la frontera norte de México*, ed. Julia E. Monárrez-Fragoso and María Socorro Tabuenca Córdoba (Mexico City: El Colegio de la Frontera Norte and Miguel Ángel Porrúa Editores, 2007), 4.

21. Chaparro, "Se reunen autoridades."

22. Karen A. Foss and Kathy L. Domenici, "Haunting Argentina: Synecdoche in the Protests of the Mothers of the Plaza de Mayo," *Quarterly Journal of Speech* 87.3 (August 2001): 237–258; http://proquest.umi.com/pqdweb?TS.

23. Astrid González, Juárez contra el crimen.

24. R. Ramos, M. Orquiz, and A. Mena, "Exigen regular grupos civiles," *El Diario*, Ciudad Juárez, April 21, 2004.

25. Ibid.

26. Ibid.

27. Ibid.

28. M. Orquiz, J. M. Cruz, and A. Mena, "Basta de denigrar a Juárez: Sectores," *El Diario*, Ciudad Juárez, March 22, 2004.

29. Ibid.

30. Servando Pineda, "Los mitos de las muertas de Ciudad Juárez," www.nortedeciudadjuarez.com, July 29, 2004.

31. Orquiz, Cruz, and Mena, "Basta de denigrar a Juárez."

32. Ibid.

33. Orquiz, Cruz, and Mena, "Basta de denigrar a Juárez."

34. Pineda, "Los mitos."

35. Ibid.

36. Orquiz, Cruz, and Mena, "Basta de denigrar a Juárez."

37. Ibid.

38. See Amnesty International, Mexico, *Muertes intolerables: 10 años de desapariciones y asesinatos de mujeres en Ciudad Juárez y Chihuahua* (London: Peter Benenson House, August 2003); Comisión Interamericana de Derechos Humanos, *Situación de los derechos humanos de las mujeres en Ciudad Juárez, México: El derecho a no ser objeto de violencia y discriminación*, http://www.cidh.org/annualrep/2002sp/cap.vi.juarez.htm; Comisión Nacional de los Derechos Humanos, *Recomendación no. 44/98: Caso de las mujeres asesinadas en Ciudad Juárez y sobre la falta de colaboración de las autoridades de la Procuraduría General de Justicia del Estado de Chihuahua*, May 15, 1998, http://www.cndh.org.mx/; idem, *Informe especial de la Comisión Nacional de*

*Derechos Humanos sobre los casos de homicidios y desapariciones de mujeres en el municipio de Juárez, Chihuahua,* November 28, 2003, http://www.cndh.org.mx/; Naciones Unidas, *Diagnóstico sobre la situación de los derechos humanos en México* (Mexico City: Oficina del Alto Comisionado de las Naciones Unidas para los Derechos Humanos en México, 2003); idem, *Informe de la Comisión de Expertos Internacionales de la Organización de las Naciones Unidas, Oficina de las Naciones Unidas contra la Droga y el Delito, sobre la misión en Ciudad Juárez, Chihuahua, México,* (Mexico City: Oficina de las Naciones Unidas contra la Droga y el Delito, November 2003), http://www.comisioncdjuarez.gob.mx/Portal/PtMain.php?&nIdPanel=38&nIdFooter=40.

39. "Las Mujeres de Juárez" is a *corrido* that narrates the impunity granted to the alleged perpetrators of these murders and the Mexican government's inefficiency and inability to stop violence against women.

40. SUN, "Protestarán por corrido de feminicidios," *Diario Digital,* Ciudad Juárez, April 19, 2004.

41. Caren Kaplan and Inderpal Grewal, "Transnational Feminist Cultural Studies: Beyond the Marxism/Postructuralism/Feminism Divides," in *Between Woman and Nation,* ed. Caren Kaplan, Norma Alarcón, and Minoo Moallem (Durham, N.C.: Duke University Press, 1999), 349–363.

42. *Tan Infinito como el Desierto* is a ten-episode miniseries of thirty-minute episodes. It was aired throughout Mexico in July 2004. The *telenovela* (soap opera) narrates the hypotheses that emerged at the time surrounding possible culprits and why they murdered the city's young women; see http://www.tvazteca.com/telenovelas/infinito/.

43. Ramón Chaparro, "TV serie: Procede denuncia por varios delitos," *El Diario,* Ciudad Juárez, July 11, 2004.

44. Ramón Chaparro, "Piden a TV Azteca no denigrar a Juárez," *El Diario,* Ciudad Juárez, July 8, 2004.

45. Rosa Isela Pérez. "Se suman madres contra TV Azteca." *Norte de Juárez* (1/8/04), 1–3.

46. Michel Foucault, *Defender la sociedad,* trans. Horacio Pons (Mexico City: Fondo de Cultura Económica, 2002).

47. Juan Carlos Segura, "Reflexión sobre la masacre," in *Poder y cultura de la violencia,* comp. Devalle Susana B.C. (Mexico City: El Colegio de México, 2000), 35–117, quotation on 52.

48. Donncha Kavanagh, Majella O'Leary, and Diarmuid Giolláin, *Stories of the Subaltern,* Paper no. 02/10 (2002), 7.

49. Foucault, *Defender la sociedad,* 20–21.

50. Ibid., 21.

# CHAPTER 7

# The V-Day March in Mexico: Appropriation and Misuse of Local Women's Activism

CLARA E. ROJAS

The V-Day march, presumably a protest against the murder of over three hundred young women between 1993 and 2003, was not only a belated response to gender violence on the border, it was also, I shall argue, an appropriation and misuse of local women's activism by local hegemonic groups. Before explaining this position, however, I provide historical background.

For a decade (1993–2003), over three hundred young women (ages 12–19) from low-income backgrounds were tortured and murdered in the Mexican border city of Juárez.[1] The discovery of the murders launched a long and apparently unfruitful antagonistic process between local women activists and the authorities.[2] In 1994, faced with the official dismissal of and silence surrounding the events, the victims' families and a group of women activists began to confront the local and state authorities to demand information. In return, those in charge of the investigation hid information, blamed the victims, and, overall, tried to minimize both the events and the women's petitions.

This process of dismissal and silencing was perpetuated mainly through a demeaning process of stereotyping. For instance, the victims and their families were publicly (re)victimized by the authorities through a typical patriarchal discourse which openly blamed the victims for their "licentious" way of life. This process was reinforced and re-created by local media and other local hegemonic groups (for example, representatives of the Catholic Church).[3]

After years of marches, protests, forums, conferences, as well as national and international exposure, finally, in February 1998, the state judicial authorities offered a document which compiled their information on the murders. The files showed a pattern of uninterest, lack of effort, and/or inability to identify the victims, to classify and analyze evidence, or to conduct fo-

**Fig. 7.1.** Rigo Maldonado © 2004, "2004 V-Day March with Eve Ensler and Esther Chávez Cano." Courtesy of Rigo Maldonado.

rensic tests.[4] The deplorable state of the investigations was evidence that the authorities had no intention of trying to find the murderer(s). The evident official negligence represented in the files disclosed one of the most violent and haunting (his)tories of social injustice against girls and women.

Thus, in 2003, in Ciudad Juárez, Mexico, "reality" showed its face. The material consequences of the patriarchal discourse, articulated with race, class, and regional discriminatory beliefs and practices—pervasive throughout Mexican society—were imprinted on the murdered bodies of hundreds of low-income young women. The murders exposed and reconfirmed a long history of impunity granted and social injustice practiced by a corrupt judicial system and routinely reinforced by a misogynist environment sustained by multiple social actors—female and male—in this border community. In this apparently paralyzing scenario, since 2003, diverse local women activists, as direct participants in an extremely stressful, contradictory, and tragically ongoing story, have resisted, negotiated, and contested patriarchy.

## (Re)articulating Despair: The V-Day March

A comprehensive analysis of local women's activism during this (in)famous social protest calls for multiple ways of knowing and understanding, yet this struggle has established a paralyzing scenario of despair and skepticism among local activists. It is necessary to point out that national and international recognition and support came almost seven years after this struggle had begun; by then, political and social positions among local actors had been contested, rearticulated, and, in the process, many had been erased or in effect been dismissed. For example, when the call for the V-Day march was received, questions circulated in private conversations: What for? Isn't it too late? Why not last year, when three more victims were found? Why not seven years ago, when we were struggling to prevent more murders? Why after hundreds of victims? Who's benefiting from this march? Fair or unfair, this is how the majority of the local activists felt and how they structured their feelings. The spirit has its reasons.

Thus, from my geopolitical position as a Juarense/Fronteriza feminist rhetorician and member of the local "illuminated" middle class,[5] I offer an insider's report of what the V-Day march meant for local women's activism. Having been part of the emotions and feelings of many local activists,[6] I focus on what Raymond Williams describes as the "structure of feeling": "a process of consciousness between the articulated and the lived . . . For all that is not fully articulated, all that comes through as a disturbance, tension, blockage, emotional trouble, seems to me precisely a major source of major changes in the relation between the signifier and the signified."[7] This structure of feeling—the feelings, emotions, and hurt of local activists—has influenced our private and public reaction to any agonistic demonstrations, including the V-Day march.[8] This structure is important because it has affected, for better or worse, the way we, as local activists and scholars, participate now, or not, in the public or political sphere. This emotional state is either not readily visible to outsiders, or it is often dismissed as being too emotional, or it is attacked for being too skeptical and dismissive.

I should first explain that several weeks before the event took place, the march had already been co-opted by local nongovernmental groups, at that time (re)positioning themselves vis-à-vis the state government. These groups, sadly, many of them represented by women, have never supported the local women's struggles. On the contrary, many of them that side with the local elite have made statements to local media claiming that the issue of the "dead" (local and national euphemism for "murdered") women is hurting the city's "image." If we take a closer look at the language used by local organizers, paraphrasing the call to the march, it read: "Los invitamos a participar en el 'Día por la Paz y contra la Violencia,' que se ha denominado V-Day" (We invite you to participate in the Day for Peace and Nonviolence, which has been called V-Day).[9] Accordingly, these groups openly appropriated and misused Eve Ensler's V-Day event in Juárez by erasing the main objective of a global movement destined to stop violence against women and girls. Seemingly, this was not the goal in Ciudad Juárez. Why, for example, did Eve Ensler and her collaborators not insist on the main objective of the march by not permitting the euphemistic naming of V-Day as a "day of peace and against violence"? Such a disclaimer would have been a real political stance on their part. It was their call, but it did not happen, not in Ciudad Juárez.

This process of appropriation was also exposed, although in other terms, by Marisela Ortiz and Norma Andrade, cofounders of a local NGO, Nuestras Hijas de Regreso a Casa (May Our Daughters Return Home), which is currently working with several of the victims' families.[10] A few days before, they sent an e-mail message to Eve Ensler that read:

> As we have been the object of manipulations and accusations by the local V-Day Committee, we, as mothers, relatives and close friends of young women victims of kidnappings and murders, would like to convey to you that we have been forced to reduce or limit our 14th February program to:
>
>> a mourning Mass for the anniversary of the vanishing of Lilia Alejandra García Andrade, and to the performance of the play "Women of Ciudad Juárez," from the group Sinérgia from Los Angeles and directed by Rubén Amevizca. You are cordially invited to both of them and, in any circumstances, we hope to be able to have the short interview with you as it was proposed by your representative. It is not in our mind nor is it our intention to boycott the celebrations of V-Day you generously preside. But unfortunately we need to set ourselves aside from any organization or person representing local interests fostering or protecting abuse of power. Unfortunately again, murdering women in our city has been and is a political matter. We cannot collaborate with people who are attacking and discriminating us fiercely.[11]

Even though I have explained my reasons for believing the V-day march was manipulated by those less concerned with the victims, I recognize that, from a global perspective, a march of this magnitude was a very important international outlet for exposing one of the most violent and haunting instances of social injustice toward women and girls. It also represented the solidarity and effort of many women—and men—who came from all over the world to support the women of Juárez.

We—at least we local scholars and activists—recognized and appreciated this expression of solidarity, but to celebrate it uncritically was not easy. It was not easy because, in a benevolent process of supporting a plea for social justice, specifically for the victims and their families, the international activists were unaware that they were endorsing local dominant discourses, albeit represented by women's faces. And although with the best of intentions, those who came legitimated the self-constructed "benefactor" status of a few local women who have for so long committed their activism to local hegemonic groups, erasing many other voices. The V-Day march was an urgent reminder of Linda Alcoff's recommendation for feminists to be aware of the power of positionality.[12] Who had the power to name? Who spoke? For whom? For what purpose?

Since the V-day march, these questions have become more urgent, especially to me as a local feminist rhetorician.[13] Evidently, the march exposed the recognized local and international subject positions of those who have the symbolic power to speak, name, and represent the women of Juárez. The event only confirmed the process of (mis)representation and appropriation present in local activism. We, local women scholars, aware for some time of this process, had already taken a critical distance from a few local women activists who had become prominent figures in the social protest surrounding the femicides and who had blocked, intentionally or not, the possibility of forwarding women's rights. Moreover, our decision was also influenced by the fact that our statements related to the process of appropriation practiced by some local women activists were misinterpreted, misused, and co-opted by those representing local hegemonic groups; they used them to fracture the local women's demands. Thus our critique of the unethical stance of some of the local activists was conveniently misinterpreted as "just another fight among women" or "just another fight for resources,"[14] debilitating local women's activism.

I have discussed this issue elsewhere,[15] where I tentatively suggested that we—mainly feminists—were not prepared to make public the historical silences imprinted on the victims' bodies or to disarticulate the discriminatory practices of some of the most visible activists, specifically directed at low-income women, without hurting the efforts made by other well-intentioned women. In other words, I suggest that we were prepared in theory "with" theory, but not prepared to ground our best intentions in the spheres of political deliberation.

## Embodied Practice

Because every practice has—or must have—a responsible body, I need to say that Esther Chávez Cano and Victoria Caraveo are two of the main figures in question.[16] I will address, as fairly as possible, the "benefactor" status of internationally recognized activist Esther Chávez Cano, who was also one of the local organizers for the Día de la Paz y contra la Violencia.

Why didn't she contest the appropriation of the V-day march by local organizers? Seemingly, it was not in her best interests, as she took an uncritical position. Her attitude is understandable because, by the time the V-Day march took place, Chávez Cano was no longer recognized locally as "the" representative of Juarense women. The march gave her a forum from which to (re)position herself, albeit momentarily, via speeches to international groups and networking with local elites.

Even though we local activists have always recognized Chávez Cano as being *one* of the first local women to disrupt the government's silence surrounding the murders during the initial confrontations (1994), she is not recognized locally as *the* representative of the women of Juárez, much less of the victims or their families, who began to distance themselves from her by the end of 1998.[17] Chávez Cano belongs to the local middle class and has been publicly visible through her participation in institutional politics in Juárez. Additionally, she was an editorial writer for one of the local newspapers for several years. Thus she is a recognized public figure. It seemed almost "natural" for her to be socially constructed, by local media, as the "star" in this fight for social justice.

In the beginning, everything seemed all right, but, apparently, only to us, because by the end of 1998, almost all of the victims' families had begun to publicly distance themselves from Chávez Cano, claiming, among many other things, that she was using their murdered daughters to advance her personal projects (that is, Casa Amiga). Again, this accusation was misinterpreted as a fight over resources, but it was not that simple; it was about an unethical process of (mis)representation on the part of Chávez Cano. When some of us stopped and listened closely to the mothers' accusations, we realized that, in fact, the victims' bodies were being appropriated unethically by Chávez Cano in forums, conferences, and many other events, to obtain funds that never benefited the victims' families. When she was confronted, Chávez Cano denied it and argued that she spoke for the "the victims of violence" . . . in other words, she spoke basically for everybody in Ciudad Juárez.

Moreover, she is not recognized locally as the founder of Casa Amiga, but as a cofounder. Many social actors—local, national, and international—were part of this project. Supposedly, it was to belong to the women of Juárez. Initially, it was supposed to help the victims' families heal, but this never happened. Casa Amiga was considered a social project, not a personal one.

Chávez Cano is currently distanced from local women scholars because of our critical position toward her protagonist behavior. Yet all this does not seem to be important, because Esther Chávez Cano is still being rewarded and recognized internationally as the representative of the women of Juárez. Apparently, all the issues surrounding the murders, besides the obvious social injustice perpetuated by the state, need a closer, critical and self-reflective look at how to advance social justice, and not just the easy, comfortable action of extending charity.

Moreover, the V-Day march events were conducted on the premises of the Carta Blanca brewery, owned by the de la Vega family, one of the most powerful families not only in Juárez but in all of Mexico. Paradoxically, Mr. de la Vega is a local, state, national, and international distributor of beer and liquor. He was part of the hegemonic groups dismissing the femicide and one of the promoters of heavy drinking in Juárez. He is also known not only for his economic power, but also for his political influence. His wife, Lupita de la Vega, a socialite and director of the Federación Mexicana de Asociaciones Privadas (FEMAP, Mexican Federation of Private Associations), is also recognized internationally as a benefactor of the women of Juárez. The day after the march, local newspapers published stories about the event on the front page and in the society pages. The society pages contained a detailed story about an exclusive dinner held at the U.S. Consulate in Ciudad Juárez for Jane Fonda and Sally Field the same night of the march. All the local socialites were invited, including Esther Chávez Cano. The victims' relatives and other activists were not invited.

These are only a few examples of the factors that have created a scenario of despair and skepticism among local activists. At this point, it appears that not only local scholars but also many other women activists in Juárez have decided to respond personally to the victims' mothers or families' requests or needs, or to women's rights issues, and not to answer public calls for forums, marches, or any other event that does not have a clear objective. Therefore, since 2006, I—like most of the local activists—have kept a critical distance from agonistic activism, because, as I mentioned before, our public manifestations have been (mis)used, appropriated, and, in the most charitable interpretation, conveniently ignored. This is also why the decision to participate in the V-Day march was not an easy one.

Many of us were torn by a paradox that in many ways has kept me and other local women activists symbolically immobilized for several years now. This paradox lies in being unappreciative of the efforts of so many international activists by not attending the march or by attending the march knowing that we were supporting those who intentionally or not have appropriated the victims' bodies and the families' suffering to forward their political personas. In the end, some of us decided to march in appreciation of the solidarity of so many people who came believing they were making a difference.

We have learned—the hard way—to be very cautious about what, how, and whom we support publicly. Currently, we are reflecting on how we have been or may be complicit with those who have—intentionally or not—appropriated this fight for social justice. Seemingly, for some—hopefully, not for the majority—the victims have become a modus vivendi at the local, national, and international levels.

Apparently, during this process, the real and the symbolic were collapsed in such a way that the "real" victims were socially constructed and objectified as part of what Stuart Hall calls "the spectacle of the Other,"[18] and "the rest of" the women of Juárez were symbolically (re)positioned as victims. Both the spectacle of the victims as the other and the (mis)recognition of all local women through a process of victimization, are "un-productive sites of those who are known only through (re)interpretations and stereotypes promoted by others, who in turn write and speak for them."[19]

The process of (mis)recognition of the cultural, economic, and social diversity of so-called Third World women has been contested by many feminist scholars. They have warned us about the danger of collapsing these women into a vacuum of sameness, because in the process, we might efface local relations of power among women.[20] This is why the juarense women cannot be seen as a homogeneous group of "Third World subalterns." This (mis)representation has had serious implications in that privileged women in the locality have been uncritically and socially constructed as the benefactors when they, intentionally or not, have perpetuated oppressive practices toward underprivileged women in Ciudad Juárez.

Based on this experience, I kept coming back to Gayatri Spivak's "Can the Subaltern Speak?" In recognizing her use of the concept "subaltern" as a social position occupied by those who have been denied any social privilege, I asked who spoke and continues to speak not only for the juarense/fronteriza female subaltern, but for all the women in Juárez, and for what purpose. Granting that feminist poststructuralist discussions have rightly argued that female subalterns can, in fact, speak in the interstices,[21] the margins, the third spaces, or the liminal, based on the experience of the juarenses/fronterizas, I argue that, in order to begin to understand the (im)possibilities of subaltern speech, we have to look into the symbolic and material constraints that exclude or limit the access or visibility of their demands in the public arena of political struggle and negotiation. If we do not do this, many issues will remain, conveniently for some, (in)articulated in the structure of feeling. Consequently, the scenario will continue to be one of despair.

## Notes

1. Visit www.amnestyusa.org/women for more information. For a theoretical and systematized account of the femicides in Ciudad Juárez, see Julia E. Monárrez-Fragoso, "Feminicidio sexual serial en Ciudad Juárez: 1993–2001," *Debate Feminista* 13 (April 2002): 25; idem, "La cultura del feminicidio en Ciudad Juárez, 1993–1999," *Frontera Norte* 23.12 (January–June 2000).

2. I use the term "discovery" in reference to the moment the local community became aware of the murders, because nobody really knows for how long the local police knew about the murders, or how many other victims had been found before it became a public issue.

3. For several years, pictures of the victims' bodies were exhibited and stereotyped in the *nota roja* (sensationalist media) of local newspapers as "prostitutes," also implying that prostitutes deserved to be tortured and killed. The fact that the story of the murders appeared exclusively in the sensationalist press says a great deal about the silence surrounding the events.

4. Adriana Candia, Patricia Cabrera, Josefina Martínez, Isabel Velásquez, Ramona Ortiz, Rhory Ortiz, and Guadalupe de la Mora, *El silencio que la voz de todas quiebra: Mujeres y víctimas de Ciudad Juárez* (Chihuahua, Mex.: Ediciones del Azar, 1999).

5. Women who live in Ciudad Juárez are known nationally as juarenses. I add the term "fronteriza," which means, literally, "from the frontier," and, metaphorically, "from the border." This distinction is necessary because *frontera*, as understood by the Mexican people, marks a limit and not a space of interaction as in current poststructuralist discussions of "border." I consider it necessary to clarify this position because it does mark regional, national, and international—to mention a few—socially constructed differences, differences that have social, cultural, and political implications. For example, historically, women who live on the Mexican side of the border have been—nationally and internationally—silenced through a process of negative stereotyping as loose, available bodies, prostitutes, ignorant, and victims, among many other demeaning categories. Although the intensity of this perception depends on the local women's class, it is always present.

6. The current public image of the local women activists is one of a fragmented group that lacks solidarity, but privately we all know, talk to, and support each other. We have taken a backstage position because most of us—at least thirty local women activists and scholars—do not recognize those who claim to be representing us.

7. Quoted in Lawrence Grossberg, *We Gotta Get Out of This Place* (New York: Routledge, 1992), 409n.

8. My doctoral research—in progress at the time of the original publication of this essay—centered on documenting and analyzing the limits and possibilities of (re)constructing the political persona of the juarense/fronteriza.

9. This is male-centered language.

10. According to Julia Monárrez-Fragoso, local researcher on the femicides, the

victims' families, mainly represented by the mothers, are not a homogeneous group. On the contrary, they have also struggled with in-group conflict and fragmentation. The Nuestras Hijas group is only one of several groups representing the victims' mothers (personal communication, June 20, 2002). It was still active in 2009.

11. Nuestras_hijas@yahoo.com.mx, Ciudad Juárez, February 1, 2004.

12. Linda Alcoff, "The Problem of Speaking for Others," *Cultural Critique* 20 (1991–1992): 5–32.

13. We local women scholars are not a homogeneous group. Some of us position ourselves as feminists, others do not, but all of us work on gender issues. All of us work as researchers either at the local university (Universidad Autónoma de Ciudad Juárez, UACJ) or at El Colegio de la Frontera–Norte (COLEF), which is an internationally known research institution focused on border studies in Ciudad Juárez.

14. These kinds of statements are commonly used to explain the apparent fragmentation of the juarense activists, especially when referring to those who participate in local NGOs that depend on national or international support. Again, this type of assertion sidesteps the complexity of the demands for social justice.

15. I discuss this issue in a paper presented at the "Primer Encuentro de Estudios de las Mujeres en la Región Paso del Norte: Retos Frente al Siglo XXI" in Ciudad Juárez, November 2003. I further expand my discussion in "(Re)inventando una praxis política desde un imaginario feminista," ed. Julia Monárrez-Fragoso and Socorro Tabuenca Córdoba, eds., *Bordeando la violencia contra las mujeres en la frontera norte de México* (Mexico City: El Colegio de la Frontera Norte and Miguel Ángel Porrúa Editores, 2007).

16. Victoria Caraveo, a local activist and socialite, was the director of the Instituto Chihuahuense de la Mujer (Chihuahua Women's Institute). She is also considered one of the first activists to confront the authorities, but she was co-opted by them when she accepted the position as director of the institute. From the moment she was given the appointment, she began to dismiss and confront other activists. She has been ostracized by all the other activists.

17. I want to mention, among other representatives of the women of Juárez, Judith Galarza, independent human rights' activist; Mónica Alicia Juárez, local broadcaster; Irma Campos, lawyer; and Patricia Monrreal, community activist.

18. Stuart Hall, "The Spectacle of the Other," in *Representation: Cultural Representations and Signifying Practices* (Thousand Oaks, Calif.: Sage, 1997), 265.

19. Ibid., 265.

20. See Chandra Mohanty, "Under Western Eyes," in *Third World Women and the Politics of Feminism*, ed. Lourdes Torres, Chandra T. Mohanty, and Ann Russo (Bloomington: Indiana University Press, 1991), 51–80; Gayatri Chakravorty Spivak, "Can the Subaltern Speak?" in *Marxism and the Interpretation of Culture*, ed. Cary Nelson and Lawrence Grossberg (Chicago: University of Chicago Press, 1988), 271–313.

21. For a more a comprehensive understanding of the notion of the in-between spaces of women's speech, see Emma Pérez, *The Decolonial Imaginary: Writing Chicanas into History* (Bloomington: Indiana University Press, 1999).

CHAPTER 8

# Femicide, Mother-Activism, and the Geography of Protest in Northern Mexico

MELISSA W. WRIGHT

*What has happened in Juárez resembles what is happening throughout Mexico. Courageous individuals speaking out against human rights violations and demanding thorough investigations into abuses are being targeted in an attempt to silence them.*
—RENATA RENDÓN, AMNESTY INTERNATIONAL USA'S
ADVOCACY DIRECTOR FOR THE AMERICAS

*Testimony, as every product in our culture, is often seen as a commodity that must provide practical use.*
—NORA STREJILEVICH, "TESTIMONY: BEYOND THE
LANGUAGE OF TRUTH"

"This silence terrifies me," said Esther Chávez Cano, the director of Casa Amiga, a rape crisis center in Ciudad Juárez, the city that borders El Paso, Texas.[1] The silence she refers to is the quiet surrounding the ongoing violence against women in northern Mexico. "No one is protesting," she said. "There are no press conferences. No marches. It's like we're back in 1993."

The year 1993 marks the beginning of what is widely recognized as northern Mexico's era of femicide (*feminicidio*)—the killing of women by persons granted impunity.[2] The year also marks the beginnings of the protests that made this violence infamous around the world. As I listened to Esther, a woman in her mid-seventies, while she lay on her sofa, preparing for another round of chemotherapy, I wondered if I should state the obvious. "You know, Esther," I said, "no one, anywhere, protests violence against women on a regular basis."

"Well," she said, "we used to."

Indeed, between 1995 and 2005, the northern Mexican cities of Ciudad Juárez and Chihuahua City (both in the State of Chihuahua) were renowned for protests led primarily by women; the protests shocked first the country and then much of the world with the news that women and girls were being kidnapped and murdered with impunity throughout the border region. For simplicity's sake, I refer to these protests and their protagonists as part of an "antifemicide" movement or campaign.[3] These protests took many forms and involved a variety of organizations and individuals who formed coalitions that spearheaded marches, press conferences, the creation of public monuments and memorials, artistic performances, and confrontations with public officials, among other actions.

In recent years, however, the local antifemicide coalitions have dissolved as groups or have parted ways to work on separate projects or have coordinated activities around issues other than femicide.[4] And with the disappearance of these local antifemicide coalitions, there has been a quieting of the protests across the region. Unlike in previous years, the discovery of a female body is not followed by press conferences or other public actions that keep the violence on the front pages of local dailies. Indeed, local press coverage of the femicides has waned despite evidence of enduring violence against women, an escalation of violence more generally, and impunity for criminals across the board.[5] Recent municipal and statewide elections reveal that femicide, and how candidates address it, is no longer the campaign issue that it was from 1995 to 2004.

The dissolution of local coalitions and the quieting of public protest in northern Mexico, however, does not signify a lack of activism around femicide. Instead, it indicates a shift in the geographic orientation of the movement as activists from Mexico form coalitions with organizations and individuals in other countries to raise public awareness of the problems in their country. For instance, some activists and their organizations in northern Mexico have been working on cases on behalf of victims' families to present to the Inter-American Commission on Human Rights under the Organization of American States;[6] others are working with Argentina's Equipo Argentino de Antropología Forense (Forensic Anthropology Team), a nonprofit organization that assists in the analysis of forensic data and the preparation of reports;[7] others are trying to foster regional and international support for the preservation of the public monuments to the violence and its victims in northern Mexico;[8] and still others participate regularly in academic, political, and human rights events around the world. While it is hard to place an actual number on such efforts, it seems clear to activists within the movement that, as visibility of their activism has faded locally over the last few years, it has increased outside of the country.[9]

The movement's geographic shift toward the international arena reflects the impact of two principal processes on the antifemicide movement.[10] One is the strategy of activists within and beyond Mexico to generate international political pressure on Mexican politicians in order to seek justice for the victims and their families and to prevent further crimes. This strategy is especially important when activists are harassed or receive threats, as has been the case in the antifemicide campaigns.[11] The other is a weakening in northern Mexico of the movement's coalitions, which are fragmented by political disagreements and competition for resources. In this chapter, I investigate these two processes in relation to each other in order to ask how the quieting of this movement within Mexico is connected to its internationalization and what this holds for Mexico's democracy and for women's participation in it.

As a starting point, I take my cues from activists and scholars, primarily in Ciudad Juárez and in the state capital of Chihuahua City, who express concern over the divisions that have debilitated the coalitions within the domestic campaign.[12] In my experience within this movement, such divisions are palpable in marches, academic forums, and other public events. And as one scholar based in Ciudad Juárez put it, "The in-fighting makes all of this so hard."[13] In conversations with event participants, a variety of explanations describe the quarrels as based on a range of issues from politics, class, and regional orientation, to difficult personalities among key participants. While there is no single opinion as to why the movement has so many internal fissures, there is a commonly held view that, as one activist put it, "working on local coalitions is not a good use of our energy right now."[14] Or as another activist said, "We are working on our separate projects, and we are doing important things. But it does show that there are no strong [antifemicide] coalitions here right now."[15]

Rather than regard such expressions of frustration as indicators of a "failed" movement in Mexico, I view them as part of the ongoing materialization of social movements out of the destruction of previous forms, as has been analyzed in the large literature on social movements in Latin America.[16] Therefore, I agree with those scholars who urge careful study of the infighting and divisions so common to social justice movements around the world. They argue that treating these troubles as idiosyncratic or as inappropriate for public discussion leaves gaps in the literature on social movements, on networks, on collective action, and on the realities of social justice work in past and present times.[17] Indeed, as one scholar and antifemicide activist has written, we must treat this movement as a "drama" full of "contradictions and constant transformation."[18]

And so it is in this vein that I investigate how the dramas unfolding within the local coalitions in northern Mexico are connected to the production of international ones and to a geographic transformation of this movement. I do this primarily by focusing across scales, at the connections linking the faltering of the movement domestically to its production internationally and ask how the former contributes to or limits the latter.

Toward this end, I find useful Cindi Katz's elaboration of topography as a metaphor for tracing the dynamic alignments of social movements across scales that form around particular concepts.[19] Her usage of contour lines to refer to points of social contact reflects a Marxian allegiance to the idea that connections among people are based on social, rather than essential, relationships that incorporate spatial strategies for mediating these relationships. This thinking also finds common ground with network theory, but metaphors of networks and of cartography work slightly differently. Katz refers to contour lines as a means for integrating these spatial strategies into a conceptualization of the processes that mediate social relationships across space and through time: "My intent in invoking them is to imagine a politics that simultaneously retains the distinctness of the characteristics of a particular place and builds on its analytic connections to other places along 'contour lines' marking, not elevation, but rather a particular relation to a process. . . . In this way, it is possible to theorize 'the connectedness of vastly different places made artifactually discrete by virtue of history and geography but which also reproduce themselves differently amidst the common political-economic and sociocultural processes they experience."[20]

Instead of regarding this social movement in terms of people-to-people contacts, I use Katz's formulation of contour lines to imagine the antifemicide social movement as emerging through the various efforts of different actors as they engage with similar sets of issues. These efforts include positive as well as negative interactions, as some people may prefer not to work directly with each other even as they seek justice around shared concerns.

The contour line that I identify and follow in this case is one that creates connections, including negative connections (or disconnections), within the antifemicide movement around the concept of the "public woman." By combining Marxist critiques of political economy with poststructuralist feminist interrogations of discursive production,[21] I investigate the discourse of the public woman as a technological device for producing the public woman as a material force of power that the antifemicide activists must confront at every turn. And they do so via spatial strategies for configuring and reconfiguring their alliances in relation to her. In this way, the public woman represents a contour line around which positive and negative connections form. She is a polarizing figure central to the movement, and I believe her to be key to the movement's current domestic problems as well as to its international successes.

## Public Women Versus Radical Mothers

In Mexico, the term "public woman" evokes the figure of a prostitute (*puta*) who stands for the contaminated woman who in turn contaminates all that she touches. The significance of public woman in Mexico's version of democracy is clear when contrasted to the concept of "public man" (*hombre público*), which is one way of saying "citizen,"[22] and it has been a powerful tool used by the governing elite to disparage women who work outside the home or who try to participate in the democratic process.[23]

The significance of the public-woman discourse for Ciudad Juárez, a city in which women represent a majority of the officially employed population, is readily evident. Since the inauguration of the *maquiladora* export-processing industries in the 1960s, women and girls have had to contend with widespread descriptions of themselves as public women who represent social trouble despite the regional economy's dependence on their income-generating activities.[24] Such descriptions of female workers, common to industrial cities since the nineteenth century, are hardly unique to this border city, but they have been extended more broadly to encompass women who participate in the public sector.[25] For while Ciudad Juárez is most famous around the world for its feminization of the international division of labor and for the female sex workers who have long provided sexual services for men from both sides of the border, it is also well known within Mexico for women's participation in the democratization movement in the 1980s, which eventually brought an end to the Partido Revolucionario Institucional's (PRI's) monopoly over the country's governance.[26] Consequently, in a city of women workers and women activists, the discourse that pervades the region today of public women as "social trouble" is a concept that links women who work outside the home to those who exercise democratic rights around the idea that all such women are dangerous and contaminated.

In the following, I organize the discussion of antifemicide protests around two periods that reflect different strategies that activists have used for dealing with the power of the public-woman discourse in contemporary Mexico. I refer to the first period as defined by "a politics of rights" and the second, by "a politics of mother-activism." The politics of rights represents the beginning years of the antifemicide protest in the 1990s, when its leading activists created a coalition to change the meaning of public woman by focusing on an expansion of women's rights to the city and its governance. They fought the blame-the-victim strategy that political and corporate elites used to dismiss the crimes as problems created by women on the street. And their politics of rights incorporated many of the demands of the rights-based movements that were shaking up Mexico and much of Latin America at the time. Many of the leaders of this early phase of the antifemicide campaign had years of experience in the democratization, women's rights, and agrarian movements within and beyond northern Mexico. Their organizational experience provided the initial infrastructure for helping the families and friends of victims publicize their concerns and gain access to political and economic leaders.

But as I detail below, the public woman discourse provided the principal means used by governing elites to attack this politics of rights and to cause its dissolution by the early 2000s. And this destruction created the conditions for the production of a second period of antifemicide campaigning around what I call a "politics of mother-activism."

The movement's politics of mother-activism reflects a realignment of the previous coalitions largely in response to a vicious assault on the movement by governing elites who used the public-woman discourse to demonize its leaders. While victims' family members always have been leading forces in the antifemicide protests,[27] the organization of the movement around the idea of the mother-activist as the central protagonist took hold after 2001. This strategy reveals another way of fighting the public-woman discourse, as the mother-activist in this context represents the woman who, motivated by her private experience as a mother, trespasses into the public sphere, not as a public woman but as a private one whose presence on the street indicates that something is terribly wrong in northern Mexico.

Mother-activist movements gained momentum across Latin America in the 1970s as a strategy for seeking justice in repressive political climates. As numerous other studies have shown, women who present themselves as mother-activists assume many and varied roles, often as leaders and key strategists, within social movements that also vary depending on the context and activist goals.[28]

But despite the diversity among them and their activism, mother-activists share something in common in the proclamation that their politics originate in their experiences as mothers. Their public life on the street, in short, always begins with their private one in the family. This point of origin is fundamental to mother-activism and its strategy for mitigating political hostility toward its actions. It is an activism that plays on the patriarchal concept of matronly woman as inherently *apolitical*—or as the opposite of virile male subversives—to present the image of mothers as nonthreatening to governing elites even as their demands often challenge the basic foundations of state and economy.[29] For this reason, I refer to them as "conservative radicals," as they couch radical demands within the conservative demeanor of women defined as mothers within a patriarchal context that demands female obligation to the male-headed, domestic realm.[30] That they have no counterpart in the figure of father-activists only further demonstrates the gendered dimensions of the conservative logic that girds mother-activism in the idea that mothers belong at home while men, be they fathers or otherwise, have full access as public men to all domains of political economy.

Just as in other mother-activist movements, this conservative radicalism of the antifemicide movement finds expression as the mothers demand the return of their children and an end to the impunity granted the criminals. The apparent simplicity of this demand of a mother for her child and of punishment of those who have injured this child is, of course, radical when presented against the state, which is either protecting or not pursuing the criminals in a context in which the child is known to be, or is assumed to be, dead. As such, the mothers demand the impossible both in a physical sense (that is, the return to life of a dead child) and the political sense (that is, the end of impunity in a corrupt political system, for which Mexico is still famous). For this reason, other scholars have described mother-activists as engaged in an "eternal struggle," one that can never end and that therefore can be quite dangerous to the status quo.[31] The power of the mother's appeal lies within the conservatism of her request and the promise that follows. In exchange for her child and for the disciplining of those who have injured her, the mother will return home where she belongs. She is not, like a public woman, forsaking her definition as a woman beholden to the domestic sphere. Indeed, her politics rest on a plea for the government to create the conditions by which she can return home. Thus, it is her presence on the street that exposes the social perversion, not because the mothers are socially perverse but because the situation has forced them, against the natural order of things, to leave their homes.

In this way, the mothers articulate that their politics are a reaction to a state that neither protects nor holds sacred the patriarchal family but instead creates conditions that force women to leave their homes and look for their children. Such conservative radicalism has proven to be extremely forceful in the socially conservative contexts of many Latin American countries, particularly from the 1970s to the 1990s.[32] In this way, mother-activists use the idea of the patriarchally defined mother—the woman whose duties

**Fig. 8.1.** J Guadalupe Pérez © 2005, "Marcha contra la Violencia hacia las Mujeres" (March against Violence toward Women). Courtesy of J Guadalupe Pérez.

and sexuality are bound within the home—in order to neutralize hostility against their activism and to protect them from charges that they are either political subversives or public women who threaten the foundations of family, nation, and society.[33]

But despite its disavowal of comprising public women, the mother-activist approach has been the most successful for publicizing the antifemicide movement beyond Mexico and generating protests internationally. And yet, as I endeavor to show in the following, this activism would not be possible in the antifemicide campaign without the previous round of activism organized by those who proclaimed their rights as public women in the public sphere. Tracing the contour line of the public woman reveals the intimacy binding these two periods while it sheds light onto many of the tensions that currently tear at the movement's social fabric.

## Background

In the early 1990s, when families and friends of victims began calling attention to the violence that had claimed their loved ones, they found their initial support among organizations and individuals whose own activism originated as responses to economic and political stresses of the 1970s and

1980s.[34] In Mexico's border cities, neoliberal restructuring had begun in the 1970s (a decade earlier than its official 1982 date) with the inauguration of the *maquiladora* export-processing factories as the region's economic and social development model. Ciudad Juárez, particularly, had been the test case for organizing social and economic development around the private sector and export processing. During Mexico's strong economic growth in the 1970s, Ciudad Juárez was already showing evidence of social distress as thousands upon thousands of internal migrants, most fleeing extreme rural poverty, chased dreams of a better life across the border in the United States or in the *maquiladoras* of Mexican border cities. Ciudad Juárez was the principal destination of the female migrants, who made the city notorious for its feminization of the international division of labor and whose enthusiasm for accepting poverty-level wages for long, grueling factory shifts revealed their economic desperation.

Additionally, political liberalization and fraud-free elections occurred earlier in northern Mexico than in the rest of the country, which was still in the grips of the PRI, which had ruled the country since 1929. By 1982, a democratization movement was well under way in Ciudad Juárez, where the socially conservative Partido de Acción Nacional (PAN) won the mayoral race in the city that year and laid the groundwork for capturing the state governorship ten years later.

Even as many civic organizations in Ciudad Juárez supported the democratization represented by the PAN's victory, they faced a further entrenchment of neoliberal ideologies as the PAN leadership advocated for even more extreme market-driven social reform than the PRI had.[35] To boot, the PAN added a strong dose of social conservatism focused on an orthodox Catholic definition of family values that called for a return of the patriarchal family and included a strong critique of the women who filled the streets, factories, and nightclubs of Ciudad Juárez. And in 1992, PRI and PAN legislators in Chihuahua passed a law defining abortion as a capital offense.

Within this climate, the organizations that emerged in Ciudad Juárez and in Chihuahua City were dealing with a malicious combination of the politics of production, built around the *maquiladora* export-processing model, which sought low-waged female labor, with a politics of reproduction that stigmatized those same women and girls for working outside the home and denied them basic services. Thus, while governing elites boasted of the city's low-paid women workers who did good-quality work, they simultaneously blamed these very women for working outside the home and refused to seek solutions for the lack of day care, educational and medical facilities, secure housing, dependable public transportation, and services to deal with domestic abuse and gendered violence. By the mid-1980s, more than a quarter of the city's population lived without potable water and other city services, brutality against women was on the rise, and their children were increasingly entering the ranks of a growing drug economy. In response to such troubles, Ciudad Juárez and Chihuahua City both saw, in the 1980s, a proliferation of organizations that focused on the needs of marginalized communities, single-headed families, prodemocratization, and legal aid even though the country did not have a donor base to support their activities.[36]

Such was the political and economic context surrounding the initial call to organize against the femicides in 1993, when Esther Chávez, a retired accountant from Kraft Foods and editorialist for a Ciudad Juárez daily, and Judith Galarza, a human rights activist whose sister had been disappeared during the 1970s dirty war, issued an alarm to civic leaders: according to their count, some forty women and girls had been savagely murdered in the border city.[37] Victims' families had already been protesting but were not receiving adequate attention from the media or public officials, and it was clear to Chávez and Galarza that they needed institutional support from the city's civic organizations. Chávez described their first attempt at organizing a protest this way: "We knew we had to do something, so we went to the mayor's office. And we got there and said, well, what do we do? And then we said, well, we're occupying the office! Isn't that what you do? And when the press came, they said, 'Who are you?' We didn't even have a name."[38] Within a few weeks, they came up with a name: Coordinadora de Organizaciones No Gubernamentales en Pro de la Mujer (Coalition of NGOs for Women's Rights). The coalition initially consisted of some eight organizations based in Ciudad Juárez (but some with shared networks in Chihuahua City), later growing to fourteen.[39] The participating organizations had a variety of missions ranging from concerns about community health and education to dealing with domestic violence and economic development. With the creation of the coalition in 1994 was born a new women's rights movement that took the idea of antifemicide as its central concern.

## The Politics of Rights

The coalition quickly enacted a five-point mission statement to attack practices and beliefs within political economy and cultural institutions that justified violence against women and denied them the resources to fight it. Toward meeting their goals, they organized protests and marches and occupations of public buildings. They helped the families find a public audience for their frustration with the police and for their pain, and they moved these stories of femicide from the back to the front pages of the Chihuahua and, then, the Mexican newspapers. These protests caught regional political and corporate elites off guard as the violence that they had complacently ignored was becoming the biggest story of the border.

By 1998, the *New York Times,* CNN, and other international news sources, in addition to Mexico's major newspapers, had declared to the world that Ciudad Juárez was not only a place for factory work and free trade but also was a place to murder young women with impunity.[40] And this attention was drawing connections between the murders and the insecure lives of the young factory women who worked in facilities bearing such household names as GM, Phillips, Hoover, RCA, and GE. News stories showed how factory women had to brave dark and mean streets either on their way to work for the first shift or on their way home from the second, as they struggled to support themselves and their families on poverty-level wages.[41]

All of this international attention meant that the coalition was making progress toward its goal of changing a regional political economy that presented women as disposable and docile. For the coalition was not only bringing attention to the ugly underbelly of industrial capitalism and neoliberal economic reform that combined inadequate wages with reduced public expenditures, it was also shattering a long-standing promise that regional elites had used to attract international business to the border city: that the region had an inexhaustible supply of "docile" women who put up and shut up with the best of them.[42] Suddenly, Ciudad Juárez was erupting with loud and boisterous women who were marching, yelling at public officials, blocking international bridges, painting telephone poles, protesting at factories, and, basically, raising hell.

Indeed, the coalition's public acumen forced federal and state officials to recognize the importance of their protest. In 1994, the state government appointed a special prosecutor to investigate the murders and established an office in Ciudad Juárez to handle the crimes. The coalition met with the governor, the mayor, and federal officials, and, through the 1990s, candidates running for local and statewide offices had to explain their views regarding the violence against women along the border.

But as the coalition made strides toward challenging the concept of women's disposability and docility, regional corporate and political elites struck back with a vengeance. And they used the most powerful weapon they had in their arsenal: the discourse of the public woman. Through the mid-1990s, they targeted this discourse principally at the girls and women who had been murdered and/or kidnapped. By characterizing the victims as public women who behaved like whores, regional elites attempted to dismiss the victims' legitimacy as innocent victims on the basis that they had invited their own suffering and were therefore responsible for the crimes perpetrated against them. Thus, by resorting to the age-old blame-the-victim strategy, still so common around the world for dismissing violence against women, political and corporate leaders attempted to privatize the problem.[43] The issue, they said, was a crisis of the patriarchal family as revealed by the presence of women on the streets at all hours of the day. Thus, according to such logic, the solution lay not with the state but with a reassertion of firm patriarchal domestication of mothers, daughters, and sisters.

The coalition skillfully fought this discursive attack with two principal strategies. One was to personalize the victims as a way to defeat official efforts to lump all victims into a catchall category of worthless whores. Its second approach was to portray the victims as daughters whose activities on the street were dictated by their obligations within the home. This strategy for representing victims as children had already proven effective throughout Latin America as a means of fighting the dirty wars of numerous countries, where activists had to combat the idea that the victims of state-sanctioned violence were communists and terrorists or other such social troublemakers who deserved, or even caused, the brutality that ended their lives. In Ciudad Juárez, this dirty-war rhetoric, still well remembered in northern Mexico, where numerous activists in the 1970s were disappeared or murdered by government forces, was now being applied to the femicide victims. By portraying the victims as public women, the governing elites alleged that they were a kind of cultural terrorist who bred the social terror of women loose on the streets, free to destroy the patriarchal basis of family and nation.[44]

Yet, by using a discursive strategy of presenting the victims of violence as children, the antifemicide activists turned the governing elites' social conservatism on its head, again as has been common throughout Latin America since the 1960s. In this case, the coalition was able to present victims as children (i.e., daughters) due in part to the way that the *maquiladora* model of development had been sold to the Mexican public. In the 1960s and 1970s, *maquiladora* proponents had justified the hiring of young women in factories on the basis that they would apply the "natural" female traits of servitude, docility, and dexterity to income-generating activities, and thereby reinforce their roles as mothers, wives, and daughters.[45] In other words, the proponents of the *maquiladora* model argued that factory girls would not turn into public women. Instead, the factory would serve as an extension of the patriarchal home, where patriarchal managers would over-see the continued obedience and docility of factory daughters.[46]

The coalition used this same logic in the 1990s to explain how the victims of violence were these very daughters whose familial obligations compelled them to walk the streets en route to their factory jobs. This discourse proved extremely popular in the foreign, particularly the U.S., press, as the debates on the North American Free Trade Agreement (NAFTA) in the mid-1990s had introduced the *maquiladoras* into the U.S.-American imaginary. And the portrayal of the victims as innocent daughters, above other possible identities, took hold in the domestic and international press. The occasional reference to victims as *señoritas* also reinforced the innocent daughter iden-tity, as within the patriarchal traditions of conservative Mexican families, "*señoritas*" are unwed and virginal daughters whose status will change when they leave their fathers' homes for their husbands' and become *señoras*.[47]

Consequently, the coalition's discursive strategy served many purposes. It tapped into the powerful discourse of children, which denied the govern-ment its discourse of terrorist by diverting the condemning connotations of public women. It also allowed the coalition to make a link between the violence and the neoliberal political economic policies that both exploited factory daughters and left them unprotected. On the basis of these discur-sive connections, the coalition organized a movement to demand better pay, better transportation, better housing, more respect, and more safety for the factory daughters of northern Mexico.[48] As such, the coalition turned the discourse of factory daughters into a tool for declaring the rights of women to be on Ciudad Juárez streets and deserving of protection as full partici-pants in the region's political economy. And within a year's time, the elite had clearly lost the battle over the discursive production of the victims. Not only had the coalition demonstrated the victims' innocence, but it also had used the elite's own representations of female workers as daughters as the means for creating the most significant women's rights movement in the region's history.

But as Joan Scott cautions, women's rights movements are nothing if not contradictory.[49] The strategy of turning victims into daughters provided the governing elites with a powerful counterstrategy, again traceable along the contour line of the public woman. As they were losing the battle over the discursive production of the victims, the governing elites used the public-woman discourse against the activists when they asked: If the victims were innocent daughters rather than public women guilty of their own crimes, as the activists argued, then who was authorized to search for them? Motherhood thus became the standard for determining the legitimacy of the women who were fighting for the daughters of northern Mexico, and any nonmother was fair game for being exposed as a dangerous public woman.

This strategy for attacking the coalition exploded in late 1999 and early 2000 with an accusation that the nonfamily activists in the coalition were manipulating the victims' families for their personal gain.[50] This discursive attack proved to be very powerful not only against the coalition but also against its constituent organizations, which had been critical of the federal and state governments in previous years. For the attack not only took aim at the activists for being women on the street, it also turned their ability to fund-raise, particularly internationally, into a liability. Indeed, the more successful the organizations had been in raising funds for their programs from international donors, the more vulnerable they were to the attack that they were "profiting" from the manipulation of families and the selling of their pain to an international market that was always looking for a juicy story of sex and violence along the border. As a result, governing elites succeeded in portraying the coalition as a bunch of public women who were prostituting not just families but also Mexico to an international market and, in so doing, sullied the country's reputation.[51]

The first principal target of such attacks was the childless and unmarried Esther Chávez, who was vilified for her public activities in a series of attacks over several months in the local daily, *El Norte*, in 2000.[52] "We couldn't even support her," one former member of the coalition told me in December 2006. "We didn't want to get burned with her."

The power of the public-woman discourse as a weapon against the antifemicide movement was perhaps made even more apparent in the years following the terrible discovery in November 2001 of eight female corpses, all showing torture and mutilation, in central Ciudad Juárez. The bodies were found directly across from the headquarters of the *maquiladora* association and down the street from Wal-Mart. This event galvanized a massive response from all social sectors across the state, and they were joined by domestic and international organizations in a quickly organized march, called Éxodo por la Vida (Exodus for Life), in March 2002. While the organizers of the march were leaders of the NGOs in Chihuahua City, along with members of some victims' families, they showed that the lessons of the assault on public women had been well learned. When they marched across the 370 kilometers of Chihuahuan desert, they created an image of the "domestic woman in mourning" to express their political opposition to the state government, which was doing nothing about the violence.[53] The press referred to these women as "Las Mujeres de Negro" (Women in Black).[54]

On their arrival in Ciudad Juárez, the marchers were met by thousands of protesters, and they walked through the city together, en route to one of the international bridges, where they erected a cross adorned with nails, torn clothing, mannequin parts, and photographs as grisly reminders of the savagery that ended the victims' lives.

But while the event was orchestrated by a variety of women-led civic organizations with diverse goals, the groups that came forward in the following weeks as the leading antifemicide movement's organizations were those that claimed a basis in victims' families and, particularly, in their mothers.[55] Two of the most prominent family organizations emerged out of this period: Nuestras Hijas de Regreso a Casa (May Our Daughters Return Home, Ciudad Juárez) and Justicia para Nuestras Hijas (Justice for Our Daughters, Chihuahua City). A third mothers' organization was created soon thereafter by the Chihuahua state government to present another version of mother-activism.

By 2003, the mother-activists and their organizations were traveling nationally and internationally to bring attention to the violence. Yet the various organizations remained distinct, reflecting different political approaches to mother-activism and different conceptualizations of justice in relationship to it. Justicia para Nuestras Hijas, based in Chihuahua City, has focused most directly on the state government and its responsibility in relation to the crimes. Some of the organization's members are active in the legal aid organization that helped give rise to Mujeres de Negro, and they have formed the Centro de Derechos Humanos para las Mujeres (Center for Women's Human Rights) in Chihuahua City, which, among other activities, works directly on specific legal reforms to create better protections for women and their families in marginal communities.

While the family organization is independent of these other NGOs, this concentration on formulating demands and change at the level of the Chihuahua state government (which is responsible for homicide investigations and prosecutions) reveals cross-fertilization among the legal aid and family organizations. The Ciudad Juárez group, Nuestras Hijas de Regreso a Casa, is independent of any other Mexican organization and is the most internationally visible. Its members have traveled internationally giving talks, participating in documentaries, and speaking before the United Nations, Amnesty International, and international human rights commissions. While its members have met with state and federal officials, the organization does not focus as much as does the Chihuahua-based group on statewide judicial reform. Rather, its emphasis has been more on generating international pressure on the federal government as well as organizing workshops and therapy for the victims' families. The mothers organized via the government entity Instituto Chihuahuense de la Mujer are less involved in political activism than are the other two groups and focus more on the victims' mothers and their families.[56]

While clearly distinct from one another, the different family organizations share a common explanation for the origins of their mother-activism within the mothers' experience of loss. Unlike the organizations of the coalition, they are made up of private women. And while this explanation presents a shield against accusations that they are troublesome public women, it has not laid a foundation for creating strong coalitions among the organizations. Indeed, the divisiveness around the public woman that wrought the demise of the coalition has continued to plague efforts to create coalitions among the family organizations. As one early leader in the antifemicide campaign announced in a Chihuahua newspaper in 2003: "There are pseudo-organizations and pseudo-leaders who benefit [*lucran*] not only politically, but also from the donations that they receive in bank accounts in the name of women assassinated in Ciudad Juárez. The time has come to identify a difference [between the public and private women] in order to clean up the image of the NGOs."[57]

The discourse of the public woman is once again front and center as tensions fly over whether family organizations should work with nonfamily ones, how to use donated funds, whether domestic violence counts as femicide, and whether the mothers should be confrontational with public officials, among other issues. The most common way to voice such debates has been through a discourse of who represents the "real" victims' mothers versus who has "sold out" to or been manipulated by the activist publicwomen organizations.

These tensions came to widespread attention in the days preceding an international protest organized by groups within and outside of Mexico to take place in Ciudad Juárez on February 14, 2004. A group of NGOs in Ciudad Juárez and Chihuahua City, including family and nonfamily groups, had coordinated with regional and international organizations such as Amnesty International and Eve Ensler's V-Day Foundation to organize several events, including a performance of the *Vagina Monologues,* a march across the international bridge between Mexico and the United States (where Ciudad Juárez and El Paso meet), and speeches from high-profile Mexican and U.S. celebrities. In the weeks leading to the event, however, the mothers associated with the Instituto Chihuahuense de la Mujer criticized some of the principal organizers for "profiting from the memory of their daughters."[58] Targeted in the attacks were the Mujeres de Negro and Esther Chávez, who were accused of "not being capable of understanding the pain that the mothers feel from their losses."[59] But the recriminations were also directed at mothers associated with the Ciudad Juárez organization Nuestras Hijas de Regreso a Casa, whose codirector had to defend the fiscal activities of her organization against the claims that it also was "profiting" from the deaths. In this context, to be guilty of such profiting was to be discredited as a public woman who was, essentially, prostituting the pain of the families in the public market.[60]

However, in those same days, similar accusations had been made by Nuestras Hijas de Regreso a Casa as it publicly broke ranks with the February 14 coordinators and declared that the family organization would be holding an alternative event in Ciudad Juarez simultaneous with the originally planned one. The organization explained its dissatisfaction with the event organizers in an online posting. It criticized the other local activists for yielding to the pressures of women's rights activists in the United States, who were concerned with domestic violence and sexual taboos, who engaged in inappropriate fund-raising events that took advantage of the mothers, and who excluded the legitimate mothers from the planning of the event.[61] The accusations were, in other words, that the event had been taken over by public women who were furthering their feminist agenda for women's rights at the expense of the mothers' concerns for their children.

These claims were disputed by the event organizers, but the impasse was never resolved. On the day of the event, the mother-activists parted ways.[62]

The Ciudad Juárez mothers' group held its activities in one part of the city, the Chihuahua City organization participated in the originally scheduled protest in another part of the city, and the mothers working with the Instituto Chihuahuense de la Mujer left town altogether and embarked on a weeklong government-sponsored trip to Mexico City. Participants from within and outside of Mexico who wanted to support the antifemicide cause had to choose between the simultaneous events. Some tried to support both efforts, and many talked of the confusion and despair caused by the public divide that exposed deep rifts within the movement.[63] As one activist put it to me during the February 14 activities, "This is the beginning of *another* end" to the antifemicide movement in the region.

While other protests have occurred since then, none have attempted to re-create the breadth of coalitions and events envisioned by the V-Day planners. But to appreciate fully the meaning of these divisions among the mother-activists, their corresponding organizations, and the other antifemicide protesters, we must push the analysis a step further into an examination of how the public-woman discourse as used by activists within the movement has a different emphasis from that used by the governing elites.

While the latter used the discourse as a means for silencing protesters,

**Fig. 8.2.** J Guadalupe Pérez © 2007, "Madres en Oración en el Campo Algodonero" (Mothers Praying in the Cotton Field). Courtesy of J Guadalupe Pérez.

the activists used it as a means for bringing attention to the exploitation of labor that they endured as participants in the nonprofit sector of global capitalism. So although the reaffirmation of the virtuous private woman (versus the antithetical public version) still held within the activists' use of the discourse, the mother-activists articulated a radical dimension not intended by the elites as they voiced a critique of capitalist exploitation from a "mothers'" point of view. And this critique has much to do with the tensions emerging in northern Mexico in relation to the success of the movement internationally.

### The Labor of Mother-Activism

To see this critique within the mother-activist use of the public-woman discourse, we must begin with the labor of mother-activism. The making of a story out of one's pain, loss, and anger is a labor-intensive endeavor that requires mental and sometimes physical strength, preparation, and the willingness to perform publicly. In the antifemicide campaign, the mother-activists work hard to produce their testimonies and make them accessible. Some have traveled nationally and internationally and have spoken at a wide variety of events. Many have talked of the exhaustion they experience and how difficult it can be to tell their personal stories in front of a crowd. Many must overcome fear of speaking in public and adapt to unfamiliar surroundings to perform their testimony. In other words, their performances require the time, dedication, and energy that fit within the category of activities commonly known as "work," as they transform their emotions as mothers who have lost a child into a public rendition of a story recognized as "testimony." In this usage, "testimony" does not refer to its legal definition of providing evidence under oath but to the meaning of "*testimonio*," the Spanish term developed as a human rights instrument during Latin America's dirty wars of the twentieth century.[64] In such contexts, testimony is a first-person account of a human rights violation that has been sanctioned by the state; hence, the testifier is not providing testimony in a state-sponsored court of law but in the realm of public opinion as a way to foment moral outrage over state-sponsored abuses.[65]

Testimony is simultaneously the assertion of a personal and collective identity. Its power derives from its first-person narrative structure based on the authenticity of personal experience, but its *significance* lies in its claims that the personal represents a collective experience.[66] Testimony, as one Argentine activist/author/torture survivor has written, communicates the "intimate, subjective, deep dimension of horror" that one person feels on behalf of many.[67] With this understanding, testimonial speech is a description of events whose veracity lies in the personal experience of the testifier. For example, in her famous testimonial, *I, Rigoberta Menchú*, Menchú tells a story of torture and atrocity at the hands of the Guatemalan military, which stands as a collective experience for millions of indigenous peoples who have suffered state-sanctioned violence around the world. Her testimony later became a source of controversy when others challenged her first-person experience of the atrocities she described.[68]

At issue in the controversy was not whether the human rights violations had occurred but whether they had happened *to her*. Testimony stakes its validity on this question. For this reason, it is critical that the strategy of mother-activism be based on the testimony of those who have actually lost daughters to the violence that counts as femicide. Their loss in Mexico speaks to the loss of other mothers in other places at other times whose children have been murdered by assassins protected by a corrupt state. So while others may know their stories, under the terms of *testimonio* no one else may tell them. Only the mothers may lay claim to representing this larger collectivity.

The practice of mother-activist testimony within the antifemicide movement reinforces this idea as it tends to flow through emotional renderings of the experiences that connect mother-activists to an audience around the idea of a human rather than a political connection. Certainly, this is a prominent message within the antifemicide campaign, as mother-activists talk of their daughters and of their anguish and outrage over the treatment of their children and over the government's indifference to the brutal crimes. These testimonies frequently unfold through expressions of anger along with intense sadness and tears, to which the audience almost always visibly responds in kind, its anger palpable and tears flowing. The emotional experience reinforces the mother-activists' assertions that their motivations lie not in the political realm but in their experience as mothers.

But since the mother-activists are the only ones who can provide the testimony based on events that they have experienced and since mother-activism relies on the emotional force of their testimonies, the mothers must constantly tell and retell their stories. As they do so, they provide a steady reassurance that the politics with which they are engaged are those that transcend politics because their politics originate in the fundamental human connection of a mother to her child. Their demands for the return of their children, for an end to corruption, and for an end to legal impunity are radical in northern Mexico today. Such demands question the legitimacy of a state that does not protect its citizens or its families and that does not bring criminals to justice.

But the mothers cloak their radicalism within a promise to return home once the violence, the legal impunity, and the corruption end. In this way, the mothers are telling a story that has been told many times before by mother-activists in parts of Mexico, Argentina, El Salvador, Chile, and other places over the decades. Their stories, in other words, are already well known, as they seek radical changes while promising not to become radical themselves.[69]

Indeed, the familiarity of this message is born of its repetition, which underscores the mother-activist's iconic status as a figure who represents a collective of mothers past and present who have taken to the streets to protect their children. And, in this way, the mother-activists' stories fulfill another requirement of *testimonio:* they follow a "systemizing" structure that signifies the genre of mother-activism.[70] While the details of the terrible events vary from one mother to the next, the audience that hears their stories recognizes the basic structure of the story. The stories may be shocking in the awful details that they entail but they are rarely surprising, as mothers describe their grief, their anger, and their subsequent political activism as natural outcomes of the most natural relationship—that of a mother and her child, something that is recognizable around the world as fundamental to human society.

Consequently, as the mother-activists follow the basic contours of mother testimonial speech, they fulfill the audience's expectations for what this kind of speech entails.[71] They have liberty with the details but not with the general outline of their story, which must meet the expectation that their political activism derives from their experience as mothers. It is not a story that questions the meaning of motherhood but, instead, one that reaffirms it as a fundamental and transparent relationship that transcends political and other social differences and that links mother-activists in one part of the world to those in another. Accordingly, their stories are familiar not because these particular mothers have told them before but because other mothers in other places have told similar stories as part of their activism.

In this way, the mother-activists demonstrate how testimonies, as an author in *Human Rights Quarterly* puts it, resemble a commodity that "provides practical use,"[72] as mother-activists generate audiences that are already familiar with the stories that the mothers are going to tell. It is the familiarity of these stories that underscores their popularity. As one activist in Ciudad Juárez said, "The mothers tell the same stories because that's what the audience wants to hear, even though they have heard it before."[73] The mothers tell their stories, which have already been heard, as a means of generating an audience that can hear this testimony and react by supporting the movement with human and material resources. Such resources arise from the networks of social activism that link local and global organizations and individuals within the general contours of social movement funding, where organizations with access to donor bases (usually in the "First World/Global North") and to the tax-deductible structures that facilitate fund-raising, turn themselves into the funders of causes in those places (often called the Third World/Global South) lacking the capital base and the requisite tax benefits.[74]

By appealing to an international audience, mother-activists are also helping create those connections for channeling donations from one part of the world to another. And to make these connections, mother-activists must impress on their audience not only the worthiness of the cause in and of itself but also its worthiness in relation to other causes that also desperately need the funding. For those tax-deductible donations that gird donor giving around the world are, like any capital resource, scarce, and competition for them can be fierce.[75]

Social justice causes exist in the nonprofit domain of global capitalism and are not immune to the requirements for competition that apply to any social entity within the system.[76] Consequently, the mothers' repetition of testimony is a "productive act," in the sense meant by Judith Butler, for producing a cause that can compete in the international market of human rights causes.[77] The repetition of their stories is not merely to "inform" but also to "produce" mother-activists as the antifemicide movement's symbol or, to use Jean Baudrillard (2001), as its "commodity-sign."[78] They give the movement its brand name, or, as an activist and scholar in Ciudad Juárez put it, "The mothers sell this cause."[79]

Consequently, the mother-activist strategy requires a constant supply of mothers who are willing to do the work of mother-activism and compete for resources. So, while many of the mother-activists in the movement assume a variety of roles across organizations (not only in the mother-activist ones), when they present their testimony, they must constantly reproduce themselves as mothers above any other possible identity. In effect, they must continually work to put their testimony into circulation and make the connections between their individual experience and that of a larger collectivity so as to reproduce the brand of mother-activism that sets their cause apart from others.

But since testimony circulates only if it is heard, creating an audience for mother-activists is as crucial as the act of testifying.[80] This work of audience creation includes the labor of numerous activists, including but certainly not limited to those who identify themselves as mother-activists. In other words, victims' mothers, their supporting organizations, and all of the other individuals and organizations that have participated in the antifemicide movement and who make it possible for mother-activism to circulate as a practical commodity through the international circuits of social justice campaigns are working in a labor process required for producing and selling their cause.

According to Marx, the social relations of labor also include all of the labor embodied in the technology and other entities required for the organization of any particular labor process. With this analysis, Marx demonstrates how labor processes are built on relations that bind workers from different places in time. The labor process within the antifemicide movement is no different. Indeed, by using the discursive analysis of poststructuralism, we can see how the previous battles over the identification of victims as either worthless whores or innocent daughters represent part of this labor process. Such was the labor of many in the politics-of-rights period within the antifemicide movement as activists tirelessly fought the government's rendition of victims as public women. By transforming the victim's image from that of worthless whore into that of innocent daughter, these activists created the context through which mother-activism could and did emerge as the movement's prominent political strategy.

Such labor, without a doubt, is a requirement for the successful production of a cause based on mother-activism, since, in the absence of innocent children, mothers do not wield the moral force of mother-activists. When the children are tainted by a discourse that condemns them for the violence that ended their lives, their mothers appear as women who mourn the loss of children who went down a bad path. Such mourning rarely provides the basis for political activism.

Another example of such a situation is found in Ciudad Juárez, where the young men and women who die as part of the violent drug economy that ravages the city are not represented by mother-activists or family organizations. Even though many of these young people come from working-poor families and from the same neighborhoods as many of the femicide victims, they do not count as innocent victims within a discourse of drug violence that always blames the victim. These victims are regarded as guilty of their own murders by virtue of an association with the illegal drug economy, so their families do not have the moral ground that justifies the claims presented by mother-activists on behalf of their innocent children.

Once again, however, true to the commodity form as described by Marx, regardless of all the work required by mothers and others to produce mother-activism, the mother-activist image emerges via a woman's testimony as a commodity that hides the social relations of its own production. Instead of seeing all of the labor that goes into its making, the mother-activist image appears to emerge as the natural outcome of a mother's experience in losing a daughter. The mother-activist does not seem to be the product of social labor but, rather, an outcome of the natural order of things. So even as the mothers exert tremendous energy, along with countless others, to produce their testimony and put it into circulation as the harbinger of a particular kind of cause, the mothers' own stories deny the exercise of this very labor.

Marx's analysis alone does not reveal the full dimension of this paradox. Yet again, the tools of poststructuralist feminism show how the discourse of the public woman creates a context in which mother-activism must always deny the labor that goes into its making. This requirement derives from the initial acceptance by mother-activism of the patriarchal definition of motherhood as a natural relationship rather than as a principal component of something that could be called "reproductive" or "domestic" labor. To acknowledge motherhood as a form of "work," along with other domestic tasks associated with social reproduction, is to reinforce feminist demands that women's labor within the home be recognized as such. Instead, mother-activists echo the patriarchal refrain of motherhood as a natural, rather than a political, relationship. The conservative radicalism articulated by mother-activists is achieved when the labor of motherhood, including a mother's fight for her children in repressive political contexts, is rendered invisible. Only then does the mother-activist emerge as a symbol of a movement based not on public labor but solely on the private duties, emotions, and obligations of domestic women. As a result, the discourse of the public woman against which mother-activism sets itself establishes the terms by which all the labor—of the mothers and other activists, past and present—must recede from view if mother-activism is to succeed as a political strategy, since to acknowledge the labor is to acknowledge the social relationships binding public to private women in the antifemicide campaign.

Yet it is this very invisibility of the mothers' labor that, again paradoxically, lies at the heart of the critiques that many mother-activists and their supporting organizations use against each other and against other activist groups as they struggle over the making of an antifemicide movement in northern Mexico. As one mother-activist complained at a July 2007 protest, "It's exhausting and hard (work to protest) . . . while other people profit in our name . . . and fill their pockets with money."[81] These remarks were directed against domestic and international activists, some of them other mother-activists and their organizations. What these remarks reveal (and they are by no means unique to this particular event) is how mother-activists compete against each other in the making of their cause even as they suffer from the same problem as any laborers under conditions of capitalism: they do not have access to the resources that their own commodity generates through its circulation. Rather, ensnared within the confines of the public-woman discourse, these mothers must deny the labor they put into their activism even as they speak of how hard they work, how their work creates a marketable image, and how they do not receive the resources generated from its circulation through the international circuits of nonprofit capitalism.[82] Hence, and to use a bit more of Marx, the mothers and other activists who have worked to create the mother-activist face the paradox that the fruit of their labor confronts them like a commodity, as something that circulates beyond their control and that hides their labor, which it embodies. Mother-activism emerges in this way as an "object," alienated from the many public and private women who made it.[83]

Such was the case during the 2004 V-Day protest in Ciudad Juárez, when the activists who had participated in the antifemicide protests as mother-activists and those who supported them parted ways.[84] They were caught in the crosshairs of the public-woman discourse, which dictates the terms by which mother-activism must materialize as a politics that denies the very labor required to create it, even as mother-activists work so hard to generate international resources in the extremely competitive market of social justice causes. As groups compete for scarce resources, they do so by reproducing the very discourse that so beleaguered the antifemicide campaign from its beginnings, during the early period of the politics of rights. They continually reaffirm the legitimacy of a public-woman discourse that ceaselessly vexes the antifemicide movement of northern Mexico.

## Conclusion

Early marketing of the Jennifer López film *Bordertown*, a fictionalized account of the crimes in Ciudad Juárez, included an endorsement and appearance by one of the mother-activists at the film's opening. Amnesty International shows photos of Ms. López on its Web site surrounded by additional mother-activists whose significance is clear. Their image, and the stamp of authenticity it conveys, is part of the film's marketing strategy. To make such an observation is not to criticize the practice.[85] Rather, it is to acknowledge the capitalist context in which nonprofit causes and their organizers must operate. And it is to turn attention to how the pressures and internal contradictions of capitalism are inescapable even for organizations that do not share the signature characteristic of capitalist entities: the accumulation of profit. They must compete within this context, which means that they must, in one way or another, participate in the generation of profit even if they cannot keep those profits for themselves. This participation can occur in numerous ways, but one of the most common versions lies within the production and marketing of causes that attract tax-deductible donations, which are, after all, crucial for the preservation of capital in contemporary capitalism. The organizations and individuals within the antifemicide movement certainly demonstrate many of the stresses created by capitalist market pressures on their relationships.

Yet as this movement also reveals, a critique of capitalism does not adequately explain the tensions that are tugging at the movement's social fabric. As I have tried to show, only by appreciating the significance and durability of the public-woman discourse in contemporary Mexico can we begin to sort through the complex social relationships within the movement's productive destruction. Without an understanding of this discourse, the battles over the victims' innocence make no sense in a country where homicide is already and always has been a capital offense. Likewise, this discourse tells us why mother-activism is a powerful political strategy not only in Mexico but also elsewhere.

To be sure, the repetition of this discourse provides plenty of evidence for Judith Butler's claim that "to repeat" is "to produce," since the public woman who lives and breathes through the stories about her is as much a part of the material reality of northern Mexico as is industrial capitalism. Indeed, I believe it impossible to understand the capitalist processes of the region without appreciating who the public woman is and what she stands for. And equally impossible is a comprehension of what the antifemicide organizations are really fighting as they coalesce and disintegrate around the contour line of the public woman.

As the antifemicide movement shows, mother-activism represents a powerful tool for women as they fight for social justice in a context in which women's public participation is dismissed as socially perverse. Indeed, mother-activism offers a political identity for women who prefer to present themselves as mothers in the public sphere and who otherwise might not engage in political activism. It has proven to be an extremely effective identity for integrating women into political praxis. But when this identity is the *only* one recognized as legitimate within a social movement, other forms of women's activism are silenced. For this reason, the government's deployment of the public-woman discourse as a means for discrediting non-mother-activists has been central to efforts to silence their activism and, in effect, to remove them from engaging in Mexico's democratic process. When presented as a response to the public-woman discourse, mother-activism actually reinforces many of the strategies used to silence women and exclude their participation in the public sector. So one of the challenges for mother-activism as a political strategy is to figure out how to recognize the relationships binding public to private women in their social justice work.

To highlight the limits of this strategy is simply to recognize it as a political strategy that, like any other, has advantages and disadvantages. As has been well demonstrated regarding citizens'-rights movements, of which the first politics-of-rights period is an example, such strategies also reproduce the exclusions on which citizenship always depends.[86]

All of this is to say that there never seems to be one best way to organize social justice campaigns. For this reason, it seems essential, as Iris Marion Young famously wrote, that coalitions form across different approaches as a flexible political tactic.[87] The women of northern Mexico's antifemicide campaign have no choice but to engage with the discourse of the public woman, as it is a weapon that can be pointed at any time at any woman who ventures onto the street as she works, walks, or participates in her country's democracy. Strategizing against the deployment of this weapon seems a crucial step for the building of effective coalitions across public and private women that can ground the international geography of the antifemicide movement within local political practice.

## Notes

Author's note: This chapter was prepared for the Urban Geography Plenary Lecture presented at the Association of American Geographers' (AAG) Annual Meeting in San Francisco in March 2007, cosponsored by *Urban Geography* and the Urban Geography Specialty Group of the AAG. I would like to thank Sarah Hill, Geraldine Pratt, Fernando Bosco, Rosalba Robles, Julia Monárrez, Guadalupe de Anda, Esther Chávez Cano, Irma Campos, Alma Gómez, Lucha Castro, El Centro de Derechos Humanos de la Mujer, Graciela Ramos, Marisela Ortiz, Nuestras Hijas de Regreso a Casa, and the graduate students in the globalization seminar at the Universidad Autónoma de Ciudad Juárez for their comments on my ideas as I have developed this chapter. I am also grateful to the Fulbright–García Robles committee for providing the support that allowed me to write this research in Mexico; the opinions expressed here do not necessarily reflect those of the organization. I am solely responsible for any errors in this document.

1. Esther Chávez Cano, Ciudad Juárez, personal communication, April 2007.
2. Julia Monárrez-Fragoso, "Feminicidio sexual serial en Ciudad Juárez: 1993–2001" *Debate Feminista* 25 (2002): 279–305; available as "Serial Sexual Femicide in Ciudad Juárez: 1993–2001" at www.womenontheborder.org/articles.
3. In other publications, I have referred to this movement as Ni Una Más, a slogan meaning "Not One More," which has been used over the years as a campaign title for various antiviolence protests in northern Mexico. However, not all antifemicide protests use this moniker, which emerged several years after activists had protested the violence under different slogans and campaign titles.
4. The Mesa de Mujeres (Women's Network) in Ciudad Juárez is an example of a coalition of activists involved in antifemicide work but who are not addressing that issue exclusively in their joint work.
5. "Desaparecen 124 personas en trece meses," *El Norte de Ciudad Juárez* (February 23, 2007).
6. Nuestras Hijas de Regreso a Casa (May Our Daughters Return Home) and the Asociación Nacional de Abogados Democráticos (the National Association of Democratic Lawyers) are working on such cases.
7. Alma Gómez of the organization Justicia para Nuestras Hijas (Justice for Our Daughters) is working with the Argentine forensic team and helped bring them to Mexico.
8. The Network without Borders for Women's Life and Liberty, created at

the "Feminicide = Sanctioned Murder" Conference held at Stanford University in May 2007, has coordinated a set of resolutions, including the protection of the monuments.

9. I have arrived at this impression after talking with activists in Ciudad Juárez and Chihuahua City from 2003 to the present.

10. While much has been written on the limits to any particular set of categories, such as "movements" or "networks" or "coalitions," to describe the dynamic social relationships that connect activists across global and local scales (June Nash, "Social Movements and Global Processes," in *Social Movements: An Anthropological Reader,* ed. June Nash [Oxford: Basil Blackwell, 2005, 1–26]), I see no way around using some of the terms, and I do not have the space here to deconstruct their meaning for this movement, even though this issue is relevant to the topics I discuss. So, despite the pitfalls, I use the term "social movement" in addition to the concept of spatial alignments as explained in theories of networks (B. Latour, *Reassembling the Social* [Oxford: Oxford University Press, 1995]) to refer to the antifemicide protests.

11. Amnesty International, *Muertes intolerables: México: Diez años de desapariciones y asesinatos de mujeres en Ciudad Juárez y Chihuahua* (London: Amnesty International, 2003); idem, "Amnesty International Demands Protection and Justice for Mexican Activists, Attorneys Threatened in Probe of Juárez Murders," press release, June 28, 2007, http://www.amnestyusa.org/document.php?lang=e&id =ENGUSA20070628006.

12. I began investigating and participating in the antifemicide protests in Ciudad Juárez in 1996, when I joined the faculty of the Universidad Autónoma de Ciudad Juárez (UACJ). I have lived and worked in Ciudad Juárez on and off since that time and completed a visiting appointment at the UACJ as a Fulbright–García Robles Scholar for 2006–2007. Many of my observations come from conversations with activists in northern Mexico and from participation in a variety of events over the years.

13. Rosalba Robles, Ciudad Juárez, personal communication, February 2004.

14. Anonymous source, Ciudad Juárez, personal communication, May 2004.

15. Speaker Irma Campos, director, 8 de Marzo (March 8), Chihuahua City, personal communication, February 2007.

16. S. Álvarez, A. Escobar, and E. Dagnino, *Cultures of Politics, Politics of Cultures: Re-Visioning Latin American Social Movements* (Boulder, Colo.: Westview, 1998); J. Nash, "Social Movements and Global Processes," in *Social Movements: An Anthropological Reader,* ed. J. Nash (Oxford: Basil Blackwell, 2005), 1–26.

17. M. Edelman, "When Networks Don't Work: The Rise and Fall and Rise of Civil Society Initiatives in Central America," *Social Movements: An Anthropological Reader,* ed. J. Nash (Oxford: Basil Blackwell, 2005), 29–45.

18. C. Rojas, "La retórica de menosprecio," *Revista de la Frontera* 2 (2006): 5–8, quotation on 5.

19. Cindi Katz, "Vagabond Capitalism and the Necessity of Social Reproduction," *Antipode* 33 (2001): 708–727.

20. Ibid., 721.

21. Particularly important are Joan W. Scott, *Gender and the Politics of History* (New York: Columbia University Press, 1989); Judith Butler, *Bodies That Matter*

(London: Routledge, 1993); Geraldine Pratt, *Working Feminisms* (Philadelphia: Temple University Press, 2004).

22. I would like to thank Soccoro Tabuenca for pointing out this linguistic contrast to me.

23. Debra Castillo, "Border Lives: Prostitute Women in Tijuana," *Signs* 24 (1999): 387–433; Melissa Wright, "Public Women, Profit, and Femicide in Northern Mexico," *South Atlantic Quarterly* 105 (2006): 681–698.

24. See also Castillo, "Border Lives"; Debbie Nathan, "Work, Sex and Danger in Ciudad Juárez," *NACLA Report on the Americas* 33 (November–December 1999): 24–32.

25. L. Lamphere, *From Working Daughters to Working Mothers* (Ithaca, N.Y.: Cornell University Press, 1987).

26. Elsa P. Hernández Hernández, "La participación política de las mujeres en el gobierno local: El caso de las regidoras de Juárez, 1980–2001," Master's thesis, Universidad Autónoma de Ciudad Juárez, 2002.

27. The first formally organized family organization, *Voces sin Eco* (Voices without an Echo), emerged in 1998 out of the coordinated efforts of family members, some of whom had been actively protesting and challenging governing elites for some years. The group disbanded in 2001.

28. Diane Taylor, *Disappearing Acts: Spectacles of Gender and Nationalism in Argentina's "Dirty War"* (New York: Columbia University Press, 1997); C. Bejarano, "Las Super Madres de Latino América: Transforming Motherhood by Challenging Violence in Mexico, Argentina and El Salvador," *Frontiers: A Journal of Woman Studies* 23 (2002): 126–140; M. Bouvard, *Revolutionizing Motherhood: Las Madres de la Plaza de Mayo* (Lanham, Md.: SR Books, 2002); Fernando Bosco, "Human Rights Politics and Scaled Performances of Memory: Conflicts among the Madres de Plaza de Mayo in Argentina," *Social and Cultural Geography* 5 (2004): 381–402; idem, "The Madres de Plaza de Mayo and Three Decades of Human Rights Activism: Embeddedness, Emotions and Social Movements," *Annals of the Association of American Geographers* 96 (2006): 342–365.

29. Taylor, *Disappearing Acts;* Joan W. Scott, "Feminist Reverberations," *Differences* 13 (2002): 1–23.

30. See also T. Neuman, "Maternal 'Anti-Politics' in the Formation of Hebron's Jewish Enclave," *Journal of Palestine Studies* 33.2 (2004): 51–70, available from International Module, ProQuest, October 9, 2007; N. Craske, "Ambiguities and Ambivalences in Making the Nation: Women and Politics in 20th-century Mexico," *Feminist Review* 79 (2005): 116–133.

31. Álvarez et al., *Cultures of Politics.*

32. Taylor, *Disappearing Acts.*

33. Scott, "Feminist Reverberations"; Neuman, "Maternal 'Anti-Politics.'"

34. Through the 1970s, it was extremely difficult to form civic organizations independent of the authoritarian PRI, whose governing apparatus depended on a politics of co-optation. Most efforts to resist organizations independent of the PRI met with hostility if not violent repression. A series of events beginning with Vatican II and prodemocracy campaigns in the 1960s, trade unionism in the 1970s along with a radical urban guerrilla movement in the north, the economic crisis of

the 1980s, and the 1985 earthquake that devastated Mexico City forced the PRI to loosen its grip on civic organizations.

35. This sort of paradox was not experienced on a national level until the PAN's federal victory in 2000.

36. The practice of anonymous donation is still uncommon in Mexico, and organizations have few domestic options, besides government sources, for raising funds.

37. María Elena Vargas, who was a founding member of the feminist organization 8 de Marzo in Chihuahua City, was also key in these early days for creating the original list of names that was used to demonstrate that a crime wave against women was in effect.

38. Esther Chávez Cano, Ciudad Juárez, personal communication, January 2007.

39. M. Pérez García, "La Coordinadora en Pro de los Derechos de la Mujer: Política y procesos de cambio en el municipio de Juárez (1994–1998)," Master's thesis, Universidad Autónoma de Ciudad Juárez, 1999.

40. Deutsche-Presse Agentur, *International News* (October 23, 1997); CNN Today, *Ten Gang Members Confess to Rapes and Beatings in Ciudad Juárez, Mexico, but Deny Murder Charges*, 13:00 PM ET, May 8, 1998; S. Dillon, "Rape and Murder Stalk Women in Northern Mexico," *New York Times* (April 18, 1998), late edition–final, sec. A, 3.

41. Dillon, "Rape and Murder."

42. María Patricia Fernández-Kelly, *For We Are Sold, I and My People: Women and Industry in Mexico's Frontier* (Albany: State University of New York Press, 1983); Leslie Salzinger, *Genders in Production: Making Workers in Mexico's Global Factories* (Berkeley and Los Angeles: University of California Press, 2003); Melissa Wright, *Disposable Women and Other Myths of Global Capitalism* (New York: Routledge, 2006).

43. Monárrez-Fragoso, "Feminicidio sexual serial"; María Socorro Tabuenca Córdoba, "Dia-V permanente en Ciudad Juárez," *El Diario de Ciudad Juárez* (March 2, 2003).

44. Wright, "Public Women."

45. Fernández-Kelly, *For We Are Sold*; Salzinger, *Genders in Production*.

46. Wright, "Disposable Women."

47. Debbie Nathan, "The Missing Elements," *Texas Observer* (August 30, 2002): 1–9, www.womenontheborder.org/Articles/Senorita.

48. Pérez García, "La Coordinadora en Pro de los Derechos de la Mujer."

49. Joan Scott, *Only Paradise to Offer: French Feminists and the Rights of Man* (Cambridge, Mass.: Harvard University Press, 1997).

50. Ibid.; Wright, "Public Women."

51. And the elites blamed the coalition and its supporters for the economic downturn in the late 1990s, when, in response to the U.S. recession and competitive prospects in China, Ciudad Juárez began to see a net loss of *maquiladora* jobs as industries closed or relocated operations (Wright, "Disposable Women").

52. Esther Chávez Cano, personal communication in her home in Ciudad Juárez, December 2006.

53. Wright, "Disposable Women."

54. These Mujeres de Negro are not directly affiliated with other Women in Black organizations.

55. The roots of the Mujeres de Negro were in feminist, rural legal aid, antiprivatization, and prodemocracy groups. Two of its leaders had served in statewide office, and many of the women were known for their activism in public politics. But immediately, the Mujeres de Negro group was vilified by the governing and other regional elites for prostituting family pain for their own political and economic gain. See D. Piñón Balderrama, "Lucran ONGs con muertas [NGOs profit with deaths]," *El Heraldo de Chihuahua* (February 23, 2003). And so while the Mujeres de Negro still organized events and presented a public image of female domesticity and mourning, the group's leaders spoke through the family-based organization Justicia para Nuestras Hijas when articulating their demands for public accountability and an end to the violence.

56. At the time of this writing, many of the mothers who worked through this institute had left the organization along with its first director, Victoria Caraveo, who also was the founder of the organization Mujeres por Juárez, a group with its origins in the protests against the high rates charged by utility companies.

57. F. Meza Rivera, "Sí reciben donativos las ONGs," *El Heraldo de Chihuahua* (February 25, 2003).

58. R. Chaparro, "Se reúnen autoridades con madres de víctimas: Lucran ONGs con feminicidios, acusan," *El Diario de Ciudad Juárez* (January 22, 2004).

59. Ibid.

60. See, e.g., C. Guerrero and G. Minjares, "Hacen mito y lucro de los feminicidios," *El Diario de Ciudad Juárez* (July 22, 2004).

61. Nuestras Hijas de Regreso a Casa, *January 15 Letter to Eve Ensler* (2004), http://amsterdam.nettime.org/Lists-Archives/nettime-l-0401/ msg00055.html.

62. For an insightful analysis of this day and the many complex relationships at play in the V-Day event, see Clara Rojas, "The V-Day March in Mexico: Appropriation and Mis-Use of Local Women's Activism."

63. As a participant in these events, I spoke with many who expressed dismay over these divisions.

64. George Yúdice, "Testimonio and postmodernism," *Latin American Perspectives* 18 (1991): 15–31.

65. In Latin America, testimony has been a significant way for women to represent their own experience in political and cultural contexts.

66. Yúdice, "Testimonio and postmodernism"; N. Strejilevich, "Testimony: Beyond the Language of Truth," *Human Rights Quarterly* 23 (2006): 701–800.

67. Strejilevich, "Testimony," 701.

68. S. Schwartz, "A Nobel Prize for Lying," *The Globe and Mail* (December 30, 1998).

69. Taylor, *Disappearing Acts*; Craske, "Ambiguities and Ambivalences"; K. Snyder, "Mothers on the March: Iraqi Women Negotiating the Public Sphere in Tanzania," *Africa Today* 53 (2006): 78–91.

70. Strejilevich, "Testimony."

71. Ibid.

72. Ibid., 703.

73. Rosalba Robles, Ciudad Juárez, personal communication, January 2007.

74. See also K. Ghimire, "Introduction: Financial Independence among NGO's and Social Movements," *Development* 49 (2006): 4–10; E. Morena, "Funding and the Future of the Global Justice Movement," *Development* 49 (2006): 29–33.

75. Ibid.

76. M. Joseph, *Against the Romance of Community* (Minneapolis: University of Minnesota Press, 2002).

77. Judith Butler, *Bodies That Matter: On the Discursive Limits of Sex* (New York: Routledge, 1993).

78. Jean Baudrillard, *Selected Writings* (Cambridge, U.K.: Polity Press, 2001).

79. Anonymous source, Ciudad Juárez, personal communication, March 2004.

80. Yúdice, "Testimonio and postmodernism."

81. L. Sosa, "Recriminan a ONGs madres de asesinadas," *El Diario de Ciudad Juárez* (July 6, 2007), http://www.diario.com.mx/nota.php?notaid=a1bdd8b2 8665bf0a4eeb99538d6f5932.

82. Chaparro, "Se reúnen autoridades"; G. Salcido, "Denuncian ser usadas para fines electorales," *El Diario de Ciudad Juárez* (January 22, 2004); Sosa, "Recriminan a ONGs."

83. Karl Marx, *Economic and Philosophical Manuscripts* (New York: Penguin Books, 1844).

84. Salcido, "Denuncian ser usadas."

85. In the spirit of full disclosure, I make tax-deductible contributions to Amnesty International.

86. W. Brown, *States of Injury* (Princeton, N.J.: Princeton University Press, 1995).

87. Iris M. Young, *Justice and the Politics of Difference* (Princeton, N.J.: Princeton University Press, 1990).

**PART THREE**

*TESTIMONIOS*

# CHAPTER 9

# "The Morgue Was Really from the Dark Ages": Insights from a Forensic Psychologist

CANDICE SKRAPEC

As a professor of criminology, my area of research is serial murder in different countries. In 1999, I was invited to go to Ciudad Juárez to lend my knowledge and assistance to the state judicial police there. I was also allowed to take some students along to provide them with internship opportunities.

Once there, I found that the officers were in tremendous need of resources. And when I say resources, I mean particularly training, but also equipment. With a city the size of Ciudad Juárez, which at that time was about 1.5 million people, there was just one van, one crime lab van, to service the entire city. There were no provisions for analyzing DNA evidence. Everything had to be sent out. The morgue was really from the Dark Ages.

But perhaps most importantly, I saw that they especially needed training in the area of identification, processing, and storage of evidence for purposes of subsequent prosecution of criminal suspects, because without that you cannot make your case. So we may have identified some viable suspects that are responsible for these crimes, but the judicial system requires that we have the evidence to back up our accusations. And that is what impressed me most immediately—this was sorely lacking. Some evidence was being collected, but in fact, there was no one place that housed all of it. The evidence was not cataloged in any systematic way, what little there was, so it really needed to be developed from the ground up.

I reviewed every file on each of the cases of missing women and bodies found between 1992 and 2002. Some of the women's bodies have not been identified: we do not know who those women or girls were, but by and large, I've had the opportunity to see each of those cases. In terms of what my sense is of what has been going on since, and, I would stress, *before* 1993, because we did go through all the police records for 1992, my impression is that nothing changed in 1993 other than the media picked up that these murders were occurring.

**Fig. 9.1.** J Guadalupe Pérez © 2003, "Parte del Trabajo de Reconstrucción Facial Realizado en Seis Osamentas por el Especialista Frank Bender" (Forensic Facial Reconstruction Carried Out on Six Skeletal Remains by Specialist Frank Bender). Courtesy of J Guadalupe Pérez.

The picture I have is that a number of individual men have killed women and girls in this city for many years, not unlike what goes on in other large cities. But in addition to this, we have groups of men who have been perpetrating these crimes, which is unusual, because each member of such a group is a potential threat to every other member of the group as a potential witness against him. We are not accustomed to seeing that. I suspect these murders are being committed by groups of individuals, as well as single perpetrators, and I suspect two or three groups of men whose members are drawn together by their involvement in drug trafficking.

I think it is reasonable to believe that the "Railway Killer," Rafael Reséndez-Ramírez, has perpetrated some killings in Juárez because of his ties to the city before he started his crimes in the U.S. His killings included sexual violation of victims. He was older when he was caught in the U.S., leading me to think that he was killing in Mexico when he was younger. (After all, these kinds of sex killers tend to start their crimes at an earlier age than he was when he was caught in the U.S.) I suspect he was an opportunist and found that the crimes had bigger payoffs in the U.S., so once he started in the U.S., he found it more "profitable" to stay and commit his crimes here. I therefore believe he is a viable suspect in some of the earlier

Juárez murders, before he came into the U.S. on his crime spree, but I do not think he killed a large number of women in Juárez.

Then we have Sharif, who was only incarcerated for one case, although he was suspected in many others.[1] Right now, if you look at the actual status of these cases, only he and El Tolteca have been arrested, incarcerated, and convicted. All of the others—Los Rebeldes, Los Choferes—none of them have been convicted, and they've been incarcerated for years awaiting trial.

You cannot make a case stick in court without evidence, unless you have a system that has a tradition of making its cases otherwise. What can you rely on if you do not have physical evidence? You rely on confessions. And of course, there is much talk about many confessions being coerced. I am not in the position to speak to that because I have not been in a situation to have witnessed any of that, but I have observed that there has been very little in the way of any kind of evidence that could be brought forward in a courtroom to prosecute those cases. So they must be relying on confessions.

That is not good enough, in my opinion. I do truly believe—I am hopeful—that that is being recognized. We have to see, as much as we can, that we must essentially change the culture of the criminal justice system together, help each other, because we all live in this world together. Violence against women in one country, in one city, Ciudad Juárez, is violence against women everywhere, so we must collaborate, not compete. I think we have learned some things in North America that may be helpful to prosecuting the men responsible for perpetrating these crimes. It does require a systematic look at evidence, and I see the culture beginning to change. For example, I have been invited to provide training not just for *los peritos* [medical and forensic experts]—the individuals who collect evidence at the crime scenes, not just the police investigators, the agents who investigate these cases, not just the psychologists who work in the Special Victims Unit, but also the judges. And that signals to me, at least with my limited experience, that for the first time, we are really seeing someone in an administrative position paying attention to what is needed. Of course, there is always the reality of the follow-through or the lack thereof. We can go through the motions and provide the training, but there still is a tradition built largely on necessity: How do you make your case if you don't have evidence? If your confessions are forced?

Ciudad Juárez is a hotbed of drug trafficking. That goes hand in hand with prostitution and with other kinds of crime, including homicides. I think we really have to be aware of the entire picture. There have been claims that these murders are related to Satanic rituals, snuff films, organ trafficking—certainly anything is possible, but, truly, I think this is more basic than that. Organ trafficking requires a degree of sophistication that we are not seeing. I have seen the autopsy reports and viewed autopsies of victims, and there is no indication of any careful excision, removal, preservation, ice, etcetera, that would be required for any kind of organized criminal activity engaged in organ trafficking. The indications are not there.

In terms of ritualistic activity, there have been some odd cases of evidence on occasion that look rather bizarre, but again, nothing that would suggest, specifically, any kind of activity repeated in other cases, any ritualistic behavior that would be Satanic or something of that nature. I must qualify this all by saying that the murders that I have been most interested in are those of the women and the girls who have been killed and sexually violated. I have not attended to domestic homicides, prostitution-related murders, or drug-related homicides. I hope someone is and that there are people doing that, but with these other killings, indeed, the crime scenes are like what we see in North America in cases involving the sexual violation of the victims. I am suggesting that the motive may be less sensational, and, in fact, more like what we are accustomed to seeing: sexual violations of victims for purposes of personal gratification on the part of the offenders who then discard the bodies.

We see these kinds of murders, that kind of rage, evidenced everywhere against women, and particularly these kinds of sexual homicides. So Ciudad Juárez is not atypical in that regard, but my sense of the data, what it suggests to me, is that the proportion of the murders that are committed in this city every year that are sex-related homicides is higher than in other places I have observed and where I have worked with police departments.

In terms of the psychology of the offenders, I think we have a two-pronged picture here. One is of individual offenders working alone, and that tends to be someone with a different psychological makeup from those men who are killing in groups. There are some significant differences, at least that we've observed relative to other cases. On the one hand, of the men that I am interviewing—I have been interviewing incarcerated serial killers in different countries for about eighteen years now—the vast majority worked alone. I have had the opportunity to essentially get a sense of, psychologically, who they are, applying my training and experience as best as I can. I have not had the opportunity to spend any time with men who kill in such groups. For a psychologist such as myself, this collective behavior is very intriguing. Just practically speaking, they increase the risk of being identified if someone else could point the finger at them. It enhances their risk. So why would they do that? This may suggest a difference in Ciudad

Juárez that, culturally, could help us to understand how such groups of men could come together for the purpose of killing, and do so repeatedly.

It perhaps is, in large measure, attributable to a devaluation of the woman, the female, in society. It's not such a big deal when they kill a woman because the worth of the woman really has not been established in society as anything of importance. However, if you were to kill anyone who is higher up in the drug cartel or something like that, then you would not talk about it because that person was valued, had importance in the society. There would be ramifications—you would be essentially the target; a rival drug group might go after you.

But what we have seen is that, by and large, these murders have gone by unprosecuted. This tells the perpetrators of these crimes that they can essentially continue to conduct business as usual, which includes the killing of women and girls in this city. And that is part of what must change.

I have been in Ciudad Juárez working for La Procuraduría [the District Attorney's Office] for about a total of eight months, and I know there are people who have been working diligently to make a difference. This is a doable proposition. The murders will never stop. One murder is always too many, but we can do a much better job of collaborating, of collecting the positive forces (not antagonistic, competing forces), to solve future cases. But it's going to require much "fancy dancing" around feelings, egos, and politics.

I have been engaged in my research for the last eighteen years, seeking to understand how an individual can come to a place where he can not just kill someone and perhaps torture her, etcetera, but then fantasize between killings. This is something that really excites them: they look forward to the next one; they plan the next one. This is something on which they spend a lot of psychic energy: *killing*. Even though they are not killing most of the time, they're thinking about it.

Certainly, there are things that reduce our inhibitions, like alcohol and drugs, and they can be part of the picture with some of these group-related activities. We're learning a great deal about this from biological studies of the brain. Additionally, some people in effect have brains that function differently from those of the rest of us.

Let me give you an example of how impulsive some people are. You may have a tendency toward acting on impulse more than me as a result of your genetic makeup. That is biologically based. Now, the impulses that you may have, like most of us, are not going to involve urges to kill women. It may be like eating an entire pie in one sitting. You know that you should not do such a thing, perhaps because of a concern about weight. Some days you may succumb to that urge and say I cannot believe I ate the whole thing, but, by and large, you do not. You inhibit that behavior because it is bad for you. We have those inhibitions; we have brakes. In general, the brain expends much more energy stopping us from doing things than it does in facilitating our actions. By and large, I look at these men who engage in chronic, serially violent behavior as men who have faulty braking systems. They lack the mechanism that would keep such urges in check.

But there remains another question: Where does the urge to kill come from in the first place? This is an entirely different question. We are becoming more adept with medications at altering people's ability to control their behavior so they are capable of taking a step back and processing the anticipated behavior first, not jumping in with both feet. They may ultimately decide to do it anyway, but it is not like a reflex. They have control over their impulse. That is, at least in part, biological.

But what gives shape to those impulses? Where do they come from in the first place? How do females become so devalued that they are not human? And when you observe the way in which some of the bodies are left, it is truly dehumanizing. With such defiling of the victims, you know that these killings are coming from a place of rage, a tremendous sense of the need to control women. And in Ciudad Juárez, I have heard theories, speculations, that the women, largely working in *maquiladoras* (in fact, slightly more than half of the *maquiladora* workers are women because of manual dexterity and that sort of thing), may be threatening to a traditional Mexican society where women have been largely expected to be in the home. Men ask, "What are they doing out there making money?" Perhaps, although not in Ciudad Juárez, it has been an issue that women take jobs from the men. In any case, they are certainly not getting the administrative jobs. Regardless, it is possible that the movement of women out of the home and into the workforce is creating a disruption in society as usual, and that some men are threatened by that. I do not know. Maybe that is something for sociologists to study more closely. It may, however, explain the nature of the bond that groups of men have when they kill women together.

I would argue that it is the psychology of the individual killers, ultimately, that we need to understand. These environmental factors—the poverty, the devaluation of women, etcetera—are all around each one of us and they affect each one of us in different ways. I suspect the real keys to the puzzle are going to be revealed to us through biological research, essentially to see what is making these men much more prone to violence than others.

I also believe that we need to be very clear about the distinction between men operating alone and those operating within a group. There certainly appears to be an element of machismo involved in both cases. This is particularly evident where victims had been kept alive for a period of time while being abused and tortured, signaling a strong need to control the victim. This suggests that the offender does not feel confident in himself, so he is doing these things essentially to show, to demonstrate, his prowess and power.

With groups of men, cultural differences notwithstanding, a parallel thing may be occurring where they are demonstrating their machismo to each other. Essentially, their mind-set is, "I can do this. Can you do this?" Certainly, that is one of the things all of us want to know: How can anyone do this? So the attitude of "Well, I can do it. Can you?" becomes a demonstration of machismo. And some of the men, I would believe, who have gotten caught up in these circles are participating with the "help" of drugs and alcohol that serve to lower their inhibitions.

Usually, even when you see two people perpetrate homicides, serial homicides, by and large, one of them is inevitably much more dominant; the other one is a follower. In the case of drug-related gangs, the people in positions of power (by virtue of money or some kind of status) establish the "rules" that the others are expected to follow. Some of the followers would be inclined to behave that way anyway, and this gives them a vehicle for committing these kinds of crimes. It is condoned and accepted by other members of their group—and by the greater society—because we are not prosecuting them. We are allowing this to continue. So the men who are committing these killings together have a camaraderie of sorts that reinforces the acceptability of this behavior. And then, outside of these groups, we have a society that is not responding in any effective way.

So, with the lack of prosecutions in these cases, a powerful signal is being sent that this behavior is, by and large, acceptable in Juárez and, arguably, in the greater society of Mexico.

One of the cases that had the greatest impact on me involved a girl whom the coroner believed to be between nine and eleven years of age. We do not know if she was sexually assaulted because her remains were only bones. But, of course, I believe she was sexually assaulted. She was left at the outskirts of Ciudad Juárez, where it was just fortunate that her remains were found. No one ever came to report a child missing within that time frame. We do not know who she was, and likely never will.

When you drive in Ciudad Juárez, you see all these young women hoping to work in the *maquilas*. That is part of their aspirations. They appear happy with life. But they are all vulnerable—every one of them.

**Fig. 9.2.** J Guadalupe Pérez © 2004, "Víctima en un Baldío de la Zona del Cristo Negro" (Victim in an Empty Lot by the Cristo Negro Zone). Courtesy of J Guadalupe Pérez.

I avoid using the term "random" when I speak about serial murder because most serial killers take time to select particular victims—victims chosen to meet specific and idiosyncratic desires of the offender. For example, one offender was not inclined to engage in the sexual assaults of older female victims within the group; although he participated in kidnappings, he did not participate in the actual murders of those women. But with younger victims, with girls, that was his thing. In this particular case, I suspect this man also sexually assaulted girls on his own—when he was not with the group.

It is not over in Juárez, and it never will be. Forgive that pessimism, but we are humans, and among us will always be individuals—not just men, but also women—who are capable of perpetrating horrendous crimes against other people. So, no, it is not over now, and it never will be. However, I have seen, very slowly, some important changes taking place within the criminal justice system in Juárez that ultimately have the potential to make a major impact on this kind of criminal activity. This is likely, however, to have the effect of displacing these kinds of crimes to another city. Again, the people who perpetrated these crimes do not just stop because they might get caught; they will go somewhere else, where it is less likely they will be caught. They are among us; that's who they are, that's how they are in the world. To improve the situation in Ciudad Juárez, the entire criminal justice system has to change, not just the police who are investigating the cases. Perhaps most important is the need for society to examine its role in the perpetuation of these murders.

I am, in fact, hopeful that we will have a significant impact on the way these men conduct their business of crime and, ultimately, on the disposition of these cases, so that we do not just apprehend them and keep them in jail, but also prosecute them so that they are never permitted to walk freely in society again.

## Notes

Editor's note: These comments were transcribed from an interview conducted by Lorena Méndez with Candice Skrapec at "The Maquiladora Murders, Or, Who is Killing the Women of Juárez?" Conference held at the University of California, Los Angeles, October 31–November 2, 2003, organized by Alicia Gaspar de Alba. The editor would like to express her gratitude to Lorena Méndez for sharing her videotapes of the conference.

1. Since these comments were given in 2003, a few other suspects have been incarcerated, though not all have been convicted. In 2001, two bus drivers, Víctor Javier García Uribe, also known as "El Cerillo," and Gustavo González Meza, also known as "La Foca," were arrested for the murder of eight women found dumped in a cotton field. González Meza died of an unnecessary hernia operation in 2004. García Uribe was released in 2005. Sharif died in the Chihuahua City jail in 2006. For details about other suspects, see Chap. 3, n5 in this volume.

# CHAPTER 10

# "We'll See Who Wins"

EVA ARCE

My daughter worked helping the mothers of missing and murdered women. She helped in any way she could, making punch at Christmas or things like that. She would often say, "Poor mothers. They must be suffering so much for their missing daughters." But I don't think she ever imagined that she was going to be a victim herself.

In my daughter Silvia's case, they notified me that she hadn't returned home after the fourth day she had gone missing. It was four days later that the man she had been living with and her son came to see me. I saw them walk back and forth and hold onto the tree, and the boy would say to his father, "Tell her, Dad, tell her," and the man would say, "No. You tell her."

This grabbed my attention, so I said, "What's wrong? Why won't you just tell me?" So then the man told the boy to tell me, and he said, "Well, Grandma, it's that my mom hasn't returned home since Wednesday, when she went to collect the rent from the tenants."

So I told them that we should go look for her. And the man didn't look worried at all. He said, "No. Where are you going to go right now? It's too early. Everything is closed right now." I told him it didn't matter and that we had to go look for her right away. So we went. We went to go look for some of her acquaintances, and they told me they hadn't seen her. That night, I went to the place where she went to collect the rent, and they told me she had been there at about 6:00 PM, but that they hadn't seen her since that day and they didn't know her whereabouts. And that's the way it went until I went to go file a missing persons report with the police.

What I didn't like was that, while I was filing the report, the man Silvia lived with was outside talking, and they wrote everything he said in that report. When the police called me in to the Sex Crimes Office, the report was

**Fig. 10.1.** J Guadalupe Pérez © 2005, "Muñeca, Colonia Puerto de Anapra" (Doll, Puerto de Anapra Neighborhood). Courtesy of J Guadalupe Pérez.

no longer there. I had to file another report, and they said they were going to continue looking for her.

I believe the police officers knew who had taken Silvia and where she was being held because, later on, some young women testified that the chief of the PGR [Procuraduría General de la República, Attorney General's Office] and some of the men who worked for him had kidnapped them, along with Silvia and several other young women, and that they were held captive.

Since that young woman escaped, she didn't want to testify, but when she saw us looking for Silvia, she said she would testify. She did and she let it be known that the police chief had kidnapped her and beat her and had repeatedly told her, "This is where we want to see you. This is how we want to see you and have you."

But the moment arrived when the same man who had kidnapped her came to pick her up and take her somewhere else. He said, "Oh, there you are, you [expletive]. They threw her out and threw four hundred pesos at her as they warned her, "You better not open your mouth. Here's this money to shut you up, and you better not say anything because, if you do, we're going to kill you, your son, and your entire family." She nonetheless gathered the courage to tell everyone who had been responsible for her and many other women's kidnappings. She said she was afraid, though, that they had already killed Silvia and several other women. She said all this in the report, but the report was kept for four years, and it never came to light or to the public.

It was a long, arduous time waiting, and we would visit the police station often, going in and out of the offices. Sometimes police officers would walk by and say, "We'll see who wins." I went to see the attorney general to see how the investigations were going. They kept on saying they had nothing. She told me to go see a police officer whom they called "El Diablo." I went to see him and he asked me, "Why are you looking for her? You're here waiting all this time . . . Don't look for her anymore. She's off having fun, getting drunk and doing drugs. What you should do when she gets home is take her to a rehabilitation center." I continued, but I was very upset that that man had said such things to me.

Two months later, I heard that Silvia's sons were not living at home. I went to talk to their father, Octavio, to see what was going on, but when I got there, only his brother and grandfather were there, and they refused to speak to me. I repeatedly asked about the boys' and Octavio's whereabouts, but they wouldn't tell me. I threatened to bring the authorities to make them tell me where my grandchildren were. As I was leaving, his brother told me not to say anything, that he would tell his sister to let me see the children. I kept on asking where Octavio was, and he wouldn't tell me. Finally, he told me not to say anything, but that the ones who took Silvia came to get him. So it was then that I found out that they all knew what had happened to Silvia.

After I found that out, I went to get the children and I went to the Police Department. I spoke to Suly Ponce and told her all about how Octavio knew about my daughter's disappearance. She told me I couldn't prosecute him because he was in El Paso/Sierra Blanca [Texas], and they would have to call Washington, DC, Foreign Relations, and Mexico City offices to see if they could go speak to him in Sierra Blanca. I told them I could go talk to him, but that first I wanted them to follow through and get through all this red tape.

They never did anything. Needless to say, I was very upset with them. The report has always been there, yet they don't follow through with the investigations. We would go back and forth to the police to find out what they had discovered, but there was always nothing. They said the report had no lines of investigation, but I told them it did, because I had contributed to those investigations. I had taken some state prosecutors to gather some testimonies that stated that the police chief and other men had ordered them to kill some people and bury them where no one could find them. That cassette tape was nowhere to be found. They kept on saying that they didn't know where it was, but we kept on urging them to investigate.

Lucha Castro took the case, and we opened up the report again. I always argued that they could follow up on those testimonies that said that Silvia and other women had already been killed. I later found out that the PGR chief was detained in Veracruz, Mexico, and I urged them to go question him while he was there, but they never wanted to. They have since taken out lots of evidence and testimonies from the police file—all sorts of pictures, interviews, and evidence that I had gathered are no longer there. I followed up on the police chief. They had said he was crazy, that he was being treated by a psychiatrist at an institution. I wrote to them seeking to find out what doctor was treating him, what hospital he was in. It was all a lie. His partners were paying and making this up to get him out of jail because he had been sentenced to twenty-three years of prison. Right now, he is free. I was seeking funds to go to Mexico City and go see him, but then I got word that he was out and that he wasn't being punished.

Then they told me that someone was detained in San Antonio, Texas, and that they were going to extradite him here to Juárez to get his confession, but they never did. They took him out through Laredo, Texas, and he never got to Juárez. There is another person I wanted them to investigate. He was working in the [Rio Grande] Valley with some of those other men in that tape that was recorded, but they never followed up on him. Even though I had investigated and I had testimony from people who had last seen Silvia, nothing was ever done or followed up on. They just kept on saying they would do it but never did. I went to the police station on a daily basis, and sometimes I'd be there all day. I even took my little grandchildren. I'd leave them playing there in a corner while I went in to talk.

Because of all of the things I've said and done, I've suffered a lot of harassment. People have followed me, threatened me, and beaten me. But I've lost a daughter, and I'm not going to step down. I'm going to continue fighting and moving forward. I'm going to continue confronting the government even if it sends people to beat me and do all kinds of things to me; I'm going to continue confronting these events. It's very hard and very saddening to know that these people took my daughter and killed her and they continue to go unpunished and protected.

Last year, I got in an argument with a representative from the PGR. I asked him what they were going to do with those people who took my daughter. He said, "I'm not going to do anything. I'm not going to obligate them to say anything if they don't want to say anything."

So I said, "Then why do you invite us to this gathering if you're saying you're not going to do anything? I'm leaving, then, only this time, don't follow me and beat me up." I said this in front of everybody, all kinds of public officials.

He rudely retorted, "I'm not going to do anything."

I said, "Because you're self-interested. You receive money for it and you protect him because you're all the same and you work for the same people, and that's why you're not doing anything."

A federal agent also went to my house last year. He was there for a while speaking to my grandson, Silvia's son. Three days later, my grandson was murdered. My son told them about their mother. Ever since she had disappeared, neither the children's father nor his family looked after them. They didn't know where they slept, if they ate, or if they had any shoes. I was poor, but I took care of them as best I could. But unfortunately, my grandson grew up. As he matured, he realized what had happened to his mother, and he was very disturbed. It wasn't until those judicial agents came to speak to him that he opened up and took them to where he used to live with his father. Three days later, he was dead. It's going to be a year now.

What does this all mean? It means that the government knows everything and they themselves are involved in all this, and that's why they don't want to speak to us or help us.

I'm not receiving any financial support from the government. I refused it because they came asking for my grandchildren's birth certificates. They told me that, because my daughter is considered missing, I might not get anything. I told them I didn't want their money—I wanted my daughter here with me, and I wanted her alive, not dead. Besides, I told them, I'm the one who's carrying out these investigations all by myself without your help.

I went to see Soberales and I asked him if we couldn't punish these men because they were officials, then what could we do to them? That's when they followed me, beat me, and landed me in the hospital. I had to undergo surgery for some of the blows that I took. They've done so much to me. They surround my house and follow me.

One evening while I was gone, someone came to my house with Silvia's photograph and told my younger daughter that they wanted me to go identify my daughter's body at a hotel. I got very tense and nervous. I couldn't believe they came to my house to personally take me out. Unfortunately, I wasn't home, but the next day, I went to the PGR. I attended a meeting with several Mexican attorneys and other people from the United States. Some of the police officials said that it had probably been some American

**Fig. 10.2.** Laura Molina © 2005, "Justice for the Women of Juárez." Courtesy of Laura Molina.

reporters who went to my house and played a practical joke on me. I told him it was no joke—that I could identify the man who went to my house as a police officer. I had seen his picture on the wall.

My daughters warned me, "Let's get out of here, Mom, because they're going to kill us." There's a lot more to say, but that's just one of the many long stories and problems we've gone through in Ciudad Juárez.

## Note

Editor's note: Eva Arce spoke at the "Femicide = Sanctioned Murder: Gender, Race, and Violence in a Global Context" Conference held at Stanford University on May 18, 2007. Her testimony was transcribed and translated by Georgina Guzmán.

# CHAPTER 11

# "The Government Has Tried to Divide Us"

PAULA FLORES

In my daughter María Sagrario's case, a presumed suspect has now been apprehended. Two years ago, in February 2005, José Luis Hernández Flores was charged with killing my daughter. This April marked a year since he's been sentenced. He was sentenced to twenty-seven years.

We have continued to work to find the other people responsible, since he's not the only one. From the beginning, he has said that there were two other people, if one can call them people, and that he wasn't the main culprit. Police authorities have not followed those leads or made any further investigations. We family members were the ones who were able to find this suspect. We had to undertake our own investigations.

We had suspicions about this man from the start, but the authorities never did anything. The authorities have tried to brainwash us by telling us over and over again that he is the only culprit, that he was working alone, because they want to close the case. I think twenty-seven years is nothing compared to all the pain he's caused us. But I'm afraid. I'm afraid that with that sentence, the authorities want to tell us that he's the main one and the only one.

On April 10, 2007, I was able to file my complaints before the Inter-American Commission on Human Rights. I presented all the irregularities that had transpired in María Sagrario's case. We are going to gather all that information into a document. As a mother, it was very hard for me to make that decision, to carry through with all this and go before the commission, because of the way our government is. I hope it will not be this way, but I fear that they might want to file a countersuit against all of us family members. Everything we do must be backed up by documents.

In terms of the investigation, nothing is new. Nothing has happened; there are no leads or follow-ups. The authorities don't call us to tell us if they're investigating or not. It's clear to us that they aren't doing anything. In the past, I could count on my husband to help me, but now he's not here. That support is not here anymore, but I am still determined to continue seeking justice. I hope, if God wills it, those lawsuits that we mothers have presented to the commission will be followed up on and will lead to some result, some transcendence, so that, that way, the authorities will pay more attention to us, give us some answers.

We family members want our protests to become permanent—we want the crosses to be painted and maintained. I want to thank the many people who have supported our protest by promoting the black cross on a pink background that Voces sin Eco began. I want the campaign to stay alive. Many people say that Voces sin Eco didn't create much "echo," but I think it did. I think it created a lot of echo because the crosses are there and they speak on a global scale, and the crosses continue to mark Ciudad Juárez as a city of violence. The authorities and people who were born in Juárez are irked by these crosses, but it is a way in which we continue to remember. We are going to continue giving the crosses life, retouching all of the crosses in Juárez's empty lots, because it is one way to remember all of the women and our murdered little girls.

Unfortunately, some of us mothers of victims can focus on nothing but our pain. But I, as María Sagrario's mother, wanted to work with the community. Today, one of the things I thank God for is that there is now a preschool named after María Sagrario and that, in this way, María Sagrario has not died. María Sagrario continues to live in every one of those preschool children.

It would be great if each one of us mothers could do something meaningful, something that would commemorate each of our daughters forever. We could name other schools after other victims. This is one of the ways you could lend your support. I also ask for your support in continuing to give life to those crosses.

It's been brought to my attention that there are parts of the city where there is no electricity. This is true, because our own government has not been responsive to our demands, which constitute preventive measures. I don't know in what ways you are able to assist us in order to demand that the government implement preventive measures, that it provide electricity. When María Sagrario was murdered, that's what happened; she had to walk through dark streets in Lomas de Poleo because there were no streetlights. The town was still part of those communities that did not have electricity. I don't know in what way we could become involved in order to meet these communities' needs.

Above all, I want you to keep supporting us so that the authorities continue the investigations. I hope that one day not too long from now, we will be able to perform a DNA test on my daughter's body, which was never performed. I no longer trust the Argentine authorities because they were collaborating with the state government. We knew that as long as they were in power we were not going to have a sound investigation. I did not want to submit myself to that, after all the mistakes that they've committed: after they made a mistake about Sagrario's tomb; after they did what they wanted; after they gave us a negative DNA test. As a mother, I think I will always doubt whether it is my daughter's body or not. I hope that the opportunity to perform the DNA test surfaces soon, because my husband is already buried alongside Sagrario's grave, so I would like to at least have that satisfaction one day.

Another thing that I presented before the Commission on Human Rights was the monetary compensation that they gave us as mothers of the victims because they thought that they were going to silence us with money. They thought that, with money, they were going to make amends for the great injury that they inflicted on us. Before we received that compensation, which they later called "economic assistance," they made us mothers sign a form stating that we did not have a right to a DNA test and that we understood that the bodies which we had received were those of our daughters. I brought this problem to the media's attention and I denounced it in the newspaper *Norte de Ciudad Juárez*. I was the first mother to denounce this because I didn't think it was just.

Even though I didn't want a DNA test anymore, I didn't think it was just that they made us agree to these terms and to something that we were not asking for, because we never asked for money. Even today what I want is justice; I want Sagrario's murderers. There is no money that can repair the great damage that they've done. The only way they can repair the damage is when I see Sagrario return, when I open the door and I see her enter our home. But not with money.

Moreover, I filed a report on this form with the Mexican Internal Affairs Commission when they came. I asked how it could be possible that they were making us agree to this, but I still haven't received a response. The claim has been filed with the commission and I hope it will come through, because I want to have the right to that DNA test and I want to be certain that Sagrario's body lies in that tomb that I visit.

I don't know what's going to happen, but it is in this manner that the government has attempted to silence us. It has divided us family members and organizations, and it's worked very well.

I have always maintained that the government has divided us—especially when Guadalupe Martínez and María López Urbina worked there as prosecutors. They would hold meetings and only invite certain mothers. Those of us who didn't get invited felt left out. One time, Amnesty International was there, and even though I argued and screamed at them, in front of the press, to let me in the meeting, they still didn't let me attend. That's how they pit us against each other: we say, "How come she gets this and I don't?"

Another thing that has silenced and divided us is the money that has been given to us, even though we never asked for it. Even when it came to giving us the money, they separated us. They gave each family an appointment on a different day and at a different time. There were about fifteen different public officials there—Marga Lindo, Connie Velarde, Attorney Espejo from María López Urbina's office. They filmed us that day, but I personally felt it was psychological torture to film us receiving money that we never asked for. As I've said to the External Relations Committee, I want justice, and they can have their money back.

I used that money to help my daughters. They're married now and live on their own, but they also suffered Sagrario's loss along with my husband and me. Unfortunately, many mothers are in great need of that money, and they think that, because they've received it, they no longer have the right to speak out and demand justice.

We were also given financial assistance to set up our own business. I set up a dry-goods and grocery store with the loans they gave my family. We have to work hard to pay off those loans, and that's another source of worry. I worry about having to pay back 120,000 pesos to the federal government. I had to buy a lot of things I'm not going to make profit on, like a refrigerator, a scale—many of the things you have to invest in to set up a store. We know we have that obligation, and that's how the government has tied our hands.

There are some mothers who had only one daughter to help them, and when their sole daughter died, they were left alone. Fortunately, I have many daughters to help me, but those mothers without a daughter are stuck there in their stores; they're there all day waiting on customers. That's one way the government has managed to keep us confused and on the margins, so we won't be out protesting and seeking justice. I know this because I've spoken to many of the mothers in Lomas de Poleo, and when I ask them to come with me to some event, they say, "I can't. The store responsibilities won't let me go anywhere. I barely have time to go home and eat." This is one of the government's strategies, and it's worked very well.

But also, organizations have divided us. For example, if we've joined a certain organization and we go seek out another organization, they tell us, "You're in such and such organization, so you shouldn't come here. Go back to so and so organization." We shouldn't be divided by our own organizations. For example, I am also part of an organization that is named after María Sagrario, but this foundation's objective is to improve the community's well-being and promote education. The women in this foundation do not focus on the crimes. Sometimes I think that we all steer away from the crimes. I work with the women in the community, but don't work on anything having to do with the crimes, like going to look for bodies. The community work we do is very different, and it has served as a source of therapy for me. I never thought that there was ever going to be a preschool named after María Sagrario in Lomas de Poleo. A woman in our community petitioned to name the school after my daughter because of all of the work I'd done, and I am grateful to her to this day. That is why I say that we can do things to unite us, not divide us.

I think that as mothers we have felt alone. We've felt that we've been fighting against such an insidious problem all alone. There are moments when we say to ourselves, "Enough is enough," and our daughters say, "There, Mom, let it go." But I reply to my daughters, "No, I'm going to die fighting because I want to see Sagrario's murderers."

One thing is clear: they didn't just kill Sagrario, because Sagrario's physical characteristics and the manner in which she was killed were similar to other girls. Thus, I will continue to seek justice for Sagrario. I know that everything that people are doing—organizing, becoming involved—none of it is in vain. All of this will serve to make the authorities pay some attention to these crimes.

**Note**

Editor's note: Paula Flores spoke at the "Femicide = Sanctioned Murder: Gender, Race, and Violence in a Global Context" Conference held at Stanford University on May 18, 2007. Her testimony was translated and transcribed by Georgina Guzmán.

# CHAPTER 12

# Las Hijas de Juárez: Not an Urban Legend

RIGO MALDONADO

## Art as Political Practice

In 1999, I started hearing stories of the disappearances of girls in the border town of Ciudad Juárez, Mexico. I would hear these stories from family members and blow them off as being part of another urban legend, like the infamous Chupacabra.[1] However, long after the Chupacabra was laid to rest, reports about the missing women in Juárez continued. I checked the archives of the *Los Angeles Times* and alternative newspapers to prove that the stories were a hoax. I was not able to locate any news articles. Even the Internet presented few findings.

The disappearance of the women in Juárez seemed so surreal to me. How could this have been happening for ten years and no one know about it? Would I hear of this horrific tale on an episode of the *X-Files,* or were the women really disappearing?

Two years later, in the spring of 2001, my friend Victoria Delgadillo invited me to an event at Self Help Graphics in downtown Los Angeles, organized by a group named Viejaskandalosas. The group included artists, writers, and performers who were trying to shed light on the disappearance of many women in Ciudad Juárez. Artwork was displayed around the community room, and very little was said about the disappearances in Juárez. Viejaskandalosas' founder Azul Luna spoke of a weekend caravan that would go from Los Angeles to Juárez for an art exhibit and a solidarity march in support of the missing women.

More than a dozen people met on Olvera Street in Los Angeles for the caravan. Spanish-language media documented the people who held signs that read "¡Ni Una Más!" "Justicia para las Mujeres de Juárez" [Not one more! Justice for the women of Juárez]. Many onlookers paid little atten-

**Fig. 12.1.** Rigo Maldonado © 2002, "Crosses in the Desert." Courtesy of Rigo Maldonado.

tion to the signs; some of the people who held the signs looked confused or unsure of what they were doing. Three vans and one car made the trip. Most of the people in the van were artists who were going to perform at the Instituto Nacional de Bellas Artes [National Institute of Letters]. In the middle of the night, we embarked on a road trip that would reenergize my dormant activism.

Artist Raúl Baltazar, Érica Elizondo, Victoria Delgadillo, and I drove for sixteen hours. To try to stay awake, we had many discussions, many of them having to do with gender, sexuality, and the essence of being Chicano/a. Before the road trip, most of our interactions were during gallery events, parties, or other social gatherings. This was one of the first times we were able to listen and talk to one another about growing up, our purpose as artists, and our ambitions in life. Through Victoria's knowledge of metaphysics, I learned as she spoke about the importance of creating a balance in our artwork and activism. Sixteen hours later, we finally reached our destination: the El Paso/Juárez border.

As we crossed the *línea,* I noticed that the hills in Ciudad Juárez were packed with shanty homes built one on top of another and that, at the outer edges, iron gates surrounded nondescript buildings, what I assumed to be *maquiladoras.* Throughout the city, telephone poles were painted with black crosses on pink backgrounds.[2] Some were barely noticeable, while others seemed freshly painted. One for each girl or woman who had died, we were told. As people went on with their daily activities, these crosses stood out.

Along with the crosses, I noticed posters of missing girls. The handwriting said it all: "Se Busca" (Missing) or "¿La han visto?" (Have you seen her?). Images of the girls varied from poster to poster. Some were pictured in school uniforms, others as *quinceañeras,* and several identification photos had been enlarged, giving a ghostlike appearance to the missing.

The crosses and posters made an inexplicable impact on me. I could not concentrate on why I was in Juárez; I could only remember the crosses and the young girls' faces. I then realized that this was no longer a legend; it was true, in fact, that women were disappearing in masses in Ciudad Juárez.

That night we met with a group of local artists who housed us while we were in Juárez. The artists shared horrific tales, some I had been hearing about. One story that was ingrained in my head was that of Armine. She lived next to a small creek with tall vegetation. In the early hours of the morning, she heard a woman cry out for help, screaming until her voice was muffled. Armine called the police, pleading that they investigate the cries. The police told her that the district she lived in was not in their jurisdiction and hung up. Too fearful to act any further, Armine and her roommate did no more, nor did any of their neighbors. This had happened before. Later they would read of another missing girl.

There was an agreed-upon silence in Juárez; no one dared to speak out. "If someone speaks out, they would then have to live in constant fear that their life might be taken at any moment," we were told.

Juárez is kind of a trip. When we were there, we went on an expedition trying to locate bodies, and there we were up in the hills, and it is amazing to see the difference. If you look south, you see Juárez and the shanties, but if you look north toward El Paso, it's very hopeful; you see all these buildings and freeways. It looks really beautiful, and I think that is these women's hope, that one day they will be there, on the other side. It's sad when you're in that situation, where you are stuck right there and where the financial situation is very extreme, literally, the rich and the poor. It is like seeing your future and not really getting to it because you're stuck somewhere else.[3] It seems like a movie. I had to go over there to see for myself. I didn't have to see a dead body, but you sense it. People are scared, and it's sad to see people like that.

Holding banners, we marched over the downtown bridge that ties Juárez to El Paso at the border. Some people honked their horns in support of us while others ignored our pleas for justice. As we marched, some of us began to speak with mothers of the victims who marched along with us. We could

**Fig. 12.2.** Rigo Maldonado © 2002, "Banda Civil Group [Group of Civilians] Preparing to Walk the Desert in Search of Bodies." Courtesy of Rigo Maldonado.

overhear them speaking about their daughters, and one mother in particular spoke about how she blamed herself for what had happened. This woman was the mother of Laura Berenice Ramos Monárrez. Érica interviewed the mother as she spoke of her daughter, her love of Banda El Recodo, and her dedication to the family. She said that she felt guilty because God took her daughter because she was a bad mother.

Even the most basic conversation in Spanish separated Raúl, Victoria, and me from these mothers; our emotions and lack of vocabulary vexed us and prevented us from finding the appropriate words to offer sympathy. We stood in silence as we began to grasp the overwhelming magnitude of what these women were experiencing and the events that were plucking the lives of so many young women from Ciudad Juárez. The reported count of women found that day: 310; hundreds more were still missing.

After marching in silence, Raúl, Victoria, and I processed all of the information we had just witnessed. As artists, we wanted to do something in return, for the living victims and, at the same time, to honor the spirits of the women who were no longer there. The original concept was that Victoria and Raúl would paint a portrait of Laura Berenice, and I would create a frame for it. After the portrait was complete, we had an idea to do a caravan through California, Arizona, New Mexico, Texas, and then into Juárez. We

**Fig. 12.3.** Rigo Maldonado © 2002, "La Cruz de Laura Berenice" (The Cross of Laura Berenice). Courtesy of Rigo Maldonado.

would stop in major cities and use the portrait to bring attention to the violence that was occurring in Juárez. The final stop would be in Laura Berenice's neighborhood, where the portrait would be on permanent display.

The ride back home was quiet, as this horrific tale of murdered and missing women became true. We returned to Los Angeles a little drained but full of hope. The images of the land, the people, the crosses, and women kept appearing in my mind. When I closed my eyes, I would see the images of the women and imagine their final moments on earth. We could not hold our silence and began talking to friends, colleagues, and family. With our creative energies, we were determined to expose the issue in Los Angeles to create international pressure and to help our people in Ciudad Juárez.

## Art as Spiritual Practice

My exposure to the art world began with a high school field trip to the UCLA Wight Gallery in 1990. The Chicano Art Resistance and Affirmation (CARA) exhibit finally validated my existence through the eyes and hands of other artists.[4] The artwork exhibited challenged many stereotypes of Chicanos/as. We were no longer Vírgenes de Guadalupe or Aztec warriors carrying a dead princess. Our art was no longer just the plaster figurines you could buy at the border at Tijuana. The CARA exhibit affirmed our political, social, historical, and cultural contributions to the United States.

In the artwork, my understanding of art, which was for rich white people and inaccessible, was broken that day. I no longer had to imagine myself in drawings and paintings in galleries and museums; the images I saw that day represented my political, social, and cultural being.

Of all the artwork at the gallery, I felt most connected with Amalia Mesa-Bains's installation titled *An Ofrenda to Dolores del Río.* The artist had conceptualized the altar as the movie star's dressing table, complete with trinkets, photographs, and even a real cup of coffee, as though the actress had simply stepped out of the room and would return to finish applying her makeup. I stood in front of the altar for half an hour, absorbing every little detail of the installation. The way the fabric draped, how the items were placed and the imagery used, the pervasive smell of rose petals gathered in clumps at the foot of the table. The piece gave me a nostalgic feeling and a feeling of deep connection because I had done this type of artwork all along. As I stood in front of Mesa-Bains's masterpiece, I thought to myself, "I have been an artist all my life; I just didn't know I was creating art."

Growing up, my family's use of religious iconography throughout the house made our home look like an installation. As a child, I spent hours arranging and rearranging the *santos*, never realizing I was creating displays in my own home.

After the CARA exhibit in the early 1990s, I began researching my cultural traditions and found one in particular that I did not know much about. I began to focus my research on the Day of the Dead. In 1994, after a friend's tragic death due to gang violence, I remembered Mesa-Bains's altar to Dolores del Río. Instantly, I started collecting photographs, items my friend liked when he was alive, and created my first altar. Like many artists, I used the process of creating as a form of spirituality and healing.

Nowadays, however, the Day of the Dead has become a commercial commodity throughout California. Sponsors have seized this as another opportunity to market their products to the Chicano community. During the 2002 Day of the Dead in Los Angeles, a $1,000 cash prize altar competition was held at the Hollywood Cemetery. The winning entry was an altar dedicated to actress Hattie McDaniel. Watermelons, black-faced stereotypical images, and fried chicken decorated the elaborate altar. In the center lay a coffin. Inside the coffin was a skull adorned with a red handkerchief tied around it, adding to the Aunt Jemima syrup bottle caricature. The artist was dressed in a green "southern belle" dress and enormous bonnet, wailing over the coffin. When asked why he decided to dedicate the altar to Hattie McDaniel, the artist stated, "I had the antebellum dress"!

I felt ill. Not only was it insulting to the memory of Hattie McDaniel to display her as nothing more than a wide-eyed servant, it was insulting to the celebration as a whole. Day of the Dead has been attracting mainstream artists, New Agers, goths, and many who have no idea of the importance and traditions of the celebration. Sponsors are treating it as another Cinco de Mayo, another opportunity to sell beer, food, and unnecessary trinkets. In a Day of the Dead celebration, a life deserves neither prize money nor ranking.

In 2003, when Judy Baca, creative director of the Social and Public Art Resource Center (SPARC), asked me to curate an exhibit for the Day of the Dead show for SPARC, I knew I did not want to perpetuate this commercialized aspect of the celebration. I had never been a curator for a show, but felt that it was something that needed to be done. With SPARC's commitment to provide space for social and political issues, I found it to be a venue in Los Angeles that I could use to bring a greater awareness of the tragedies that were occurring in Ciudad Juárez. I agreed to curate a Day of the Dead show at SPARC only if it dealt with the issues of the women of Juárez, and only if I could cocurate it with Victoria Delgadillo. Both Victoria and I felt

**Fig. 12.4.** Rigo Maldonado © 2003, "Cross Installation outside Social and Public Art Resource Center in Venice, California," "Las Hijas de Juárez" Exhibition. Courtesy of Rigo Maldonado.

that the Day of the Dead was an appropriate and meaningful way to honor the 320-plus women's lives lost on the Juárez border. These women were never given a proper celebration of their lives; now it was their turn to have their names and stories known:

> The terror of these unjust deaths ripples violently through Juárez, yet most residents remain quiet for fear of the ramifications that speaking out could cause. Maquiladoras shrug their shoulders and simply wave in new bodies that will replace those that are missing. Investigators dance in sloppy circles around evidence and leads while the madness that rips these bodies apart spirals out of control.
>
> The artists participating in the Hijas de Juárez art exhibit have decided that they will be the echoes of the voices that have been muffled and gagged. It is their hope that their art pieces will engage the general public to mobilize for the goal of bringing an end to the abductions, rapes and murders that remain unsolved to this day.[5]

In the "Hijas de Juárez" exhibit,[6] we wanted each artist to come up with his or her own conclusion about the violence that was occurring in Ciudad

Juárez. We made it a point that it was not a women's issue, a Mexican issue, or a social class struggle; it was a human rights epidemic that needed international pressure to stop the violence against women in Juárez.

## Notes

Author's note: To see a slide show of artwork from the "Hijas de Juárez" exhibition and to learn about other efforts that I am involved with to raise consciousness about the femicides in southern California, see my Web site: www.rigomaldonado.com.

1. Besides having a really cool name, the Chupacabra, or goatsucker, is a phenomenon that started in mid-1995 and is legendary in Central and South America, Puerto Rico, and the southwestern United States. Something strange was killing all the livestock (mostly goats), draining all their blood. The deaths were mysterious, and people became very frightened. I remember that, during this hysteria, a mother in Santa Ana, California, would not allow her daughter to go to the prom because of fear of the Chupacabra. It was so talked about that T-shirts, masks, movies, and even *corridos* were created to bring media attention to this creature.

2. I cannot stand pink anymore. I'm almost embarrassed by choosing that color to represent the women in Juárez, because I'm adding to the gender association that pink is for girls.

3. The University of Texas at El Paso lies directly across the border from some of the oldest and more established of the Juárez *colonias,* or shantytowns, underscoring the north/south and rich/poor differentials of that border.

4. For a thorough analysis of the CARA exhibition, see Alicia Gaspar de Alba, *Chicano Art: Inside/Outside the Master's House: Cultural Politics and the CARA Exhibition* (Austin: University of Texas Press, 1998).

5. Excerpt from curators' statement, by Victoria Delgadillo and Rigo Maldonado, http://www.rigomaldonado.com/rigomaldonado.com/femicides_.html.

6. To pay homage to the then 320+ women of Juárez, Mexico, who had been abducted, raped, and murdered, SPARC in Venice, California, hosted the "Hijas de Juárez" exhibition. The exhibit ran from November 3, 2002, to February 21, 2003, and included installations, altars, works on paper, digital art, and sculpture. Artists in the show included, among others, Judith Baca, Yreina Cervántez, Alma López, Raúl P. Baltazar, Ester Hernández, Azul Luna, Daisy Tonantzin, Rigo Maldonado, and Victoria Delgadillo. Outreach programming included a community discussion with artists and activists, a candlelight vigil and protest on the Day of the Virgen de Guadalupe, and "Call to Action" readings and performances by writers such as Alicia Gaspar de Alba and Claudia Rodríguez and performance artists like Raquel Salinas. With this exhibition and its related programming, SPARC launched a yearlong project known as "The Juárez Project" to bring awareness to the plight of the murdered women in Juárez and to engage and mobilize the general public in Los Angeles around the issue.

# Goddess Murder and Gynocide in Ciudad Juárez

JANE CAPUTI

*With the serpent of fire he [Huitzilopochtli] struck Coyolxauhqui,*
*he cut off her head,*
*and left it lying there*
*on the slope of Coatepetl.*
*The body of Coyolxauhqui*
*went rolling down the hill,*
*it fell to pieces,*
*in different places fell her hands,*
*her legs, her body.*
—FLORENTINE CODEX

*Mexican women are often seen as objects to be used and discarded, to be thrown*
*on the rubbish heap, as literally happens in Ciudad Juárez.*
—ELIANA GARCÍA, DEPUTY, PARTIDO DE LA REVOLUCIÓN DEMOCRÁTICA

The cover of the program for the 2003 "Maquiladora Murders" Conference at the University of California, Los Angeles, focusing outrage on the ongoing rape, torture, and murders of hundreds of women in Ciudad Juárez, features original art by Alma López—a drawing titled *Coyolxauhqui's Tree of Life* (see Figure i.4). This artwork references key figures and symbols: the Aztec Moon Goddess, who was decapitated by her brother; the Cosmic Circle; and the Tree of Life. The last is a common theme in Mexican folk arts, originally in those used for ritual purposes.[1]

The conference Web site explains López's work in this way: "Coyolxauhqui is the Aztec Warrior Moon Goddess, who was brutally dismembered by her brother Huitzilopochtli (the Sun God) for uprising against patriarchy." In this way, López's image re-members the Goddess whom Gloria Anzaldúa has identified as the "first sacrificial victim."[2] She revives Coyolxauhqui and restores her to her rightful symbolic place of cosmic center. In so doing, López asks us to consider not only the political and socioeconomic, but also the *spiritual* meanings of this ongoing male sacrifice of the women and girls of Juárez.

This, precisely, is the purpose of this Afterword. I consider the murders as a form of ritual blood sacrifice, a modern enactment of the core patriarchal myth of Goddess murder. I ponder the ways that these gynocidal acts are involved in an overall pattern of soul murder as well as the ways that feminist activism (material and spiritual) works to undo this pattern and re-member Coyolxauhqui and all she represents.

Many activists against violence toward women use the word "femicide" to name men's murders of women *as women*.[3] Femicides are a form of hate crime, murders of women by men that are motivated by misogyny as well as by masculinist notions of manhood, honor, love, pride, pleasure, religion, culture, and sense of ownership of women. Femicides take many forms, including honor killings, witch burnings, selective destruction of female fetuses and infants, boyfriends and husbands killing their girlfriends and wives, and stranger sex killings. But "femicide" alone does not name the full agenda behind this pattern of violence. The word "gynocide," first used by Mary Daly and Andrea Dworkin in the 1970s, serves this purpose.[4]

"Gynocide" resonates linguistically and politically with "genocide," and it is meant to. "Genocide" signifies not only the literal killing of a group of people, it also means the planned and systematic destruction of their traditions, language, spirituality, morale, memory, and sense of self and culture. This type of systematic violence, serving as a form of social control, also has been directed against women as a group in patriarchal cultures. The complete elimination of women is not the point of gynocide. After all, even patriarchal men (and it is important to note that not all men support patriarchal values) rely on women for sex, reproduction, nurturance, menial and unpaid labor, and other kinds of care in the home and in society at large. The aim of gynocide is not to destroy all women, but to destroy women as a spiritual, political, and cultural force and to obliterate women's group identity, with a shared history, responsibility, consciousness, and sense of values and purpose.[5]

"Gynocide" does not just sound like "genocide." The two are linked historically. First of all, the sexual violence that characterizes gynocide also is a basic component of genocide.[6] Second, the motivation for genocide is sometimes rooted in gynocidal imperatives.

Paula Gunn Allen writes that, prior to various waves of patriarchal colonization, worldwide, there were what she calls "gynocracies"—woman-centered tribal societies."[7] Gynocratic cultures, Allen avers (marked among many North American societies prior to the European conquest), value peacefulness, harmony, cooperation, health, and general prosperity and are based in nonhierarchical notions of relationship between humans and all of creation. European and European American genocide against Native North Americans, Allen insists, was rooted not only in a desire for land and riches, but also in gynocide. Conquerors needed to destroy these gynocratic social systems, religions, and values with which patriarchy (and its practices of domination, ownership, and overkill) could not coexist.[8] They also sought to destroy the very memory of these alternative ways of being and knowing.

According to June Nash,[9] prior to Aztec patriarchal dominance, women in ancient Nahua culture constituted a spiritual, political, and cultural force. But some among the Aztecs were, Davíd Carrasco notes, "plagued by a sense of illegitimacy and cultural inferiority."[10] Trying to build themselves up, they became imperialist, oppressed women, and rewrote the sexually egalitarian Nahua mythology. The new mythology justified patriarchal domination, hierarchy, and perpetual warfare. Rituals of human sacrifice enacted the myths and inculcated these values.

In one central myth, Coatlicue, the serpent-skirted origin Goddess of Life, Sustenance, Death, and Rebirth, is sweeping a temple. She is impregnated when a ball of feathers falls from the sky. Coatlicue's daughter Coyolxauhqui is supposedly shamed by her mother's inappropriate behavior and rallies her four hundred sisters and brothers to kill their mother. The action of the myth takes place on Coatepec (Serpent Mountain). As Coyolxauhqui charges up the sacred mountain, Coatlicue gives birth to Huitzilopochtli—the Sun and War God. He emerges fully grown, quickly dresses, and arms himself. He pounces on Coyolxauhqui, decapitates her, and deliberately disrespects her, leaving her head where it fell and letting her body break into pieces as she tumbles down the mountain.

This is the official narrative anyway, but I have to wonder what Coyolxauhqui might say about the incident were we listening to her side of the story. The Sun/War God not only kills Coyolxauhqui, he dismembers or disarticulates her. He stops her, scatters her, and silences her. Significantly, the word "disarticulation" connotes both dismemberment and the loss of the power of speech.[11] Mythographers do relate that Coyolxauhqui had actively questioned who it was who had fathered what Coatlicue carried in her womb. Some say that Coyolxauhqui actually was trying to warn Coatlicue of a plot against her and that Huitzilopochtli decapitated her specifically to silence her. Afterward, the grieving Coatlicue placed the shining head of her daughter into the night sky, where she became the Moon. Obviously,

Coyolxauhqui endures. As the Moon, we can face her and perhaps even hear her as she speaks to us still.

The patriarchal order begins in this mythic moment of Goddess murder and dismemberment—as well as in the concomitant deification of War. This sequence of events in the attack on Coyolxauhqui was invoked, scholars suggest, by the Aztecs as a mythic model (among several) for their actual blood sacrifices.

Huitzilopochtli decapitates Coyolxauhqui on top of Coatepec, a sacred mountain that was understood as an axis mundi, the "center, axis, and symbolic 'navel of the earth.'"[12] An axis mundi is a terrestrial space that functions as an "existentially centered point of ontological transition between cosmic planes."[13] It is a place where one can experience the underlying unity of the realms of sacred and mundane, inner and outer, universal and particular.

In order to reference the foundational event of Huitzilopochtli's murder of Coyolxauhqui at this cosmic center, Aztec religious and political leaders sought to make their capital and ceremonial city of Tenochtitlan into a corresponding axis mundi. They constructed a temple, the Templo Mayor, as a direct model of Coatepec. An image of Huitzilopochtli sat at the top of the Templo Mayor, while a massive circular stone carving depicting the decapitated and disarticulated Goddess Coyolxauhqui lay at the foot of its stairway.

The most common sacrifices under Aztec rule were animals that were decapitated. But the most valued were human victims, captured warriors as well as women and children. Victims were escorted up the temple stairs and held down so a priest could cut through the chest wall and pull the heart from the chest, offering it to the Sun (Huitzilopochtli). Their bodies were then sent tumbling down the stairs in memory of the fall of Coyolxauhqui's body. Female victims often were decapitated. Davíd Carrasco, in his extensive study of Aztec sacrifice, reports that archeologists also found the decapitated skulls of young women placed around the Coyolxauhqui stone and comments, "The suggestion is that there was a ritual reenactment of the myth [of Coyolxauhqui's murder] at the dedication of the stone sometime in the latter part of the fifteenth century."[14]

Modern Western people might suppose that human sacrifice is a thing of the past, something done only by the "primitive others" of history, those "rightfully" defeated by the supposedly civilized and civilizing Europeans. But when I look at my own European American culture, then and now, I see human sacrifice everywhere.

When the Spanish, English, and other European conquerors came to

**Fig. a.1.** Alma López © 2009, digital drawing of the Coyolxauhqui stone. Courtesy of Alma López.

what is now known as the Americas, their cultures were engaged in actions that can be understood as forms of blood sacrifice: inquisitions against Jews and "heretics"; the burning of women as well as some men, children, and animals as "witches"; public torture and executions, which, as one historian notes, took on the "aspect of religious rites" while also serving to impress upon the populace the growing power of the state.[15] More recently, we can point to lynchings; genocides or ethnic "cleansings" against those whom oppressors designate as dangerous, dirty, and savage; state-sponsored executions; as well as corporate and military production and dumping of environmental pollutants leading to early death, particularly for the dispossessed. All of these are forms of human sacrifice to Gods of Purity, Power, Profit, and Progress, as well as War.

Mary Daly provocatively claims that "patriarchy is itself the prevailing religion of the entire planet, and its essential message is necrophilia."[16] Most of us are conditioned to understand men's violence against women, including lethal violence, as just "things as they are." But femicide is another form of modern blood sacrifice to the patriarchal God(s).[17]

## Goddess Murder/Blood Sacrifice

Before the figure of the god [Huitzilopochtli] . . . were piled bones made of amaranth dough, and these were covered with the same mantle that covered the image [of the god]. This was adorned with designs of bones and parts of the body of a dismembered person. (Sahagún). It may be that the limbs decorating the cape are yet another reference to the dismemberment of Coyolxauhqui.
—EDUARDO MATOS MOCTEZUMA

I killed 40 prostitutes in Mexico and all I got was this bloody T-shirt.
—SAYING ON A T-SHIRT SOLD BY WWW.SINFULSHIRTS.COM

The Aztec myth figuring a Goddess as a sacrificial victim has resonance not only with other Aztec narratives (of Cipactli and Tlaltecuhtli), but also with many other cultural myths from around the patriarchal world.[18] Goddess murder, for example, is celebrated in the triumphal narrative of the slaughter of the Goddess Tiamat (who took the form of a marine serpent) by her grandson Marduk in the ancient Babylonian epic.

Mircea Eliade references this myth of Goddess murder as a "creation" myth—and one that directly inspires human sacrifice: "*One becomes truly a man only by conforming to the teaching of the myths, that is, by imitating the Gods.* . . . We have seen that certain blood sacrifices find their justification in a primordial divine act; *in illo tempore* the God had slain the marine monster [the Goddess] and dismembered its body in order to create the cosmos. Man repeats this blood sacrifice—sometimes even with human victims" (original emphasis).[19] This type of myth is not really about quintessential creation or creativity. Rather, it refers to the inauguration of a new world order: Goddess murder is the deed that makes the patriarchal man—and his world.

And such myths do not simply remain in the past, colorful stories no one really takes seriously from religions no one supposedly believes in anymore. Rather, they continue, taking new forms and featuring new personae but still doing what these myths are supposed to do—perpetually establish and maintain patriarchal power and models of manhood. They also provide scripts for reenactment. For example, the world-renowned killer of prostitutes, "Jack the Ripper," has taken on the dimensions of a folk hero, inspiring both adulation and imitation.[20]

Jack the Ripper and other femicidal killers are not priests, at least not officially; they are criminals. But it is important to recognize that not all blood sacrifice needs to be officially blessed. René Girard reminds us that "in many rituals the sacrificial act assumes two opposing aspects, appearing at times as a sacred obligation to be neglected at grave peril, at other times as a sort of criminal activity."[21] The murders of women and girls in Juárez are crimes, but, at the same time, they can be understood as patriarchal sacrificial rituals.

Nancy Jay writes of blood sacrifice around the world and concludes that it is an exclusively male activity.[22] The reasons for such sacrifice are based in patriarchal definitions of men and women, as well as in men's fears and insecurities. Patriarchal cultures define women as a sex opposite to men—inferior, unclean, and dangerous. There must be, then, Jay notes, some way for men who align themselves with that system to rid themselves of the perceived dreadful consequences of having been born of woman, including continuing dependence on female reproductive and sustenance powers as well as the inevitability of death, as all who are born of woman also die. Blood sacrifice is embraced by some men because it enables them to fancy that they have purged those negative consequences of having been born of woman. Blood sacrifice becomes their ritual way of connecting generations of fathers and sons, separating men from the mother-powered cycle of birth and death, and allowing men to achieve a sense of dominance, control, purity, individualistic ego, and even immortality. Femicidal killers, like the ones who have targeted the women and girls of Juárez, are one of the most recent versions of this kind of blood sacrifice. Generally, such sacrifice takes one of two forms. In the first, the sacrificer seeks to use the victim as a source of spiritual strength, trying to take her or his energy for himself.[23]

With this knowledge, we can go back to the story of Coyolxauhqui. In the myth, Huitzilopochtli was unsatisfied with merely killing his sister and her allies; he wanted to both obliterate and absorb them. To accomplish this, he took their costumes and their symbols and "introduced them into his destiny, he made them his own insignia." Davíd Carrasco calls this an act of "symbolic possession" by which Huitzilopochtli "transformed their obliteration into his own power."[24] Subsequently, the actual sacrificial rites performed by Aztec priests were intended, Carrasco continues, to "absorb" the "souls of victims" into the city, temples, statues of the gods, and so on.[25] Follow-up to the actual sacrifices at times included ritual cannibalism and dramatic wearing of the flayed skins of victims. Priests wore female skins deliberately to impersonate Goddesses and to claim their power for themselves.

A persistent rumor about the killings in Juárez speaks of them as forms of human sacrifice, maybe some kind of Satanic ritual.[26] This perception stems, in part, from the fact that many of the bodies are found naked or partly clothed, their clothing and effects carried away. Many also are left in a grievous state of mutilation and dismemberment—their breasts sliced away, their nipples chewed off, eyes removed, genitals torn up, limbs scattered. These practices, whether the killers are conscious of their implications or not, replicate the overtly sacrificial goal of taking a victim's energies and making them the killer's own.

These corporeal depredations also are ways of ritually disregarding the victims. Huitzilopochtli deliberately disrespected Coatlicue's body, letting it roll down the hill and come apart like so much trash. This is reminiscent of the second kind of blood sacrifice, in which a victim is treated as "unclean and is cast away."[27] The Juárez murders, like so many other instances of mass or serial murder of women, closely conform to this model whereby Goddess is turned into garbage.

Since the days of Prohibition, Juárez has been a place for First World visitors to come and indulge in any number of illicit pleasures (alcohol, guns, drugs, sex). It is also the site where global capital has been *making a killing* to the tune of billions of dollars in annual profit. From the Border Industrialization Program in the 1960s to the North American Free Trade Agreement in the mid-1990s, transnational companies have "taken advantage," as they say, of this border, at the expense of the exploited female labor force and the environment, which is left with a toxic stew of violence, despair, and industrial waste. Because pollution laws are conveniently lax, the factories can emit fumes and dump waste without much concern or oversight. For all these reasons, the U.S.-Mexico border has been made into something of an international sacrifice zone.

There is also a specifically gendered context pertinent to our understanding of the Juárez crimes. Debbie Nathan points to the ways that traditional Mexican patriarchal sexual norms and politics deem men to be providers leading public lives and having license to have sex outside of marriage, while women are supposed to be chaste and remain in the private sphere:

> For people who cling to this double standard, a woman who works for wages or has extramarital sex may be marked as a whore and considered fair game—if not for murder, then for violence. In Juárez, where narcotrafficking, the sex trade, and globalization have eaten away at the social fabric, women are particularly vulnerable. Against this cultural backdrop,

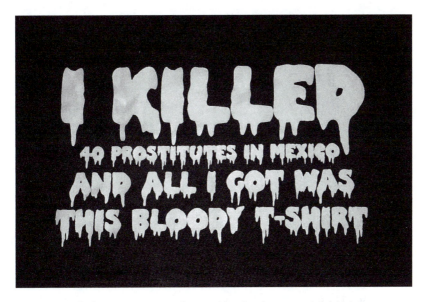

Fig. a.2. "I Killed 40 Prostitutes T-shirt" sold online by www.sinfulshirts.com. Courtesy of Jane Caputi.

Mexican border cities have developed a bar and brothel economy to satisfy U.S. tourists' desire for cheap alcohol, narcotics, and prostitutes. As a result, Juárez and other border communities have a longstanding and humiliating "sin city" image throughout Mexico. As one person told Pablo Vila, a University of Texas–San Antonio sociologist, Juárez needs to be cleaned up by getting rid of evil things: not only the bars, but "the women." The maquila murders may be taking this sentiment to a chilling extreme.[28]

Those misogynistic sentiments are by no means confined to predators targeting young women and girls in Juárez, but have marked similar outbreaks of serial sex murder of women in England, Iran, Guatemala, and the United States.[29]

Still, there is no reason to suppose that it is only Mexican men who are committing these femicides. In the United States, at least 86 percent of the men who sexually attack Native American and Alaskan Native women are non-Indians, mostly white men.[30] White men deliberately target indigenous women; they are motivated presumably not only by racism and misogyny, but also because they know that these crimes often are overlooked by the police and the criminal justice system. The English-language T-shirt that I cite at the beginning of this section is marketed to North American men who identify with and are amused by the idea of going to Mexico deliberately to kill women (whom they stigmatize as "whores" whatever their occupation).

The disorder and contamination in Juárez (and other cities with a legacy of colonialist exploitation) do not emanate from its "unclean" women. They are produced by sex, race, and class hierarchies, by political and police corruption, exploitative First World tourism, "savage capitalism,"[31] drug wars, environmental abuse, and the normalcy of male violence. And enmeshed in these material realities, there remain particular spiritual and ritual meanings of men sexually murdering female victims, in this case, young and fertile ones.

David Carrasco seeks to understand the intended and particular "ritual cosmo-magical" outcomes of the sacrifice of women by men in the Aztec empire. He comes to no definitive conclusions, calling for further study, but he does suggest that "male management of female powers was primarily a strategy to take female creative energy associated with the earth, plants, and fertility and redirect it, in certain cases, through ritual metamorphosis, into military needs, styles, and purposes."[32]

The title of this anthology, *Making a Killing*, suggests something similar might be happening now at the U.S-Mexico border. Is there still an intricate bond between seized and sacrificed female creative energies and the needs, styles, and purposes of conglomerates of male power—military, corporate, religious, and criminal? From a feminist-spiritualist perspective, these murders ritually reflect and serve a much larger purpose: the theft of female energy and the consolidation of patriarchal power, achieved via the ongoing and systemic rape, mutilation, contamination, and murder of women and subordinated peoples along with the creatures and elements of nonhuman Nature. Domineering and destructive men, cultures, and institutions still are always trying to seize "female creative energy" and redirect it into the crushing concerns of ego, father-dominated family, church, state, corporation, and empire. Proclaiming omnipotence, they evince what is actually impotence and parasitism, dependent as they are on the stolen energy of others.

Again, Nancy Jay understands the ritual purpose of men's blood-sacrifice rituals to be their attempt to extract themselves from the maternal cycle of birth, death, and transformation. In so doing, they claim to have become immortal. But what they truly have become is necrophilic, both lifeless *and* deathless, essentially soulless.

## Soul Murder and Symbolic Resurrection

The damage done to us now and in the future by a system that fills our heads with artificial needs so that we forget our real needs—how accurately can it be accessed? Can the mutilation of the human soul be measured? The spread of violence, the debasement of daily life?

—EDUARDO GALEANO

Gynocide appears in myriad forms, most obviously in the systematic rape and slaughter of women, but also in the rape and murder of gender-variant men who are identified as "feminine" by their male attackers.[33] Gynocide also is an underlying factor in attacks on all that patriarchal civilizations stigmatize as inferior and "feminine"—including whole peoples deemed "dirty," "savage," and "closer to Nature," and, of course, nonhuman Nature itself. At the same time, gynocide also is expressed in attempted murder of the spirit or soul.

In the mythic time of patriarchal beginnings, a male god slaughters the original creative female source, seizing her symbols in order to ritually transform her obliteration into his power. Her dismemberment signifies as well that moment when perceived differences become fused with opposition and hierarchy. In that new "split consciousness,"[34] one that is neither universal nor inevitable, unities are severed. Male is separated from and valued more highly than female, spirit from matter, mind from body, self from other, light from dark, high from low, culture from nature, and so on. This endemic splitting necessarily thwarts the body/soul's need for wholeness, the longing to express and experience the interconnectedness of all life.

Many, steeped in patriarchal perspectives, have come to believe that rape, murder, violence, and war are the inevitable expressions of "human nature." But this is precisely backward. Rather, it is patriarchal civilization's ongoing targeting of "female energies," which we can understand as the principle of life, fructification, creation, knowledge, and connectivity in both women and men, that has resulted in what Galeano calls "the spread of violence and the debasement of daily life."[35] For civilization does not just target non-human Nature; it first targets *human nature*, what we call the soul or spirit—the aspect of being that connects humans in kin and ken with the (equally enspirited) nonhuman world, which enables us to feel, to relate, to love, to empathize, to know, and to harmonize in all senses of that word. Spirit/soul is the force that enmeshes us in the field of life; spirit is the breath that we all share, the heart and center of the Sacred Hoop.

In many of the most familiar figures of religious ideas, myths, and fairy tales, for example, Cinderella, Sophia, the Shekinah, the soul or spirit is figured as female.[36] In these stories, spirit is consigned to the ashes, oppressed, enslaved, and exiled. But, the stories promise, she will return in radiance someday. Why, we might wonder, is the spirit or soul represented as a feminine force? Is this because the soul is in some essential way a feminine aspect of both females and males? Or is the soul cast as feminine precisely because, under patriarchy, it is oppressed, repressed, and murdered, that which patriarchal men must deny and even murder in order to be "men"? My guess is the latter.

Those who write of the horrors of sexual abuse speak of it as a form of soul murder, with the abuser feeding on and even obliterating the soul. Oppressors of all kinds regularly commit soul or "spirit murder" when they disregard those whose lives qualitatively depend on their regard.[37] Genocide and colonization inflict a "soul wound" on those who survive.[38]

Meanwhile, those capable of the most egregious violence are often themselves virtually soul dead, sometimes because they were victimized and, as a result, are unable to feel love of self or other.[39] But sometimes it is because, like Huitzilopochtli and all the other Goddess-slaying gods and heroes of myth and history, they feel illegitimate and insecure and have therefore sought potency in domination.

Dominators and exploiters, by definition, are broken. No longer able to generate their own energy/soul, they have to try to steal others' souls through parasitism/colonization or blood sacrifice. Of course, dominators deceive themselves. The soul cannot truly be stolen. What dominators ultimately injure if not kill off completely is their own soul. The outcome of all of this attempted soul murder, theft, exploitation, consumption, and exile of the feminine/soul is the deeply dispirited, violent, power-mad, bad-news, and broken world that passes as civilization.

Both Mary Daly and Gloria Anzaldúa have called us to "re-member" the dismembered Goddess, the World Soul, and retrieve her symbols.[40] Drawing on the story of Coyolxauhqui, Anzaldúa explicitly links Goddess murder to the experience of the split and exiled soul. As she perceives it, Coyolxauhqui "was such a threat to Huitzilopochtli . . . that he decapitated her, cut her up in pieces, and buried the pieces of her body in different places. To me that's a symbol not only of violence and hatred against women but also of how we're split body and mind, spirit and soul. We're separated. . . . My whole struggle in writing, in this anticolonial struggle, has been to put us back together again. To connect up the body with the soul and the mind with the spirit."[41] Part of this work includes what Anzaldúa calls "*conoci-*

*miento*"—consciousness work that connects the inner life of the mind and spirit to the outer worlds of action, "a kind of 'spiritual activism.'"[42]

Alma López's drawing *Coyolxauhqui's Tree of Life* is steeped in just such *conocimiento*, recalling the soul and her symbols and fusing them to political resistance. Two of the symbols in her work, the Circle and the flowering Tree of Life, also appear together in that cosmic idea of the axis mundi.[43]

The sacred tree as the axis mundi, or center of the world, appears throughout Mexican folk art, dating back to the pre-Classic period (600 BCE–200 CE). Writing on Mexican ceramics, one scholar tells us that this "celebrated form" suggests "an early recognition of the tree as *axis mundi*—a life giving force at the center of the earth that penetrates and unifies all the layers of the world."[44] The axis mundi, moreover, is the intimate and ultimate center to which one journeys in order to "gain access to the source and flow of 'reality' in the world."[45] This happens because the axis mundi is like unto the soul, the life-giving and unifying force at the center of our own being. This soul is what allows us to experience that "flow of 'reality,'" which always entails knowing and feeling the unity of all life.

Earlier, I noted that the Aztec Templo Mayor, built to commemorate and reenact the murder of Coyolxauhqui, was deliberately constructed to be an axis mundi. Alma López invokes an alternative to that gynocidal hub. Her *Coyolxauhqui's Tree of Life* displaces and decenters the blood-soaked temple and the gynocidal God/War. She restores Goddess to the unifying center, for she, as soul, is the unifying force, the context, the background and source of life. López's visual evocation of the axis mundi features Coyolxauhqui whole once again and fused with the Flowering Tree. Her face is the celestial Circle. The bodies of Earth creatures are fused to her own body as she stands on the base of the Serpent/Underworld. Coyolxauhqui's restored presence as, and at, the heart of the world unites the realms of the cosmos. Centering ourselves in this axis mundi, we experience the World Soul and hence our own souls.

When I started this chapter on the rapes, tortures, mutilations, and murders of women and girls in Ciudad Juárez, I felt conflicted. How does one write about atrocity from a distance? Contemplating this image as I come to the chapter's conclusion, I am granted, as the axis mundi is meant to do, a moment of reality allowing me to take in the understanding that *there is no distance* for any of us, really, from these murders and other atrocities. And I do not mean simply that there is a bond of compassion. Particularly for those of us in the North and living in relative safety, wealth, protection, and privilege, we have to understand, as Buddhist teacher Thich Nhat

Hanh reminds us, that our lives are like this because their lives (and deaths) are like that. Hanh reminds us: "We are not separate. We are inextricably inter-related."[46] Those of us who are safe and comfortable may be relieved that this is so, but, at the same time, if we are sane, we also have to be suffering because we know that others are suffering, and suffering unjustly. For example, others are deprived because the North takes the bulk of the resources; others are in danger because of the torturous and violent ways that world leaders supposedly keep their own citizens "secure." To be sane, and to keep our souls, those of us who are privileged have to suffer with this knowledge and also work to relieve the suffering of others and institute justice. Coyolxauhqui comes back together whenever this happens.

A model for resistance based in *conocimiento* can be found in the searchers who go to the outskirts of Ciudad Juárez and seek the broken and often scattered parts of the bodies of their loved ones. These "Super Madres,"[47] as well as other relatives, neighbors, and activists, paint the names of murdered women and girls on crosses and display photos on signs, ceaselessly petitioning officials, keeping attention on the atrocities, and getting the message out to the world. They take their private grief and make it public, demanding justice. These acts are rituals, ones that are both political and spiritual. They are rites of retrieval, remembrance, and respect, which not only remember the murdered loved ones, but also re-articulate Coyolxauhqui, hearing, and giving, her voice.

## Notes

1. Lenore Hoag Mulryan, *Ceramic Trees of Life: Popular Art from Mexico* (Los Angeles: UCLA Fowler Museum of Cultural History, 2003).

2. AnaLouise Keating, ed. *Gloria Anzaldúa: Interviews/Entrevistas* (New York: Routledge, 2000), 257.

3. Jill Radford and Diana E. H. Russell, eds., *Femicide: The Politics of Woman Killing* (New York: Twayne, 1992).

4. Mary Daly, *Beyond God the Father: Toward a Philosophy of Women's Liberation* (Boston: Beacon Press, 1973); Andrea Dworkin, *Woman Hating* (New York: E. P. Dutton, 1973).

5. See also Mary Daly, with Jane Caputi, *Websters' First New Intergalactic Wickedary of the English Language* (Boston: Beacon Press, 1987), 77.

6. Andrea Smith, *Conquest: Sexual Violence and American Indian Genocide* (Boston: South End Press, 2005).

7. Paula Gunn Allen, *The Sacred Hoop: Recovering the Feminine in American Indian Traditions* (Boston: Beacon Press, 1986).

8. Jane Caputi, "Overkill: Why Excess and Conflict Are Both Sexy and Sacred," *Journal for the Study of Religion, Nature and Culture* 1.3 (Winter 2007): 277–292.

9. June Nash, "The Aztecs and the Ideology of Male Dominance," *Signs: Journal of Women in Culture and Society* 1.21 (1978): 349–362.

10. Davíd Carrasco, *City of Sacrifice: The Aztec Empire and the Role of Violence in Civilization* (Boston: Beacon Press, 1999), 71.

11. It is significant that a synonym for "dismemberment" is "disarticulation." One of the meanings of the adjective "articulate" is "possessing the faculty or power of speech" (*Webster's Third New International Dictionary* [Springfield, Mass.: Merriam-Webster, 1986]).

12. Carrasco, *City of Sacrifice*, 59

13. Paul Wheatley, cited in ibid., 30.

14. Ibid., 62.

15. Julius R. Ruff, *Violence in Early Modern Europe, 1500–1800* (Cambridge: Cambridge University Press, 2001), 29.

16. Mary Daly, *Gyn/Ecology: The Metaethics of Radical Feminism* (Boston: Beacon Press, 1978), 39.

17. Jane Caputi, *The Age of Sex Crime* (Bowling Green, Ohio: Bowling Green State University Popular Press, 1987). See also my film, *The Pornography of Everyday Life*, 2006, distributed by Berkeley Media, www.berkeleymedia.com; and Jane Caputi, "The Gods We Worship: Sexual Murder as Religious Sacrifice," in *Goddesses and Monsters: Women, Myth, Power and Popular Culture* (Madison: University of Wisconsin Press/Popular Press, 2004), 182–208.

18. The first epigraph is from Eduardo Matos Moctezuma, *The Great Temple of the Aztecs: Treasures of Tenochtitlan* (London: Thames and Hudson, 1988), 140.

19. Mircea Eliade, *The Sacred and the Profane: The Nature of Religion*, trans. W. R. Trask (New York: Harper and Row, 1957), 100.

20. Caputi, *The Age of Sex Crime.*

21. René Girard, *Violence and the Sacred*, trans. P. Gregory (Baltimore, Md.: Johns Hopkins University Press, 1977), 1.

22. Nancy Jay, *Throughout Your Generations Forever: Sacrifice, Religion, and Paternity* (Chicago: University of Chicago Press, 1992).

23. E. O. James, "Sacrifice," in *Encyclopedia of Religion and Ethics*, ed. J. Hastings (New York: Scribner's, 1926), vol. 21, 1–6, esp. 1. See also the explanation of exploitation given by Iris Marion Young, "Five Faces of Oppression," in *Theorizing Feminisms*, ed. Elizabeth Hackett and Sally Haslanger (New York: Oxford, 2006), 3–16.

24. Carrasco, *City of Sacrifice*, 63.

25. Ibid., 148.

26. Simon Whitechapel, *Crossing to Kill: The True Story of the Serial-Killer Playground* (London: Virgin Books, 2001), 50–53.

27. James, "Sacrifice," 1.

28. Debbie Nathan, "The Juárez Murders. Amnesty Now," www.amnestyusa.org/amnestynow/juarez/html, 2003.

29. Caputi, "The Gods We Worship."

30. Jodi Rave, "Failure to Protect," *Amnesty International* (Summer 2007): 10–13.

31. Eduardo Galeano, "To Be Like Them," in *Juárez: The Laboratory of Our Future*, ed. Charles Bowden (Denville, N.J.: Aperture Foundation, 1998), 121–129.

32. Carrasco, *City of Sacrifice*, 210.

33. Extract from Galeano, "To Be Like Them," 129.

34. Susan Griffin, "Split Culture," in *Healing the Wounds: The Promise of Ecofeminism*, ed. Judith Plant (Philadelphia: New Society Publishers, 1989), 7–17.

35. Galeano, "To Be Like Them."

36. Harold Bayley, *The Lost Language of Symbolism*, 2 vols. (New York: Barnes and Noble, 1912, 1996).

37. Patricia Williams, "Teleology on the Rocks," in *The Alchemy of Race and Rights: Diary of a Law Professor* (Cambridge, Mass.: Harvard University Press, 1991), 55–79.

38. Eduardo Durán and Bonnie Durán, *Native American Postcolonial Psychology* (Albany: State University of New York Press, 1995).

39. James Gilligan, *Violence: Reflections on a National Epidemic* (New York: Vintage Books, 1996).

40. Daly, *Gyn/Ecology*, 39.

41. Anzaldúa, in Keating, *Gloria Anzaldúa*, 220.

42. Ibid., 178.

43. The Circle and the Flowering Tree of Life also appear together in Black Elk's vision of the Sacred Hoop. See John G. Neihardt, *Black Elk Speaks: Being the Life Story of a Holy Man of the Oglala Sioux* (Lincoln: University of Nebraska Press, 1988).

44. Delia A. Cosentino, "The Tallest, the Fullest, the Most Beautiful: The Tree in Pre-Columbian and Colonial Mexico," in *Ceramic Trees of Life: Popular Art from Mexico*, ed. Lenore Hoag Mulryan (Los Angeles: UCLA Fowler Museum of Cultural History, 2003), 30–49, quotation on 33.

45. Carrasco, *City of Sacrifice*, 30.

46. Thich Nhat Hanh, *The Heart of Understanding* (Berkeley, Calif.: Parallax Press, 1988), 38.

47. Cynthia Bejarano, "Las Super Madres de Latino América: Transforming Motherhood and Houseskirts by Challenging Violence in Juárez, Mexico, Argentina, and El Salvador," in *Violence and the Body: Race, Gender, and the State*, ed. Arturo Aldama (Bloomington: Indiana University Press, 2003), 404–429.

# Selected Bi-national Timeline of the Juárez Femicides

# SELECTIVE BI-NATIONAL TIMELINE

## U.S.

| | |
|---|---|
| **1989-1993** | George H. W. Bush (R) President of U. S. |
| **1992** | U.S. President George H. W. Bush, Canadian Prime Minister Brian Mulroney and Mexican President Carlos Salinas meet in San Antonio, TX, on December 17 to sign NAFTA. |
| **1993-2001** | Bill Clinton (D) President of U.S. |
| **1993** | • U.S. House of Representatives approves NAFTA on November 17 by a vote of 234 to 200. |
| | • NAFTA signed into law by President Clinton on December 8. |
| **1994** | NAFTA implemented January 1. |
| **1998** | • *NYTimes* publishes "Rape and Murder Stalk Women in Northern Mexico" in April, its first coverage of the Juárez femicides. |
| | • The May/June issue of *Ms.* magazine publishes "The Maquiladora Murders" by Sam Quiñones. |
| | • Publication of *Juárez: The Laboratory of Our Future* by Charles Bowden. |
| **1999** | ABC 20/20 special "Silent Screams" is aired on national television in January. |
| **2000** | First *Washington Post* article on femicides, "Bright Lights, Dark City," is published in June. |
| **2001-2009** | George W. Bush (R) President of the U.S. |
| **2001** | Release of "Señorita Extraviada" documentary by Lourdes Portillo. |

## EL PASO

| | |
|---|---|
| **1999** | • 620 registered sex-crime offenders in El Paso County 1995-1999.* |
| | • New Mexico State University "Burials on the Border" conference held in October. |
| **2000** | 745 registered sex-crime offenders.* |
| **2001** | • 5 year old Alexandra Flores kidnapped from a Wal-Mart, raped, and murdered by registered sex offender. |
| | • 751 registered sex-crime offenders.* |
| | • Cross-border Coalition Against Violence born in late 2001. |
| **2002** | Diana Washington Valdéz's award-winning exposé, "Death Stalks the Border," published in *El Paso Times* in June. |

| 1994 | 1995 | 1996 | 1997 | 1998 | 1999 | 2000 | 2001 | 2002 |
|---|---|---|---|---|---|---|---|---|

## CIUDAD JUÁREZ

| | |
|---|---|
| **1993** | First 17 bodies discovered in Juarez.** |
| **1994** | • 300 maquiladoras, 75% U.S.-owned, employ 220,000. 60% are women. |
| | • Special prosecutor appointed to investigate murders. |
| | • Coalition of NGOs for Women's Rights founded by Esther Chávez Cano and Judith Galarza. |
| **1995** | Abdul Latif Sharif, Egyptian chemist "mastermind," arrested. |
| **1995-1998** | Juárez City Council and Police Department's "Prevention Campaigns" for keeping young women safe against predators. |
| **1995-1999** | Ramón Galindo (PAN) mayor of Cd. Juárez. |
| **1996** | Los Rebeldes gang arrested in sting operation. |
| **1997** | 107 total bodies found since 1993.** |
| **1998** | Chihuahua judicial authorities release murder files to the press. |
| **1999** | • "Los Choferes" band of bus drivers arrested. |
| | • Jesús Manuel Guajardo, "The Toltec," arrested. |
| | • Publication of *El silencio que la voz de todas quiebra* by Adriana Candia, and six other women journalists. Police files closed after this publication. |
| **2001** | • 8 bodies found in cotton field in front of AMAC (Maquiladora Association) building. |
| | • Victor Javier Garcia Uribe & Gustavo Gonzalez Meza arrested for the crimes. |
| | • Nuestras Hijas de Regreso a Casa founded. |
| | • State legislators reverse a change to the Mexican penal code that would have shortened sentences for rapists judged to have been provoked by their victims. |

## MEXICO

| | |
|---|---|
| **1965** | Border Industrialization Program (BIP) implemented. |
| **1988-1994** | Carlos Salinas (PRI) President of Mexico. |
| **1992-1998** | Francisco Barrio (PAN) Governor of Chihuahua. |
| **1994** | • Tratado de Libre Comercio de América del Norte (NAFTA) goes into effect. |
| | • Chiapas uprising on New Year's Day, after the Zapatista Army (EZLN) leader Subcomandante Marcos declares NAFTA is a "death sentence" to Indian peoples of Mexico," launches 12-day "war" on the Mexican state in protest. |
| **1994-2000** | Ernesto Zedillo Ponce de León (PRI) President of Mexico. |
| **1998-2004** | Patricio Martinez García (PRI) Governor of Chihuahua. |
| **1999** | Publication of *Las Muertas de Juárez* by Victor Ronquillo. |
| **2000-2006** | Vicente Fox (PAN) President of Mexico. |

# OF THE JUÁREZ FEMICIDES

| 2003 | • U.S. Congresswoman Hilda Solis leads delegation to Juárez with Dolores Huerta, visits victims' families, NGOs, public officials, maquiladoras and crime scene sites. Introduces HR 466 to Congress encouraging U.S. involvement in binational effort. |
|---|---|
| | • Texas passes HCR 59 committing to binational cooperation in investigations. |
| | • "Gender, Justice, and the Border" conference held at Arizona State University-West in April. |
| | • "The Maquiladora Murders, Or, Who Is Killing the Women of Juárez?" conference held at UCLA , Oct. 31-Nov. 2. |
| 2004 | Mexico Solidarity Network launches Caravan for Justice to raise consciousness about the femicides across the United States. |
| 2005 | Publication of *Desert Blood: The Juárez Murders* by Alicia Gaspar de Alba. |
| 2006 | • DVD release of "The Virgin of Juárez," dir. Kevin James Dobson, starring Minnie Driver. |
| | • HR 4437, the House bill that includes the criminalization of undocumented immigrants and the construction of a border wall, signed into law by President G.W. Bush in October. |
| 2007 | • Release of "Border Echoes," doc. by Lorena Mendez and "On the Edge: The Femicide in Ciudad Juárez," doc. by Steev Hise. |
| | • Publication of *The Daughters of Juárez: A True Tale of Serial Murder* by Teresa Rodríguez and Diana Montañe. |
| 2008 | DVD release of "Bordertown," dir. Gregory Nava, starring Jennifer Lopez, Antonio Banderas, and Martin Sheen. |
| 2009-present | Barack Obama (D) President of the U.S. |

| 2003 | El Paso police department teams up with Mexican officials to set up first-ever binational hot line for people on both sides of the border to call in anonymous tips about the slayings of women in Juárez. |
|---|---|
| 2006 | • J. Paul Taylor Social Justice Symposium, "Justice for Women," held in March at New Mexico State University. |
| | • English publication of Diana Washington Valdéz's *The Killing Fields: Harvest of Women* |
| | • President Bush announces that he will send 6,000 National Guard troops to help monitor El Paso/Juárez border for one year. |
| 2007 | • Nine displaced NAFTA workers (La Mujer Obrera advocacy group) launch hunger strike in Chamizal National Memorial. |
| 2009 | • *El Paso Times* reports Edgar Alvarez Cruz, sentenced to 26 years in prison for the murder of Silvia Gabriela Laguna Cruz in 1998, is denied an amparo, or relief from his conviction (August). Alvarez is also a suspect in the 2001 cotton field murders. |

| | 2003 | 2004 | 2005 | 2006 | 2007 | 2008 | 2009 |
|---|---|---|---|---|---|---|---|

| 2002 | • 267 bodies found since 1993.** |
|---|---|
| | • Mario Escobedo Anaya (bus drivers' attorney) killed by state police. |
| 2003 | • Amnesty International "Intolerable Killings" report released in August. |
| | • Instituto Chihuahuense de la Mujer releases Chihuahua Homicides Unit's "Homicidios de Mujeres: Auditoría periodística"; counts 231 murders 1993-2003. |
| | • David Meza Argueta arrested and tortured for allegedly killing his cousin Neyra Azucena Cervantes. |
| 2004 | • V-Day border march led by Eve Ensler, Jane Fonda, Christine Lahti, and Sally Field, largest march in region's history. |
| | • Nuestras Hijas de Regreso a Casa reports 361 total murdered women. |
| 2006 | • Abdul Latif Sharif dies in jail. |
| | • David Meza Argueta released from prison, finally acquitted of all charges after almost 3 years in jail. |
| | • Las Cruces-based Amigos de las Mujeres de Juárez helps start local anti-trafficking coalition on the border. |
| 2007 | • Victims' mothers file complaints to Inter-American Commission on Human Rights |
| | • 407 bodies found since 1993.** |
| | • Mexico's Maquiladora Industry Conference names Juárez as the top maquiladora center in Mexico. |
| 2008 | • 300,000 march for non-violence. |
| | • Esther Chávez Cano awarded Mexico's National Human Rights Award. |
| 2009 | • 39 more bodies found (as of June 24).*** |
| | • **According to Casa Amiga statistics, total body count estimated upwards of 600 women and girls.** |

| 2003 | National Commission of Human Rights in Mexico reports 2000 women disappeared. |
|---|---|
| 2004-present | José Reyes Baeza (PRI) Governor of Chihuahua. |
| 2006-present | Felipe Calderón (PAN) President of Mexico. |
| 2005 | Publication of *Cosecha de Mujeres* by Diana Washington Valdéz. |
| 2006 | • Federal Attorney General (PGR) declares Juárez femicides a "black legend" spoiling tourism and commerce on the border. |
| | • Indymedia releases new documentary, "Bajo Juárez: Una Ciudad Devorando a Sus Hijas," directed by Alejandra Sanchez Orozco and Antonio Cordero. |
| 2007 | • Indigenous Intercontinental Conference, Sonora. |
| | • Publication of *Bordeando la violencia contra las mujeres en la frontera norte de México*, edited by Julia Monárrez Fragoso and María Socorro Tabuenca Córdoba. |
| 2009 | • Publication of *Trama de una injusticia* by Julia Monárrez Fragoso. |

Thanks to Allison Wyper & Tom Bryan

*SOURCE: *El Paso Times*    **SOURCE: Grupo Ocho de Marzo    ***SOURCE: Casa Amiga

## APPENDIX B

# The Juárez Femicides in Print, Film, and Music: A Partial List

### Books (by publication date)

Fuentes, Carlos, and Alfred J. Mac Adam. *The Crystal Frontier: A Novel in Nine Stories*. New York: Farrar, Straus, and Giroux, 1997.

Benítez, Rohry, Adriana Candia, Patricia Cabrera, Guadalupe de la Mora, Josefina Martínez, Isabel Velázquez, Ramona Ortiz. *El silencio que la voz de todas quiebra: Mujeres y víctimas de Ciudad Juárez*. Ciudad Juárez: Ediciones del Azar, 1999.

Ortega, Gregorio. *Las muertas de Ciudad Juárez: El caso de Elizabeth Castro García y Abdel Latif Sharif Sharif*. Mexico City: Distribuciones Fontamara, 1999.

Ronquillo, Víctor. *Las muertas de Juárez: Crónica de una larga pesadilla*. Mexico City: Planeta Mexicana, 1999.

Whitechapel, Simon. *Crossing to Kill: The True Story of the Serial-Killer Playground*. 3rd ed. London: Virgin Books, 2002.

González Rodríguez, Sergio. *Huesos en el desierto*. Barcelona: Editorial Anagrama, 2002.

Amnistía Internacional/Amnesty International. *México: Muertes intolerables*. London: Amnesty International Publications, 2003.

Alcalá Iberi, María del Socorro. *Las muertas de Juárez: La voz viva de las muertas*. Mexico, D.F.: Editorial Libra, 2004.

Bard, Patrick. *La Frontera: Una novela de denuncia sobre las muertas de Juárez*. Trans. José Antonio Soriano. Mexico City: Grijalbo Mondadori, 2004.

Gaspar de Alba, Alicia. *Desert Blood: The Juárez Murders*. Houston, Tex: Arte Público Press, 2005.

Agosín, Marjorie, Celeste Kostopulos-Cooperman, and Guadalupe Morfín. *Secrets in the Sand: The Young Women of Ciudad Juárez*. Buffalo, N.Y.: White Pine Press, 2006.

Wright, Melissa W. *Disposable Women and Other Myths of Global Capitalism*. New York: Routledge, 2006.

Washington Valdez, Diana. *The Killing Fields: Harvest of Women: The Truth about Mexico's Bloody Border Legacy*. Los Angeles: Peace at the Border, 2006.

Monárrez-Fragoso, Julia Estela, and María Socorro Tabuenca Córdoba, eds. *Bor-

*deando la violencia contra las mujeres en la frontera norte de México.* Mexico City: El Colegio de la Frontera Norte and Miguel Ángel Porrúa Editores, 2007.

Rodríguez, Teresa, Diana Montané, and Lisa Beth Pulitzer. *Hijas de Juárez: Un auténtico relato de asesinatos en serie al sur de la frontera.* New York: Atria Books, 2007.

Botha, Ted. *The Girl with the Crooked Nose: A Tale of Murder, Obsession, and Forensic Artistry.* New York: Random House, 2008.

Duarte, Stella Pope. *If I Die in Juárez (Camino del Sol).* Tucson: University of Arizona Press, 2008.

Staudt, Kathleen A. *Violence and Activism at the Border: Gender, Fear, and Everyday Life in Ciudad Juárez.* Inter-America Series. Austin: University of Texas Press, 2008.

Monárrez-Fragoso, Julia Estela. *Trama de una injusticia: Feminicidio sexual sistemático en Ciudad Juárez.* Mexico City: Editorial El Colegio de la Frontera Norte, 2009.

## Films (by release date)

*Borderline Cases: Environmental Matters at the United States–Mexico Border.* Dir. Lynn Corcoran. Bullfrog Films, 1997.

*Performing the Border.* Dir. Ursula Biemann. Women Make Movies, 1999.

*The Border.* Dir. Paul Espinosa. Espinosa Productions, 2000.

*Maquila: A Tale of Two Mexicos.* Dir. Saul Landau and Sonia Ángulo. Cinema Guild, 2000.

*Writing Desire.* Dir. Ursula Biemann. Videocassette. Women Make Movies, 2000.

*Remote Sensing.* Dir. Ursula Biemann. Women Make Movies, 2001.

*Señorita Extraviada* (aka *Missing Young Woman*). Dir. Lourdes Portillo. Xochitl Productions, 2001.

*Juárez: Desierto de esperanza.* Dir. Cristina Michaus. Tenzin, S.C., 2002.

*Las Muertas de Juárez.* Dir. Enrique Murillo. Perf. Salvador Pineda. Laguna Productions, 2002.

*Tan infinito como el desierto* (telenovela). Dir. Albino Corrales and Néstor Galván. TV Azteca, 2004.

*Juárez: Stages of Fear.* Dir. César Alejandro. Stages of Fear Joint Venture, 2005.

*Preguntas sin respuesta.* Dir. Rafael Montero. Instituto Mexicano de Cinematografía, 2005.

*Bajo Juárez: La ciudad devorando a sus hijas.* Dir. Alejandra Sánchez, Foprocine, Instituto Mexicano de Cinematografía, Pepa Films, Universidad Nacional Autónoma de México, 2006.

*Bordertown.* Dir. Gregory Nava. Perf. Jennifer López, Martin Sheen, Antonio Banderas. Möbius Entertainment, 2006.

*On the Edge: Femicide in Ciudad Juárez.* Dir. Steve Hise. Illegal Art, 2006.

*Virgin of Juárez.* Dir. Kevin James Dobson. Perf. Minnie Driver, Angus Macfadyen, Esai Morales, Ana Claudia Talancón. Las Mujeres LLC, 2006.

*Border Echoes—Ecos de una Frontera: The Truth behind the Juarez Murders.* Dir. Lorena Méndez-Quiroga. Peace at the Border Films, 2007.

*Backyard/traspatio.* By Sabina Berman, dir. Carlos Carrera ("The Crime of Padre Amaro"), perf. Jimmy Smits, 2009.

## Music (by release date)

Amos, Tori. "Juárez." *To Venus and Back.* Atlantic Records, 1999.

At the Drive-In. "Invalid Litter Department." EMI International, 2001.

Downs, Lila. "La Niña." *Border/La Línea.* Narada World, 2001.

Mujeres en Fuga. "El Boulevard de los Sueños Destrozados." *Brujas.* Ediciones Pentagrama, 2004.

Los Tigres del Norte. "Las Mujeres de Juárez." *Pacto de Sangre.* Fonovisa, 2004.

El TRI. "Las Mujeres de Juárez." *35 Años.* WeaRock, 2004.

*De Mariposa a Cruz—Juárez: Stages of Fear* (original soundtrack). Perf. Ruben Blades, Alejandra Guzmán, José Feliciano, Alejandro Lerner, Diego Verdaguer, Emilia Navaira, Carina Rico, Little Joe, Jenni Rivera, Fernando Arau, Eduardo Palomo, Colin Hay, César Alejandro, Rogelio Martínez, Celeste Carballok, Amy Pietz, Joe Jackson, Cecilia Noel, Andy Lauer, Taylor Negrón, Laura Zamora, Ignacio Elizavetsky, Juan Namuncura, David Shark, Francisco Romero, Marcelo Rod-Che, César Zamora. Fonovisa, 2005.

Los Jaguares. "Madera." *Crónicas de un Laberinto.* Sony International, 2005.

# Notes on Contributors

EVA ARCE is a human rights activist and the mother of Silvia Arce, who disappeared in Juárez on March 11, 1998, with a friend, Griselda Mares. The Washington-based Inter-American Commission on Human Rights has accepted her case.

ELVIA R. ARRIOLA is associate professor of law at Northern Illinois University and executive director of Women on the Border. Her articles include "Of Woman Born: Courage and Strength to Survive in the Maquiladoras of Reynosa and Río Bravo, Tamaulipas" (2001), "Looking Out from a Cardboard Box" (2000), and "'Voices from the Barbed Wire of Despair': Women in the Maquiladoras, Latina Critical Legal Theory, and Gender at the U.S.-Mexico Border" (2000).

JANE CAPUTI teaches women's studies at Florida Atlantic University and explores the spiritual meanings of gynocide. She is the author of *The Age of Sex Crime* (1987); *Gossips, Gorgons, and Crones: The Fates of the Earth* (1993); and *Goddesses and Monsters* (2004).

IRASEMA CORONADO is an associate professor in the Department of Political Science at the University of Texas at El Paso. She is coauthor, with Kathleen Staudt, of *Fronteras No Más: Toward Social Justice at the U.S.-Mexico Border* (Palgrave, 2002). Her most recent book is *Políticas: Latina Public Officials in Texas* (University of Texas Press, 2008). She served as cochair of the Coalition against Violence toward Women and Children on the Border. Her research interests continue to evolve around the role of women in politics and cross-border cooperation at the local level in the U.S.-Mexico border region. She is the recipient of a Border Fulbright and in 2009 was teaching and researching at the Universidad Autónoma de Ciudad Juárez.

PAULA FLORES is an activist in the community of Lomas de Poleo in Ciudad Juárez. She is the mother of María Sagrario González Flores, who disappeared on March 11, 1998. Paula runs the María Sagrario Foundation, an organization that established a kindergarten, Jardín de Niños María Sagrario González Flores, in Juárez.

ALICIA GASPAR DE ALBA is a native of the El Paso/Juárez border and a professor of Chicana/o studies, English, and women's studies at the University of California, Los Angeles, where she also serves as the chair of the César E. Chávez Department of Chicana and Chicano Studies. She has published eight books, among them the award-winning novels, *Sor Juana's Second Dream* (University of New Mexico Press, 1999) and *Desert Blood: The Juárez Murders* (Arte Público Press, 2005). Her most recent historical novel, *Calligraphy of the Witch*, was released by St. Martin's Press in fall 2007. For more about Gaspar de Alba's work or to sign an online petition to put an end to the Juárez murders, see www.desertblood.net.

GEORGINA GUZMÁN is a PhD candidate in English at the University of California, Los Angeles. Her dissertation examines second-generation Chicana/o children's empathy, recognition, and (dis)identification with their immigrant parents and their racialized labor in twentieth-century Chicana/o literature.

ALMA LÓPEZ is a Mexican-born Chicana artist, activist, and visual storyteller. She holds an MFA from the University of California, Irvine (1996). Her work ranges from serigraphs, paintings, and photo-based digital prints to public murals and video. Since the 1992 Los Angeles uprisings, López has been engaged in collaborative public art-making that helps to bridge black and brown communities. She has designed posters for national and international events, and her artwork has appeared on the covers of more than twenty publications. Her most recent video documentary is a twenty-minute short titled *Boi Hair*. To see samples of her diverse work, see her Web site: www.almalopez.com.

Born in the shadow of Disneyland in Orange County, California, artist RIGO MALDONADO explores the plastic interplay between traditional craftsmanship and twenty-first-century notions of gender, identity, body politics, and culture. Maldonado incorporates a baroque sensibility to create complex and fanciful works of art dealing with religion, sexuality, and popular culture. His dynamic installations incorporate sculpture, video, fashion, and photography to create an iconic aesthetic of social consciousness. In 2003, he cocurated, with Victoria Delgadillo, the groundbreaking "Hijas de Juárez" exhibit at the Social and Public Art Resource Center in Venice, California. His work has been exhibited at galleries and public spaces throughout the Southwest, Mexico, China, and Guatemala. To learn more about his work, see his Web site: www.rigomaldonado.com.

LAURA MOLINA was born in East Los Angeles in 1957. She studied art and filmmaking at the California Institute of the Arts and was trained as a Disney animator. Her projects have included a self-published comic book, *Cihualyaomiquiz the Jaguar* (1996), a reaction to California's Proposition 187 and featuring an avenging Mexican American superheroine. She is mentioned in *The Great Women Cartoonists,* by Trina Robbins. Her biography and five of her paintings are included in *Contemporary Chicano and Chicana Art,* published by Bilingual Review Press in 2002.

JULIA E. MONÁRREZ-FRAGOSO has a PhD in social sciences with a specialization in women's studies and gender relations from the Universidad Autónoma Metropolitana. She is currently a level I national researcher at El Colegio de la Frontera Norte in the northeast region, with headquarters in Ciudad Juárez. Her area of research is feminism and violence. She has published various articles on this subject, and her dissertation, "Feminicidio sexual sistémico: Víctimas y familiares, Ciudad Juárez 1993–2004," received an honorable mention from the National Women's Institute in the 2006 Sor Juana Inés de la Cruz, First Feminist of the Américas Dissertation Contest. In 2005–2006, she researched, wrote, and edited *Sistema socioeconómico y geo-referencial sobre la violencia de género en Ciudad Juárez, Chihuahua: Propuestas para su prevención* for the Commission to Prevent and Eradicate Violence against Women in Ciudad Juárez. She is coauthor, with María Socorro Tabuenca Córdoba, of *Bordeando la violencia contra las mujeres en la frontera norte de México* (2007). Her book *Trama de una injusticia: Feminicidio sexual sistémico en Ciudad Juárez* was published in 2009.

CLARA E. ROJAS holds a PhD in rhetoric and professional communication from New Mexico State University. She is an associate professor in the Department of Humanities at the Universidad Autónoma de Ciudad Juárez. She teaches discourse analysis, feminist theories, and Mexican women's history. Her research is focused on the analysis of public discourse from a feminist rhetorical perspective, and she looks at the rhetoric of media popular culture, specifically, audience reception of Mexican women's magazines and other media products. She was awarded a two-year grant by the Consejo Nacional de Ciencia y Tecnología (National Council of Science and Technology) and the government of the State of Chihuahua to investigate the relationship between text and audience reception centered on the analysis of violence-prevention literacy. She may be contacted by e-mail at crojas@uacj.mx.

MARIAN E. SCHLOTTERBECK graduated from Oberlin College with highest honors in history with a thesis on popular representations of women and *maquiladoras* in Ciudad Juárez. She is completing a PhD in Latin American history at Yale University. Her dissertation examines the intersections between labor organizing and popular mobilizations in the Chilean city of Concepción between 1960 and 1980.

CANDICE SKRAPEC, PHD, is a psychologist and criminologist who has researched serial murder and consulted as an investigative profiler since 1984. She is an associate professor in the Department of Criminology at California State University, Fresno, and is coordinator of the forensic and behavioral sciences track of the emerging Joint Doctoral Program in Forensic and Behavioral Sciences (with the University of California, Davis). For more than two decades, Dr. Skrapec has interviewed incarcerated serial murderers in different countries. Like the rest of us, she is interested in what makes them tick. Her quest to answer this question has taken her on an incredible journey into the minds of scores of offenders. She has worked extensively with and trained police in Canada, Mexico, and the United States and is regularly asked to consult with law enforcement officers, attorneys, the media, movie and documentary producers, and authors of fact and fiction books—particularly in the areas of criminal psychology, serial murder, and investigative profiling. Dr. Skrapec is a recognized expert in the field of forensic behavioral science and has presented before many international audiences. Police from departments around the world contact Dr. Skrapec to assist in active and "cold" criminal cases.

KATHLEEN STAUDT, PHD, is professor of political science and director of the Center for Civic Engagement at the University of Texas at El Paso. She teaches courses on the border, public policy, women/gender, democracy, and educational leadership. Staudt has published twelve books and edited collections, five of which focus on the U.S.-Mexico border, including *Violence and Activism at the Border: Gender, Fear, and Everyday Life in Ciudad Juárez* (University of Texas Press, 2008). She is active in community organizations, including Interamerican Foundation affiliate Border Interfaith, the Paso del Norte Civil Rights Project, and the Coalition against Violence toward Women at the Border.

MARÍA SOCORRO TABUENCA CÓRDOBA has a PhD in Hispanic languages and literatures from the State University of New York at Stony Brook, and a Master's degree in Spanish literature from the University of Texas at El Paso. She has been a researcher at El Colegio de la Frontera Norte since 1992, where she was the dean for the northwest region (1999–2007) and the regional director in Ciudad Juárez (1995–2001). She has been a member of the Sistema Nacional de Investigadores (National Researchers System) since 1994. Tabuenca Córdoba is the author of *Mujeres y fronteras: Una perspectiva de género* (1998); coauthor of *Lo que el viento a Juárez: Testimonios de una ciudad que se obstina* (with Ricardo Aguilar, 2000), *Border Women: Writing from la Frontera* (with Debra Castillo, 2002); *Gobernabilidad e ingobernabilidad en la región Paso del Norte* (ed. with Antonio Payán, 2004); and *Bordeando la violencia en la frontera norte de México* (with Julia Monárrez-Fragoso, 2007). Her publications are on Chicana and Mexicana border women's literatures, and she has also written on discourses about Juárez femicides and border images in Mexican film and Juárez's cultural production. Her current research is on the representations of Ciudad Juárez in film and narratives.

STEVEN S. VOLK, professor of history and chair of Latin American Studies at Oberlin College, is completing a book on the historical memory in the United States of the overthrow of Chilean president Salvador Allende on September 11, 1973.

MELISSA W. WRIGHT is an associate professor in the Departments of Geography and Women's Studies at The Pennsylvania State University. She has also been affiliated with El Colegio de la Frontera Norte–Ciudad Juárez, and was a visiting scholar at the Universidad Autónoma de Ciudad Juárez from 2006 to 2007 as a Fulbright–García Roble recipient. Her book, *Disposable Women and Other Myths of Global Capitalism,* was published by Routledge in 2006, and she has published articles in a variety of journals in geography, women's studies, anthropology, and cultural studies.

# Index

# Reprints and Permissions